ON PROCLUS AND
HIS INFLUENCE
IN MEDIEVAL PHILOSOPHY

PHILOSOPHIA ANTIQUA

A SERIES OF STUDIES
ON ANCIENT PHILOSOPHY

EDITED BY

J.J. MANSFELD, D.T. RUNIA
W.J. VERDENIUS AND J.C.M. VAN WINDEN

VOLUME LIII

ON PROCLUS AND
HIS INFLUENCE
IN MEDIEVAL PHILOSOPHY

EDITED BY

E.P. BOS AND P.A. MEIJER

ON PROCLUS
AND HIS INFLUENCE
IN MEDIEVAL PHILOSOPHY

EDITED BY

E.P. BOS AND P.A. MEIJER

E.J. BRILL
LEIDEN • NEW YORK • KÖLN
1992

The paper in this book meets the guidelines for permanence and durability of the Committee on Production Guidelines for Book Longevity of the Council on Library Resources.

ISSN   0079-1687
ISBN   90 04 09429 6

CONTENTS

BIBLIOGRAPHY

PREFACE

On 7 and 8 september 1989 a symposium was held at the University of Leiden to celebrate Professor L.M de Rijk's 65th birthday. The title of this symposium was *On Proclus' thought and its Reception in the Middle Ages*. In the present volume the proceedings are published.

The contributions are divided in two parts. The first part is about Proclus' thought, the second about its reception in the Middle Ages. In each part the texts are ordered according to the chronological order of the subjects they deal with.

The editors wish to thank E.J. Brill of Leiden for publishing this book in the series *Philosophia Antiqua*.

L.M. DE RIJK

CAUSATION AND PARTICIPATION IN PROCLUS
THE PIVOTAL ROLE OF SCOPE DISTINCTION IN HIS METAPHYSICS

1 *Status quaestionis*

Quite a lot has been written about what are taken to be inconsistencies in Proclus' doctrines and arguments, and they have provoked quite a lot of irritation among modern scholars.[1] Proposition 98 of the *Elementatio* is surely not the most appropriate evidence to free our author from such charges. It is the proposition in which the author supposedly[2] outlines his solution[3] to the intricate problem of transcendence *vs* immanence of the Platonic Forms: "Every cause which is separated <from its effects> is at once everywhere and nowhere." Reading such statements might easily lead you to the middle of nowhere.

Quite understandably, at first glance at least, Dodds claims[4] that Proclus lays himself open to charges of inconsistency: the One, Proclus asserts, is unshareable (ἀμέθεκτον), yet we are told at the very beginning of the *Elementatio* that "every manifold in some way partakes of the One". For a reply Dodds refers[5] to Proclus' exposition of prop. 56, from which Dodds seems to gather that what is *proprie* ἀμέθεκτον[6] is nevertheless indirectly μέθεκτον through the μετεχόμενα it generates. Most unfortunately Dodds joins (*ibid.*) Emile Bréhier[7] in suggesting that "the ἀμέθεκτον is the intension of the concept (*sic!*, see n. 5), the μετέχοντα are its extension, and the μετεχόμενα are that which links intension with extension". Rosán is quite right in rejecting[8] such a comparison. For one thing, it would seem that the notion of intension should be associated with the μετεχόμενον rather than the ἀμέθεκτον (as Rosán

---

[1] Our colleague Dr. Piet Meijer has already drawn our attention to charges of the kind in E.R. Dodds, *Proclus. The Elements of Theology*. A Revised Text with Translation, Introduction and Commentary, Oxford [2], 211, A.J. Festugière, *Commentaire sur le Timée de Proclus*. Trad. et notes, Paris 1966 - 1968, II, 52 and K. Kremer, *Die neuplatonische Seinsphilosophie und ihre Wirkung auf Thomas von Aquin*, Leiden 1971, 212 ff.

[2] See Dodds, *Proclus. The Elements of Theology*, 211.

[3] For its historical background, see Dodds, *Proclus. The Elements of Theology*, 251 ff.; cf. 211.

[4] Dodds, *Proclus. The Elements of Theology*, 211; *cf.* below, P.A. Meijer, 'Participation in Henads and Monads in Proclus Theologia Platonica III, chs. 1 - 6', 81 ff.

[5] Dodds, *ibid.*

[6] Dodds has "a term which is *proprie* ἀμέθεκτον" as he is in a constant habit of talking about *terms* where nothing of the kind is found in Proclus. Our author definitely does not substitute logical for metaphysical labels. See for the use of "prop." and "cor." note 40.

[7] E. Bréhier, *Histoire de la philosophie*, I, 477.

[8] L.J. Rosán, *The Philosophy of Proclus. The Final Phase of Ancient Thought*, New York 1949, 89, n. 80.

remarks), for another it might reasonably be asked what on earth, from the logical point of view, should be understood by "that which links intension with extension".

The present paper aims to investigate in some more detail the transcendence-immanence antinomy. First an outline of its historical background will be presented from Plato onward through Plotinus and Jamblichus up to Proclus. Next I shall discuss Proclus' doctrine on these matters in the larger perspective of his philosophy, and focus on the intriguing notion of ἀμέθεκτον. Finally a few remarks will be added on the important role of what we might call "scope distinction" in Proclus' doctrines and dialectical arguments.

2 Causation and Participation in Plato

Guthrie's likening[9] of the causal function of Plato's transcendent Forms to Aristotle's Unmoved Mover can definitely find some support in Plato's works. Indeed, "of all the expressions with which Plato tried to convey the relationship between Forms and particulars, that of pattern and copy does seem to go nearest the root of the matter."[10] To Plato, the Forms really combine the formal, efficient and final causes in one, a conception of "cause" which was to become typical of all Platonism since then. It will suffice on this score to recall the important Neoplatonic doctrine of Reversion (ἐπιστροφή), which is what the product of an efficient cause obtains in returning to its cause which acts, then, as a goal, really desired by its effect.

In Plato's Phaedo this is, of course, not so clearly profiled as it is in later Platonism. However, the procedure is quite similar: physical things are not only said to partake of Forms and possess the latters' copies as "present in" themselves, but also to emulate the state of perfection characteristic of the Forms, albeit, of course, with a limited amount of success.

In this picture, the mutual relationship between the transcendent Forms and their instances or particulars occurring in the physical world can most aptly be described in terms of a continuous tension between causation from above and participation from below, indeed a tension which, especially in Neoplatonism, was considered the main concomitant of the ontological process.

As is well-known to every student of Plato, the notion of participation had met severe criticism from the old master Parmenides in Plato's dialogue of this name, and thus gave rise to a basic metaphysical problem (Parm. 130 e - 135 b): if participation is to be really active, the Form must be present in particulars and therefore split up; but if participation is to be ontologically effective and founded on a firm basis, the Forms must be transcendent.

---

[9] W.K.C. Guthrie, A History of Greek Philosophy.V: The Later Plato and the Academy, Cambridge etc. 1978, 146.
[10] Guthrie, A History of Greek Philosophy V, 146.

Plato has countered this problem in the central part of the *Sophist* by devising what he himself calls "a novel metaphysics" which focuses on the immanent status and activity of the transcendent Forms.[11] It seems a tenable claim that in the *Sophist* Plato solves the metaphysical problem of participation insofar as he clarifies and justifies his own talk about the Forms and their instances and instantiations, and rebukes all kinds of (basically semantic) misunderstandings on this account.[12] However, in this dialogue, the counterpart of participation or, if you like, the paradeigmatic function of the Forms, seem to be of minor concern to Plato. This is all the more striking since in the so-called "second regress argument" of the *Parmenides* (132 c - 133 a) it is precisely the Forms' pattern (or paradigm) function that is given a real roasting by Parmenides. The general line of his attack is the following: if the Forms are formal causes responsible for the specific characters of particulars which "wish" or "strive" to be as the Forms are while still remaining "of less worth" (*Phaedo* 74 d - 75 e), the latter must have some resemblance to the former, and since resemblance is a reciprocal relation you must concede that inasmuch as a particular resembles the Form, the latter, in turn, must resemble the particular; and if two things resemble each other they do so by sharing the same character, which must be held to be a Form causing this resemblance; and so on *ad infinitum*. As is easily seen, this attack is two-sided: it is effected along the lines of participation and of causation. Again, one may claim that the *Sophist* provides a reasonable solution to the first attack. But what remains a serious problem is how causation is accomplished by the Transcendent Forms and their immanent representatives. As late as in the *Phaedo* we are still left to ourselves on that score, not helped by such hesitant sentences as "beautiful things became beautiful by the Beautiful, though whether by its presence or communion or how else, I cannot say" (100 d). In the later dialogues this specific point is not clarified either.

After the *Sophist* the causation problem is given more profile in the *Philebus, Timaeus* and *Critias*. From then onwards, the Forms are, to use the happy characterization given by Guthrie,[13] "formal causes only, having resigned to a separate power (*i.e.* the Demiourgos or Maker) the quasi-efficient function which they, rather obscurely, possessed in the *Phaedo*." Guthrie seems to be right that in Plato's later period, the separateness of the *aitia* is underlined, which gives causation a remarkable touch. Guthrie also notices the striking absence of its terminological counterpart, μέθεξις, "a trouble-making metaphor (...) and one which took a severe beating in the *Parmenides*."

---

[11] See L.M. de Rijk, *Plato's Sophist. A Philosophical Commentary*, Amsterdam 1986, *passim*, esp. 103 ff.

[12] See *ibid.*, 140 ff.

[13] Guthrie, *A History of Greek Philosophy*. V, 255.

One may ask, now, if in the later dialogues participation faded into the background in favour of causation. I presume that, if so, this is of minor importance. What *was* decisive for the later development of Platonism is that causation and participation lost the relation of reciprocity they had before, when Forms were supposed to *cause* something and, by the same token, to be partaken of (μετέχεσθαι) by it, to that effect that "A causes B" implied "A is partaken of by B." In Neoplatonism, μέθεξις, meaning "*participation*"[14] became a unilateral relation, *viz.* from effect to cause, not *vice versa*, whereas cause and effect maintained causation as a bilateral relation. In other words, the transcendence of the cause was so strongly underlined that immanence was strictly opposed against it. The risk of interrupting "the great chain of being" was faced with the continuity of the great chain of causation instead.

Underlining the separatenes of the Primordial Cause and of secondary causes as well led to rethinking the notions of transcendence and immanence. This reconsideration took place together with the gradual transition from a "metaphysics of Forms" *via* a "metaphysics of Being" (or Ontology in the strict sense) to a "metaphysics of the One" (or Henology). As I have remarked elsewhere:[15] "in any final analysis Plato's doctrine of the Forms is untenable unless the the Transcendent Domain is taken as the entire Domain of Perfect BEING (or perfect GOOD), not split up into a number of distinct Forms. The distinction of them seems to concern, in as far as the Transcendent Domain is concerned, only a *potential* articulation, which might be actualised in the act of participation. Small wonder that in what moderns from as late as the nineteenth century onward have been accustomed to call "*Neo*platonism", Plato's doctrine has developed along the lines it actually did into a doctrine of *One* Principle, *One* Cause prior to both being and intelligence."

As a matter of fact such a development seems to have been initiated by Plato himself.[16] Well, the gradual transition from a metaphysics of Forms into a metaphysics of Being, which is bound to devise a hierarchic order of the whole domain of "all that is", must lead yet one step further and put *one* Principle ("the One") beyond Being. Actually, this step was taken by Plotinus[17] and remained influential throughout Neoplatonism (with the only exception of

---

[14] "taking a part"; cf. in Medieval Latin "participans" = "partem capiens" in contradistinction with μετέχον= "posthabens". For the role of the μετά *(post)* metaphor, see below 26.

[15] De Rijk, *Plato's Sophist*, 353, n. 55.

[16] For a first appearance of a metaphysics of Being rather than of Forms in Plato, see ibid.

[17] See *e.g.* Armstrong, 'Plotinus', in A.H. Armstrong, *The Cambridge History of Later Greek and Early Medieval Philosophy,* Cambridge 1967, 222 ff.; W. Beierwaltes, *Platonismus und Idealismus*, Frankfurt am Main 1972, 17 - 24. For its preparation in Middle Platonism, see J.M. Dillon, *The Middle Platonists. A Study of Platonism 80 B.C. to A.D. 220,* London 1977, 214 ff.; 346 ff.; 353 ff.; 366 ff.

Porphyry[18]) and it is not even entirely absent in Medieval thought that as a rule restored the predominance of *Ens perfectissimum* (or *Summum Bonum*) = *Causa Prima* (or *Deus*).

3 *Procession and Participation in Plotinus and Jamblichus*

On his deathbed Plotinus (c. 205 - 270) testified to his main intention as a scholar and a teacher to return the divine in man to the Divine in all.[19] For Plotinus, the object and proper aim of a philosophical life is to understand man's divine origin, to live up to this consciousness by restoring one's relationship with the divine All and thereby to attain a union with the highest Principle, the One or Good (see esp. *Enneads* V, 1). In fact, this return to man's real origin, which is ultimately constitutive of man's proper being, is viewed as a gradual communion ("unification" in the sense of "being-made-one" so to speak) rather than a straightforward union with the One, which were a contradictory conception as the One itself is unattainable. The communion, then, is (always in a imperfect way, of course) accomplished by "the knowledge of the things which proceed from it (*i.e.*the Good) and intellectual progress by ascending degrees; but we advance towards it by purifications and virtues and adornings of the soul." (*Enneads* VI 7, 36, 6 - 9, translation Armstrong[20]).

As to the material universe as a whole, *qua* domain of the Forms it is basically a world of patterned "Oneness", structured *into* a "manifold" (πλῆθος) of multifarious diversity. The lowest forms are not truly real entities, but merely the remotest reflections of true reality in the world of Intelligence. All what is is more authentic "being" according as it is closer to the One.

Plotinus' metaphysics is the mature fruit of his original re-thinking and critical analysis of the body of speculative notions he found in Middle Platonism.[21] He was the first to contrive a coherent doctrine[22] of the One or

---

[18] For Porphyry's identification of God and being (as of the Νοῦς and the One), see Armstrong, 'Plotinus', in Armstrong, *The Cambridge History of Later Greek and Early Medieval Philosophy*, 266 ff. and Lloyd, 'Porphyry and Jamblichus' in A.H. Armstrong, *The Cambridge History of Later Greek and Early Medieval Philosophy*, Cambridge 1967, 287 ff.; Beierwaltes, *Platonismus und Idealismus*, 24 - 26.

[19] See Armstrong, 'Plotinus', in Armstrong, *The Cambridge History of Later Greek and Early Medieval Philosophy*, 222 (cf. 215), whose excellent treatment of Plotinus' thought is at the basis of the present survey, as is Lloyd's invaluable and original discussion of Jamblichus, ''Porphyry and Jamblichus', in Armstrong, *The Cambridge History of Later Greek and Early Medieval Philosophy*, 272 - 325.

[20] 'Plotinus', in Armstrong, *The Cambridge History of Later Greek and Early Medieval Philosophy*, 227.

[21] Cf. Armstrong, 'Plotinus', in Armstrong, *The Cambridge History of Later Greek and Early Medieval Philosophy*, 236 ff. For these, see Dillon, *The Middle Platonists*, 43 ff.; 145 ff.; 192 ff.; 240 ff ; 272 ff.; 311 ff.

[22] Quite remarkably, Proclus' master Syrianus reports (in his Commentary on the *Metaphysics*, 166, 3 ff., ed. Kroll) that Archaenetus, Philolaus and Brotinus postulated a "unific" causal principle (ἐνιαία αἰτία) above the two principles, Monad and Dyad; among

Good (the First Hypostasis) as clearly distinguished (or rather separated) from, and existing beyond, its first product, divine Intelligence (Νοῦς) and the World of Forms.[23] He claimed his first Principle to be beyond all description, not capable, that is, of human determination, rather than vaguely and colourlessly undetermined in itself, since it is itself the principle *par excellence* of all determination (or *Peras*, "Limit") in the domain of being. It is free of any determination and limitation *qua* "infinitude"; as indeed *omnis determinatio est negatio* as the later saying runs. Since all being must be determined, and accordingly limited by its proper form, the One must be beyond Being. Unlike all his predecessors, Plotinus is quite explicit on this account.

The metaphysical impact of this development can hardly be overestimated. From then onwards, Being is no longer taken as an absolute perfection and its notion is basically associated with restriction and limitation. All what is is *some*thing, as opposed against being something else.[24] In short, as such being is a minor variant of Oneness (or "Existence Itself"), which is itself Absolute Perfection.[25]

The First Principle, then, (for which the determinations, "the One", and "the Good" are inadequate labels[26]) is the inexhaustible source ("cause") from whose overflowing profusion the whole universe of formal (rather "informed") being originates, including the ghostly and sterile forms embodied in matter, as well as forms in the sublunary world; matter is indeed absolutely negative and un-real to the extent that the positive nature of everything in the material world is entirely due to its inherent forms.

The way in which the second Hypostasis, Νοῦς or "Intelligence", proceeds from the One is preferably described in terms of the irradiation of sunlight. A similar description holds true of the other Hypostases. It is characteristic of every Hypostasis that it is of a lower rank than the source from which it immediately derives, and that its production ("procession from the cause") in no way affects or detracts the source. As basically a process of superabundance and overflow, emanation is rather the self-realisation[27] of the One as Good, a

---

them Brotinus says that it is superior to all Νοῦς and Οὐσία in power and seniority. See Dillon, *The Middle Platonists*, 121.

[23] See also the interesting observations made in Beierwaltes, *Platonismus und Idealismus*, 17 ff.

[24] In Medieval Neoplatonic metaphysics the primacy of Being is restored. There (as *e.g.* in Gilbert of Poitiers) *esse aliquid* refers to a state of imperfect being in contradistinction with the *esse simpliciter* of Perfect Being. See De Rijk, 'Semantics and Metaphysics in Gilbert of Poitiers. A Chapter of Twelfth Century Platonism (1)', in *Vivarium* 26 (1988), 87 - 100.

[25] For that reason there is some confusion in the usual talk of "being-in-some-sense" as it might suggest thet "being *simpliciter*" does not suffer from limitation. However, to the mind of ancient Neoplatonic thinkers it most surely does.

[26] See also Rist's informative chapter on the Plotinian One, *Plotinus. The Road to Reality*, Cambridge 1967, chapter 3.

[27] The usual opposition of emanation against the Christian notion of creation is rather unfortunately overstated in that it strongly suggests that notions of unconsciousness and

truth still resounding in the adage of the Christian Neoplatonists: *"Bonum est diffusivum sui."* With them too the First Principle (the Good) is defined by this expression rather than merely assigned one of its properties.

A more precise account of how the Νοῦς proceeds from the One shows that there are two "moments" in its timeless procession: the first stage is the one in which a "sight not yet seeing" proceeds from the One; in the second stage this sight turns back in contemplation upon the One, and thus is "informed" or filled with an essential content so as to become Intelligence *and* Being (*Enneads* II 4, 5; see Armstrong[28]). The way in which Soul proceeds from Intelligence (the third of the Plotinian three Hypostases) and is informed by turning in contemplation upon it, closely parallels the way in which Intelligence proceeds from the One.

The constitutive function of the "turning back" procedure (ἐπιστροφή) has become one of the main characteristics of Neoplatonism: Intelligence is Intelligence, as well as Soul is Soul and the World is the World, precisely *in that* they turn back in contemplation to their respective sources and ultimately the source of all that is, the One or Good.[29]

At the very end of the descent from the One lies matter (*Enneads* VI 4, 14 - 16). Like everything prior to it, matter is produced by the antecedent principles and so ultimately by the One. The diverse stages of this procession are in fact characterized by an ever — decreasing power of the reflections of oneness, goodness and beingness. In matter, not to be identified with potentiality in the Aristotelian sense, but rather an entirely passive receptacle of the lowest forms (the embodied forms), the descent from the One reaches its natural end; in matter, indeed, the stage of absolute "otherness" from the One or Good is attained.

Throughout the procession from the One to and through all the lower forms three things are crucial:

(1) The procession (production, causation) from the One is simply its overflow, due to its superabundance and unlimited perfection.[30]

(2) Every product (effect) constitutes itself in contemplatively turning back upon its immediate source. Thus Intelligence becomes the (always inadequate)

---

mechanism be associated with the former. For sound criticism of too loosely using the term "emanation" in this respect, see Armstrong, 'Plotinus', in Armstrong, *The Cambridge History of Later Greek and Early Medieval Philosophy,* 239 - 241 and Rist, *Plotinus. The Road to Reality,* 66 - 83.

[28] 'Plotinus', in Armstrong, *The Cambridge History of Later Greek and Early Medieval Philosophy,* 241.

[29] Rational beings are, on top of that, capable of yet another voluntary ἐπιστροφή to the One; see *e.g. Enneads,* VI 9, 8.

[30] Armstrong, 'Plotinus', in Armstrong, *The Cambridge History of Later Greek and Early Medieval Philosophy,* 241 rightly argues that "a perfection which is not creative, which does not produce or give out, is for Plotinus a contradictory and obviously untenable conception" and refers to *Enneads* V 1, 6; 2, 1 and 4, 1.

representative of the One, the Soul of Intelligence and so on; however, they can only do this by "breaking it up" and plurifying it.

(3) Throughout the procession oneness is *the* characteristic of what is produced on the lower levels. The status of lower-level entities is entirely due to the respective amount of oneness present in them: the higher the amount of oneness in them, the higher the ontic status of the entities.

As a metaphysician Iamblichus (c. 250 - 330) has firmly established (against Porphyry) the division of the second Hypostasis into Intelligence *qua* intelligible (or being) and *qua* intellectual (or noetic) content. For the present purpose, however, his introduction[31] of ἀμέθεκτα (or ἐξῃρημένα) is of greater importance. Doing this Jamblichus laid great emphasis on the strict separateness of the principles *qua* principles and thus clearly opposed transcendence against immanence, and procession against participation.

To rightly evaluate the notion of ἀμέθεκτος one has to bear in mind that in Neoplatonic metaphysics, procession is the generation of the less unified ("a smaller amount of oneness", as it were) from the more unified ("a greater amount of oneness") and ultimately from Unity itself. One scale of oneness or simplicity is represented by the triad "the principle *before* its representatives of the next level" — "the principle *qua* being their leader", — "the principle *qua* represented in each of its representations". It is within this context that the procession's counterpart, participation, comes in: what is shared (the *participatum*) is the principle *qua* divided or "split up", whereas the principle taken by itself (*viz.* preceding this stage of procession) must be indivisible and accordingly not - shared, and even unshareable (ἀμέθεκτος). Thus you have the triad: ἀμέθεκτον, μετεχόμενον, μετέχον: ἀμέθεκτον is any principle when considered quite apart[32] from its being shared in; μετεχόμενον is the principle *qua* "divided" (or rather "distributed") and immanent in the effect as the principle's instantiation; finally the μετέχον is the participant i.e. the subject that possesses the μετεχόμενον as its characteristic property, or from the viewpoint of (extensional) logic, it is each of the particular instances (individual members) of that property taken as a class.

According to Proclus' report in his commentary on the *Timaeus*[33] Jamblichus claimed that every self-subsistent[34] entity exists first unshareably

---

[31] For Jamblichus' paternity, see Proclus, *In Timaeum* II, 105, 16 - 28; 240; 313; 15 - 24. See also Festugière, *Commentaire sur le Timée de Proclus, ad locum.*

[32] I prefer the formula "quite apart" to the usual one "prior to", which has a somewhat temporal connotation which despite the frequent use of the preposition μετά = "after" is quite alien to Neoplatinic metaphysics. For the secondary connotation of μετά, see below 26.

[33] See above n. 31.

[34] Incidentally, unlike in Peripatetic thought, in Neoplatonism the term "subsistence" is used to stand for any essential *forma essendi. Cf.* Gilbert of Poitiers' use of the term "subsistentia"; see De Rijk, 'Semantics and Metaphysics in Gilbert of Poitiers. A Chapter of Twelfth Century Platonism', in *Vivarium* 26 (1988), 82 ff; 27 (1989), 6 - 16; 24 ff. For that

(ἀμεθέκτως), then as a shared form proceeding from the principle as its irradiation (ἔλλαμψις).

Two points may be made now:

(1) The descent properly speaking is described by Jamblichus in terms of "procession" and "irradiation" (κατάλαμψις), whereas the relationship as viewed from below is pictured in terms of reflection (similitude) and participation.

(2) Causation and participation are no longer entirely exchangeable notions (as with Plato himself), due to the predominant role from now onwards played by the separateness of a principle as acting as a cause; *qua* separate it is ἀμέθεκτος.

Apart from the procession of the respective Hypostases Jamblichus also has procession within each Hypostasis. So procession became associated with triadic structures,[35] among which the most famous one was that of "Being-Life-Intelligence,"[36] to the effect that Being, Life and Intelligence were considered three aspects of anything whatsoever in the universe.

Finally, in the continuous process of causation (or procession; πρόοδος), participation (μέθεξις) and reversion (ἐπιστροφή), each level of reality is connected to the one on the next higher level by containing as its highest characteristic feature a shared form which reflects the unshareable entity that identifies the next higher level. For example, there is a physical world that is a participant (μετέχον) possessing a shared soul (ψυχὴ μετεχομένη) immanent in it and on the next higher level there is unshareable Soul (ἀμέθεκτη ψυχή). Similar relationships are found on the higher levels.

4. Proclus' Refined Metaphysics

4.1 Preliminary

Every Ancient metaphysical system aimed at making manifest what the outside world "really" (ὄντως) is by uncovering its ontic principle(s) which unlike this world itself is (are) conceived of as independent, unchanging and eternal.[37] Of course, Neoplatonism is no exception to the rule. More than other philosophers the Neoplatonists tried to bridge the gap between the Principle (the One or Good) and its productions. This gap surely presents itself to any metaphysician since every metaphysical system which establishes itself firmly upon sublime Principles is bound to fall short in explaining how the sublime Principle is

---

matter, every "participant" (μετέχον) is a *rendez-vous* of several subsistences, see below 13 and 17.

[35] For the introduction of triadic structures as early as in Middle Platonism, see Dillon, *The Middle Platonists*, 30 ff.; 168 ff.; 214 ff.; 348; 356 ff.

[36] So Jamblichus, Proclus, *In Timaeum* III 145, 8 - 11. *Cf.* Festugière, *Commentaire sur le Timée de Proclus, ad loc.*

[37] For Plato's everlasting efforts to clear up the problematic situation ("transcendence vs. immanence" and "Being and not-Being"), see De Rijk, *Plato's Sophist, passim.*

capable of being the First Cause of such a trivial offspring the outside world ultimately is.

In the foregoing sections I have described this basic problem in as far as (Neo)Platonism is concerned, in terms of causation *vs* participation. Every student of Proclus knows that he has tried to solve the problem by devising a highly sophisticated and to the utmost refined ontological picture of the universe. Mainly due to the interpretation given by his master Syrianus of the first two hypotheses of Plato's *Parmenides* Proclus succeeds in describing the structure of Reality as a continuous procession (emanation) of all that is from the One or Good. In this procession-causation process the return or reversion of the inferior to the superior is the basic constitutive factor of the inferior's existence.[38] Well, such a reversion requires the transcendence of the superior on each level of the emanation of the One or Good and, by the same token, a continuous tension between transcendence and immanence is unavoidable throughout the domain of "what is" (τὰ ὄντα).

All that is is, down to the lowest level of existence (ὕπαρξις), a manifestation of the First and Foremost Principle (πρωτίστη ἀρχή), the One or Good (and this is why such later labels as John Scottus Eriugena's *theophania* are quite understandable). Primordial and all subsequent causation or procession (πρόοδος) is really nothing other than the communication or transmission (μετάδοσις) of Oneness by means of lots of "unific power" (δυνάμεις, ἑνώσεις). Both the One and the lower principles continue to transcend their effects (*Elem.* prop.75) and in this sense there is no communion (κοινωνία) or participation (μέθεξις) at all. What is actually communicated is the principle's irradiation (κατάλαμψις, more precisely "radiation from above"). This is caused by the principle's superabundance[39] and as ἔλλαμψις or immanent irradiation it is active on the lower level of existence and bestows being upon the participant; or to say it more precisely, the irradiation is constitutive of the participant's existence. *Qua* effect it is a spark immanent in the participant and, accordingly, clearly opposed against the principle's transcendence.

Let us examine now the notions of causation and participation more closely.

---

[38] See above, 7.

[39] *Cf. Elem.* 30, 25; 68, 9; 106, 17 and 112, 23 where the Principle's superabundance is described in terms of emanating power (δύναμις).

4. 2 *The Proclean Universe From the Viewpoint of Causation*

The One or Good is the single Cause of the whole universe *(kosmos)* or the total sum of everything that exists in one way or another; see *Elem.* prop. 11 - 13; 20 - 21 *et passim; Theol. plat.* I, 11 - 24 *et passim.*.[40]

The One (τὸ αὐτοέν or "Oneness itself") = *Limitation* or Definiteness itself (τὸ πρῶτον πέρας) = Infinitude itself (ἡ πρώτη ἀπειρία); see *Elem.* prop. 90. The First Principle's Infinitude is nothing but superabundant Power whose activity *qua* Providence (πρόνοια) gives rise to anything else in the universe (*Elem.* props. 87 - 96). Its Definiteness is the cause of ἕνωσις or "unific power" which constitutes the unity of an entity of lower rank and unifies it in counterbalancing as it were its self-destructive manifoldness. The First Principle, and the lower principles as well, give existence to their effects by procession (πρόοδος), and value or Goodness by making the effect revert to the cause (ἐπιστρέφειν). Reversion may be said "to restore to reality the value which was lost in the process of procession, without annihilating the individuality which procession creates."[41] Thus, reversion is equally constitutive of the effect's existence (*Elem.* props. 31 - 39, *cf.* above p. 7).[42] The δύναμις or ἕνωσις being active throughout the universe as the constitutive agent of everything's existence (ὕπαρξις) is a homogeneous power.[43] When acting above the level of Being it is called *apeiria*, whereas the power below that level is called ζωή, or Life.[44] *Qua* First and Only Cause the One or Good contains the whole universe within it potentially. Its causation gives rise to other subsistences (ὑποστάσεις) which are either dynameis or their participants. The One itself exists but *is* not ('being' indeed is something inferior to Oneness and Existence; see below 12f.); it is "beyond Being" (ὑπερουσίον).

---

[40] *Elem.* = *Elementatio theologica* quoted after Dodd's edition; prop. 1, exp. refers to Proclus' explanation of the prop.; *cor.* to the corollary added to some of them. *Theol. plat.* = *Platonic Theology* quoted after the edition by Saffrey - Westerink (henceforth S.W.).

[41] Dodds, *Proclus. The Elements of Theology*, 221.

[42] W. Beierwaltes, *Proklos. Grundzüge seiner Metaphysik,* Frankfurt am Main 1965, 343 ff. puts Proclus' doctrine of the One in its authentic perspective.

[43] For ὕπαρξις as "energy", see *e.g. Elem.* props. 9; 16; 65. F. Romano is quite right, I presume, in rejecting (*Proclo. Lezioni sul "Cratilo" di Platone. Introduzione, Traduzione e Commento,* Catania 1989, 133 - 136) "esistenza" ("existence") as the word is commonly used for rendering Proclean ὕπαρξις. He quite understandably prefers a translation such as "natura profonda", "natura essenziale" meaning singular natures rather than abstract ones. However, in order to have, as in Greek, a one-word expression I would maintain "existence" on the proviso, however, that it is taken in the specific Proclean, or rather Neoplatonic sense of "<the property of being an> existent-including-its essential-nature." The use of "essentia" as found from the 12th century onwards may be compared (see De Rijk, 'Abailard's Semantic Views in the Light of Later Developments', in *English Logic and Semantics from the End of the Twelfth Century to the Time of Ockham and Burley,* edited by H.A.G. Braakhuis, C.H. Kneepkens, L.M. de Rijk, Artistarium. Supplementa I, Nijmegen 1981, 29 - 32 and J. Spruyt, *Peter of Spain on Composition and Negation. Text, Translation, Commentary,* Artistarium, Supplementa V, Nijmegen 1989, 162, 177.

[44] See Rosán, *The Philosophy of Proclus. The Final Phase of Ancient Thought,* 109, n. 36.

What comes "after" (μετά) the One or Good is a mixture of Limitation and Infinitude (*Elem.* props. 87 - 96). The Proclean universe consists of six levels of existence below that of the One or Good.[45] On every one of these domains the causative force of the One has decreased only to come to an end on the lowest level, *viz.* that of the material world.

The first level of mixtures (μικτά) is the domain of being (τὰ ὄντα); see *Elem.* props. 87 - 103; *Theol. plat.* III, 9. Unlike the One all that is as such is not simple but "composed"[46] of one-ness (or limitation or definiteness) and the corresponding power (infinitude); see *Elem.* prop. 89. *Qua* composite all that is is not perfect in the absolute sense and, accordingly, "an existence"[47] (ὕπαρξις) of a lower rank than the One, although there is, of course, "perfect Being" as the highest existence on its own level.[48]

Thus "Being" is a notion which in itself connotes limitation and imperfect existence; being is, in other words, a minor variant of existence.[49] Yet, since being is the universal and highest characteristic of all that *is* and, accordingly, among all that is has the highest existence, the term "being" is often used by Proclus as an equivalent of "existence". In fact, existence differs from being only on the level of the One. On its own level Being is the cause of all that is. As such it is the cause co-operative with the One. (*Elem.* prop. 75, exp.) or rather acting as the representative of the One which properly speaking is the First and Only Cause.

The second and third levels of mixtures within the universe are that of Life (ζωή) and that of the Intellective Principle (Νοῦς) which are the two companions of Being in the triad subordinate to the Hypostasis of Being: "What is" — "Life" — "Intellect". At the basis of this configuration, as of the ones found on lower levels, is the post-Plotinian theory that all intelligibles have a triadic structure which on every level mirrors the fundamental triad: steadfastness (μονή) — procession (πρόοδος) — reversion (ἐπιστροφή), or limitation (πέρας) — infinitude (ἄπειρον) — mixture (μικτόν).[50]

The fourth level is that of Soul (ψυχή). This domain contains the extra-mundane Soul transcending the entire world order. As with Plotinus (*Enneads*

---

[45] Cf. Rosán, *The Philosophy of Proclus. The Final Phase of Ancient Thought*, 100 - 117. For the underlying triadic structure, the Neoplatonic "trinity of subordination", Soul — Intellective Principle — The One, see *Elem.* prop. 20.

[46] For the peculiar nature of Neoplatonic "composition" and its basically differring from Aristotelian composition, see below 15 ff.

[47] rather than "an existent" because of the formal nature of all inhabitants of the Proclean universe. For that matter, Proclus uses the same term ὕπαρξις to mean both "existence" and "existent".

[48] For "perfection" as a relative notion, see *e.g. Elem.* props. 25 and 39 and above 7.

[49] For Proclus, "being" always is "being something" or "being so and so"; see *e.g. Elem.* prop. 18; cf. above 7.

[50] For "triadic structure" in Proclus, see *e.g. Elem.* props. 146 - 148. The impact of "triadic thought" on Neoplatonism is profoundly discussed in Beierwaltes, *Proklos. Grundzüge seiner Metaphysik*, 19 - 164.

IV 3, 4) from this Soul which has no single tie with bodies, the World-Soul and the particular souls[51] derive (*Elem.* props. 184 - 211; *In Timaeum, passim)* The fifth level is that of nature (φύσις). It is an immanent but incorporeal causative force which gives birth to the material world. It is defined at *In Parm.*, 1045: "I call 'Nature' that single power ruling over the material world and presiding over change together with the Intellect and the Soul and by means of them." The sixth and lowest level is that of the material world, called Body (σῶμα), which is the ultimate effect of all preceding causes. It is itself without any causative force. As deprived of all productive Oneness it is nothing but an "appearance".

Rosán[52] is quite right in claiming that "for Proclus there is only one basic relationship that can be hold between two existing things and their powers and in terms of which all other relationships may be explained," *viz.* causation. Its nature can be best elucidated when it is taken as μετάδοσις, that is, the transmission or communication of power (δύναμις). The process of causation is systematically expounded in *Elem.* props. 25 - 39 and 97 - 112. Resuming the doctrine of the *Elementatio* and the *Platonic Theology* it may be stated that everywhere in the universe causation (procession) is due to the emanation of the sublime causative force of the One as Good, which as a continuous stream (qualitatively homogeneous but quantatively of an ever lessening power) is, on every level, the constitutive agent of any existence and, accordingly, of any particular existing on that level. Whereas in the One Definiteness (or Limitation) itself is identical with Infinitude itself, they are different entities[53] at every level posterior to the One and, accordingly, different, and to some extent even opposing agents. But because at the level of the One, the two are both formally and really identical, at all the following levels it is oneness (ἕνωσις) that brings them together and causes plurality (or multitude, or "manifold"; πλῆθος), which for Proclus is nothing but a combination of "one" and "not-one" (*Elem.* prop. 2).

Each particular in the universe is a composite or *rendez - vous* of a number of ontically different characteristics, the so-called "henads" (*Elem.* props. 6[54]; 116 - 117; 128 - 137; *Theol. plat.* I, 26; III, 3) which *qua* instantiations of oneness are as many (diminished) δυνάμεις originating from the One *via* the

---

[51] In point of fact, the sub-level of the particular souls comprises (a) the immanent souls of the seven planets and of the fixed stars, (b) those of the "gods below the moon" (*In Tim.* 255, 10) to which human souls belong as well. *Cf.* Dodds, *Proclus. The Elements of Theology,* 295 ff.

[52] Rosán, *The Philosophy of Proclus. The Final Phase of Ancient Thought,* 68.

[53] I use the neutral term "entity" for everything enjoying existence, whether a participant or a power immanent in it. It should be noticed that for Proclus, the latter is something subsistent, too.

[54] Dodds seems to be wrong in changing (at p. 6, 25 and 26) the reading of all MSS ἑνάδες into ἑνάς.

monads, that is, the leaders of each and every group (σειρά, τάξις, ἀριθμός; *Elem.* prop. 21; *Theol. plat.* II 26, 7; III 2, and *passim*).

Each particular has its own henads exclusively belonging to it as its particular constituents (*Elem.* props. 8; 21; 23; 113 - 165; esp. 102, 14 - 16; *Theol. plat.* III 1 - 6). *Qua* common elements of the members of any class of entities the participated monads "connect what is to the One which is beyond all the wholes, in the same manner as the participated intellects unite souls with the universal Intellect and as participated souls unite bodies with the universal Soul" (*Theol. plat.* III 4, 15, 20 - 24). Every manifold being a combination of one and not-one (*Elem.* prop. 2) is at the same time like (ὅμοιον *viz.* to the One) and unlike (ἀνόμοιον), *i.e.* as a (group of) subsistent entity (-ties) it is unlike, but like inasmuch as it has (participated) oneness. "Likeness binds all things together as unlikeness distinguishes and dissociates them" (*Elem.* prop. 32). All procession is accomplished through a likeness of what follows to the preceding primitive principle (*ibid.* prop. 29), or to say it otherwise, by ἕνωσις (*Theol. plat.* I 28, 120, 16 - 19). In explaining prop. 29 Proclus says (with reference to prop. 28: "Every producing cause gives subsistence to entities like to itself prior to such as are unlike") that "it is a likeness coming from the producing causes which makes the products subsistent" (*cf. Theol. plat.* III 2, 6, 14 - 21). Similarly, reversion is accomplished through likeness (*Elem.* prop. 32; *Theol. plat.* III 2).

It should be noticed then that Proclus describes the union and reversion as performed in such a manner that "the like in manifold" (τὸ ὅμοιον πλῆθος) unites itself with the One whereas the unlike is united with the One by the likeness it has within itself:

> *Theol. plat.* III 4, 15, 24 - 16, 14: For it is not possible that the unlike classes of the secondary entities should be united with the cause which transcends the manifold without an intermediate (ἀμέσως) and it rather must be that the connection should be effected through the alike entities. For the alike in the manifold inasmuch as indeed it is a manifold, has communion with the whole and inasmuch as it is like to its preceding monad, it is by nature united with the latter. Being established, therefore, in the middle of both, it [*i.e.* the like in the manifold] is united with the whole and the One which is prior to the manifold. But it contains in itself remote processions <from the One> which in themselves are unlike with regard to their own oneness, and through itself it makes revert all <members of the class> to that oneness [*viz.* that at the top of the class]. And in this manner all entities extend themselves towards the First and Foremost Cause of the wholes, the unlikes indeed through the likes and the latter through themselves. For likeness itself by itself conducts and binds the many to the One and makes revert secondary entities to the monads at the head of them. For the very being of the likes *qua* likes originates from oneness; hence, it binds manifold to that from which it is allotted its procession.

It seems useful to draw our attention to the fact that unlike the term ὅμοιον which refers to a (the) constitutive element(s) of an entity, *i.e.* its henad(s), ἀνόμοιον stands for the participant itself rather than any (putative) unlike "component". This may be gathered from the passage just quoted and also *e.g.*

from *Elem.* prop. 36 exp. (40, 5 - 6: "the more remote <effects> are less perfect, as they become unlike their causes"); I prop. 110, exp. and prop. 135, exp. 120, 10 - 11: "the participant must be like to the participated[55] in one respect and different and unlike in another." On top of that, and more importantly, one should refrain from conceiving of the composition of beings of the Proclean universe as an Aristotelian configuration of two elements such as form and matter. For Proclus, each and every procession is accomplished as a lower manifestation of the One, and oneness is the *only* true constituent of an entity. It is true, Proclus sometimes speaks of "something added" to the One (or to a lower principle), but by this "something added to the One" the author apparently understands the diminution of the One. That the addition really is something detracting from Oneness appears from quite a number of passages.[56] Throughout these passages the "addition" turns out to be an *additum* to the One and Good itself (see esp.*Elem.* prop. 10, 9 - 10) which affects it where it is present as an (immanent) irradiation at each of the lower levels of the universe. By using the term "addition" Proclus does definitely not suggest that *within* the participant there is some composition of two (preexisting) elements. Similarly, in the wellknown prop. 2 of the *Elementatio* the particular, *qua* deteriorisation of the One, is opposed against the One itself, rather than its own unific element.[57]

4.3 *The Proclean Universe From the Viewpoint of Participation*

In order to clarify the important difference between causation and participation it is useful to start with the definition of cause presented by Proclus in *Elem.* prop. 98, exp.: "For a cause is that which fills all entities that are naturally capable of taking a share in it, which is the principle of all secondary entities, and is present in all the fertile emanations of its irradiations." Thus causing appears to be co-ordinated with sharing in that the cause makes its effect share in it. Sharing indeed is that which guarantees the communion of the effect with its cause because they are mutually connected by the alike character they have. This is explained in more detail in prop. 28, exp. 32, 17 - 21:

> If they [*i.e.* cause and effect] are altogether distinct they will be irreconcilable, and nowhere will that which proceeds from the cause sympathize with it, and

---

[55] *i.e.* the immanent share it possesses; see below, 16 ff.

[56] *Elem.*, 10, 9 - 13; 108, 16 - 17; *Theol. plat.* I 11, 31, 19 - 20; II 2, 23, 11 - 12; 10, 63, 15; III 2, 10, 10 - 14; 4, 14, 19 - 22; 5, 18, 4 - 15; 20, 69, 7 - 9; see also Dodds, *Proclus. The Elements of Theology,* 195 ff., and S.W. III, 112, n. 4.

[57] Dodds' translation on p. 2, 18 - 21 in *Proclus. The Elements of Theology* ("But if it has some character other than oneness, in virtue of that character it is not-one, and so not unity unqualified") is basically incorrect in that he takes ἐκεῖνο (20) to refer to the immanent oneness of the participant. But it appears from ll. 16 - 17 ("it partakes in the One by being something beside the One") that ἐκεῖνο stands for the transcendent One. Therefore, one should rather render ll. 19 - 22: "But if it is something beside the One [i.e. added to the

accordingly the one will not partake in the other either as they are completely different. For the participated bestows upon the participant communion in that which it participates of. Well, surely it must be that what is caused (τὸ αἰτιατόν) participates in the cause as from there possessing its beingness.

This passage makes Proclus' use of the key-terms "to cause" and "to participate" quite clear. The former term is unequivocally used in that τὸ αἰτιατόν stands for the effect as opposed against τὸ αἴτιον (or ἡ αἰτία) as its cause. However, τὸ μετεχόμενον (litt. "what is participated") stands for the character communicated by the cause to the effect rather than the cause itself participated in and here designated by the formula τὸ οὗ μετέσχεν (litt. "that of which it [the participant] has taken a part"). In other words, *qua* participant the effect does participate (by definition to be sure) in the cause as its principle, and, accordingly, is called τὸ μετέχον (or τὸ μετάσχον p. 32, 20), whereas what is designated by the passive participle μετεχόμενον is the transmitted δύναμις or spark (ἔλλαμψις) deriving from the cause, rather than its source. Grammatically speaking, the subject of the active verb μετέχειν ("to partake", "to share", "to participate") is the effect or participant[58] and its indirect object [59] (referred to by a partitive genitive) is the cause; however, the subject of the passive form μετέχεσθαι is the immanent δύναμις or spark deriving from the cause and present in the participant[60] to the effect that μετέχεσθαι ὑπό = "to be possessed[61] as an immanent share by" or "to be as a share present in", rather than "to be shared of (in) by"; similarly the participle μετεχόμενον should be rendered "possessed as an immanent share" or "be an immanent share". That means that

---

One'] which is not one, then in virtue of that [*i.e.* the "something added to the One"] it is not one (...).''

[58] To be sure, this absolutely does not mean that, philosophically speaking, the participant acts as *subiectum participationis*. In point of fact, for the Neoplatonists there is no participant or any receiver before the μέθεξις. Unlike Plato who admitted the τὸ ἐν ᾧ as a (rather vague) subject of participation, Proclus has really nothing of the kind. For him, the participant does not come into existence until the very act of μετάδοσις (transmission or communication). To speak with Nicholas of Cusa (1401 - 1464), there is "reflection without a mirror" (*De docta ignorantia* II 2, ed. Hoffmann - Klibansky, 67: *"sicut imago speciei in speculo, — posito quod speculum ante aut post per se et in se nihil fit ."*

[59] For Nicholas of Methone (*Amptyxis*, 5, 17 ff.; 44, 14 ff., ed. P. Wilpert, *Quellen und Studien zur Geschichte der Philosophie,* Band V, Berlin 1967, 41); on *proprie* ἀμέθεκτον as opposed against *indirectly* μέθεκτον, see Dodds, *Proclus. The Elements of Theology,* 211.

[60] Likewise the verb μεταδίδοναι ("to communicate") is used with the partitive genitive (referring to the indirect object, the cause or principle), whereas the corresponding δίδωμι has as its direct object the transmitted δύναμις; see *e.g.* Elem. prop. 18, 20, 3 - 10: "Everything which by its mere being furnishes <something> to others is itself primitively that which it gives to the receivers. For if it gives by mere being, and so makes the bestowal (μετάδοσιν) from its own beingness, then what it gives (ὃ μὲν δίδωσι) is inferior to its own beingness <...>. Therefore, that which pre-exists in the giver himself is in a better way than what is given (τοῦ δοθέντος)." The substantive noun μετάδοσις is indiscriminately used to mean the bestowal (act) and the gift. See *e.g. Elem* p. 66, 28; 68, 2 and 7.

[61] Rosán, *The Philosophy of Proclus. The Final Phase of Ancient Thought,* 81, 54 is right in preferring the rendering "possessed" to "participated", but his preference seems to be mainly based on the fact that the participant does not share its character with something else rather than on the share's immanent status.

the term μετεχόμενον is always used to stand for the immanent power (δύναμις) or the inherent ontic principle in all that is and, consequently, is found at every level of the universe. When e.g. Proclus speaks (In Parm. VI, 1045, 11 - 12, ed. Cousin) of τὸ ἓν μετεχόμενον ὑπὸ νοῦ he describes it himself as "oneness thrown in Intelligence as a kind of seed" so that oneness immanent in the effect must be meant, not "the One participated in by Νοῦς."[62] Likewise expressions such as μετεχομένοι νόες and μετεχομέναι ψυχάι[63] (where the plural is to be noticed) should be rendered: "immanent Intelligence shares", and "immanent Soul shares" respectively.

Thus the relationship between effect and cause is transitive, whereas that between causation and participation is not. The tension between causation and participation can be best clarified by discussing the intransitivety of the latter relationship, which centres round the notion of ἀμέθεκτος or "unshareable", "unshared". Once the precise meaning of ἀμέθεκτος is established the participle μετεχόμενον does not cause special difficulties.

5 The meaning of ἀμέθεκτον and μετεχόμενον in Proclus

For Proclus any principle (the secondary ones as well as the First Principle, the One or Good) is qua transcending its effects not partaken of by them nor can it possibly be something immanent in them and, consequently, is not said to μετέχεσθαι or "to be a share present in" something else. Therefore all transcendent principles must be "exempt from being a share" since what is shareable, or rather actually shared, is the δύναμεις or sparks produced by them qua causes. Obviously, our author was influenced by Jamblichus on this account, as he himself reports (In Timaeum II 13), that Jamblichus taught that every subsistent entity exists first "unshareably" (ἀμεθέκτως), then as a participated character, proceeding from the principle as its irradiation or spark (ἔλλαμψις).[64]

Of course, the ἀμέθεκτον par excellence is the One or Good itself; see In Parm. VI, 1067; Theol. plat. III 4. However, due to the oneness transmitted by the One there is also beyond shared being, shared intelligence and shared soul, Being exempt from being shared (τὸ ἀμεθέκτως ὄν) as well as unshareable Νοῦς and unshareable Soul; see Elem. props. 161 -165. Again, Jamblichus' views on this account may be paralleled.

The statements above may be supported now by several passages taken from the Elementatio and Platonic Theology.

---

[62] Cf. Theol. plat. I 12, 56, 24 - 57, 1 quoted below 21.
[63] E.g. Theol. plat. III 2, 10, 27 ff. (see below 21) and III 4 (below 23)
[64] see above 8.

5.1 Μέθεξις c.a. in the *Elementatio*

Let us begin with the propositions 23 and 24 of the *Elementatio*.

> prop. 23: Every unshareable (ἀμέθεκτον) gives subsistence out of itself to what is possessed as a share (τὰ μετεχόμενα); and all shared subsistences (μετεχομέναι ὑποστάσεις) are linked up by an upward tension to unshareable existences (ἀμέθ-εκτοι ὑπάρξεις).

In the proof or exposition of this proposition Proclus explains the relationship the unshareable has with what is possessed as a share and the participant:

> p. 26, 25 - 28, 7: For the unshareable having the structure (λόγον) of a monad (*qua* being independent and not dependent upon something else and *qua* transcending the participants [i.e. as their leader]) generates what can be possessed as a share. For either it will remain by itself in sterility <....>, or else, it will give something of itself; and so the receiver becomes a participant but that which is given (τό δοθέν) attains subsistence by way of participation (μετεχομένως). But every share (μετεχόμενον), in getting to be related to that by which it is possessed as a share [i.e. the particular], is secondary to that which in all is equally present and has filled them all out of its own being. <....>. If <the latter> be in one out of all, it will no longer be related to all but to one <only>. Therefore, if it is both common to all possible participants and identical for all, it will be prior to all; well, that means ἀμέθεκτος.

In the next proposition (24) the hierarchy between the three is given and expounded:

> p. 28, 8 - 9; 18 - 20: Every participant is inferior to the share it has and the latter to the unshareable. For, in short, the one [i.e. the unshareable] is something one prior to the many; the other is a shared part in the many (μετεχόμενον ἐν τοῖς πολλοῖς); at the same time one and not-one, but every participant is not-one and at the same time one.

Obviously, "that which in all equally is present and has filled them all out if its own being" is opposed against "that which is given <by the unshareable *qua* cause> and attains subsistence by way of participation", *i.e.* the μετεχόμενον which unlike the unshareable *is* proper to just one participant.[65]

In the first part of the exposition it is said (28, 10 ff.) that the ἀμέθεκτον *qua* independent of something else and *qua* transcending its participants generates shares that can be possessed by participants. Hence the following picture arises: out of itself, not *qua* partaking, that is, of someting else superior to it, the unshareable generates shares which attain subsistence by participation and each uniquely belong to their own participant. This would mean, I presume, that the privative noun ἀμέθεκτος should dispose of any notion of sharing actually accomplished, both in the upward and in the downward direction, so that *qua* unshareable the unshareable is independent of any superior source of parti-

---

[65] For the connotation of "individuality", see above 8 and 13, and *Theol. plat.* III 4, 14, 11 - 15.

cipation and transcends the entities coming after it.⁶⁶ As a matter of fact, it does give rise to other entities which, accordingly, *are* its participants (and are called so as well) just as it does depend upon a superior cause itself, as is explicitly claimed in prop. 99.

All this must imply that the notion of ἀμέθεκτον should only apply within a certain scope, *i.e.* setting apart any relationship of sharing in the upward or downward direction, yet without denying or ignoring such relationships.

Elem. prop. 99 makes this even more manifest. In this passage Proclus discusses the unshareable *qua* unshareable:

> p. 88, 20 - 23: In that respect precisely in which an unshareable is unshareable, therein it does not obtain its subsistence from something else as its cause but is itself the principle and cause of all its shares. And it is in this sense (οὕτως) that in every series the principle is ungenerated.

To begin with, this proposition apparently discusses the unshareable as occurring in the series of which it is the leader (the *monas,* that is; see prop. 23). The restriction is made explicit in the closing sentence and also appears from the opening lines of the exposition: "For if it is (an) unshareable it is allotted primacy *in its own series* and does not proceed from others" (88, 24 -5). The same restriction is expressed by the statement that something is (an) unshareable *in respect of* the proper character (κατὰ τὴν ἰδιότητα), which is, of course, the proper character common to all members of the series involved and to them exclusively. Again, one has to notice the reduplicative formula: "the unshareable *qua* unshareable" (88, 20). Proclus does surely not deny or ignore that the unshareable should derive from a superior cause (this is, on the contrary, explicitly acknowledged by him). What he claims is that *qua* unshareable it does not derive from something superior as its cause. Thus causation as well as participation are out of scope and, again, any sharing is ruled out both in the upward and in the downward directions. Let us read Proclus' explanation of prop. 99:

> p. 88, 24 - 33: For if it is (an) unshareable it is allotted primacy in its own proper series, and does not proceed from others; since it would no longer be the first if it received from something else that proper characteristic according to which it is (an) unshareable. If it is, however, inferior to others and proceeds from them, it does not proceed inasmuch as it is (an) unshareable but inasmuch as it is a participant. For of the entities from which it arises, it of course partakes and it is not primitively that of which it partakes; rather it is primitively what it is in the manner of an unshareable (ἀμεθέκτως). Therefore, it is not *qua* unshareable that it originates from a cause. Indeed, inasmuch as it originates from a cause, it is a participant and not (an) unshareable. However, *qua* unshareable <it is> the cause of shares [see prop. 23], yet without being itself a participant of others.

---

⁶⁶ that is, those occurring in the same series; see below 21. For the sense of "after" (μετά), see above 8, n.3 2, and below 26.

Three things may be clear now. First, the notion of ἀμέθεκτον only applies within a certain series.[67] Second, the term does not refer to what is just un-shareable, period, but rather what from a certain point of view (*viz.* viewed as the leader of a series) is (an) unshareable. Once its relationship to its own superior cause *is* taken under consideration it is no longer an unshareable but itself a participant.

Nonetheless, what the unshareable generates out of itself (see prop. 23) does partake of it. This is even rather pregnantly expressed 60, 16 - 19: "Beauty, likeness, steadfastness and identity *being unshareables*, are yet par-taken of by their continuous participants and by their temporal participants secondarily in the same series."[68] Surely, all and everything does partake in the One, the unshareable *par excellence*. However, just as Proclus does not say that "the One is partaken of", the leader of any series is not said "to be partaken off" either (in Greek μετέχεται or μετεχόμενον). Why that? It must be because the passive forms μετέχεσθαι and μετεχόμενον are used to refer to the "share" or "part" taken rather than the source which is "shared in" or "partaken of".

This is also strongly supported by prop. 116, exp., which may seen as the crown witness for our view:

> p. 102, 14 - 16: In the first place it is evident that that [*i.e.* the One] is unshare-able; otherwise it would be a μετεχόμενον and *thereby* (διὰ τοῦτο) belong to some one thing and no longer be the cause both of that which is prior to Being [*viz.* the character, beingness] and of what is [*viz.* the participants of oneness and being-ness].

In this passage μετεχόμενον is clearly "associated", to say the least, with im-manence and individuality, as it is in the corollary of prop. 63 too:

> p. 60, 13 - 16: From this it is apparent that also the unific powers (ἐνώσεις) deriv-ing from the One which irradiate what is (ἐλλαμπόμεναι τοῖς οὖσιν ....)[69]

where it should be noticed that unlike καταλάμπειν the verb ἐλλάμπειν (as the noun ἔλλαμψις) is used to mean the *immanent shining (and sparks)* present in what exists on a lower level than its cause (see above 10).

So there is overwhelming evidence that the passive verb μετέχεσθαι and its participle should mean "be<ing> an immanent share" or "possess(ed) as an immanent share". Consequently, ἀμέθεκτος is best rendered "exempt from any sharing", a formula intended to cover both sharing and being shared. That is to say, as restricted to one particular series in the universe, any sharing in a higher

---

[67] This restriction is confirmed by passages such as 90, 20 - 2; 92, 5 - 6 and 158, 26 - 8, where the notion of ἀμέθεκτον is clearly associated with the unshareable's being an inhabitant (as the leader, to be sure) of a certain series (σειρά, τάξις).

[68] *Theol. plat.* III 2, 10, 26 ff. See also Dodds, *Proclus. The Elements of Theology*, 234 and 238.

[69] The Greek expression (*lit.* "radiating in, what is") makes the immanence of "oneness" quite manifest. See also above 10.

cause (occurring as it is in the next higher series) is out of the question, whereas to be itself an immanent share in the entities of the series of which it is the leader is impossible, since *qua* unshareable it is the transcendent cause of these entities (prop. 23).[70]

Let us now consider the use of the key - notions of participation as occurring in the *Platonic Theology*, Book I - V (Book VI not being available as yet in a critical edition.)

5.2 Μέθεξις *c.a.* in the *Platonic Theology*

As in the *Elementatio*, the participle μετεχόμενον is always used to stand for the shared character immanent in the participant. In many passages this seems to be ignored by modern interpreters who mistake it for meaning the transcendent source of participation. *E.g.* when summarizing *Theol. plat.* II 3, Saffrey - Westerink (in their excellent introduction, p. LXXXI) rather equivocally say "car le participé doit être transcendant par rapport à ses participants" where Proclus has δεῖ (...) εἶναι (...) πρεσβύτερον, (...) τοῦ μετεχομένου τὸ ἐξηρημένον which rather means: "It must be that the transcendent <cause> should be superior to the <immanent> share possessed."

Here are some informative passages taken from the first five books:

> I 12, 56, 24 - 57, 7: For what is the oneness possessed as a share by what is other than that which is the divine *in* every being and through which all entities are united with the unshareable One? For just as bodies through their life-character (τῇ ἑαυτῶν ζωῇ) are linked with Soul and as souls through their intellective character (τῷ ἑαυτῶν νοητικῷ) extend towards universal Intelligence and the first Intellection, likewise what truly *is*, through its oneness (τῷ ἑαυτῶν ἑνί) is raised to the transcendent Oneness and by this <is> inseparable from the First Cause.

Clearly, the ἓν μετεχόμενον of line 25 is the "share of oneness", just as in the subsequent lines the immanent character of oneness is parallelled with the *immanent* characters of Life and Intelligence.

In III 2 the ἀμέθεκτα are explicitly opposed against the μετεχόμενα.

> III 2, 10, 15 - 26: Therefore, in addition to what has been said, let us determine the following, which is most assuredly true, viz. that everywhere it is necessary that prior to the causes which are immanent shares (μετεχομένων αἰτίων),[71] the unshareable causes should have pre-existence in the <respective> wholes. For if it is necessary that a cause should have the same relationship to its offspring as the One has to the whole nature of beings, and that by nature it should possess this rank with regard to the secondary entities, whereas the One is unshareable as it equally transcends all beings — then it is fitting, I think, that also every other cause reflecting the superiority the One has with regard to all entities, transcends what is immanent in the secondary entities and possessed as shares by them.

---

[70] The term χωριστῶς μετεχόμενον used in props. 81 and 82 does not refer to the source of participation either; see Dodds *ad loc.* Professor C. Steel (Louvain) was kind enough to correct my previous misunderstandings on this score.

Obviously, τῶν ἐν τοῖς δευτέροις ὄντων (line 25) stands for that which is immanent in the secondary entities and the following μετεχομένων fits in quite well with it and further explains the immanence of the share.

The remainder of this chapter (which reminds us of *Elem.* props. 28 and 100) implicitly (but clearly enough) says that the unshareable cause gives subsistence to immanent shares (μετεχόμενα), shares, that is, of the specific property of the series of which the monad *qua* ἀμέθεκτον is the leader (*cf.* III 3, 13, 12 - 18, quoted below 11):

> III 2, 10, 27 - 11, 15: (...) and <on the other hand it is fitting that> every unshareable and primitive cause, when out by itself it gives subsistence to the immanent shares (μετεχόμενα), rank the monads which are like to itself above what is unlike to it in the secondary entities. I mean that, for instance, the first soul should rank the manifold of souls [*i.e.* the soul-shares] before the beings of nature, and the first Intelligence should rank the intellect-shares (μετεχομένους νοάς) before the manifold of souls. It is in this manner indeed that everywhere the very first transcendent class can have a rank analogous to the One and the secondary entities partaking of what is of a like kind as the cause will not only be analogous to the cause but they will also, through their likeness to these [*i.e.* secondary entities], be united with the unshareable principle. Therefore, prior to the forms immanent in other entities, there are forms being by themselves, and prior to the causes which are co-ordinate in a series, there are the transcendent <causes>, and prior to the immanent <monads>,[72] there are the unshareable monads. And (a corollary deriving from this proof): the transcendent causes are generative of the co-ordinate causes and the unshareable causes place the immanent monads beyond their own offspring. And what is by itself produces the powers which are immanent in other entities (τὰς ἐν ἄλλοις δυνάμεις).

In III, 3 the different roles of the unshareable henad and the (immanent) henads of beings are clarified, whereby it is also manifest that the term ἀνόμοιον ("what is unlike") stands for the unalike "substance" rather than any of its unalike constituents (whereas "the alike" always refers to the substance's immanent constituent (or the representative of its superior cause, the henad):

> III 3, 13, 6 - 18: For again, according to another way [*viz.* of considering the subject matter, *i.e.* the role of the henads] it must be that what primitively *is* should partake of the first and foremost Cause through their proximate henads. For every class of the secondary entities is connected with the preceding ones through what is like <to the latter>: bodies indeed <are alike> to the universal Soul through the particular souls [*i.e.* soul-shares], the souls <is alike> to the universal Intelligence through the intellective monads [*i.e.* Intelligence-shares], and what is (the first beings at least) <is alike> to the One through the unitary existences [*i.e.* oneness-shares]. For what is, by its own nature, is unlike to the One; for beingness (οὐσία) and what is in need of unity from outside, cannot be connected with the first and foremost Oneness and is entirely remote from it. The henads of what is, however, which were given existence from the henad

---

[71] I take αἰτίων for the genitive of neuter αἴτιον and τὰ ἀμέθεκτα as referring to causes; *cf.* in line 24 the neuter ἕκαστον.

[72] S.W. seem to take μετεχομένων (line 11) for a neuter genitive and translate "beings" (êtres). However, the constructionas well as the rhythm of the passage seem to require to supply μονάδων in order to maintain the parallellism between "causes" and "monads".

which is unshareable and so transcends the wholes, are not only able to connect what is with the One, but also make revert it to themselves.

Theol. plat. III 4 elaborates what is stated by *Elem..* prop. 116 ("Every god is shareable, except the One") and opposes the immanent henads against the un-shareable One. It opens with a basic question on this account:

> III 4, 14, 11 - 15: Well, is that manifold of henads unshareable in the same manner as the One itself, or is it possessed as an immanent share by what is and does every henad belong to just one being, so to speak as its flower, its summit and its centre around which every being has attained its subsistence?

Proclus declares himself in favour of the second option which clearly takes the μετεχόμενα as shares immanent in what is. He explains how we can agree with Parmenides' claim (in the second hypothesis of Plato's dialogue *Parmenides* 142 d 9 - 143 a 3) that the One *partakes of* Being and *is partaken of* by Being,[73] since, to his mind, two different ways of "partaking" ("participation") are found here (*ibid..*, 15, 14 - 15).[74] The author continues:

> III 4, 15, 15 - 24: For the One partakes of Being, *qua* not-being primitively one nor transcending[75] what is but irradiating from above[76] "truly being beingness" (τὴν ὄντως οὖσαν οὐσίαν). Being, however, partakes of the One as being held together by it, as being filled with divine unific power (ἑνώσεως), and as reverting to the One which *is* by itself and accordingly[77] unshareable. For the monadic shares (αἱ μετεχόμεναι μονάδες) connect what is to the One that transcends the wholes, in the same manner as the intelligence-shares (οἱ μετεχόμενοι νόες) connect the souls to the universal Intelligence and the soul-shares (αἱ μετεχόμεναι ψυχάι) connect the bodies to the universal Soul [the remainder of the text is found above 14].

The concluding part of this chapter is in full accord with the foregoing: the manifold of gods (= henads) are possessed as immanent shares by what is (p. 16, 16 - 17). Socrates' account of the nature and activity of the Good (in *Rep.* VI, 508 d 4 - 509 a 5) is referred to and explained along the same lines as in the passage just quoted: it is true, the Good does transcend Being (in the same manner as the sun transcends the visible things), but light *immanent* in intelligibles illuminates them (in the same manner as visible things become apparent through the light generated in them). Thus immanent henads are constitutive of the subsistence of beings and their reversion to the higher principles and ultimately the One or Good:

---

[73] *Cf. Theol. plat.* V 30, 110, 5 ff. For the general theme, see also *Theol. plat.* II, chs. 1 - 3.

[74] *Cf. Theol. plat.* III 24, 84, 26 - 85, 4.

[75] *i.e.* not *qua* the One but as an immanent share of oneness. For the notion of "irradiation from above", see above 10, and the next note.

[76] The irradiation comes "from above" (Greek: καταλάμπων), *i.e.* from the next higher order (in this case, the supreme level of the One). It essentially is causative, *i.e.* any product originates by the irradiation from above. See *Elem.*, prop. 163, exp., 142, 13 - 16: "(...) The henads irradiating from above the Intelligence which is divine and unshareable are intellectual, — not *qua* subsisting immanently in the Intelligence but in the causative sense (κατ' αἰτίαν) *qua* subsisting prior to the Intelligence and giving birth to it)."

[77] As often, καί is explicatively used.

III 4, 17, 4 - 12: (...) the deity proceeding from the First is shareable (μεθεκτή) as is the entire multitude of henads. And the First is truly the One-beyond-Being. However, every one of the other gods, it is true, is (just as the First) beyond Being, according to his proper existence[78] due to which he is a god, yet they are immanent shares possessed by beingness and what is (ὑπὸ οὐσίας καὶ τοῦ ὄντος). Consequently, this argument makes clear to us that while binding all what is to themselves and connecting through themselves all what is posterior to them to the One which equally transcends them all, the gods are henads, and shareable henads at that.[79]

Finally, when discussing the first hypothesis of the *Parmenides,* Proclus opposes the unshareable One against (the participants and) the henads possessed as immanent shares by those participants:

III 24, 83, 22 - 84, 3: The first and unshareable One, then, which preexists beyond the whole of things (not only beyond the participants but also the henad-shares <immanent in them>), is celebrated in the first hypothesis [*i.e* of the *Parmenides*] where it is demonstrated to be the cause of all things in an ineffable way without being itself limited in any one of all things or having any power or peculiar character of a kindred nature with the other gods.

Book IV 1 again proves that what is unshareable is only so in its own series. For instance, *qua* unshareable, Life separates primitive Being from Intelligence, and while partaking of what is, it is nevertheless possessed as an immanent share by the Intelligence (7, 19 - 21).[80] Here the opposition of causation against participation becomes patently clear in that the latter is interrupted as it were by the exemption from sharing which *qua* leader every leader of a series enjoys, whereas causation, of course, is a continuous process; see *e.g. Elem.* prop. 28: "the principle of Continuity".

At IV 6, 22, 24 - 25 immanence is clearly associated with μετέχεσθαι: unlike the demiurgic Intelligence which is unshareable, the particular intelligence which, by definition, is immanent, is said to be μετεχόμενος. At IV 19, 56, 20 ff. Proclus claims that for the present purpose of the discussion (concerning the necessity of intermediate triads) it makes no difference whether you take Intelligence *qua* possessed as an immanent share or *qua* divine, unshareable Intelligence. Finally, at IV 33, 99, 10 - 11 it is said that in the particular gods the god is not (an) unshareable (consequently, he is an immanent "god-share"), "because there is no henad separate from what is either."

Chapter V of the *Platonic Theology* is entirely in line with the foregoing books as far as the use of the terms μετεχόμενος and ἀμέθεκτος is concerned. Let it suffice to mention the most illustrative passages: V I, 8, 3 - 20; V 8, 28, 20 - 23; V 14, 7 - 11, 46, 1 - 4, 49, 12 - 17; V 15, 52, 2 - 7; V 23, 84, 13 - 22, 86, 7 -

---

[78] *i.e.* by themselves, quite apart from their immanence in other entities.
[79] *Cf. Elem.* props. 113 and 115, and *Theol. plat.* V 38, 139, 17 ff.
[80] Similarly, at p. 8, 10 ff. Life, although unshareable, is nevertheless said to partake of the intelligible monads, to be inferior to Being and to give birth, on its turn, to the unshareable Intelligence.

14; V 30, 111, 18 - 28; V 37, 136, 24 - 137, 5; V 38, 134, 20 - 21 (*cf. Theol. plat.* III 24, 83, 22 - 84, 23; quoted above 000).

Concluding this section the following may be stated:

(1) Quite in line with the common Platonic and Neoplatonic tradition Proclus uses μετέχειν with a genitive to mean "to partake of" something which *qua* pertaining to the next higher rank *transcends* the participant.

(2) The passive forms μετέχεσθαι and μετεχόμενος, however, are not used to signify the transcendent source of participation (occurring on the next higher level than that of the participant). Thus it does not mean "be(ing) partaken of", but rather stands for "be(ing) possessed as an immanent share" or "be(ing) an immanent share".[81]

(3) The privative *adiectivum verbale* ἀμέθεκτος concerns a relative (or "relational") rather than an absolute notion, to the effect that nothing is said to be ἀμέθεκτον unless with respect to its own series (on the proviso, of course, that the One is called ἀμέθεκτον with regard to the *whole* Universe and, accordingly, in an absolute manner). Its meaning should be associated with that of μετέχεσθαι. Accordingly, the privative noun ἀμέθεκτος basically discards the notion of being an immanent share, and means "not (capable of) being an immanent share". On top of that, *qua* restricted in its use to the own series exclusively, any participation in the upward direction is also out of the question. Therefore, its basic meaning seems to be "exempt from any sharing", which formula is to discard both participation in the upward direction ("not partaking itself of") and in the downward direction ("not being (possessed as) an immanent share").

(4) Proclus' extensive use of the notion of ἀμέθεκτος, which connotes the exemption of any sharing and thus aptly interrupts as it were the chain of *participated* Being, has everything to do with his constant efforts to solve the old Platonic problems surrounding the relationship between causation and participation, or rather between transcendence and immanence. Proclus has quite well seen that to underline the function of the Ideas as immanent causes is bound to be at the cost of their epistrophic function which can only be safeguarded by our sticking to their absolute, undetracted Transcendence.

---

[81] It is easily seen now that the usual charge of inconsistency against Proclus (see Dodds, *Proclus. The Elements of Theology*, 211; "τὸ ἕν is ἀμέθεκτον, yet every manifold partakes in the One" does not hold: it is based on the interpreters' failing to see the meaning of the passive form μετέχεσθαι. Dodds' intended transitive use of "participate" throughout the translation (see Dodds, *Proclus. The Elements of Theology*, 3, n. 1) is disastrous in this respect. A similar mistake is found with many interpreters of the Medievals' use of the term "participatum". So Kremer, *Die neuplatonische Seinsphilosophie und ihre Wirkung auf Thomas von Aquin*, 382; 416 ff. takes it to stand for the source of participation instead of the share. In Medieval usage "participatum" never refers to that source. See De Rijk, *La philosophie au moyen âge*, 172 ff.

(5) What I have called "the interruption of the chain of participation" and the concomitant fading into the background of the notion of "*part* -icipation" may be elucidated by the remarkable fact the prefix μετά as found in μέθεξις seems to have the sense of "after" as its secondary connotation, which is corroborated by the use of verbs such as προυπάρχειν ("to preexist") said of the Principle (or lower principles), to the effect that μετέχειν ("to share") has more or less the connotation of "to have <a character> *after* <the principle in which this character preeminently preexists>"; see *e.g. Elem..* props. 29; 53; 90, and the expositions added to props. 18; 23; 65 and 78. In this connection it should be noticed that in the Middle Ages the word μέθεξις is sometimes rendered *posthabitio* meaning "the (act of) having <the character involved> *after* (= secondary to) the cause".[82]

6. *The Basic Role of the* μετεχόμενον *for Continuity and Reversion*

As we have seen already (above 8 ff. and 19) whatever comes "after" (μετά) the One or Good is not pure Existence, but only a mixture of Limitation and Infinitude or "one and not-one" and so at the same time alike and unalike to the One: it is alike to the One in virtue of its immanent share of the Superior cause and unalike to the One *qua* participant distinct from its cause. What binds all things together is alikeness and, consequently, it is alikeness immanent in the lower entities that is at the basis of all reversion to the Superior. Indeed, alikeness not only causes lower entities to be subsistent, it also makes them revert to their Principle, the One (see esp. *Elem.* props. 28 - 32; *Theol. plat.* I 28, III 2 and III 4; above 14 ff.; *In Timaeum* II, 313, 19 - 21).

The law governing the entire process of procession and reversion (which is, to be sure, just *one* process)[83] is commonly called the "Law of Continuity";[84] also for its sources). Dodds rightly remarks,[85] that this law "provides the justification for the Jamblicho-Procline methods of mean terms." Proclus is in a constant habit of defending his multiplication of entities and the introduction of triads of entities overlapping the distinct levels of the universe by reference to what Dodds[86] labels "the law of mean terms", *viz.* that two doubly disjunct terms "AB" and "not-A not-B" cannot be continuous, but must be connected by an intermediate term, either "A not-B" or "B not-A", which

---

[82] See William of Moerbeke's translation of the *Elementatio* (ed. H. Boese, Louvain 1987), *passim*, where ἀμέθεκτος is rendered: *amethectus, imparticipabilis, imparticipatus, non-posthabens* (!). Of course, William also uses the word *participatio*. In this connection Thomas Aquinas' paraphrasis in *De causis* is noteworthy: "secundum quandam posthabitionem, idest consecutionem , sive participationem (ed. Saffrey, 79, 23 - 4)."
[83] See Dodds, *Proclus. The Elements of Theology*, 219.
[84] See Dodds, *Proclus. The Elements of Theology*, 216, also for its sources.
[85] See Dodds, *Proclus. The Elements of Theology*, 216.
[86] See Dodds, *Proclus. The Elements of Theology*, Introd., XXII.

forms a triad with them.[87] The law of the mean terms is aptly accompanied by the well-known adage laid down in *Elem.* prop. 103: "All entities are in all, but in each according to its proper nature."[88] In point of fact, the adage focusses on the intensional aspect of what is dealt with in the Law of Continuity and the Law of mean terms in particular. In this connection it may be asked what precisely is understood by "proper nature". Proclus uses the adverb, οἰκείως, meaning litterally "of the house<hold>", "properly belonging". So the adverb determines the manner in which everything is in all as a manner precisely adapted to the receiver.[89] That means that the δύναμις or ἕνωσις is transmitted by the superior in a form less intense (see *Elem.*. props. 7 and 8; *Theol. plat.* III 2), but nonetheless remaining like the cause.

It is in this triangle of tension that the triad ἀμέθεκτον — μετεχόμενον — μετέχον comes in, the relationships between whose members are the subject of *Elem.* prop. 24 (see above 18.). The μετεχόμενον mediates[90] between the cause *qua* unshareable and the effect *qua* participant, but definitely not as between two pre-existing elements. Rather, *qua* representative of the superior cause the μετεχόμενον constitutes the effect and thus acts as the participant's immanent cause. *Qua* immanent share it is the representative of the transcendent cause which *qua* transcending its effect is unshareable. At the same time, *qua* "like to the cause" (ὅμοιον) the μετεχόμενον binds itself and the participant to the superior cause and, ultimately, to the One and so realizes Reversion in the universe.

Continuity and Reversion are not only discussed in *Elem.* props. 28 - 31, but also in *Theol. plat.* III 2, which deals with what Proclus later (III 3, 11, 23) calls axioms, basic for the theory of the henads. There are four:

- all procession and reversion are effected by likeness (6, 15 - 7, 25); *cf. Elem.* props. 28 - 29; 32; *In Parm.* VI, 1043, 9 - 29.
- each monad produces a manifold that is co-ordinate with it (7, 26 - 9, 11): *cf. Elem.* prop. 21
- the effects are more numerous according to their greater distance from the One (9, 12 -10, 14); *cf. Elem.* prop. 25.
- the unshareables are superior to the immanent shares (10, 15 - 11, 15); *cf. Elem.* prop. 24.

---

[87] The principle is laid down in *Elem.* prop. 28 (see above 15) and *Theol. plat.* III 2, p. 22 (see below 15) and applied in *Elem.* props. 40; 55; 63; 64; 132; 166; 181 and *Theol. plat.* I 28; III 2; III 4 and elsewhere.

[88] This adage is at the basis of *Elem.* props. 121; 124; 125; 128; 129; 134; 140; 141; 170; 176; 177; 195; 197. It is frequently commented on by Medieval authors; see also Dodds, *Proclus. The Elements of Theology*, 254.

[89] *Cf.* the later scholastic adage: *quicquid recipitur, recipitur ad modum recipientis.*

[90] This is of course quite another thing than saying that "the μετεχόμενα link intension with extension" (Dodds, *Proclus. The Elements of Theology*, 211 see above 1).

The first axiom discusses the law of continuity and the intermediate media ("the likes"). Proclus argues that the effects (or participants) are connected with their principles ("the unshareable causes") by immanent shares which act as their (immanent) causes. Again,[91] it appears that the expression "unlikes" refers to the participants, whereas the "likes", being the shares of the character involved, are immanent in the participants which they make revert to, and unite with, their superior causes and ultimately the One:

> III 2, 6, 14 - 7, 1: Well, this is, I think, more than anything else apparent to those whose conceptions are not distorted, that everywhere, but especially in the divine orders, the emanations that are secondary are accomplished through the likeness the secondary emanations have to their proper principles. For Nature and Intelligence, as every generative cause, by nature produce, prior to their unlikes,[92] their likes and unite them with themselves. For if it is necessary that the procession of beings be a continuous one and that no vacuum intervene either in incorporeal entities or in bodies, it must be that what proceeds in every natural order proceed through likeness. For it is by no means right that the effect be identical with its cause; for the remission and deficiency of the unific power (τῆς ἐνώσεως) of the producing cause generate secondary things.

Next Proclus shows why it is necessary that there are such intermediate entities, which can connect the effects with their causes from which they are properly speaking separated; and this connection must take place in order to maintain continuity in the universe:

> ibid., p. 7, 1 - 13: For again, if that which is secondary were identical with that which is first, by the same token (ὁμοίως) the two of them would be the same, and one would not be the cause, nor the other the effect. If, however, the one by its very being has the exuberance of the productive power while the other has the deficiency of the produced power, it is by nature (a) that they are separated from each other, (b) that the generative cause is superior to the generated thing, and (c) that there is no identity of entities that differ so greatly. If the secondary is not identical with what is first, then: if it is only different <from the latter>, the two will not be united with each other, nor will the one partake of the other, since[93] connection and participation (ἡ γὰρ συναφή καὶ ἡ μέθεξις) surely are the communion (κοινωνία) of the entities connected and the concord (συμπαθεία) of the participants with the shares (τὰ μετεχόμενα).[94]

Subsequently, Proclus starts from the alternative option that the effect is at the same time the same as and different from what is the first:

> ibid., 7, 13 - 27: If it lacks sameness and is overwhelmed by the power which is contrary to sameness, it will no longer be the One that is the leader of the procession of what is nor will every generative cause in the order of the Good preside the secondary entities; for the One is not the cause of division but of friendship and the Good makes revert generated entities to their causes. Well, rever-

---

[91] See above 27.
[92] *Elem.* prop. 28.
[93] The same view is found at *Elem.* 110, 7 - 9.
[94] In the parallellous passage of the *Elementatio* (prop. 28, exp., 32, 17 - 20) the μετεχόμενα are said to bestow upon the participant a communion with that of which it partakes.

sion and friendship of the entities secondary to the primitives are effected by
likeness, not by unlikeness. If therefore the One is the cause of the wholes and if
the Good in the manner of what is transcendent is desirable to all entities, it will
everywhere bestow subsistence upon its products through likeness to the antecedent causes, in order that not only the procession be through the One but also
the reversion of what proceeds be to the Good. For without likeness there will
never be generation nor reversion of the products to their proper principles.

7. Scope Distinction in Neoplatonic Doctrine and Procedure

Every student of Proclus is well acquainted with his relaxed attitude towards
statements that, as they stand, are flatly contradictory as affirming thesis and its
antithesis at the same time. Famous examples are *Elem.* prop. 2 and the exposition added to prop. 24. Prop. 2 runs: "All that partakes of the One is both one
and not-one." In the exposition added to this proposition Proclus concedes that
"being one" is meant as "being one according to participation" whereas "being
not-one" stands for "not being the One itself." To be sure, it is a reasonable explanation but the simple reader still might ask why the proposition itself is so
provocatively formulated. The exposition of prop. 24 concerns a famous trias
and discusses the relations existing between the participant, the source of
participation and the immanent shared character (see above 18 ff.) The latter is
described as a character present in the many (ἐν τοῖς πολλοῖς), which is at the
same time "one, yet not-one" and the participant as "not-one, yet one" (Dodds'
translation).

Quite naturally, all such contradictory sentences may prove to be only
seemingly so, once they are provided with the appropriate qualifications. For
that matter, quite a number of statements may be true "from a special point of
view." Basically, Neoplatonic argument appears to be sympathetic towards this
principle. However, Neoplatonic dialectics is not a matter of logical negligence
or tolerance, rather it is focussed on quite respectable purports. In this concluding section I shall attempt to analyze and evaluate Neoplatonic dialectics from
the philosophical point of view.

It should be remarked at the outset that such a procedure, which to a con-
siderable extent may be parallelled to what in modern usage is called "scope
distinction", does not amount to merely considering one and the same object
from different angles, or something like looking at the moon first from the
front and then from the back. Rather, scope distinction concerns an object *qua*
whole, one time observed from one aspect proper to it and another time form
some other angle. The observer need not change his standpoint at all. That is
not saying that scope distinction in metaphysical matters has nothing to do with
the observer; rather, to the Neoplatonists, it is because of the basic deficiency
of all human observation and consideration that scope distinction is unavoid-

able in any philosophical analysis. We owe to Beierwaltes[95] a profound inquiry into the truly philosophical impact of dialectical method and its relationship to triadic thought in Proclus. Reading his fine observations will refrain the modern reader of Proclus from mistaking his dialectical analysis including what I have labelled scope distinctions for a purely logical exercise.

7.1 Two Famous Cases of Scope Distinction in Proclus

In order to clarify "scope distinction" as a philosophical procedure in Proclus it is useful to select two peculiar examples from the overwhelming multitude occurring in his works; their amount is in fact so overwhelming that it frequently annoys modern scholars rather than provoking their admiration for the man's logical acumen.

Our first example is found in the well-known discussion of the notion of ἀμέθεκτος; see above p. 17 ff. As we have seen in our discussion of *Elem.* props. 23 and 24 (above, 17 ff.), this notion only applies within a certain scope, *viz.* setting apart any relationship of sharing, both in the upward and in the downward direction, whereas, nonetheless these relationships are neither denied nor ignored. Prop. 99 of the *Elementatio* is still more explicit on this score in dealing with the ἀμέθεκτον *qua* ἀμέθεκτον:

> prop. 99, exp., p. 88, 20 - 23: Precisely in the respect in which an unshareable is unshareable, it does not obtain its subsistence from something else as its cause but is itself the principle and cause of all its shares. And it is in this sense (οὕτως) that in every series the principle is ungenerated.

Proclus' speaking of "to partake of an unshareable" follows along the same lines; *e.g.* in *Elem.* 60, 16 - 19 (see above, 20) and *Theol. plat.* III 2, 10, 26 ff. (see above, 22) Nor is Proclus denying or ignoring that what is ἀμέθεκτος itself partakes of a superior entity (except, of course, for the ἀμέθεκτον *par excellence*, the One). Any unshareable below the level of the One originates from a superior cause, he agrees, but not *qua* unshareable; see above, 19 ff.

All this surely does not involve a contradiction. Rather, unshareableness obtains within a certain scope, *i.e.* it is only said of an entity when it is taken as the leader of its series and with regard to the members of this series. Thus the notion of ἀμέθεκτος basically serves to qualify (and interrupt, as it were) the chain of participation as opposed against the unqualified chain of causation. To put it shortly, any transcendent cause is ἀμέθεκτος, whereas its representative on the next lower level is nevertheless μετεχόμενον (*i.e.* an immanent share also acting as a causal constituent[96] of the entity involved), originating, by definition, from the transcendent cause but by no means detracting or diminishing the

---

[95] Beierwaltes, *Proklos. Grundzüge seiner Metaphysik*, 240 - 270.
[96] For a cause being both transcendent and immanent, see *Elem.* props. 9 - 14; 26; 56 - 60.

latter's original power and status, so that the transcendent cause is the *source* of participation, yet without being its *object*.

Our second example concerns the distinction between *monas* and *henas*. [97] In Plato's *Philebus* (15 a 6 - b 1) these terms are indiscriminately used to stand for the Forms. Plotinus alludes (*Enneads* VI 6, 9, 33) to this passage when calling the Platonic Forms *henades*. Proclus mentions (*In Parm*. IV, 880, 30 - 38) this twofold use of henas = monas as found in the *Philebus* but adds an explanation of his own, saying that the Forms are monads with regards to the One by itself, and henads with regard to their products and the wholes of which they are the leaders. That means that changing the point of view implies assigning different names to the same entity. Apparently, from this viewpoint monads are the Forms taken as the leaders of a series, whereas henads are the same Forms *qua* acting as immanent characters.

To be sure, Proclus himself uses "henad" in a larger sense comprising both the transcendent, unshareable Henad ("the One") and various (shareable) henads in the lower *strata*.[98] For Proclus, the monad is the unshareable leader of a series giving birth to all the members of the series and making them revert to itself (*Elem*. props. 21; 23; 64; 69 exp.; 100 exp.; 108; 110; 115 exp.; 181 exp.; 204 exp.). Of course, the distinction between *monas* and *henas* in Proclus is closely related to the specific role of the notion of ἀμέθεκτον and his view of the transcendence-immanence issue.

7.2 *Scope Distinction Deliberately Applied and Recommended*

One need not be surprised at all to find "scope distinction" quite frequently practiced in the *Elementatio*.[99] The work is written in the geometric manner with propositions and their respective deductive proofs, so as to make us expect the frequent use of sagacious distinctions. In *Platonic Theology,* fruitful distinctions based upon considering one and the same entity from different angles is not uncommon either. We have seen several passages of this kind in our foregoing discussions.[100]

In his extensive commentary on Plato's *Parmenides* Proclus, apparently in the wake of his master Syrianus, describes and recommends scope distinctions as deliberately and succesfully applied by Plato's spokesman (*In Parm*. VI,

---

[97] I am much indebted to the excellent discussion of this item in Saffrey - Westerink III, *Introd.* XI - XVII.

[98] See the useful survey in S.W., III. *Introd.* XV - XVII, where sub 4 "l'hénade supérieure à l'intellect" in *In Tim.* I, p. 3, 28 and p. 436, 18 (*cf. Elem.* prop. 109) should be ranged sub 1 (the transcendent One), I would presume. Proclus adopted the doctrine of the divine henads from its inventor, Syrianus. See S.W., *ibid.*, LI ff. For Proclus' henology, see also *ibid.*, LXVI - LXXII.

[99] Analysis including (scope) distinctions is found in the *Elem. e.g.* props. 2; 5 exp.; 9; 26; 30; 35; 46; 61 as against 26; 65 - 69; 88 ; 98; 99; 107; 123; 124; 130; 134; 141; 162; 176; 186; 195.

[100] See above 21 ff. To add *e.g. Theol. plat.* I 14, 67, 2 - 5; II 9, 59, 5 - 25.

1049, 37 - 1050, 25).[101] Parmenides, Proclus claims, takes (in the second hypothesis of the dialogue, 142 b - 155 e) his starting-point from the Parmenidean One, *i.e.* oneness appearing *in* things and considers it one time *qua* one, another time *qua* "one and being", and another time *qua* being that partakes of the One, whereby he constantly maintains the well-known conditional premiss: "if the One *is*." Well, to stick to that premiss is impossible unless one examines it successively in different ways. Varying the respective conclusions, then, amounts to alternately assuming different properties of the One, and those, on top of that, now affirmatively and then negatively. Like his master Syrianus Proclus divides the second hypothesis of the *Parmenides* into fourteen parts (according to the natural articulations to be found in Plato's text, they claim, rather than "hacking off its parts" as does the clumsy butcher of *Phaedrus* 265 e). These parts which elucidate fourteen properties of the One clarify, by the same token, the fourteen strata of the hierarchy of gods, of which each one is presided by its own divine henad.

7.3 *The Philosophic Impact of Scope Distinction in Neoplatonism*

The One of Neoplatonism is beyond Being and beyond Knowledge as well (see *Elem..* props. 123 and 162, and *e.g. Theol. plat.* II 4).[102] From prop. 123 ("All that is divine is itself ineffable and unknowable by any secondary entity because of its unific power that is beyond Being") can be gathered that knowability is essentially linked up with the level of Being and, consequently, knowledge as such must be something defective with regard to plain ineffability precisely because Being is a minor variant of Existence (see above, 6 and 12). Indeed for Proclus, Reality itself is beyond grasp and secret, and has itself a proper mode of "Knowledge" which transcends any intelligibility, including human knowledge. This is explicitly stated in *Elem.* props 121 and 162:

> prop. 121: All that is divine has (...) a mode of knowledge which is secret and incomprehensible to all secondary entities alike.

> prop. 162: All those henads which irradiate true Being are secret *and* intelligible: secret as connected with the One intelligible *qua* immanent shares of being.

In the exposition added to prop. 93 the association of Infinitude with incomprehensibility is explained, and it appears that lower entities, too, are incomprehensible inasmuch as they partake of Infinitude:

> p. 84, 3 - 10: For to whomsoever anything is infinite, to him it is also uncircumscribed. But among things which have Being each is determinate both to itself and to all principles prior to it. It remains therefore that the infinitude in such entities is infinite only to inferior entities <...>, as to escape the grasp of any of

---

[101] See also S.W., *ibid.*, XLVII - LI.

[102] For the hermeneutics of the ineffable in Neoplatonism, see F. Romano, 'L' ermeneutica dell' ineffabile' in *Questioni Neoplatoniche* a cura di Franscesco Romano e Antonio Tiné, Catania 1988, 13 - 26.

them; <...> it has something that for secondary entities is secret and incomprehensible.

See also *Elem.* prop. 11 exp.:

p. 12, 26 - 28: For nothing infinite can be apprehended and the causes being unknown there can be no knowledge of their consequents either.

The same doctrine occurs elsewhere, *e.g. Theol. plat.* III 1; *In Timaeum* I 3, 28 and 436, 18.

On the other hand, dialectical analysis of the lower existents is our only access to Reality, as appears from the second part of *Elem.* prop. 123:

p. 108, 26 - 28: (...) but it [*viz.* all that is divine] may be apprehended and known through the entities that partake of it; therefore only the First Principle is completely unknowable *qua* not being present as an immanent share <in other entities>.

So Proclus can conclude (prop. 123, exp.) that "nevertheless from the entities dependent upon the gods the character of their distinctive properties may be inferred, *and with cogency*; for differences of the participants are determined according to the distinctive properties of their immanent shares".[103]

Of course, such an analysis of entities composed of Limitation and Infinitude provides some real insight but nonetheless cannot help distorting things by the same token. Hence the frequent use of quasi-contradictory statements or rather simultaneous affirmations of thesis and antithesis[104] which indeed distort Reality one no less than the other, and the concomitant application of scope distinction in Neoplatonic authors.

Still one final hindrance from having a clear insight into this procedure should be cleared away. It concerns the relationship between logic and metaphysics in Neoplatonism, especially in Proclus. A.C. Lloyd[105] has rightly remarked that "Proclus' philosophy is marked by a more extreme realism than seems possible to most modern readers and which probably outdid any earlier Platonism." In this connection it is significant that in Ancient thought in general the conviction that there is, and should be, parallellism between thought and Reality is predominant. That is to say, thinking is not just a logical exercise in making all kinds of (possibly) ficticious distinctions; rather it is naturally apt to uncover the real articulations in all that is.[106] It is Reality that imposes the real articulations and divisions upon human thinking. Hence

---

[103] *Cf.* Proclus, *On Providence and Fate,* cap. 4 where "understanding" (διάνοια) is defined as that which is concerned with the relationships between entities.

[104] Small wonder that Hegel was really interested in Proclus' philosophy. See the profound observations by Beierwaltes, *Platonismus und Idealismus,* 154 - 187, concerning these two thinkers.

[105] Lloyd, 'Porphyry and Jamblichus', in Armstrong *The Cambridge History of Later Greek and Early Medieval Philosophy* , 307.

[106] For the Platonic background of this basic view, see *e.g.* Plato, *Phaedrus,* 265 d - e, and, in general, De Rijk, *Plato's Sophist,* 126 - 138.

Proclus' appeal to people "whose conceptions are not distorted" (οἱ ἀδια-στρόφοι).[107] In fact, his severe attack on those who mistook the hypotheses of Plato's *Parmenides* for just logical exercises is in the same line of thought (*Theol. plat.* II, 8 - 10; *In Parm.* VI 23, *et al.*).[108] Small wonder that Proclus does not think much of people who take logical acumen to be the proper source of the Real principles of the Universe. Instead "the Principles do not have their existence from logical inventiveness (κατ' ἐπίνοιαν) but from Existence (καθ' ὕπαρξιν).They are principles just by themselves and not due to our thinking" as our author argues for in his commentary on the *Parmenides* (VI, 23, 1054, 27 - 31).[109]

So we may conclude that in spite of his logical abilities Proclus still remains a true metaphysician, and that following the best Platonic traditions.

---

[107] *Theol. plat.* III 2, 6, 14 - 15 (see above 28). For the notion of "undistorted", see *Theol. plat.* I 4, 22, 3; I 6, 29, 9; I 17, 81, 14 - 15. This notion is clearly associated with Proclus' preference for the conceptions common to all men. See *e.g.* his *On Providence and Fate*, capp. 4 - 6.

[108] *Cf. e.g.* Proclus, *In Cratylum*, cap. 7 ed. Pasquali, and F. Romano, *Proclo. Lezioni sul "Cratilo" di Platone. Introduzione, Traduzione e Commmento, ad locum.*

[109] For the relationship between conceptual and philosophical notions, see also Rosán, *The Philosophy of Proclus. The Final Phase of Ancient Thought,* 69.

H.D. SAFFREY

ACCORDER ENTRE ELLES LES TRADITIONS THÉOLOGIQUES: UNE CARACTÉRISTIQUE DU NÉOPLATONISME ATHÉNIEN.*

Les philosophes de l'Antiquité tardive, que nous avons accoutumé d'appeler "Néoplatoniciens", ne revendiquaient pour eux-mêmes que le titre "Philosophe platonicien". Ils avaient l'ambition d'exposer dans toute sa pureté la philosophie de Platon. Pourtant, puisqu'ils avaient donné à cette philosophie le statut d'une théologie, ils furent naturellement amenés à la confronter aux autres traditions théologiques grecques et barbares. Une page célèbre du livre de Hans Lewy nous avait alertés sur ce point[1], et les travaux récents de Luc Brisson[2] et de Dominic O'Meara[3] nous ont rendus sensibles à cet aspect de retour aux sources de la philosophie grecque tardive. Les philosophes de l'École néoplatonicienne d'Athènes avaient déjà parfaitement conscience de cet enjeu de leur recherche.

Marinus, le successeur de Proclus à la tête de l'École, le 17 avril 486, jour du premier anniversaire de la mort de son Maître, prononça publiquement un éloge funèbre.[4] Malheureusement, depuis l'édition d'Émile Portus en 1618, nous avons pris l'habitude de désigner cet éloge sous le titre de *Vita Procli*. Le propos de Marinus, qui avait intitulé son discours: *Proclus ou Sur le bonheur*, n'était pas d'écrire une biographie, mais de montrer que son héros avait atteint le bonheur suprême par la pratique parfaite de toutes les vertus dont il énumérait les six degrés: naturelles, éthiques, politiques, purificatives, contemplatives et théurgiques. En arrivant aux vertus contemplatives, celles de la vie philosophique qui permet d'atteindre la vision des modèles contenus dans l'Intellect divin, il décrit l'activité de Proclus de la façon que voici: "Le philosophe, non seulement n'eut aucune peine à pénétrer toute la théologie, tant grecque que barbare, et celle qui est cachée sous les fictions des mythes, mais

---

* Je remercie mes amis, Luc Brisson et Philippe Hoffmann, qui ont bien voulu relire ce texte et me faire des remarques très utiles.

[1] *Cf.* H. Lewy, *Chaldaean Oracles and Theurgy*, nouvelle édition par M. Tardieu, Paris 1978, 483 - 484.

[2] *Cf.* L. Brisson, 'Proclus et l'Orphisme', dans: *Proclus, lecteur et interprète des Anciens*, Paris 1987, 43 - 104.

[3] *Cf.* D.J. O'Meara, *Pythagoras revived. Mathematics and Philosophy in Late Antiquity*, Oxford 1989.

[4] *Cf. Marini Vita Procli* (...) recensuit (...) Ioh. Franc. Boissonade, Lipsiae 1814, 1: Μαρίνου Νεαπολίτου Πρόκλος ἢ Περὶ εὐδαιμονίας. Est-ce pour se démarquer de ce genre de l' éloge funèbre que Damascius, au début de sa *Vita Isidori*, proteste ne pas vouloir "chanter des béatitudes" (αἴδειν μακαρίας), mais écrire une véritable "biographie" (βιογραφία), dans l' *Epitoma Photiana*, § 8?

aussi, pour ceux qui veulent et peuvent la comprendre, il la produisit au jour, expliquant toutes choses sous l'inspiration des dieux et mettant toutes ces théologies en accord (εἰς συμφωνίαν ἄγων)."[5] L'accord des théologies est ainsi présenté comme l'effort ultime du philosophe Proclus. Et dans son discours, Marinus fait ici une allusion très précise. Voici comment nous pouvons la reconnaître.

Cinq siècles plus tard, un auteur anonyme a compilé cette vaste encyclopédie que nous appelons la *Souda*. Un savant byzantin qui a lu, attentivement et dans l'ordre, les notices consacrées à Proclus et à Syrianus, a aussitôt remarqué que les catalogues des titres d'ouvrages attribués à ces deux philosophes sont presque identiques.[6] Il l'a noté dans la marge de son exemplaire. Karl Praechter a su reconnaître cette annotation quand il a interprété les mots εἰς τὰ Πρόκλου, qui se lisent dans la notice de Syrianus, comme une glose incorporée au texte, et signalé que, dans la grécité byzantine, ces mots sont équivalents à l'expression ἐν τοῖς Πρόκλου.[7] Notre lecteur byzantin de la *Souda* ne pouvait manquer de remarquer que la liste des ouvrages attribués à Syrianus avait déjà été donnée comme celle des livres écrits par Proclus. Dans cette liste commune, on trouve deux titres qui attirent spécialement l'attention.

Le premier désigne un livre intitulé: *Sur la théologie d' Orphée* (Εἰς τὴν Ὀρφέως θεολογίαν). Or, nous savons pertinemment par Marinus que Proclus s'était refusé à composer un commentaire sur les poèmes théologiques attribués à Orphée.[8] Dans ses cours, il se contentait des explications de Jamblique et de Syrianus. En effet, dans un rêve, il avait vu son maître Syrianus qui lui interdisait d'écrire un nouveau commentaire. Alors Marinus eut recours à un subterfuge. "Je le priai, dit-il, de consigner ses opinions en marge des livres de Syrianus (le commentaire de Syrianus était en deux livres). Comme notre très bon Maître s'est laissé convaincre et qu'il mit des notes dans les marges du commentaire de Syrianus, nous avons obtenu dans le même livre une collection de toutes leurs opinions, et ainsi il y a des scholies et commentaires de Proclus sur Orphée, d'un nombre de lignes qui n'est pas petit." Pour le dire en passant, voilà un texte qui devrait conforter la thèse de Nigel Wilson sur l'histoire des scholies. Il y avait donc dans la bibliothèque de l' École d'Athènes un exemplaire du Commentaire de Syrianus sur la Théologie d'Orphée, augmenté des notes de Proclus sur le même sujet.[9] Comme les Anciens n'avaient pas, sur

---

[5] *Cf. ibid.,* Chap. 22, 18, éd. J.F. Boissonade.

[6] *Cf. Suidae Lexicon* éd. A. Adler, pars IV, Lipsiae 1935, 210, 5 - 22, notice sur Proclus = P 2473, et 478, 21 - 479, 8, notice sur Syrianus = S 1662.

[7] *Cf.* K. Praechter, 'Das Schriftenverzeichnis des Neuplatonikers Syrianos bei Suidas', dans *Byzantinisches Zeitschrift* 26 (1926), 253 - 264, reproduit dans *Kleine Schriften,* Hildesheim - New York 1973, 222 - 233.

[8] *Cf.* Marinus, *Vita Procli,* chap. 27, 22, éd. J.F. Boissonade.

[9] Ce commentaire est perdu, mais on peut considérer que Syrianus, Proclus et Damascius l'ont utilisé lorsqu'ils citent ou interprètent les *Discours sacrés en vingt-quatre*

la propriété littéraire, les mêmes pratiques que les Modernes, on pouvait à cette époque attribuer ce livre aussi bien à Syrianus qu'à Proclus.[10] C'est ce qu'a fait le bibliographe bien informé qui est à la source de la *Souda*.

Le second titre qui attire l'attention dans la *Souda* est le suivant: *Accord d'Orphée, Pythagore, Platon, avec les Oracles Chaldaïques, en dix livres* (Συμφωνία Ὀρφέως Πυθαγόρου Πλάτωνος πρὸς τὰ Λόγια, βιβλία δέκα).[11] La présence de ce même titre parmi les oeuvres, et de Syrianus, et de Proclus, doit s'expliquer de la même façon. Que Syrianus ait été considéré par Proclus comme le véritable auteur de ce traité, on doit l'admettre, puisque Proclus le cite une fois dans la *Théologie platonicienne* (IV 23, 69, 12). Syrianus y est présenté comme "le véritable Bacchant", c'est-à-dire comme le philosophe par excellence au dire de Platon dans le *Phédon* (69 d 1 - 2),[12] le philosophe-modèle, inspiré par les dieux, mieux que Jamblique et Théodore d'Asiné, pour faire briller la doctrine platonicienne en accord avec les *Oracles Chaldaïques*. Et Proclus n'a eu qu'à imiter ce modèle. Il l'a fait avec ardeur, et donc cet ouvrage de l'*Accord d'Orphée, Pythagore, Platon avec les Oracles Chaldaïques*, entrepris par Syrianus, mais aussi revu et augmenté par Proclus, leur appartenait légitimement à tous deux. Le titre de ce traité, qui est tout ce que nous connaissons de ce livre, contenait la formule de tout un programme de recherches dont nous allons voir qu'il fut en effet celui de Syrianus et de Proclus. Sous leur impulsion, ce sera même une partie importante du programme de toute l' École néoplatonicienne d'Athènes.

Pour examiner comment ce programme a été exécuté, il ne sera pas inutile de passer en revue les divers membres de l'École Athénienne en essayant de déterminer, chaque fois que c'est possible, l'usage qu'ils prétendent faire des

---

Rhapsodies attribués à Orphée, dans le reste de leur oeuvre. Les fragments ont été réunis par O. Kern, *Orphicorum fragmenta*, Berlin 1922, 140 - 248. Sur leur mise en situation dans les écrits de Proclus, *cf.* L. Brisson, *Proclus et l'Orphisme*, 53 - 91: "Le témoignage sur l'Orphisme dans l'oeuvre de Proclus". Le fait que Marinus dise que Proclus "rapportait dans ses explications ce qu'ont dit Jamblique et Syrianus," n'implique pas qu'il y ait eu un commentaire de Jamblique sur Orphée. Il pouvait connaître certaines opinions de Jamblique par l'intermédiaire de Syrianus. Sur les scholies, *cf.* N.G. Wilson, 'A Chapter in the History of Scholia', dans: *Class. Quart.* 17 (1967), 244 - 256, et 'The Relation of Text and Commentary in Greek Books', dans *Il Libro e il Testo*, Urbino 1984, 103 - 110.

[10] On connaît l'anecdote rapportée encore par Marinus, *Vita Procli*, chap. 12, selon laquelle Plutarque d'Athènes engage Proclus à mettre au net son cours sur le *Phédon*, en lui disant: "Une fois achevées ces scholies, on attribuera à Proclus aussi un commentaire sur le *Phédon*." Pour d'autres exemples du même procédé, *cf.* Ch. Faraggiana di Sarzana, 'Le commentaire à Hésiode et la Paideia encyclopédique de Proclus', dans *Proclus, lecteur et interprète des Anciens*, Paris 1987, 21 - 41, en particulier 21 - 23. Voir aussi Olympiodore, *In Phaedonem*, lect. 9, § 2, 8 - 10.

[11] J'accepte tacitement l'excellente correction de W. Kroll, *De oraculis Chaldaicis*, Vratislaviae 1894, 7, n. 1. En effet, dans le texte de la *Souda*, le titre se présente dans les deux cas sous la forme: Συμφωνία Ὀρφέως Πυθαγόρου Πλάτωνος περὶ τὰ Λόγια. Kroll, dans sa note, écrit: πρὸς scripsi pro περί, *cf.* Damascius I 324. 14; la faute doit s'expliquer par une abréviation mal résolue.

[12] Sur ce point, *cf.* le commentaire de Damascius, *In Phaedonem* I, § 172, avec la note de Westerink.

traditions théologiques autres que la tradition platonicienne, et du rapport qu'ils établissent entre elles. Naturellement nous devons tenir compte du fait que nous ne possédons plus qu'une faible partie de la production des maîtres de cette École, et que, par conséquent, nous devrons résister à la tentation de tirer des conclusions trop catégoriques de cette enquête.

Paradoxalement, c'est par un philosophe de l'École d'Alexandrie que nous devons commencer. Mais le paradoxe n'est qu'apparent, car Hiéroclès a été un élève, et peut-être le plus ancien élève, du fondateur de l'École d'Athènes, Plutarque d'Athènes.[13] Il semble bien que les traités conservés de lui aient été composés, sinon au temps où il résidait à Athènes, du moins sous l'influence directe de ce séjour. En effet, son traité perdu, intitulé *Sur la providence, le destin et la relation entre la liberté et le gouvernement divin,* est connu par les notes de lecture consignées par Photius dans sa *Bibliothèque*, codices 214 et 251. Dans son ouvrage, il rapporte qu'il a été l'élève de Plutarque d'Athènes, et il écrit en faisant usage de la doctrine et des méthodes de l'École. La composition de ce traité doit remonter aux environs de l'année 415. Or Photius, dans le rapport qu'il en fait,[14] détaille les matières abordées dans les sept livres de cet ouvrage. Tandis que les trois premiers donnaient des exposés sur la doctrine de Platon et sur les objections qui lui avaient été opposées, "le quatrième livre, dit Photius, veut mettre en accord (εἰς συμφωνίαν συνάγειν) avec la doctrine de Platon ce qu'on appelle les *Oracles Chaldaïques* et les préceptes sacrés (de la théurgie); le cinquième livre rattache, à Orphée, à Homère et à tous les autres poètes-philosophes connus avant la venue de Platon, la philosophie platonicienne concernant les sujets traités."[15] Ce texte est évidemment très important puisqu'il nous révèle d'une façon incontestable une partie du programme de recherches de Hiéroclès, qui est exactement le même que celui de Syrianus et de Proclus. Et puisque Hiéroclès et Syrianus ont tous deux été les disciples de Plutarque d'Athènes, nous sommes conduits à penser que c'est lui qui leur avait appris cette manière de faire de la philosophie en

---

[13] Sur Hiéroclès, *The Prosopography of the late Roman Empire*, II, *s.v.* Hierocles 1, et L.G. Westerink dans: Reallexikon für Antike und Christentum, Bd.15, *s.v.* Hierokles II (Neuplatoniker).

[14] *Cf.* Photius, *Bibliothèque*, t. III, Paris 1962 (éd. R. Henry), pour le cod. 214, 125 - 130, et t. VII, Paris 1974, pour le cod. 251, 189 - 206. Pour Plutarque d'Athènes, maître de Hiéroclès, *cf.* cod. 214, 173 a 37 - 39. Ce traité est dédié à Olympiodore de Thèbes (*ibid.* 171 b 22 - 32) dont nous savons qu'il séjourna à Athènes en 415, après son ambassade couronnée de succès chez le roi des Huns. Ce fut vraisemblablement l'occasion de la rencontre entre Hiéroclès et Olympiodore, et le traité doit être daté de ce moment ou peu après. Sur Olympiodore, *cf.* A. Cameron, *Literature and Society in the Early Byzantine World*, London 1985, par l'index, *s.v.* Olympiodoros of Thebes, car l'auteur est revenu sur ce personnage dans plusieurs de ses travaux, et J.F. Matthews, 'Olympiodorus of Thebes and the History of the West (A.D. 407 - 425)', dans *Journal of Roman Studies* 60 (1970), 79 - 97.

[15] *Cf.* Photius, *Bibliothèque*, cod. 214, 173 a 13-18. Sur ce texte, voir I. Hadot, *Le problème du néoplatonisme alexandrin, Hiéroclès et Simplicius*, Paris 1978, 67-72. Malheureusement il n'y a aucun extrait de ces livres IV et V dans le cod. 251. Ce texte a été enregistré par Kern, *Orphicorum Fragmenta,* test. 237.

recherchant l'accord des traditions les plus anciennes avec la doctrine platonicienne. Et nous savons que Plutarque d'Athènes est le fondateur de l'École néoplatonicienne d'Athènes.

De Hiéroclès, nous avons conservé un autre ouvrage qui confirme ce que nous venons de dire. Il s'agit d'un traité élémentaire pour les débutants dans l'étude du néoplatonisme. Il est significatif que, dans ce but, Hiéroclès compose un commentaire sur les *Vers d'Or*, un écrit néopythagoricien qui pourrait dater du IIe siècle après J.-C.[16] Pour Hiéroclès, cette pièce de 71 vers contenait toute la doctrine de Pythagore sur le monde des dieux encosmiques (p. 8, 3). Maintenant, en faisant appel au *Carmen Aureum* pour en faire une introduction à la philosophie, Hiéroclès se montrait un parfait disciple de Jamblique. Car Jamblique a consacré tout un chapitre de son *Protreptique* à l'examen des *Vers d'Or*.[17] Si nous voulons une preuve que, dès les débuts de l'École d'Athènes, on a suivi la tradition de Jamblique, en voilà une qui a une grande signification. Comme on le sait, le *Protreptique* est une sorte de pot-pourri dans lequel Jamblique a juxtaposé des textes pythagoriciens, platoniciens et aristotéliciens qui lui convenaient. C'était déjà d'une certaine manière marquer un accord entre eux. Avec Hiéroclès, le travail est bien plus élaboré; chaque fois qu'il le peut, Hiéroclès introduit de vrais parallèles entre son texte et le *Timée* ou le *Phèdre* de Platon. Il cite: "Timée, le personnage du dialogue de Platon, le maître précisément des doctrines pythagoriciennes" (p. 6, 1); il se réfère à l'opinion de "Platon et de Timée le Pythagoricien" (p. 53, 1), il affirme que "Platon est en accord (σύμφωνος) avec ce que dit Empédocle le Pythagoricien" (p. 98, 20), enfin il proclame: "Voilà la doctrine des Pytha-goriciens que justement Platon a divulgué plus tard (dans le *Phèdre*)" (p. 111, 13 - 14). Et lorsqu'il s'agit de commenter les vers 67 et 68 qui ordonnent l'abs-tinence de certains aliments comme moyens de purification et de libération de l'âme, Hiéroclès commente ces vers[18] à l'aide des *Oracles Chaldaïques* et des préceptes sacrés de la télestique, dont Photius dit qu'il avait fait aussi usage dans le *De providentia*.

---

[16] C'est la conclusion de P.C. Van der Horst, *Les vers d'or pythagoriciens,* Leyde 1932, xxxiv - xxxviii.

[17] *Cf.* Jamblique, *Protreptique*, Paris 1989, chap. 3, 43.17 - 48.19 éd. des Places. Jamblique est le premier à citer ces vers sous le titre Χρυσᾶ Ἔπη, 43, 21, *cf.* Van der Horst, *op. cit.,* xxxvi. On connaît, par la tradition arabe, un autre commentaire sur les *Vers d'Or.* On ne sait pas encore comment le situer par rapport à celui de Hiéroclès, car il est attribué à Proclus. Ce Proclus pourrait être, soit Proclus de Lycie, soit Proclus de Laodicée. *Cf.* N. Linley, *Ibn At-Tayyib, Proclus' Commentary on the Pythagorean Golden Verses*, Buffalo 1984, et L.G. Westerink, *Proclus commentateur des Vers d'Or,* dans: *Proclus et son influence*, Zürich 1987, 61 - 78.

[18] Il faut lire tout le texte dans *Hieroclis in Aureum Pythagoreum Carmen Commentarius*, ed. F.W. Koehler, Stutgardiae 1974, 110, 10 - 118, 17, presqu'entièrement traduit par A.J. Festugière, 'Contemplation philosophique et art théurgique chez Proclus', dans *Studi di Storia religiosa della tarda Antiquità*, Messine 1968, 5 - 18, reproduit dans *Études de philosophie grecque,* Paris 1971, 585 - 596.

Hiéroclès a été de la première génération des disciples de Plutarque; quant à Syrianus, il est entré un peu plus tard dans l' École où il a été non seulement disciple mais aussi maître, avant de succéder à Plutarque à la mort de celui-ci en 431 - 432. Devenu chef de l' École, il a dû enseigner le cycle complet des études philosophiques. Marinus, de nouveau, nous en apporte le témoignage. En effet, au chapitre 13 de son Éloge de Proclus, il rend compte ainsi de la vie de l'École:[19] "En moins de deux années complètes, Syrianus lut avec Proclus tous les traités d'Aristote, ceux de logique, d'éthique, de politique, de physique, et celui qui les dépasse tous, sur la science théologique." Ce dernier traité est évidemment la *Métaphysique,* et il nous reste une trace de cet enseignement, le cours de Syrianus sur les livres BΓMN.[20] Marinus poursuit: "Puis, quand il eut été bien introduit par ces ouvrages comme par des sortes de sacrifices préparatoires et de petits mystères (remarquez le vocabulaire religieux employé par Marinus), le faisant avancer d'une manière régulière et non, comme le dit l'Oracle, *en sautant les étapes,* il l'amena peu à peu à la mystagogie de Platon, et lui fit obtenir l'époptie, dans les initiations réellement divines qu'on trouve chez lui, par les yeux non troublés de son âme et le sommet immaculé de son intellect." Derrière ce langage allusif, nous reconnaissons le programme des leçons portant sur les dialogues de Platon, établi depuis Jamblique, à savoir les dix dialogues préparatoires à la lecture finale du *Timée* et du *Parménide*, le dialogue époptique par excellence,[21] dont Syrianus donnait une exégèse nouvelle et meilleure que toutes les précédentes. Les dialogues préparatoires étaient dans l'ordre: *Alcibiade, Gorgias, Phédon, Cratyle, Théétète, Sophiste, Politique, Phèdre, Banquet, Philèbe.*[22] De cet enseignement aussi, qui dura sûrement plusieurs années, nous avons quelques restes, le morceau principal étant les notes d'un cours sur le *Phèdre*, prises par un disciple, Hermeias, mais il ne faut pas négliger les nombreuses références fournies par Proclus dans ses commentaires *Sur le Timée* et *Sur le Parménide*.

Nous allons y revenir. Mais auparavant, je voudrais puiser, dans le discours de Marinus, une autre information significative. Celle-ci se trouve au chapitre 26, au moment où l'orateur aborde la présentation des vertus théurgiques de son maître, qui suivent les vertus contemplatives: "Voilà, dit-il, les vertus que Proclus pratiquait alors qu'il suivait les cours du philosophe

---

[19] *Cf.* Marinus, *Vita Procli,* cap. 13, p. 11, éd. J.F. Boissonnade.

[20] *Cf. Syriani in Metaphysica commentaria,* éd. G. Kroll, Berlin 1902, avec le compte-rendu de K. Praechter, dans *Göttingische gelehrte Anzeigen*, 165 (1903) 513 - 530, reproduit dans *Kleine Schriften*, 246 - 263 .

[21] Le *Parménide* qualifié d'époptique, *cf. In Parm.* I, 617, 25 et V, 993, 18; *Théol. plat.* I 10, 44, 6.

[22] *Cf.* L.G. Westerink, *Anonymus Prolegomena to Platonic Philosophy,* Amsterdam 1962, XL, et A.J. Festugière, 'L'ordre de lecture des dialogues de Platon aux Ve/VIe siècles', dans *Museum Helveticum* 26 (1969), 281 - 296, reproduit dans *Études de Philosophie grecque*, 535 - 550.

Syrianus et qu'il étudiait les uns après les autres les ouvrages des Anciens. Mais, de la théologie Orphique et Chaldaïque, il n'avait reçu de son professeur que quelques éléments et, pour ainsi dire, des semences, parce que Syrianus n'avait pas encore eu le temps de le familiariser avec les poèmes. Voici pourquoi: à lui et au philosophe syrien, Domninus, Syrianus avait proposé d'expliquer, ou bien les poèmes d'Orphée, ou les *Oracles*, et leur avait laissé le choix; mais comme ils n'avaient pas pu se mettre d'accord et n'avaient pas fait tous les deux le même choix, Domninus choisissant les poèmes d'Orphée, notre héros, les *Oracles*, de ce fait le Grand Syrianus se trouva empêché (de réaliser son projet), et aussi parce qu'il ne survécut que peu de temps — Proclus n'avait donc reçu de son Maître, comme je viens de le dire, que le point de départ pour cette étude." On le voit: Marinus ici nous fait le récit de la dernière année de la vie de Syrianus.[23] Ayant achevé le cycle platonicien, le professeur voulait aborder avec ses disciples l'étude des poèmes théologiques, ceux d'Orphée et les *Oracles*. Nous apprenons que sont alors disciples de Syrianus, le syrien Domninus et le lycien Proclus. Domninus est sans doute l'aîné des deux puisque son choix l'emporte, lorsque le Maître leur propose de décider quel cours ils veulent entendre. Ce sera Orphée. Il y aura donc un commentaire de Syrianus sur la Théologie d'Orphée. Mais la mort prématurée de Syrianus a eu deux conséquences. La première: il n'a jamais pu enseigner les *Oracles Chaldaïques* à Proclus; la seconde: le temps lui a manqué pour donner à son cours sur le poème d'Orphée toute l'ampleur souhaitable. Cette circonstance explique donc le désir exprimé plus tard par les élèves de Proclus d'avoir de lui des compléments au travail de Syrianus, comme je l'ai rappelé plus haut. Ce que nous venons d'apprendre par Marinus, nous allons le retrouver en examinant les travaux de Syrianus qui nous sont parvenus. Il élabore l'accord de la tradition platonicienne avec celle venant d'Orphée, mais il ne fait presque jamais appel aux *Oracles*.[24]

Tournons-nous d'abord vers le Commentaire de Syrianus sur la *Métaphysique*. En B 1, 996 a 1 - 2, Aristote se pose la question de savoir si les principes sont limités en nombre ou en espèces. Aussitôt Syrianus examine la question en passant en revue les principes selon Platon et Philolaos, le limitant et l'illimité, selon Orphée, l'Éther et le Chaos, et selon Pythagore, Proteus et la Dyade, principes qui suivent le premier qui a nom, l'Un ou le Bien.[25] Il ne dit pas ici, mais plus loin, que le nom du premier principe chez Orphée est Χρόνος,

---

[23] *Cf.* Marinus, *Vita Procli*, chap. 26, 20, éd. J.F. Boissonade, et M.-O. Goulet - Cazé, 'L'arrière-plan scolaire de la *Vie de Plotin*', dans: *Porphyre, La Vie de Plotin I,* Paris 1982, 277 - 280.

[24] Sauf erreur, j'ai relevé trois références aux *Oracles* dans l' *In Met.*, à savoir: 14, 35 - 36 = fr. 108, 89, 16 - 17 = fr. 8.3, 126, 24 = fr. 37, 2 - 8 (une paraphrase); également trois références dans l' *In Phaedrum* (d'Hermeias), à savoir: 110, 5 = fr. 174, 157, 19 = fr. 23, 184, 21 = fr. 53. 2.

[25] *Cf.* Syrianus, *In Met.*, 9, 37 - 10, 11.

le Temps.[26] Il conclut: "Tout ce que l'on dit au sujet des principes pythagoriciens, on dit la même chose (ταὐτὸν ... εἰπεῖν) des principes orphiques et platoniciens," marquant ainsi l'accord des trois traditions. Mais c'est surtout dans
le commentaire sur les livres M et N que Syrianus multiplie les rap-
prochements. Le livre M commence par un long exposé de la métaphysique pythagoricienne,[27] Platon et Pythagore οὐ διαφωνοῦσι (p. 83, 12). Pour Syrianus, οἱ
ἄνδρες sont l'appellation commune de Platon et des Pythagoriciens, et le
véritable péché d'Aristote est que sa philosophie est en désaccord (τὸ διάφωνον
ἔχουσαν, p. 60. 28) avec la leur qui est plus "époptique", allusion, nous le
savons, au Parménide auquel la Metaphysique ne saurait être comparée. Pour
conclure l'explication des chapitres 2 et 3 du livre M, qui traitent du nombre
mathématique, Syrianus ne trouve rien de mieux que de recopier purement et
simplement les κεφάλαια du De communi mathematica scientia de
Jamblique.[28] Du même coup, notre commentateur se révèle à la fois disciple de
Jamblique et dévot des Pythagoriciens. Dans la section qui suit et qui traite des
Idées que Platon, dit notre auteur, "à la suite des Pythagoriciens a nommées
Nombres Idéaux," Syrianus cite le fameux Hymne sur le Nombre, qui semble
être un bien commun aux Pythagoriciens et aux Orphiques.[29] Dans le
commentaire sur le livre N, lorsqu' il arrive à l'allusion qu' Aristote lui-même
fait aux Poètes Anciens en 1091 b 4 - 6, il énumère les Règnes Orphiques qui
se succèdent depuis le premier, celui de Phanès, jusqu'au troisième, celui
d'Ouranos, en citant chaque fois les vers correspondants du poème des
Rhapsodies Orphiques pour souligner les accords entre Pythagore et Orphée.[30]

La lecture de ce commentaire sur la Metaphysique laisse l'impression que
les citations des Poèmes Orphiques que l'on y rencontre, sont plutôt
décoratives. Il n'en va plus de même avec le commentaire sur le Phèdre.[31]Sans
doute la tradition manuscrite l'attribue au disciple Hermeias, mais il ne fait
aucun doute qu'Hermeias nous a laissé une rédaction extrêmement fidèle du
cours de son maître Syrianus. Le plus souvent, il est désigné par l'appellation
de ὁ φιλόσοφος ou ἡμεῖς, une fois avec cette précision révélatrice: "nous qui
admirons ici encore la doctrine de Jamblique."[32] Nous entendons les étudiants

---

[26] Cf. Syrianus, ibid., 43, 23 - 24.

[27] Cf. Syrianus, ibid., 81, 31 - 83, 31.

[28] Cf. Syrianus, ibid., 101, 28 - 102, 35 = Jamblique, De comm. math. scientia, 3, 7 - 8,
6 (depuis le κεφ.β΄ jusqu'au κεφ. λγ΄). Sur ce livre de Jamblique, cf. D. O'Meara, op. cit.,
44 - 51.

[29] Cf. Syrianus, ibid., 106, 15 - 26 = Kern, Orphic. fr. 315 = H. Thesleff, The
Pythagorean Texts of the Hellenistic Period, Åbo 1965, 173.

[30] Cf. Syrianus, ibid., 182, 11 - 28.

[31] D'une manière générale, cf. A. Bielmeier, Die neuplatonische Phaidrosinterpretation, Paderborn 1930.

[32] Cf. Hermeias, Hermiae Alexandrini In Platonis Phaedrum Scholia, ed. P. Couvreur,
Paris 1901, 136, 19. Sur la fidélité d'Hermeias à Syrianus cf. K. Praechter, art. 'Hermeias'
13, dans Pauly-Wissowa, 15 (1912), 732 - 735.

qui réagissent pendant le cours, Hermeias et Proclus, chacun deux fois,[33] et même nous voyons une fois le professeur prendre à témoin son auditoire.[34]

Ce commentaire sur le *Phèdre* est une explication suivie, phrase par phrase et souvent mot par mot. Il est d'autant plus intéressant de repérer les développements exégétiques. Le plus important pour nous intervient dans le livre II, tout entier consacré à l'enthousiasme.[35] Dans l'explication du mythe de l'ascension du lieu supracéleste par les âmes divines et humaines sous la conduite de Zeus, nous rencontrons un long excursus sur la question:"Qui est Zeus et qui sont les douze dieux?" [36] L'auteur donne d'abord les opinions de ses prédécesseurs (les douze sphères, leurs âmes, leurs intellects, le soleil et les signes du zodiaque). Pour Jamblique, Zeus est le démiurge du *Timée*. Syrianus (nous croyons que c'est lui qui parle alors) introduit une nouvelle exégèse "en suivant, dit-il, Platon et les Théologiens" (p. 136, 25 - 26). Aussitôt nous sommes transportés dans le monde des divinités Orphiques.[37] Il y a un Zeus transcendant, et en dessous il y a trois Zeus, qui reçoivent les noms de Zeus, Poséidon et Plouton, et chacun de ces trois Zeus tient sous lui quatre divinités qui fournissent successivement l'être, la vie, la garde contre toute déchéance et la conversion. La dynastie des dieux Orphiques est rappelée: Éther, Chaos, Oeuf primordial, Phanès, premier roi; Zeus n'arrive qu'en quatrième position dans la succession des règnes, après ceux d'Ouranos et de Cronos.[38] Sans doute, pour la première fois, le mythe du *Phèdre* est clairement interprété en termes orphiques, et Homère est aussi invoqué à côté d'Orphée. Lorsqu'il commente le passage dans lequel Platon dit que pas un poète du passé n'a chanté dignement le lieu supracéleste (247 c 3 - 4), Syrianus accorde que c'est vrai s'il s'agit des poètes humains d'ici-bas, mais les poètes inspirés des dieux, Orphée et Homère, Hésiode et Musée, eux, ont chanté convenablement la vie des dieux, instruits qu'ils sont par Apollon et le choeur des Muses.[39] Dans la suite du texte, cette exégèse exposée ici *ex professo*, réapparaît souvent. Dans les correspondances qu'il établit entre Platon et Orphée, Syrianus remarque que ce que l'un dit négativement, l'autre l'avait exprimé affirmativement, ou inversement. Dans la *Théologie platonicienne* lorsque Proclus fera l'exégèse de ce même texte du *Phèdre* pour y trouver la première triade des dieux

---

[33] Pour Hermeias, *cf. ibid.,* 24, 6 et 154, 21; pour Proclus, 92, 6 et 154, 28.

[34] *Cf. ibid.,* 185, 29 - 31.

[35] *Cf.* O. Ballériaux,'Syrianus et la télestique', dans *Kernos* 2 (1989), 13 - 25. On doit remarquer que le thème de l'enthousiasme est déjà celui du livre III du *De mysteriis* de Jamblique.

[36] *Cf.* Hermeias, *In Phaedrum,* 135, 26 - 139, 25.

[37] Dans ce contexte j'ai compté vingt appels à "Théologie", ou au "Théologien" ou à "Orphée". L'accord de Platon et des Théologiens est souligné deux fois, en 136, 25 et 148, 18.

[38] *Cf.* Hermeias, *In Phaedrum,* 142, 10 - 13.

[39] *Cf. ibid.,* 146, 25 - 147, 6. Dans le *In Remp.* I, 71, 2 - 6, Proclus dit que le thème de l'accord doctrinal entre Platon et Homère (κοινωνία τῶν δογμάτων) était un sujet souvent développé par Syrianus dans ses cours.

intelligibles-intellectifs, il résumera très exactement le travail de Syrianus, en disant:[40] "Notre Maître aussi est d'avis de diviser cette triade en trois monades, et il montre ce résultat en suivant les Théologies Orphiques."

Malgré la perte de la plupart de ses autres travaux, nous sommes en droit de considérer ces deux écrits de Syrianus comme des exemples représentatifs de sa manière de commenter les textes anciens. En effet, si nous lisons les commentaires de Proclus, qui mettent si souvent à contribution ceux de son Maître, nous constatons qu'il procédait toujours en recherchant l'accord de Platon avec le théologien Orphée. Il avait devant les yeux les *Discours Sacrés en vingt-quatre rhapsodies*, et nous avons déjà dit qu'il en avait composé un commentaire qui était, dans l'École néoplatonicienne d'Athènes, l'ouvrage de référence sur ce texte, et qu'il avait intitulé *Sur la théologie d'Orphée*.

Ce titre peut-il nous mettre sur la voie qui nous mènerait à découvrir les raisons de cette faveur pour la théologie d'Orphée. N'est-ce pas justement parce qu'il venait de découvrir dans la deuxième hypothèse du *Parménide* la théologie de Platon? Dès le début de l'École et de l'enseignement néoplatonicien à Athènes, sous l'impulsion de Plutarque, ce dialogue, en effet, et plus précisément l'exégèse des hypothèses, a été l'objet d'une étude soutenue qui a connu deux rebondissements.[41] Le premier est dû à Plutarque qui est l'auteur d'une interprétation nouvelle dans laquelle il réussissait à concilier l'enseignement des Anciens qui comptaient neuf hypothèses, avec l'apport de Théodore d'Asiné établissant la correspondance entre les hypothèses qui posent l'existence de l'Un et celles qui la nient. Le second est le pas gigantesque que Syrianus a fait sur ce chemin, en ayant l'idée d'analyser la structure interne des deux premières hypothèses et d'en découvrir les articulations rigoureuses.[42] Il obtenait ainsi deux résultats fondamentaux: premièrement, tout ce qui est nié dans la première hypothèse se trouve affirmé dans la deuxième, et deuxièmement, la deuxième hypothèse comporte quatorze conclusions déduites les unes des autres, qui caractérisent les quatorze classes d'êtres, composant toute la hiérarchie des dieux.[43] Avec cette exégèse, il venait de retrouver chez Platon la "Chaîne d'Or" liant tout le monde divin, "chaîne d'or", expression anciennement forgée par Homère et Orphée.[44] Syrianus découvrait que la deuxième hypothèse du *Parménide* contient une "théogonie". Le mot est explicitement prononcé par Proclus.[45]

---

[40] *Cf.* Proclus, *Théol. plat.* IV 16, 48, 19-22.

[41] *Cf.* H.D. Saffrey, 'La *Théologie platonicienne* de Proclus, fruit de l'exégèse du *Parménide*'', dans *Rev. de Théol. et de Phil.,* 116, 1984, 1 - 12.

[42] *Cf.* Proclus, *Théol. plat.* I 10, 42, 10 - 43, 21.

[43] *Cf.* Proclus, *In Parm.* VI, 1061, 31 - 1062, 20, et *Théol. plat* . I 11, 52, 20 - 53, 22.

[44] *Cf.* Homère, *Ilias* VIII 19, et Orphée, fr. 166. 2. Sur le thème de la "Chaîne d'Or", *cf.* P. Lévêque, *Aurea Catena Homeri*, Paris 1959.

[45] *Cf. Théol. plat.* I 12, 55, 11 - 18 et III 23, 82, 1 - 2."Cette hypothèse n'est rien d'autre qu'une génération et une procession des dieux", et *apud* Damascius, *In Parm.,* 118, 34: "Proclus dit tout à fait bien que Platon s'est proposé d'écrire une théogonie", et 221, 26.

Dès lors, la comparaison avec les Théogonies anciennes s'imposait, celles d'Homère et d'Hésiode, et plus encore celle d'Orphée, réputée la plus ancienne et consignée dans le poème tenu alors pour authentique des *Rhapsodies* au nombre de vingt-quatre, sur le modèle des vingt-quatre chants de l'*Iliade*. Car en même temps que l'on élaborait des concordances, on établissait aussi des dépendances. Dans la *Vie Pythagoricienne*, Jamblique avait donné à Pythagore un ancêtre spirituel prestigieux en la personne d'Orphée, tout en reconnaissant d'autres influences venues des prêtres Égyptiens et des mages Chaldéens.[46] Chez Proclus, probablement inspiré par Syrianus, cette donnée biographique devient une véritable généalogie:[47] "Toute la théologie grecque, dit-il, est fille de la mystagogie d'Orphée: Pythagore le premier avait appris d'Aglaophamos les initiations relatives aux dieux, Platon ensuite a reçu des écrits pythagoriciens et orphiques la science toute parfaite qui les concerne." Orphée, Pythagore et Platon forment une succession qui assure la transmission continue de la théologie grecque, sous ses trois noms significatifs: mystagogie, initiation, science. Avec le *Parménide* de Platon, la théologie devient une science! Naturellement, comme toutes les sciences, elle doit avoir une portée universelle. Puisque les Théologies anciennes concernaient évidemment les dieux encosmiques et sublunaires, c'est dans ce domaine que les premières correspondances pouvaient le mieux s'établir. De fait, on les trouve dans le *Commentaire sur le Timée*. Mais en raisonnant par analogie, à l'aide du fameux principe:[48] "Tout est dans tout, mais en chacun selon son mode propre," on pouvait appliquer les mêmes relations divines en les transposant à tous les degrés et expliquer ainsi les textes du *Phèdre* ou du *Philèbe* par ceux d'Orphée ou de Philolaos, sans compter cette mine de comparaisons et d'équivalences entre les noms des dieux qu'offre le *Cratyle*.

Nous avons dit que l'Accord d'Orphée, Pythagore, Platon, avait été un programme de recherche pour l'École Néoplatonicienne d'Athènes, nous comprenons maintenant comment et pourquoi ce programme a été réalisé. Toutefois, il est utile de faire remarquer que cet accord était pour une large part un accord préétabli. Cela ni Syrianus ni Proclus ne le savaient, mais la critique historique l'a clairement révélé depuis. Prenons un exemple. Proclus avait délibérément fait précéder son *Commentaire sur le Timée* de l'écrit du Pseudo-Timée de Locres *Sur la nature*. Il dit:[49] "Cet écrit je l'ai mis en tête de mon Commentaire pour que nous soyons en mesure de savoir où le *Timée* de Platon dit les mêmes choses, où il a ajouté, où il est en désaccord, et que nous

---

Le mot n'est pas prononcé mais il est clairement suggéré en *In Parm.* VI, 1061, 23 - 1062, 11.

[46] *Cf.* Jamblique, *De Vita Pythagorica*, chap. 28, § 145 - 151, 81, 20 - 85, 20, éd. Deubner.

[47] *Cf. Théol. plat.* I 5, 25, 26 - 26, 4 avec la n. 3 (138 des *Notes complémentaires*).

[48] *Cf.* Proclus, *El. Théol.*, § 103, avec le commentaire de Dodds, 254.

[49] *Cf.* Proclus, *In Tim.* I, 1, 13 - 16.

recherchions avec exactitude la cause du désaccord (τῆς διαφωνίας)." De fait, la lecture des livres que nous avons conservés, montre que Proclus a été très attentif à cette question et qu'il n'a eu à relever aucun désaccord profond. On pouvait s'y attendre puisque nous savons aujourd'hui que le traité du Pseudo-Timée était précisément calqué sur le plan et le contenu du *Timée* de Platon. Il y avait donc entre les deux une harmonie préétablie.[50] La même observation pourrait être faite pour d'autres traités néopythagoriciens. Destin étrange que celui du Néopythagorisme. Si c'est pour justifier la thèse du plagiat de Platon envers Pythagore qu'à partir de IIIe siècle avant J.-C. on a composé cette quantité de faux néopythagoriciens, qui en vérité démarquaient la doctrine même de Platon, à l'inverse, à partir du IVe siècle après J.-C., on a lu dans ces faux néopythagoriciens la preuve évidente qu'il existait une harmonie fondamentale entre Platon et Pythagore. Il faut le redire: on découvrait alors une harmonie préétablie qui élevait l'accord entre ces philosophes au rang d'une révélation. Walter Burkert a raison de dire:[51] "Le matériel traditionnel qui avait été entassé sous le nom de Pythagore, quoique mal digéré et mutilé, fut de cette façon élevé à une dignité nouvelle et revêtu d'une autorité sans précédent. Toute cette littérature apocryphe entrait dans la sphère du religieux". Toute proportion gardée, on pourrait en dire autant des Poèmes Orphiques, que l'on appellerait aussi bien néo-orphiques, si l'on pouvait les comparer aux véritables *Discours Sacrés* plus anciens.

L'accord des trois plus grands théologiens de la Grèce était déjà en soi un résultat impressionnant, mais puisque les savants néoplatoniciens disposaient en plus d'oracles divins, il était nécessaire de confronter cet accord à la révélation des dieux qui parlent.[52] Car, et Proclus le dit plusieurs fois, les dieux sont évidemment les mieux placés pour dire ce qui les concerne, ils savent de quoi ils parlent.[53] C'est la raison pour laquelle l'autorité des dieux radicalise celle des sages et des savants, car on n'a pas le droit de refuser sa foi au théurge auquel les dieux ont délivré leur message.[54] Il faut donc croire les Oracles. Et puisque les *Oracles Chaldaïques*, du moins certains d'entre eux, révèlent aussi la théogonie et la cosmogonie, ils se présentent comme une référence ultime à laquelle l'accord des Théologiens doit être soumis. Cette confrontation pouvait

---

[50] *Cf.* W. Marg, *Timaeus Locrus, De natura mundi et animae*, Leiden 1972, 93 - 99, qui a étudié toutes les citations par Proclus de Timée de Locres dans le commentaire. Noter la formule employée en *In Tim.* II, 188. 12 - 13: μηδὲν διάφωνον εἶναι θέλοντες. Pour la correspondance étroite entre le *Timée* de Platon et le faux néopythagoricien, *cf.* R. Harder, dans Pauly-Wissowa, VI A (1936), col. 1203 - 1226.

[51] *Cf.* W. Burkert, *Lore and Science in Ancient Pythagoreanism*, Cambridge (Mass.) 1972, 96.

[52] *Cf.* Proclus, *In Crat.* § 71, 35, 4 - 5.

[53] *Cf.* Proclus, *In Parm.* VII, 512.97 - 98 Steel, *In Remp.* II, 236.4 - 5, *De Prov.* I 1, 110, 1 - 2 éd. Boese; Damascius, *In Parm.*, 131, 3 - 5, et *Théol. plat.* V, Introduction, xiii, n. 1.

[54] *Cf.* Proclus, *In Tim.* III, 63, 24 et 83, 16, *In Remp.* II, 220, 18 et 236, 10, et déjà Jamblique, *De myst.* V 23, 234, 7 - 8.

être d'autant plus facile et féconde que les Oracles utilisés par Syrianus et Proclus avaient, on le sait, un caractère nettement platonicien.[55] Julien le Théurge y faisait parler l'âme de Platon! Il n'est donc pas étonnant que, dans cette circonstance, Proclus admire "l'identité de langage entre le *Timée* et les *Oracles*."[56] La méthode en recherche théologique était par conséquent toute tracée. Chaque fois, rechercher l'accord de Platon, Pythagore et Orphée et, pour finir, confronter cet accord aux *Oracles*. C'est ce que nous voyons Proclus faire continuellement dans ses commentaires et dans la *Théologie platonicienne*. Syrianus avait indiqué cette dernière étape de la recherche d'une manière inchoative,[57] Proclus devait la mener à son terme d'une manière systématique. Par exemple, nous avons vu que Syrianus avait commenté le mythe du *Phèdre* par les textes parallèles des poèmes Orphiques; Proclus, dans la *Théologie platonicienne*, prolonge cette exégèse en commentant ce même mythe par les *Oracles Chaldaïques*. [58]

Accorder entre elles les traditions théologiques a donc été la méthode communément suivie dans l'École d'Athènes. Il nous reste à montrer, comme je l'ai annoncé, que ce fut une caractéristique de cette École, c'est-à-dire que cette méthode ne fut pas pratiquée avant les Néoplatoniciens Athéniens. Elle est tout à fait étrangère à l'esprit de Plotin. Dans les *Ennéades*,[59] le nom Ὀρφεύς n'apparaît jamais ni non plus l'adjectif ὀρφικός, et sur les cinq références aux *Orphica* signalées dans l'Index de l'édition Henry-Schwyzer, quatre le sont par l'intermédiaire de Platon qui est seul la véritable source, la dernière est une allusion à un élément bien connu du mythe,[60] à ce que Proclus appellera plus tard "la légende divine", θεομυθία.[61] Ensuite, d'après l'index de Kern, les seules références à Orphée chez Porphyre se rencontrent dans le *De antro Nympharum*.[62] Elles sont au nombre de trois et manifesteraient au mieux

---

[55] *Cf.* H.D. Saffrey, 'Proclus, diadoque de Platon', dans *Proclus, lecteur et interprète des Anciens*, Paris 1987, XI - XXVIII, en particulier XXII - XXVII.

[56] *Cf.* Proclus, *In Tim.* I, 318, 20 - 21.

[57] *Cf.* par exemple, Proclus, *In Tim.* III, 247, 26 - 249, 26: opinion de Syrianus en accord avec les Théologiens.

[58] *Cf.* Proclus, *Theol. plat.* IV 9, 27, 5 - 31, 16: Accord de Platon et des *Oracles Chaldaïques*.

[59] *Cf.* J.H. Sleeman et G. Pollet, *Lexicon Plotinianum*, Leiden - Leuven 1980. Le nom de Pythagore est cité quatre fois, mais toujours en sa qualité de philosophe.

[60] *Cf.* J. Pépin, 'Plotin et le miroir de Dionysos' (*Enn.*, IV 3 [27], 12, 1 - 22) dans *Rev. Intern. de Phil.* 24 (1970), 304 - 320. On peut admettre que Plotin soit le premier à commenter *Tim.* 35 à l'aide du mythe du démembrement de Dionysos, mais ce n'est pas établir une correspondance entre des théogonies. Une sixième référence a été ajouté par H.R. Schwyzer, 'Corrigenda ad Plotini Textum', dans *Mus. Helv.* 44 (1987), 204, mais à mon avis elle ne porte pas.

[61] *Cf.* Proclus, *In Tim.* III, 223, 16.

[62] *Cf.* Seminar Classics 609 of SUNY at Buffalo (= L.G. Westerink), *Porphyry, The Cave of the Nymphs in the Odyssey*, Buffalo 1969. Ces trois références sont: 8, 32 -10. 2 (omise par Kern); 16, 13 - 16 (= fr.192), 18, 3 - 19 (= fr.154). De son côté, H. Lewy, *Chaldaean Oracles and Theurgy*, 456, exagère démesurément le rôle de Porphyre comme introducteur des *Oracles Chaldaïques*.

un accord entre Homère et Orphée. Deux de ces références renvoient encore à la légende, une seule comporte la citation de deux vers dont il est impossible de déterminer s'ils appartenaient aux *Rhapsodies* ou à un *Discours Sacré* antérieur. Il s'agit d'ailleurs encore d'un élément de la légende, que l'on pourrait appeler "le piège du miel" qui enivre Cronos au moment où il va être castré par Zeus. L'auteur n'en tire aucune application métaphysique, mais seulement une leçon de morale.

En un sens limité, on pourrait faire de Jamblique l'initiateur de la méthode théologique qui sera pratiquée à Athènes. Il est bien connu que c'est Jamblique qui a fait entrer Pythagore, entendez les apocryphes néopythagoriciens, comme une autorité sur un pied d'égalité avec Platon. Dominic O'Meara vient de consacrer un livre entier à ce sujet,[63] et je ne peux que renvoyer le lecteur à cette étude très complète. Non seulement Jamblique a composé un ouvrage en dix livres *Sur le Pythagorisme,*[64] mais il a fait entrer le Pythagorisme dans ses commentaires sur Platon. En revanche, Orphée n'intervient que comme une figure mythique,[65] et dans ce qui nous reste de son oeuvre Jamblique ne cite jamais aucun vers des *Rhapsodies.* L'empereur Julien dira une fois que Jamblique aimait les mythes touchant aux initiations transmis par Orphée, le fondateur de l'initiation la plus sacrée, celle d'Éleusis.[66] Jamblique avait composé aussi une *Théologie Chaldaïque* sur laquelle nous ne savons pratiquement rien, mais on peut présenter le *De mysteriis* comme une recherche de l'accord entre la théologie Égyptienne et la théologie Chaldaïque. Néanmoins Jamblique ne s'attaque jamais à des comparaisons de textes platoniciens avec les vers des poèmes Orphiques ou des Oracles Chaldaïques. C'est en ce sens que nous croyons pouvoir dire que la recherche approfondie et systématique de l'Accord d'Orphée, Pythagore et Platon avec les Oracles Chaldaïques est une originalité de l'École néoplatonicienne d'Athènes. Non seulement cette caractéristique est à l'origine de l'ouvrage connu sous ce titre comme l'oeuvre conjuguée de Syrianus et de Proclus, mais c'était la méthode habituelle en théologie dans cette École.

Après Proclus, cette méthode théologique a continuée d'être pratiquée dans l'École. Marinus la mentionne dans son discours, comme je l'ai dit en commençant, Damascius la suit dans son *Commentaire sur le Parménide.* Par le même Damascius, nous faisons la connaissance du personnage de Sarapion,

---

[63] Ce livre est cité *supra,* n. 3.

[64] Cet ouvrage a été étudié d'une manière plus complète que précédemment par O'Meara, grâce à de nouveaux fragments qu'il a retrouvés chez Psellus, voir les chap. 2, 3 et 4 de son livre.

[65] *Cf.* J.M. Dillon, *Iamblichi Chalcidensis in Platonis dialogos Commentariorum fragmenta,* Leiden 1973. Au fr. 74 (p. 188), je crois qu'il faut arrêter ce qui concerne Jamblique à la ligne 7 après le mot ἀληθείας. La phrase qui commence par ῥητέον δ̕οὖν (...) marque le début de ce que Proclus lui-même veut dire sur Orphée et Pythagore.

[66] *Cf.* Julien, *Oratio* VII, *Contre Héraclius,* 12, 217 C. Ce texte manque dans les témoignages nn. 102 - 104 réunis par Kern sur Orphée, fondateur des mystères d'Éleusis.

un ami de son maître Isidore et un ermite païen, qui "poursuivait sans cesse la vérité et était naturellement contemplatif (...). Il ne possédait et ne lisait que le seul Orphée (...)."[67] Nous savons aussi qu'à Alexandrie, à la fin du Ve siècle, le philosophe Asclépiadès, qui est bien connu par le mémoire de Jean Maspéro,[68] avait composé une Συμφωνία τῶν Αἰγυπτίων πρὸς τοὺς ἄλλους Θεολόγους, dont nous pouvons bien penser qu'elle était faite sur le modèle de la Συμφωνία de Syrianus et de Proclus.

Voilà donc un aspect du néoplatonisme qui n'est pas souvent mis en valeur, et que l'on devrait appeler un "retour aux sources", ou du moins à ce que l'on croyait alors être des sources. Ayant repris possession avec Plotin de tous les dialogues de Platon et singulièrement du *Parménide*, les Néoplatoniciens ont inauguré une tradition ininterrompue d'exégèse platonicienne. Comme c'était naturel, au temps où l'on faisait de Platon un disciple de Pythagore, un retour à Pythagore devait faire l'objet de l'effort principal de Jamblique, qui reconstitua un corpus entier des doctrines pythagoriciennes. Et puisque Pythagore avait été initié par Orphée, et que l'on disposait alors des *Rhapsodies Orphiques* que l'on croyait anciennes, Syrianus donna l'explication de cette Théogonie en la considérant comme l'origine première des doctrines pythagoriciennes et platoniciennes. Enfin Proclus, comprenant que les Oracles des dieux avaient une autorité supérieure à toutes les autres et disposant du corpus des *Oracles Chaldaïques* qui faisaient parler les dieux eux-mêmes, acheva ce retour aux sources de la théologie avec le traité de l'*Accord d'Orphée, Pythagore, Platon avec les Oracles Chaldaïques*. Ce fut la Renaissance du Ve siècle.

Mille ans plus tard, Marsile Ficin travaillait à sa traduction latine de tous les dialogues de Platon. Ce fut la Renaissance du XVe siècle. Il y a cinq années, en 1984, Florence a célébré le cinquième centenaire de cet événement: *Marsilio Ficino e il Ritorno di Platone*.[69] On pouvait voir à cette occasion que ce "retour de Platon" avait été en même temps celui de Pythagore, d'Orphée, des Oracles. Ficin lui-même recherchait la "Concorde des philosophies" dans un retour à la *Prisca Theologia*.[70] Plus encore, Pico de la Mirandola et ses

---

[67] *Cf*. Damascius, *Vita Isidori*, fr. 41 = Souda IV, 324, 19 - 20.

[68] *Cf*. J. Maspéro, 'Horapollon et la fin du paganisme égyptien', dans *Bull. Inst. Franç. d'Arch. Or.,* 11 (1914), 163 - 195; voir aussi *Prosopography of the late Roman Empire*, II, *s.v.* "Heraiscus". Cette "Symphonia" est mentionnée par Damascius, *De princ.,* 324, 12 - 15.

[69] Il y eut une exposition à la Biblioteca Laurentiana et un Colloque, *cf*. le catalogue de l'exposition, *Marsilio Ficino e il Ritorno di Platone*, Manoscritti Stampe e Documenti, Firenze 1984, et les actes du colloque *Marsilio Ficino e il Ritorno di Platone* a cura di G.C. Garfagnini, Firenze 1986.

[70] *Cf*. F. Purnell jr., 'The Theme of Philosophic Concord and the Sources of Ficino's Platonism', dans *Marsilio Ficino e il Ritorno di Platone*, 397 - 415, et plus anciennement l'ouvrage fondamental de D.P. Walker, *The Ancient Theology* , London 1972. Noter cette opinion de Ficin: *"Tota Priscorum philosophia nihil est aliud quam docta religio"*, *cf*. *Opera omnia* I, 854.

disciples, Francesco Zorzi et Agostino Steuco, qui composaient des *De concordia mundi totius* et des *De perenni philosophia*, deux thèmes liés de la Renaissance Italienne,[71] permettaient que s'inscrivent dans les oeuvres d'art leur espoir et leur culte de l'Accord parfait. En architecture, c'était l'église de San Francesco della Vigna à Venise,[72] en peinture la décoration par Raphaël de la Stanza della Segnatura au Vatican.[73] Ils avaient appris, selon les mots de Zorzi que je vous livre dans la savoureuse traduction de Guy Le Fevre de la Boderie[74] que Platon et "même Aristote, quand en sa Métaphysique (N 4, 1091 b 10) il discourt de la connaissance de Dieu, révèrent les Pères Chaldéens, pour ce qu'ils avaient été appris par les Oracles, lesquels (comme dit Proclus, illustré de ne sais quelle lumière) ayant banqueté chez Dieu et vivant en une pure splendeur, intruits et informés selon les apparences et simulacres du Tout, parfaits et fermes, tenaient pour des bourdes et contes de vieilles les opinions affirmatives et les raisons appuyées en doctrine humaine."

---

[71] *Cf.* Ch.B. Schmitt, '"Prisca Theologia" e "Philosophia Perennis": due temi del Rinascimento italiano e la loro fortuna', dans *Il pensiero italiano del Rinascimento e il nostro tempo*, Firenze 1970, 211-236.

[72] *Cf.* A. Foscari e M. Tafuri, *L'armonia e i conflitti. La chiesa di San Francesco della Vigna nella Venezia del '500*, Torino 1983.

[73] *Cf.* E. Wind, *Art et Anarchie*, Paris 1988, 88 - 89 et n. 113.

[74] *Cf. L'harmonie du monde* , par G. Le Fevre de la Boderie, Paris 1578, 349.

CARLOS STEEL

LE *SOPHISTE* COMME TEXTE THEOLOGIQUE
DANS L'INTERPRETATION DE PROCLUS

Dans l'introduction à sa *Théologie platonicienne,* Proclus distingue chez Platon quatre types de discours théologiques: le discours inspiré, le symbolique, celui par images, et enfin, ce qui est l'apanage des philosophes, le discours dialectique, lequel utilise des concepts abstraits comme un-multiple, identité-altérité et être, et établit par des raisonnements nécessaires toutes les classes divines à partir du premier principe. C'est la théologie "scientifique", dans laquelle Platon a excellé plus que tout autre philosophe. Comme modèle de ce discours scientifique Proclus présente deux dialogues, le *Sophiste* et le *Parménide.*[1] C'est évidemment dans le *Parménide,* qu'on trouve l'exposé le plus rigoureux et le plus systématique de cette théologie, du moins si on sait interpréter ce dialogue comme il faut. Dans ce seul dialogue, dit Proclus, "apparaissent d'une manière parfaitement claire tous les principes de la science théologique", et on y démontre "la génération des dieux et de tout ce qui existe à partir de la cause ineffable de l'univers."[2] On peut donc dire (avec H.D. Saffrey) que "la théologie platonicienne de Proclus est fruit de l'exégèse du *Parménide.*"[3]

L'importance capitale de la lecture du *Parménide* pour la formation du Néoplatonisme a été reconnue depuis longtemps. Je n'y reviendrai donc pas: qu'il me suffise de renvoyer aux études de Saffrey et Westerink. Dans cette communication, je voudrais examiner comment Proclus a interprété cet autre dialogue dans lequel on trouve un exposé scientifique de la théologie, le *Sophiste.* S'il est loin d'avoir l'importance du *Parménide,* la doctrine qui y est développée constitue néanmoins, selon les mots mêmes de Proclus, "une préparation (προτέλεια) aux mystères du *Parménide.*"[4]

Qu'il existe entre ces deux dialogues beaucoup de connexions, cela ressort tout de suite de leur composition dramatique. En effet, dans le *Sophiste,* l'orateur principal est "originaire d'Elée, et il appartient au cercle de Parménide

---

[1] *Cf.* Proclus, *Théologie platonicienne* I 4, p. 18, 12 - 24 (je cite le texte selon l'édition et la traduction de H.D. Saffrey - L.G. Westerink). Dans ce chapitre, Proclus étudie les quatre "tropoi" de l'enseignement théologique de Platon. Voir la note 2 de S-W à la p. 17 (compl. p. 136). Selon Proclus, c'est Platon qui a le premier développé une théologie "scientifique": voir I 4, p. 20, 19 - 20.

[2] *Cf. Theol. plat.* I 7, p. 31, 22 - 27.

[3] H.D. Saffrey, 'La Théologie platonicienne de Proclus, fruit de l'exégèse du *Parménide'* dans *Revue de théologie et de philosophie,* 116 (1984), 1 - 12.

[4] *Cf. Theol. plat.* III 21, p. 73, 10 - 12: προτέλεια γάρ ἐστι τῶν Παρμενίδου μυστηρίων τὰ τοῦ Ἐλεάτου νοήματα.

et de Zénon"[5] qui, eux, jouaient les premiers rôles dans le *Parménide*. Il est donc évident que ces deux dialogues sont complémentaires et qu'ils nous présentent ensemble la doctrine de l'Ecole Italique; école qui, selon Proclus, s'adonnait à la contemplation de l'être intelligible.[6] En outre, le *Sophiste* nous permet de corriger et de compléter certaines thèses défendues par le Parménide historique et nous aide ainsi à mieux comprendre la portée du *Parménide* platonicien. "Ce que le jeune Socrate du *Parménide* n'était point en âge de faire, ce que le Socrate vieillard du *Théétète,* par un hommage de reconnaissance et d'admiration pour son noble adversaire du *Parménide*, ne voulait point faire, l'étranger éléate le fera: après bien des hésitations, il se résoudra au "parricide" et réfutera la thèse fondamentale de Parménide."[7] Il démontrera que, d'une certaine manière "le non-être est et l'être n'est pas" (241 d). C'est la réfutation de la conception parménidienne de l'être, l'introduction de la pensée et du mouvement dans l'être, ainsi que l'exposé sur la communauté des genres de l'être qui en découle, qui ont toujours retenu l'attention des interprètes. Le *Sophiste* était considéré comme un texte ontologique: il avait d'ailleurs reçu comme sous-titre: "περὶ τοῦ ὄντος". Nous savons quelle importance Plotin a accordé aux arguments de l'Eléate dans l'élaboration de sa conception de l'Etre comme identique à la Pensée.[8] Mais, à notre grand étonnement, ce ne sont pas ces pages célèbres sur la vie, la pensée et le mouvement dans l'être qui ont le plus intéressé Proclus. Il acceptait comme évidente l'interprétation dite "néoplatonicienne" de ce texte (qui y reconnaît un mouvement et une vie "intelligible"), et n'avait pas besoin d'y revenir. (Il est certain qu'il appuierait la position de Mme de Vogel contre le prof. de Rijk!).[9] Ce qui l'intéressait dans le *Sophiste,* ce n'était pas sa théorie de l'être, son ontologie, mais la doctrine de l'Un qu'on trouve dans la discussion des thèses pluralistes et unitaires (242 c - 245 e). C'est par cette discussion *héno*logique que le *Sophiste* a pour lui une signification *théo*logique.

Je me limiterai donc ci-dessous à présenter l'interprétation proclienne de cette seule section du dialogue, sans oublier pour autant que le *Sophiste* était également important pour la théorie de la dialectique et pour le statut de la

---

[5] *Cf. Sophiste* 216 a 3 - 4, passage souvent cité par Proclus dans son commentaire sur le *Parménide*: col. 649, 37 - 38; 672, 25 - 29; 681, 11 - 13; *cf.* 1078, 14 - 15.

[6] *Cf. In Parm.* 629, 24 - 630, 14; 659, 30 - 36.

[7] A. Diès, *Introduction* à l'édition du *Sophiste*, Paris 1950, 268. Pour le *Sophiste,* j'utiliserai la traduction d' A. Diès et celle de L. Robin (Paris 1950).

[8] Sur l'utilisation du *Sophiste* par Plotin, voir J.M. Charrue, *Plotin, lecteur de Platon,* Paris 1978, 205 - 229.

[9] Sur cette discussion, voir L.M. de Rijk, *Plato's Sophist. A philosophical Commentary*, Amsterdam 1986, 13 - 21: "A Tantalising Problem concerning Plato's Sophist." Les références au fameux passage 248 d - e sont rares chez Proclus; *cf. In Parm.* 1152, 38 - 1153, 7: δῆλός ἐστι κίνησιν αὐτῷ (= τῷ ὄντι) τινα τὴν νοητικὴν δήπου συγχωρῶν ὑπάρχειν, ἣν καὶ Πλάτων οἶδεν etc.; et *In Tim.* I, 417, 13 - 21.

négation (question capitale dans la théologie négative).[10] Dans mon exposé, je
distinguerai trois parties. D'abord je présenterai l'interprétation que Proclus
donne de la section 242 c -245 e, pour autant qu'on puisse la reconstruire en
s'appuyant sur des informations dispersées dans son oeuvre. (En effet, on n'a
pas gardé de commentaire sur le *Sophiste*, et il est même probable que Proclus
n'en a jamais composé).[11] Ensuite, j'examinerai l'apport du *Sophiste* à
l'interprétation du *Parménide*. Enfin, je relirai le *Sophiste* à la lumière du
Parménide, ce qui nous fera découvrir d'autres doctrines théologiques.

1. *L'interprétation de Sophiste 242 c - 245 e*

Afin d'arriver au renversement de la thèse de son "père" Parménide, l'Etranger
d'Elée commence par examiner le concept de l'être. Il veut d'abord montrer
que les philosophes, anciens et contemporains, n'ont jamais su éclaircir le
problème de l'être. Dans cet examen critique, il présente les théories
précédentes sous forme de deux oppositions: d'abord il confronte la position
des pluralistes (comme Empédocle) à celle des monistes (comme Parménide)
(242 c - 245 e), puis, il nous fait assister au combat entre les matérialistes et les
"amis des Formes" (245 e - 249 d). Comme je viens de le dire, Proclus ne s'est
guère intéressé à ce dernier combat, sur l'interprétation duquel les savants
modernes ont beaucoup polémiqué. C'est la critique de la position pluraliste et
surtout la discussion avec le monisme de Parménide qui a retenu son attention.
L'étranger y démontre que les deux doctrines, malgré leur opposition, sont
aussi incohérentes l'une que l'autre. Au lieu d'élucider ce que nous signifions
par le terme "être", elles rendent ce concept encore plus obscur. Il semble donc
que cette discussion conduise à un constat absolument *négatif*; c'est d'ailleurs
ce qui ressort de la conclusion de l'Eléate: "Ainsi est-ce par myriades et
myriades interminables que surgiront, en chaque cas, les difficultés (ἀπορίαι)
pour qui définit l'être, soit par quelque couple, soit par une stricte unité." Et le
jeune Théétète est du même avis: "Les apories s'enchaînent sans cesse l'une à
l'autre, et de plus en plus grand, de plus en plus inquiétant est le doute qu'elles
projettent, à mesure, sur chaque solution émise."[12] Le seul fruit de la discussion
aura été de rejeter comme insuffisantes les théories anciennes de l'être, et de

---

[10] Sur la dialectique dans le *Sophiste,* voir *In Parm.* 622, 22 - 24; 634, 30 - 33; 637, 9 -
12; 649, 36 - 651, 9 (texte important); 653, 32 - 654, 14; 654, 34 - 655, 12; 656, 2 - 14; 989,
14 - 17. Sur le statut du non-être et de la négation, voir *In Parm.* 1072, 19 - 1074, 21; *Theol.
plat.* II 5, p. 38, 13 - 39, 5 et l'importante note complémentaire de Saffrey-Westerink à la p.
39, 1 (p. 99 - 100).
[11] Le seul texte qu'on pourrait invoquer pour prétendre que Proclus a composé un
commentaire sur le *Sophiste*, se trouve dans *In Parm.* 774, 24 - 26: ὅπως δὲ χρὴ τὴν ἀμιξίαν
αὐτῶν (sc. les genres suprêmes) καὶ τὴν μίξιν ἐκλαμβάνειν, ἴσως καὶ εὐκαιρότερον ἐν ταῖς τοῦ
Σοφιστοῦ διελθεῖν ἐξηγήσεσιν. Cependant, ce texte ne prouve pas que Proclus a réellement écrit
un tel commentaire; tout au plus montre-t-il que Proclus a eu l'intention de le faire. *Cf. In
Tim.* III, 12, 27 - 30 où Proclus renvoie à son futur commentaire sur le *Parménide*.
[12] *Soph.* 245 d 12 - e 5 (trad. Diès).

problématiser encore plus le concept de l'être. C'est donc, comme souvent chez Platon, une discussion aporétique qui, en tant que telle, ne mène à aucune thèse positive.

Telle n'est pas la lecture néoplatonicienne de ce texte, comme en témoignent déjà Porphyre et Jamblique.[13] Proclus, en tout cas, pensait que, dans cette section du dialogue, Platon démontre d'une façon dialectique, par le biais d'une critique des positions antérieures, les deux thèses capitales de son système. D'abord, par la critique des pluralistes, il établit que la multiplicité des êtres remonte à un principe unique, la monade de l'être, l'être absolu; et ensuite il montre, par la critique de Parménide, que cet être premier lui-même dépend de l'hénade qui transcende tout ce qui existe.[14] Le caractère critique et aporétique de la discussion ne saurait donc nous cacher qu'elle conduit à établir d'une manière scientifique deux thèses capitales: la causalité de l'être premier par rapport à la multiplicité des étants, et la causalité de l'un par rapport à l'être. C'est cette double transcendance qui caractérise essentiellement le néoplatonisme. Les deux parties de la démonstration correspondent donc exactement aux deux parties de la critique, celle de la thèse pluraliste mène à l'affirmation de l' ἓν ὄν, celle de Parménide à la position de l'Un absolument un. Suivons Proclus dans les détails de son interprétation, en rappelant d'abord brièvement l'argument de Platon. (Je suppose dans la suite, comme Proclus, que la position défendue par l'Eléate est celle de Platon lui-même).

Aux philosophes qui affirment "que le Tout est le chaud et le froid ou quelque couple de cette sorte", Platon demande ce qu'ils entendent par le mot εἶναι (243 e - 244 a 3): "Quand vous dites que ce couple est l'être, que voulez-vous nous faire entendre par 'être'?" On ne saurait appeler "être" l'un ou l'autre terme du couple, soit le chaud soit le froid, et dire que l'un et l'autre des deux "sont" "d'une façon semblable" (ὁμοίως). Car si l'on identifie l'être et le chaud, l'autre terme du couple, le froid, sera aboli de l'être (en effet, il ne pourrait être que pour autant qu'il soit chaud). Il n'y aura donc plus qu'un seul principe: l'être = chaud. Il est également impossible d'appeler "être" l'ensemble du couple "froid et chaud". Car, ainsi encore, on réduira les deux principe à l'unité. Il reste donc comme seule possibilité d'affirmer que l'être est un τρίτον παρὰ τὰ δύο ἐκεῖνα, "un troisième terme en dehors de deux en question". Pour sauver la dualité des principes, les philosophes dualistes sont en fait obligés de poser l'être comme un troisième principe. Ce qui montre à l'évidence l'incohérence de leur position.

---

[13] Sur l'interprétation de Porphyre, voir le témoignage de Proclus, *In Tim.* I, 393, 27 - 31; sur celle de Jamblique, voir *In Tim.* I, 230, 4 - 16 (fr. 29, éd. Dillon).

[14] *Cf. Theol. plat.* I 4, p. 18, 13 - 20: ἐν τῷ Σοφιστῇ (...) διαλεκτικῶς ἀγωνιζόμενος καὶ ἀπορῶν πρὸς τοὺς παλαιοτέρους, ἐπιδείκνυσιν ὅπως τὰ μὲν ὄντα πάντα τῆς ἑαυτῶν αἰτίας ἐξήρτηται καὶ τοῦ πρώτως ὄντος, αὐτὸ δὲ τὸ ὂν μετέχει τῆς ἐξηρημένης τῶν ὅλων ἑνάδος, καὶ ὡς πεπονθός ἐστι τὸ ἓν ἀλλ' οὐκ αὐτοέν. On trouve une analyse plus détaillée de l'argument dans *Théol. plat.* II 4, p. 34, 12 - 35, 9: cf. aussi la note complémentaire de S.W. à la p. 34, 2 (p. 96 - 97).

Proclus reconnaît dans cet argument critique "une preuve méthodique" qui démontre que les êtres multiples, bien qu'ils diffèrent les uns des autres par leurs natures spécifiques (comme "froid" ou "chaud"), remontent tous, en tant qu'ils sont des "êtres", à un principe unique, l'être premier.[15] Voici comment il présente cet argument dans la *Théologia platonica* II, 4: "Lorsque nous nommons être le chaud ou le froid ou bien le repos ou le mouvement, nous ne dénommons pas chacun d'eux être comme étant l'être même; car si le repos était l'être même, le mouvement ne serait pas de l'être, et si le mouvement était l'être même, le repos n'aurait pas part à l'appellation d'être."[16] Si tous les étants, si différents soient-ils, peuvent être dénommés "être" "d'une manière semblable", sans qu'aucun d'eux soit l'être en tant que tel, il faut admettre que "l' être est un troisième terme duquel dérivent ces deux principes, puisqu'ils sont de l'être: car chacun d'eux est un certain être (τι ὄν), non purement et simplement être (ἁπλῶς ὄν)."[17] Il est donc évident que le fait d'être pour les êtres multiples "vient d'une chose une, l'être à titre premier". Et cela même qui est "cause pour toutes choses de leur être (οὐσίας αἴτιον)" et qui est participé par tous, ne peut être qu'unique, seul de son espèce.[18]

Cet argument de Proclus — il dira de Platon — n'est pas sans nous rappeler certains textes de S.Thomas dans lesquels celui-ci démontre l'existence de Dieu comme la *"causa essendi"* qui n'est pas tel ou tel être, mais le *"simpliciter esse"* et l'acte même de l'être. Cependant, pour Proclus cette cause de l'être n'est pas encore la première cause. Car, si elle est bien l'être à titre premier, elle n'est pas l'un de la même manière. En effet, l'être premier n'est pas l'Un en soi, mais il est un par participation. Il faut donc que l'Un absolument un existe au delà de l'être. Cette conclusion est démontrée dans la suite de la discussion du *Sophiste*, là où se fait la critique du concept de l' être-un de Parménide. En effet, Proclus retrouve dans ce texte (244 b 6 - 245 d 11) trois arguments en faveur de l'existence de l'Un au delà de l'être.[19]

Le premier argument (244 b 6 - d 13) part de la notion de l'être-un (ἓν ὄν). A ceux qui disent, comme Parménide, que le tout (πᾶν) est un, il faut demander si ce qu'ils entendent par "être" est la même chose que ce qu'ils entendent par "un". S'ils sont conséquents avec leur thèse moniste, ils diront que "un" et "être" ne sont que deux noms pour désigner une même chose: l'être-qui-est-un

---

[15] On trouve un excellent résumé de cette "preuve méthodique" dans *In Tim.* I, 448, 3 - 11 (trad. Festugière, II, 329). Voir aussi *Theol. plat.* II 4, p. 34, 12 - 24 et *In Parm.* 709, 16 - 27.

[16] *Theol. plat.* II 4, p. 34, 17 - 22 (traduction modifiée).

[17] *In Tim.* I, 448, 8 - 10: εἰ δὲ ἑκατέρα, ἄλλο τι εἶναι δεῖ τὸ ὄν, ἀφ' οὗ ταῦτα ὄντα ἐστί· τούτων γὰρ ἑκάτερον τὶ ὄν ἐστιν, ἀλλ' οὐχ ἁπλῶς ὄν (trad. Festugière).

[18] Cf. *Théol. plat.* II 4, p. 34, 22 - 26. Sur la thèse selon laquelle l'être à titre premier ne peut être qu'unique, voir *In Tim.* I, 448 - 449.

[19] Proclus donne un excellent résumé de son interprétation dans *Théol. plat.* III, 20. Ce texte sera évidemment à la base de tout notre exposé qui suit.

(τὸ ἓν ὄν).[20] Cependant, cette réponse est indéfendable. En effet, si on n'admet aucune multiplicité dans les êtres, il n'est même pas possible de nommer les choses. Car nommer présuppose déjà deux réalités: la chose et son nom. Si l'on accepte la thèse de Parménide, "toute multiplicité et toute division seront éliminées, et aucune chose n'aura de nom ni de définition, mais le nom apparaîtra identique à la chose, et le nom ne sera pas le nom d'une chose, mais le nom sera le nom d'un nom."[21] Celui qui veut éviter cette conséquence absurde, devra accepter avec Platon que la notion de l'être et celle de l'un soient différentes. Si Parménide use de ces deux termes pour dénommer la totalité une de l'être, il montre par là que cet être-un est caractérisé par une certaine multiplicité, et qu'il diffère donc de l'Un au sens propre et à titre premier, l'absolument Un qui transcende l'être-un.

Le second argument (244 d 14- 245 d 11) s'appuie sur la notion du "tout entier" (ὅλον). En effet, Parménide parle aussi de l'être comme d'un ὅλον: l'être est "semblable à la masse d'une sphère bien ronde de toutes parts". Mais, comme le fait remarquer Platon, si l'être est tel, "il a un milieu et des extrémités, et, ayant cela, il a, de toute nécessité, des parties." Mais cette multiplicité ne doit pas l'empêcher d'être affecté du caractère de l'unité (πάθος τοῦ ἑνὸς ἔχειν). L'être est donc "un, en tant que total (πᾶν) et entier (ὅλον)". Cependant, ce qui est ainsi affecté d'unité, ne peut être l'un lui-même (τὸ ἓν αὐτό). Car l'un véritable, correctement défini, ne peut être dit que "indivisible" (ἀμερές). Une totalité constituée de multiples parties, même si elle s'est unifiée au maximum, ne répondra jamais à la définition correcte de l'un. Proclus en conclut: "Par conséquent, le tout entier (ὅλον) ne peut être considéré comme l'un-en-soi (αὐτοέν). En effet, l'un-en-soi transcende toutes les parties et la totalité, tandis que le tout subit l'un comme un effet. C'est même pour cela qu'il est appelé ὅλον: car le tout n'est pas l'un-en-soi."[22] Enfin Proclus développe un troisième argument en s'appuyant sur la notion du "total" (πᾶν). En effet, pour Parménide l'être-un n'est pas seulement un tout entier, mais aussi un totalité qui enveloppe une multiplicité de parties. Le concept de πᾶν ("total") implique une divisibilité plus grande encore que celui de ὅλον ("entier"). (Car une entité peut être ὅλον ("entière"), sans être un total

---

[20]On traduit généralement l'expression τὸ ἓν ὄν par "l'un-qui-est"; cette traduction se justifie par l'usage de cette expression dans la deuxième hypothèse du *Parménide* (142 d 1 - 5): "dans cette formule, 'il est' se dit de l'Un qui est (τοῦ ἑνός ὄντος); 'un' se dit de l'être qui est un (τοῦ ὄντος ἑνός); or, ce ne sont point choses identiques que le 'être' et le 'Un', mais attributs d'un sujet identique, celui de l'hypothèse: l'Un qui est" (trad. L. Robin). Cependant, dans notre texte du *Sophiste* (244 d 14), il ne s'agit pas de l'Un qui est, mais de l'être considéré en tant qu'unité. Evidemment, les deux traductions sont équivalentes puisque l'un participe à l'être et l'être participe à l'un (Cf. *Theol. plat.* III 24, p. 84, 26 - 85, 4).

[21]*Theol. plat.* III 20, p. 69, 16 - 20.
[22]*Theol. plat.* III 20, p. 71, 1 - 5; *Cf.* aussi *In Parm.* 1078, 21 - 1079, 5; 1102, 35 - 39.

comprenant des parties multiples).[23] Il est donc a fortiori évident que ce qui est un comme un "total" (πᾶν) ne peut être l'un-en-soi, mais qu'il subit l'un comme un effet. Il faut donc admettre que l'Un existe au delà du total.

Malgré leur point de départ différent, la structure du second et celle du troisième argument sont absolument identiques. Chez Platon, on ne trouve d'ailleurs aucune distinction entre un second et un troisième argument. Les termes πᾶν et ὅλον sont utilisés dans le même texte (245 a 3), sans qu'ils impliquent une différence essentielle. Proclus ne cache d'ailleurs pas que c'est lui qui a introduit cette distinction: ἡμεῖς διείλομεν.[24] Nous verrons plus loin pourquoi.

En tout cas, une chose est claire. Pour Proclus, il ne s'agit pas dans ce texte d'une simple réfutation de Parménide. Platon y démontre d'une façon scientifique l'existence de l'Un absolu. Si l'on peut admirer la finesse et la cohérence de cette herméneutique, il est douteux que telle ait bien été l'intention de Platon lui-même. Pour Platon, il s'agissait avant tout de montrer l'incohérence de la philosophie de Parménide qui n'avait qu'un concept confus de l'être. Bien qu'il appelle l'être indistinctement "un", "entier" et "total", il est évident que le terme "un" ne s'y applique pas "selon sa définition exacte". On ne peut donc dire sans contradiction que "l'être est un" ou que "l'un est tout". Je ne crois pas que Platon ait voulu démontrer dans ce texte que l'un véritable est au delà de l'être-un. S'il a si bien distingué l'un véritable de l'être qui subit l'unité, c'est pour mieux critiquer la thèse de Parménide que "tout est un". A. Diès croit même que, dans ce texte, Platon détruit définitivement la conception parménidienne de l'Un-tout, qu'il avait commencé à réfuter dans le *Parménide* (en démontrant que l'hypothèse de l'un conduit à des résultats contradictoires: la première contre la deuxième hypothèse).[25] Nous verrons dans la seconde partie que Proclus défend une interprétation radicalement différente. Pour lui, en effet, le passage du *Sophiste* que nous venons d'analyser, apporte une confirmation magnifique à la thèse de l'unité qui fut examinée dans le *Parménide*. D'ailleurs l'intention ultime des deux dialogues n'était pas de réfuter Parménide, mais de compléter et de perfectionner sa philosophie par l'introduction de l'Un absolu au dessus de l'Etre-un.

---

[23] Sur la différence entre τὸ πᾶν et τὸ ὅλον, voir *Theol. plat.* III 20, p. 68, 7 - 13; 71, 7 - 10; III 27, 95, 14 - 16.

[24] *Theol. plat.* III 20, p. 71, 13. Il est possible que la distinction entre les trois arguments remonte déjà à Jamblique: voir *In Tim.* I, 230, 10 - 12.

[25] Voir son Introduction à l'édition du *Sophiste*, 285: "Platon en profite pour détruire définitivement la conception parménidienne de l'Un-Tout, qui est en même temps l'Un absolu."

2. Ce que le Sophiste apporte au Parménide

Il est bien connu que le point faible de l'exégèse néoplatonicienne du *Parménide* était le statut et l'objet de la première hypothèse. En effet, la position d'une unité absolue semble conduire à des conclusions impossibles (ἀδύνατα). Car après avoir démontré qu'on ne peut rien affirmer de cet un, qu'on n'en peut rien savoir et rien dire, qu'il n'est pas et qu'il n'est même pas un, Parménide demande si toutes ces conclusions au sujet de l'un sont bien "possibles". Et on lui répond: "Non!".[26] En s'appuyant sur ce passage du *Parménide*, certains platoniciens avaient conclu que l'un de la première hypothèse, l'un uniquement un, est absolument inexistant (ἀνυπόστατος). On aurait donc tort d'y reconnaître, comme Plotin ou Proclus, une référence à l'Un absolu. Selon ces gens, le premier principe ne peut être que l'un qui est l'objet de la seconde hypothèse, l'être-un ou l'un-qui-est.

D'ailleurs, disaient-ils, selon ses propres mots, Parménide prend comme point de départ de la discussion dialectique "sa propre hypothèse", lequel était l'être-un, et pas l'Un absolu.[27] Et dans son poème il montre qu'on peut dire et penser l'être-un, et pour le caractériser, il n'utilise que des affirmations, jamais des négations. Dans la première hypothèse, par contre, on n'arrive qu'à des conclusions négatives, ce qui montre encore que l'Un absolu ne peut exister.[28] Il est bien vrai, répondra Proclus, que Parménide dans le dialogue commence par poser comme hypothèse son propre un, l'un-qui-est, mais il ne s'y arrête pas, il remonte de cette hypothèse à cet Un qui est inconditionné (*anhypotheton*), l'Un absolu. "En effet, après avoir pris l'un-qui-est, il trouve la cause qui est avant l'être un lui même, en appuyant sa pensée sur le 'un' et en n'utilisant le 'est' que selon sa valeur démonstrative, afin de pouvoir faire une proposition."[29] "C'est d'ailleurs sur ce point que Parménide tel qu'il est présenté par Platon diffère de l'auteur du poème: celui-ci ne considère que l'être un et dit que cet être un est la cause de toutes choses, tandis que le premier regarde vers l'Un, en remontant de l'un-qui-est à ce qui est seulement un et avant l'être."[30] L'enchaînement des négations ne nous conduit pas à une impossibilité, mais nous fait remonter vers la cause première, l'Un au delà de tout être. Il ne s'agit pas ici d'un simple dispute entre exégètes. C'est une thèse

---

[26] *Parm.* 142 a 7 - b 1.

[27] *Parm.*137 b 2 - 3: ἀπ' ἐμαυτοῦ ἄρξωμαι καὶ τῆς ἐμαυτοῦ ὑποθέσεως περὶ τοῦ ἑνὸς αὐτοῦ ὑποθέμενος. L' interprétation de ce passage a posé beaucoup de problèmes à Proclus, car il y revient souvent: *cf. In Parm.* 638, 19 - 36; 1032, 26 - 1035, 32 (commentaire *ad locum*); 1049, 40 - 1050, 31; 1077, 19 - 1079, 26; 1093, 19 - 1094, 17.

[28] *Cf. In Parm.* 1077, 19 - 1078, 13.

[29] *In Parm.* 1093, 33 - 36: τὸ ἓν ὂν λαβὼν (...) τῷ ἑνὶ τὴν διάνοιαν ἐπερείδων, τῷ δὲ ἔστι κατὰ μόνην χρώμενος τὴν δεικτικὴν (*correxi*: δεκτικὴν *codd.*) φαντασίαν, ἵνα ποιήσῃ λόγον, εὑρίσκει τὴν πρὸ αὐτοῦ ἑνὸς ὄντος αἰτίαν.

[30] *In Parm.* VII, 496,15 - 18, ed. Steel: "Et hac differt qui apud Platonem Parmenides ab eo qui in versibus, quia hic quidem ad unum ens aspicit et hoc ait esse omnium causam, hic autem ad le unum, ab uno ente ad solummodo unum et ante ens sursumcurrens."

essentielle du Néoplatonisme qui est en question. En effet, ceux qui nient que la première hypothèse ait une réalité comme objet, identifient l'être absolu et l'Un absolu et considèrent en fait l'intellect comme le premier principe. Nous savons par la *Théologie platonicienne* II, 4 que cette opinion fut défendue par Origène, le condisciple de Plotin à l'école d'Ammonius. Proclus est plusieurs fois revenu sur cette position pour l'attaquer violemment. Car, comme il le dit, "une telle doctrine est bien éloignée de la philosophie de Platon et est toute remplie des innovations péripatéticiennes."[31] Dans l'introduction au volume II de la *Théologie platonicienne*, Saffrey et Westerink ont rassemblé et étudié les textes les plus importants qui concernent cette dispute.[32] Or, il est remarquable que, dans cette discussion, Proclus revient chaque fois à l'argumentation du *Sophiste* pour montrer que l'un de la première hypothèse n'est pas une impossibilité, mais une réalité, et quelle réalité!

Pour démontrer leur thèse, ses adversaires avaient présenté l'argument de Platon dans la première hypothèse sous forme d'un raisonnement conditionnel (συνημμένον). Si l'Un absolu existe, il n'est pas un tout, il n'existe pas en lui-meme, etc.; il n'est même pas l'un ni l'être. Puisque toutes ces conclusions sont impossibles, il semble que Platon montre par ce raisonnement que l'hypothèse de l'Un absolu est impossible. Dans sa réponse, Proclus commence par rappeler les règles logiques du συνημμένον. L'impossibilité d'une conclusion peut provenir de deux causes: ou bien la marche du raisonnement n'était pas formellement correcte, ou bien l'hypothèse de base était impossible. En dehors de ces deux cas, il faut admettre la conclusion comme possible. Eh bien, pour ce qui est du raisonnement de la 1e hypothèse, on peut facilement montrer qu'il est formellement correct. Reste donc à examiner si l'hypothèse de l'Un absolu est vraie. Or, il faut l'avouer, la vérité de cette hypothèse n'est jamais démontrée en tant que telle dans le *Parménide*. Dans la première hypothèse, Parménide examine simplement les conséquences qui résulteraient de la supposition d'une unité absolue. Si, dans la suite, cette hypothèse semble conduire à des absurdités, bien que le raisonnement soit correct, elle se révélera ainsi comme fausse. L' ἀδύνατον des conséquences nous oblige donc à rejeter cette hypothèse. C'était là l'argument principal d'Origène et de ses disciples.

Pour y riposter, Proclus se voit obligé de chercher ailleurs chez Platon un argument qui prouverait la vérité de l'hypothèse de l'Un absolu. Il trouve cet argument précisément dans la section du *Sophiste* que nous venons d'examiner: "Or, l'hypothèse que l'Un existe est vraie, et l'Etranger d'Elée lui-aussi montre que la non-existence de l'Un conduit à une absurdité, à savoir qu'existerait seulement ce qui a subi l'un comme effet," et non pas ce qui est véritablement

---

[31] *Theol. plat.* II 4, p. 31, 19 - 22.
[32] Voir l' Introduction à la *Théol. plat.* II, p. XII - XX avec traduction et commentaire des textes suivants: *In Parm.* 1064, 21 - 1066, 16; VII, 515, 66 - 81; 499, 6 - 31.

un.[33] Et pourtant, lorsqu'on voit que quelque chose participe d'un certain caractère (πάθος), sans l'être lui-même, il faut admettre que ce caractère existe aussi en soi, en tant que tel, et est antérieur à ce qui le subit comme effet: le véritablement bien, le véritablement égal, et chacun des formes. Et tout comme nous posons l'être en soi, le seul à "être" véritablement, ainsi il faut admettre aussi qu'existe l'Un en soi. Ou est-ce que l'un seul ne serait qu'un simple "nom", celui par qui toutes choses existent?[34]

L'analyse par l'Etranger du ἕν ὄν comme un πεπονθὸς τὸ ἕν démontre donc l'existence de l'Un absolu. Qu'il s'agisse bien là du même principe que dans la première hypothèse du *Parménide*, c'est évident par la définition que l'Etranger donne de l'Un véritable: "le totalement indivis". En effet, c'est précisément cela qui est démontré dans la première hypothèse au sujet de l'Un, à savoir "qu'il n'a pas de parties", et c'est de cette première conclusion que toutes les autres découlent.[35]

Le recours au passage du *Sophiste* est donc capital pour tous ceux qui veulent comprendre la signification *théologique* du *Parménide*. A celui qui croit que la première hypothèse "aboutit à des conclusions impossibles", Proclus recommande: "qu'il se rappelle aussi ce qui est écrit dans le *Sophiste*, dans le passage, où l'Etranger, mettant à l'épreuve la thèse de Parménide sur l'être, et démontrant qu'il ne peut pas être un, et surtout d'après Parménide lui-même qui dit que l'être est tout (ὅλον), conclut clairement: 'il faut, en effet, que le véritablement un soit indivisible'. Si donc le véritablement un n'est pas sans subsistance, ce n'est pas en vain que l'Etranger critique Parménide par cet argument. C'est lui (sc. l'Un de la première hypothèse) qui est le véritablement Un, de sorte qu'il est aussi indivisible, de sorte qu'il n'a pas de parties, et tout ce qui suit. Car, une fois qu'on a démontré cela (c'est-à-dire, qu'il est indivisible), toutes les conclusions de la première hypothèse suivent; de sorte qu'elle est toute entière vraie et qu'elle s'applique seulement au véritablement Un, c'est-à-dire, la cause de tous les êtres."[36]

---

[33]*In Parm.* 1065, 15 - 19. Chez Cousin, le texte de ce passage est très corrompu; je l'ai corrigé d'après les manuscrits et la version latine: δηλοῖ δὲ καὶ ὁ Ἐλεάτης ξένος ὡς εἰς ἄτοπον ἀπαντῶν τὸ μὴ εἶναι τὸ ἕν, τοῦ τὸ ἕν πεπονθότος μόνου ὑφεστῶτος, πανταχοῦ τοῦ ἀληθῶς προυπάρχοντος τοῦ πεπονθότος αὐτὸ καὶ οὐκ ἀληθῶς προυπάρχοντος. Saffrey et Westerink (*Theol. plat.* II, p. XIII, n. 6) avaient déjà proposé la conjecture ἀπαντῶν au lieu de ἀπάντων, mais ils avaient interprété cette forme comme le nominatif *masculin* du participe. D'où leur traduction: "L'Etranger arrive à la non-existence de l'Un comme à une conclusion absurde, à savoir (...)." Je considère la forme ἀπαντῶν comme le nominatif *neutre* du participe.

[34]*Cf. In Parm.* 1087, 29 - 34.

[35] *Cf. in Parm.* 1065, 19 - 24 (cf. Saffrey-Westerink, Introduction à *Theol. plat.* II, p. XIV).

[36] *In Parm.* 1087, 13 - 27. Encore un texte très corrompu chez Cousin! Je l'ai corrigé d'après les manuscrits et la version latine: Εἰ δέ τις ἀδύνατα συνάγειν οἴεται τὴν ὑπόθεσιν ταύτην (διὰ ταῦτα) ἀναμνησθήτω, καὶ τῶν ἐν Σοφιστῇ γεγραμμένων, ἐν οἷς ὁ Ἐλεάτης, βασανίζων τὸν περὶ τοῦ ὄντος λόγον τοῦ Παρμενίδου καὶ δεικνὺς ὡς οὐ δύναται εἶναι ἕν, καὶ μάλιστα κατ' αὐτὸν ὅλον λέγοντα τὸ ὄν, ἐπήγαγε σαφῶς· ἀμερὲς γὰρ πού δεῖ τὸ ὡςἀληθῶς ἕν (εἶναι. Εἰ δὲ οὐκ ἀνυπόστατον τὸ ὡς ἀληθῶς ἕν,) μήδε μάτην ἐγκαλεῖ τῷ Παρμενίδι διὰ τούτων. Ἐκεῖνο ἔστι πού τὸ ὡς ἀληθῶς ἕν· ὥστε καὶ ἀμερὲς etc.

Ailleurs, dans son commentaire sur le lemme 137 c, Proclus fait remarquer que la démonstration en *Sophiste* 244 d 14 - 245 b 11 et celle du passage du *Parménide* peuvent être interverties: elles sont ἀντίστροφα. Car dans le *Sophiste,* Platon démontre: "si le tout est, il n'est pas véritablement un", et dans le *Parménide*: "si l'un est véritablement un, il n'est pas un tout". Il est donc évident que l'Etranger et Parménide parlent du même Un. On ne peut donc rejeter l'argument de Parménide dans la première hypothèse et accepter celui du *Sophiste.* "De deux choses l'une: ou bien il faut refuser de croire que les arguments du *Sophiste* expriment la pensée de Platon, ou bien il faut accepter aussi les arguments développés ici (dans le *Parménide*), et considérer que tel est bien le premier principe selon Platon, et que le véritablement Un est le Premier."[37] L'utilisation des formes de l'impératif de la troisième personne dans ce passage montre avec quelle émotion Proclus s'adresse aux interprètes de Platon qu'il considère comme déviants. Il en ressort que le sujet lui tenait à coeur: il savait que c'était le point faible de sa magnifique construction théologique, laquelle était basé sur l'échafaudage de l'exégése du *Parménide*. Nous comprenons alors pourquoi il revient sans cesse sur la question, comme s'il voulait conjurer ses lecteurs de ne pas suivre les platoniciens hétérodoxes. Je cite encore une autre de ses exhortations: "les Platoniciens devraient voir que Parménide démontre ici par le concept de l'un, la thèse qu'ailleurs (dans le *Sophiste*) le sage disciple de Parménide, ramenant à la vérité l'opinion de celui-ci, a prouvée, et ils ne devraient pas condamner la première hypothèse de *parler dans le vide*, mais chercher à quelle réalité appliquée, cette hypothèse est vraie, et ils devraient l'apprendre de Platon."[38]

Voilà pourquoi Proclus considérait le *Sophiste* comme une προτέλεια aux mystères du *Parménide*. Loin de le considérer, comme A. Diès, comme la destruction définitive de la conception parménidienne de l'Un-Tout, il y reconnaissait l'apport le plus solide à la doctrine de l'Un en soi que le *Parménide* avait révélée.

3. *Le Sophiste relu à la lumière du Parménide*

Si le *Sophiste* est bien une προτέλεια au *Parménide*, il est également vrai que, une fois qu'on est initié aux mystères qui nous y sont revelés, on relira le *Sophiste* dans une autre lumière et on y découvrira des doctrines théologiques qu'on ne pouvait pas y voir avant. En effet, c'est dans le *Parménide* que Platon a développé le discours le plus scientifique et le plus systématique sur les

---

C'est surtout l'omission ‹Εἰ - ἕν› qui rend le texte grecque de Cousin inintelligible. D' où la traduction absurde de J. Dillon (Princeton 1987, 436): "But perhaps the criticism of Parmenides here is undeserved: for he after all referred to 'the truly one'."

[37] *In Parm.* 1103, 6 - 10.

[38] *In Parm.* 1079, 18 - 26 (trad. de Chaignet corrigée): καὶ ἐδεῖ τοὺς Πλατωνικοὺς (...) μὴ καταψηφίζεσθαι τῆς πρώτης ὑποθέσεως ὡς κενολογούσης (...).

hénades divines et sur tous les niveaux d'être qui y participent. C'est donc à cet exposé qu'il faut rapporter les données souvent vagues et apparemment incohérentes que fournissent les autres dialogues sur les principes divins, pour exprimer leur vérité d'une façon scientifique.[39]

Ainsi, en confrontant notre texte avec le *Parménide,* nous reconnaîtrons dans les trois attributs qui sont successivement niés de l'Un véritable (ἓν ὄν, ὅλον, πᾶν) les propriétés qui caractérisent les trois triades intelligibles. On trouve en effet l'exposé systématique de ces trois ordres dans les premières conclusions de la deuxième hypothèse, laquelle enseigne la procession de tous les ordres divins, depuis le sommet de l'ordre intelligible jusqu'aux âmes divines. Car il existe une correspondance admirable entre les conclusions qui sont déduites de la deuxième hypothèse et les processions des ordres divins. Ainsi la première triade intelligible correspond à la première conclusion (si l'un est, il a part à l'être: 142 b 5 - c 7): c'est l'un-qui-est, la monade de l'être ou l'essence intelligible. La seconde triade correspond à la seconde conclusion: si l'un est, il est une totalité et il a des parties (142 c 7 - d 9). C'est la caractéristique de la vie intelligible. La troisième triade, enfin, se manifeste par la troisième conclusion: si l'un est, il est une multiplicité infinie de parties (142 d 9-143 a 3). C'est l'ordre de l'intellect intelligible.[40]   Eh bien. Dans le *Sophiste* 244 b -245 b Platon a exprimé la même doctrine sur les triades intelligibles. En effet, afin de montrer que l'Un en soi transcende même le sommet de l'être, Platon a construit son argumentation "selon les trois triades intelligibles". Car il a démontré sa transcendance en le séparant de l'un-qui-est, du tout entier, et de la totalité, et dans cet ordre. Les trois attributs niés manifestent donc indirectement les propriétés des trois ordres intelligibles qui procèdent les premiers de l'Un. "Ainsi que nous l'avons appris dans le *Sophiste,* dit Proclus, le premier ordre c'est l'un-qui-est, au second rang vient le tout entier, au troisième le total".[41] Le discours négatif du *Sophiste* vient donc heureusement compléter la théologie négative de la première hypothèse du *Parménide.* En effet, dans le *Parménide* les négations de la première hypothèse ne commencent qu'à partir du sommet de l'ordre intellectif.[42] Puisque le *Sophiste* est par excellence le dialogue qui démontre l'existence de l'Un au delà de l'être, on pouvait s'attendre à trouver dans ce dialogue aussi le discours négatif sur l'être intelligible.

Cependant, pour établir dans son exégèse une correspondance parfaite entre le *Sophiste* et le *Parménide* au sujet de l'ordre intelligible, Proclus est obligé de remanier l'argumentation de l'Etranger. Comme je l'ai déjà re-marqué, il est difficile de distinguer dans le texte un troisième argument basé

---

[39] *Cf. Theol. plat.* I 12, p. 55, 23 - 56, 10.
[40] *Cf. Theol. plat.* III, 23-26 (*cf.* l'analyse chez S.W., p. CXII - CXIII).
[41] *In Parm.* 1085, 24 - 26. Proclus a développé cette interprétation dans *Theol. plat.* III, 20.
[42] *Cf. Theol. plat.* II 10, p. 62, 19 - 63, 7.

sur la notion du πᾶν. Le sens de πᾶν que Proclus retient ici (en le distinguant de ὅλον) "le totalement divisé qui rassemble un très grand nombre de parties" s'explique avant tout par une concordance forcée avec le *Parménide* et le *Timée*. "Ce qui est appelé dans le *Timée* le 'Vivant-en-soi' et le 'complet' (παντέλειον) et dans le *Parménide* 'multiplicité infinie', est appelé dans le *Sophiste* 'totalité divisée en une multiplicité d'êtres' (παντότης)." Toutes ces désignations, dit Proclus, qu'on peut recueillir dans divers dialogues, sont en fait "les rejetons d'une science unique et tendent vers l'unique vérité intelligible".[43] On peut admirer cette recherche de cohérence, cet effort pour systématiser Platon. Il me semble pourtant que, même si on veut suivre Proclus dans cette herméneutique, la base textuelle pour retrouver la troisième triade intelligible dans le *Sophiste* est trop maigre.

C'est par rapport à l'être intelligible que Proclus interprète aussi le passage célèbre sur les "cinq genres de l'être" (γένη τοῦ ὄντος): l'essence, le mouvement et le repos, le même et l'autre (250 a 8 - 251 c 7). On connaît l'interprétation originale que Plotin a donné de ces "genres de l'être". Selon lui, ils caractérisent essentiellement l'Intellect (νοῦς) "qui est à la fois intelligence et être, pensée et chose pensée, intelligence parce qu'elle pense, être parce qu'elle est pensée" (V, 1, 4, 31 s). Comme le dit très bien E. Bréhier, "Plotin déduit la nécessité de ces principes, des conditions de la pensée intellectuelle comme telle; pas d'intelligence, si l'intelligence ne pense pas l'être; pas de pensée, s'il n'y a pas d'alterité, c'est-à-dire la distinction entre chose pensante et chose pensée, s'il n'y a pas d'identité, c'est-à-dire le caractère commun à toute chose pensée, s'il n'y a pas de mouvement, puisque la pensée est un mouvement, et s'il n'y a pas de repos, puisqu'on ne pense que l'identique."[44] Dans cette interprétation Plotin est évidemment influencé par cette autre page célèbre, celle qui introduit le mouvement comme propriété de l'être (248 e - 249 c).

Toute différente est l'interprétation de Proclus. Bien qu'il ne nie pas que les genres se manifestent au niveau de l'intellect, il croit qu'ils se situent à titre premier, mais sous un mode caché et indivis, au niveau de l'être intelligible. En effet, il s'agit avant tout des caractéristiques les plus générales de l'être en tant qu'être, et non pas de la pensée. Pour Plotin, ce serait évidemment une opposition fausse vu l'identité qu'il admet entre la pensée et l'être. Selon Proclus, par contre, l'être premier est au-delà de l'intellect, et c'est pour cette raison qu'il faut considérer les cinq genres comme propriétes de l'être, c'est-à-dire des ordres différents de l'intelligible.[45] La première triade est certainement

---

[43] *Theol. plat.* III 27, p. 95, 11 - 17. C'est en s'appuyant sur le παντελές du *Timée* (30 d 2, 31 b 1), que Proclus a pu développer la notion du πᾶν dans notre passage du *Sophiste* (*cf. Théol. plat.* III 20, p. 68, 10 - 11: τρίτον ἐκ τοῦ παντελοῦς ἐπιχειρεῖ), bien que le terme παντελές manque dans le passage du *Sophiste*).

[44] E. Bréhier, Notice à *Ennéade* V, 1, 9.

[45] *Cf. Theol. plat.* I 11, p. 52, 2 - 10; III 19, p. 64, 21 - 65, 13; *In Parm.* 1173, 7 - 1175, 29 (*Cf.* J. Dillon, 'Porphyry and Jamblichus in Proclus' Commentary on the *Parmenides*'

l'*essence* laquelle, aux dire de Platon lui-même, "n'est ni en repos ni en mouvement" (250 c 6 - 7). Les quatre autres genres se manifestent seulement dans les processions de deuxième et de troisième rangs. La deuxième triade a en elle le *mouvement* et le *repos,* puisqu'elle est la vie qui demeure en repos et qui procède; tandis que dans la troisième triade se trouvent *le même* et *l'autre;* "en effet elle doit à l'altérité intelligible d'être une multiplicité *tout à fait complète* (παντελές), tandis qu'il doit au même son caractère unifié et sa capacité d'embrasser ensemble les parties".[46]

Cette interprétation du texte est certainement très manipulée, et je crains que les commentateurs modernes y perdent tout leur intérêt pour Proclus, s'ils avaient encore un peu de sympathie pour lui dans la première démarche de son exégèse. Cependant, il faut voir comment cette interprétation, si forcée qu'elle nous paraisse, témoigne encore d'un effort admirable pour rendre cohérente et systématique la pensée de Platon qui est dispersée en quantité de dialogues. Puisque le *Sophiste* est essentiellement une discussion sur l'être, il est évident qu'il faut y trouver l'enseignement de Platon sur les ordres de l'intelligible.

Le philosophe Leibniz écrivait dans une lettre à N. Remond, qui était comme lui un grand admirateur de Platon: "Si quelcun reduisoit Platon en système, il rendroit un grand service au genre humain."[47] Proclus, en tout cas, croit avoir rendu ce service à l'humanité. Et même si nous répugnons parfois aux détails de ses interprétations manipulatrices, nous devons lui être reconnaissants pour cette systématisation monumentale qu'est la *Théologie platonicienne.* Comme le disait déjà un admirateur médiéval, Berthold de Moosburg: "Son excellence et son absolue supériorité sur les autres platoniciens apparaissent à l'évidence dans ce qu'il a su ordonner les théorèmes de Platon et les expliquer très subtilement une fois qu'il les a ordonnés."[48]

---

dans: *Gonimos. Neoplatonic and Byzantine Studies presented to L. Westerink,* ed. by J. Duffy and J. Peradotto, New York 1988, 39 - 42).

[46] *Theol. plat.* III 19, p. 65, 5 - 12, *cf.* aussi III 16, p. 56, 10 - 16 et *In Parm.* 1154, 32 - 34.

[47] Lettre à N. Remond (datée du 11 février 1715) éditée par C. Gerhardt, *Die philosophischen Schriften von G.W. Leibniz,* III, 1887, 637.

[48] Texte de Berthold de Moosburg cité chez A. de Libera, *Introduction à la mystique rhénane,* Paris 1984, 321.

P.A. MEIJER

PARTICIPATION IN HENADS AND MONADS IN PROCLUS' *THEOLOGIA PLATONICA* III, CHS. 1 - 6 *

INTRODUCTION

The notion of *participation* (μεθέξις) was introduced by Plato in order to bridge the gap between the ideas and their products. It has been problematic ever since — even for Plato himself, as the first part of the *Parmenides* and the *Sophist* testify. The term "participation" in itself is misleading: it suggests that particular instances each possess one of a number of *parts* into which a transcendent idea has been broken up. Actually, however, "participation" refers to a formative principle which has descended from the idea while leaving its source undiminished. This formative principle is *in* the particular and may therefore be labelled an "immanent form."[1] Already in Plato's *Phaedo* (102 b) we find as examples of this immanent form the smallness or greatness in us.

Neoplatonic philosophers had difficulties with the notion in their own different ways. They attempted to harmonize and elaborate Plato's various statements about participation, and to construct a coherent system out of them. Participation was now called upon to explain not only the relation between the ideas and the particulars, but also, going beyond Plato, the relation between the inhabitants of the transcendent world itself, *i.e.* mind and soul; and yet other realities besides mind and soul were explained in terms of participation, such as Henads and monads[2] and their relationships with other things. Neoplatonic thought on this subject may be said to culminate in Proclus.

In the first part of this paper I shall explain my view on the position of Henads and monads in Proclus in general, and on the problems concerning the participation in Henads and monads raised by *Theol. plat.* III, 1 - 6, his fullest discussion of the position of the Henads, in particular. My conclusion will be that one should carefully distinguish between two meanings of μετεχόμενος, (1)

---

* I am very much indebted to Dr. J. Spruyt, Dr. E.P. Bos, Dr. J.M. van Ophuijsen and Mr. F.A.J. de Haas for criticism and advice concerning earlier drafts of this paper and correction of my English.

[1] I use the terminology of L.M. de Rijk, *Plato's Sophist. A philosophical commentary*, Amsterdam 1986. I am much indebted to the excellent treatment of the problems of participation in Plato in his second chapter.

[2] Since monads are not Gods, but only divine, I do not use capitals for them.

"immanent idea", and (2) "participated in" (*i.e.* by what may be termed "participants").[3]

Some modern scholars, Dodds, Festugière, and Kremer in particular, have raised objections to Proclus' system of participation and accused him of inconsistency. In the last section of my paper I shall try to refute their criticisms.

1 *Proclus' system of participation*

According to Proclus the Henads[4] are Gods; monads, however, are of a lower rank, are not Gods, but merely divine: they are no more than ideas or hypostases, such as mind, soul, and nature.[5] Henads rule over monads.[6]

As divine representatives of the God who is the One, Henads are participated in by mind, soul and nature; by contrast it is assumed by many modern scholars[7] that monads are not participated in (ἀμέθεκτος). Certainly participation in a Henad by a monad, or by a hypostasis such as mind or soul, raises difficulties, but participation in a monad by the members of the group (σειρά, ἀριθμός) is no less problematical. Proclus often calls the monad itself "imparticipable" or "unparticipated" (ἀμέθεκτον).[8] Monads, then, seem to be free from participation, but none the less they are participated *in* by participants (μετέχοντα). This is a highly intriguing expression of the problem —

---

[3] L.M. de Rijk acknowledges only the first meaning, "immanent form"; see below 72.

[4] This holds true only for the complete Henads (αὐτοτελεῖς ἑνάδες) of prop. 64 of the *Elementatio Theologiae*, *cf.* E. R. Dodds, *Proclus. The Elements of Theology*, Oxford 1933, 60. On this proposition see below 69.

[5] *Cf. e.g. Theol. plat.* III 2, 11, 10, and *Elementatio*, prop. 22, p. 26, 10 ff. and 63, p. 60, 16 ff. See also K. Kremer, *Die neuplatonische Seinsphilosophie und ihre Wirkung auf Thomas von Aquin,* Leiden 1971, 211 ff. I shall state several objections to Kremer's account of Proclus' theory of participation, below 81 ff.

[6] *Cf. In Parm.* VI, 1047, 26 ff.: "Not only with them but in all other cases we can find the monads as leading the numbers (ἀριθμός, series) which belong to them, and the Henads of the monads being the most basic origins of the things (πραγμάτων: πράγματα is not confined to denoting sensible things but may also denote transcendent "things")": Καὶ οὐκ ἐπὶ τούτων μόνων, ἀλλὰ καὶ ἐπὶ τῶν ἄλλων πάντων ὁμοίως ἂν εὕροιμεν τὰς μὲν μονάδας ἡγουμένας τῶν οἰκείων ἀριθμῶν, τὰς δὲ τῶν μονάδων ἑνάδας ἀρχὰς κυριωτάτας τῶν πραγμάτων ὑπαρχούσας. In line 29 S(affrey)W(esterink: "Introduction" to *Theol. Plat.* III, p. lxvi, n. 4), comparing Moerbeke's translation "*ante* monades", propose to insert πρὸ before τῶν μονάδων, a correction which is perhaps not indispensable. Morrow and Dillon in their translation (G.R. Morrow and J.M. Dillon, *Proclus' commentary on Plato's Parmenides*, Princeton 1987, 406) unaccountably leave out an important part of the sentence: ἡγουμένας τῶν οἰκείων ἀριθμῶν, τὰς δὲ τῶν μονάδων ἑνάδας, and translate "but in every other case we would likewise discover the monads being the most proper principles of things," which makes the monads instead of the Henads the true principles of things. With this translation Proclus' earlier remark "for everywhere the first principle is the One", which provides the foundation of the sentence just quoted, loses its demonstrative force. In fact the One is represented by Henads, not by monads, as the basic and essential origins of everything.

[7] Kremer, *Die neuplatonische Seinsphilosophie und ihre Wirkung auf Thomas von Aquin,* 210.

[8] These expressions represent two aspects of the same reality: what is unparticipated is simultaneously imparticipable, and vice versa.

which originates with Plato: see the first part of the *Parmenides* — of the relationship between the independent idea on the one hand, and the entities which depend on that idea for the individual characteristic of their being, on the other hand.

Alongside the concepts of μετέχον and ἀμέθεκτον there emerges a third entity, which is the μετεχόμενον, a term I will render literally below as "what is participated in". This third entity is explained in propositions 23 and 24 of the *Elementatio Theologica* as that form of the idea which is immanent in an entity — be it a transcendent one or a particular one in our world.[9] Incidentally it should be noted that the usual[10] translation of μετεχόμενον as "what *can be* participated" or "participa*ble* " must be rejected: the Greek language does not permit any such rendering, which would constitute a unique instance of a participle requiring to be interpreted as an *adiectivum verbale*.

However, "immanent form" is not the only meaning of the word μετεχόμενον, as I hope to show in what follows: it also denotes the entity from which something descends to the participant, for instance the mind from which a "part" descends to a (lower) soul; this constitutes another meaning of the Greek participle μετεχόμενος, as "that which is participated *in*". The participle μετεχόμενος thus denotes two things which belong to different categories. The first (hereafter: μετεχόμενος I), "what is participated", is the immanent form, the second (or μετεχόμενος II), "what is participated in", is the *entity* with which the immanent[11] form originates. It is most important to distinguish between these two uses. By μετεχόμενος (I) something is said about the participant, by μετεχόμενος (II) about an entity of a higher rank, that which is participated *in*. Μετεχόμενος (II) will play a major role below, but we shall first turn to μετεχόμενον (I) or immanent form.

---

[9]A curious terminological mistake in connection with the notion of participation is made by Rosán in his valuable book on Proclus' philosophy, *The Philosophy of Proclus. The Final Phase of Ancient Thought*, New York 1949, at p. 81, n. 56, where, commenting on prop. 18 of the *Elementatio*, he claims that whereas the passive (τὸ χορηγούμενον, *i.e.* that to which the characteristic is given) is employed for the μετέχοντα — which is correct —, the active voice of the verb χορηγεῖν (τὸ χορηγοῦν) is sometimes used for "the possessed characteristic" (the middle tense μετεχόμενον), which is incorrect. The μετεχόμενον as τὸ χορηγοῦν should be considered as the "giver", since it gives itself to what possesses it. This way of presenting the relationship of participation is advertised by Rosán as one more fit to account for the respective positions of cause and effect than Proclus' more usual terminology of μέθεξις, μετεχόμενον etc. A reading of prop.18 and of other propositions (*Elementatio*, page 10, 20; p. 20, 3; p. 68, 7 and 12; p. 108, 11; p. 164, 28) in which the terms τὸ χορηγοῦν and τὸ χορηγούμενον occur, shows Rosán's interpretation to be mistaken: it appears that τὸ χορηγοῦν is always the bestowing entity, and in fact τὸ χορηγούμενον is "that (which *something* is) bestowed upon", the recipient — which, it should be noted, appears in the *Elementatio* only once.

[10] *E.g.* Kremer, *Die neuplatonische Seinsphilosophie und ihre Wirkung auf Thomas von Aquin*, 212: μετεχόμενον (= das Partizipierbare); he also uses "participabilis".

[11] C. Guérard, 'La Théorie des Hénades et la Mystique de Proclus', *Dionysius*, 6 (1982), 78, n. 33 refers to *In Rem publ.* I, 259, 3, and 260, 9, 28, for the μετεχόμενος as meaning both μετεχόμενος (I) and μετεχόμενος (II). I do not find μετεχόμενος (II) here.

The μετεχόμενον (I) belongs to a particular entity which, as a participant, possesses a particular μετεχόμενον, which comes to it from the ἀμέθεκτον. In *Elementatio*, prop. 23, p. 26, line 30, it is said that τὸ δὲ μετεχόμενον πᾶν, τινὸς γενόμενον, ὑφ' οὗ μετέχεται, δεύτερόν ἐστιν τοῦ πᾶσιν ὁμοίως παρόντος (sc. the unparticipated): "Every *participatum, becoming a property of that particular by which it (the participatum*[12]*) is participated, is secondary to that which is equally present in all (sc.* the ἀμέθεκτον)."[13] For Proclus an entity cannot have the immanent form of its "neighbour", which is informed by an immanent form of its own.

All this leads to the tripartite system we have described, and to the paradox of an unparticipated model which, notwithstanding its "imparticipability", in virtue of its power (δύναμις) not only bestows on the participants the individual characteristic of the model, but is also held responsible for their subsistence as their cause.

A clear illustration of this tripartite system is found in Proclus' treatment of time in the *Elementatio*, prop. 53, where eternity as unparticipated (ἀμέθ-εκτον) is said to be prior to the *participata* (μετεχόμενα) in the eternal, which (μετεχόμενα) are in turn prior to the participating entities (μετέχοντα). This holds good not only for entities in the transcendent realm, but also for the temporal realities of our world, since time (ἀμέθεκτος χρόνος) is prior to the temporal in temporal things (μετεχόμενος χρόνος in τὸ ἔγχρονον, which is called μετέχον), and the temporal in temporal things is prior to the temporal things themselves. Both eternity and time are the same everywhere and in everything, whereas the participated eternity and the participated time subsist only in those entities by which the participata are participated.[14]

Returning to Henads and monads, one might wonder to what extent they are related to, or fit into, this system of participation, and whether they can be called μετεχόμενος. We shall deal with this question in the next sections.

---

[12] It is not clear what the subject is, as far as there is any specified subject, of ὑφ' οὗ μετέχεται. Presumably it is the μετεχόμενον; see below note 56.

[13] On this phrase see below 82.

[14] prop. 53: Πάντων τῶν αἰωνίων προυπάρχει ὁ αἰών, καὶ πάντων τῶν κατὰ χρόνον ὁ χρόνος προυφέστηκεν.

Εἰ γὰρ πανταχοῦ πρὸ τῶν μετεχόντων ἐστὶ τὰ μετεχόμενα καὶ πρὸ τῶν μετεχομένων τὰ ἀμέθεκτα, δῆλον ὅτι ἄλλο μὲν τὸ αἰώνιον, ἄλλο δὲ ὁ ἐν τῷ αἰωνίῳ αἰών, ἄλλο δὲ ὁ καθ' αὑτὸν αἰών, τὸ μὲν ὡς μετέχον, τὸ δέ ὡς μετεχόμενον, ὁ δε ὡς ἀμέθεκτος. Καὶ τὸ ἔγχρονον ἄλλο (μετέχον γάρ), καὶ ὁ ἐν τούτῳ χρόνος ἄλλος (μετεχόμενος γάρ), καὶ ὁ πρὸ τούτου χρόνος, ἀμέθεκτος ὤν. Καὶ τούτων μὲν ἑκάτερος τῶν ἀμεθέκτων πανταχοῦ καὶ ἐν πᾶσιν ὁ αὑτός· ὁ δὲ μετεχόμενος ἐν ἐκείνοις μόνον, ὑφ' ὧν μετέχεται. Πολλὰ γὰρ καὶ τὰ αἰώνια καὶ τὰ ἔγχρονα, ἐν οἷς πᾶσιν αἰών ἐστι κατὰ μέθεξιν καὶ χρόνος διῃρημένος. Ὁ δὲ ἀδιαίρετος αἰών καὶ ὁ εἷς χρόνος πρὸ τούτων, καὶ ὁ μὲν αἰών αἰώνων, ὁ δὲ χρόνων χρόνος, τῶν μετεχομένων ὄντες ὑποστάται.

2 Independent and dependent Henads

According to Guérard[15] the Henads are pure μετεχόμενα, *participata*. In itself this is not improbable. A passage of the commentary *In Parm.* 1069 6 - 8 informs us about participation by Henads: καὶ οὐδὲν ἄλλο ἐστιν ἕκαστος τῶν θεῶν ἢ τὸ μετεχόμενον ἕν, where it is said that each Henad is the participated One.[16] If the Henads are actually to be regarded as μετεχόμενα, one must ask which type of μετεχόμενα Proclus has in mind. In *In Parm.* 1069, 6 - 8 Proclus cannot, I think, have the *participatum* (μετεχόμενος I) in mind. For if this were the case, we meet with a difficulty. It cannot be μετεχόμενος I, for then the Henad would, according to prop. 23, belong to its participant and requires the participant as its substratum. In the passage of the *In Parm.* quoted, however, Henads seem to be independent,[17] which squares with prop. 64 of the *Elements*. According to prop. 64, which opens with a discussion of monads before it proceeds to the treatment of the position of Henads, a monad which functions as origin (and is ἀμέθεκτος) generates two types of lower entities. On the one hand it generates so-called *complete existents* (αὐτοτελεῖς ὑποστάσεις), existing in their own right and independently; on the other hand it generates *in*complete existents (ἀτελεῖς ὑποστάσεις). The complete existents subsist in themselves and do not need any other, lower (καταδεεστέρων) entity for their substratum (... δέονται δὲ οὐδὲν τῶν καταδεεστέρων εἰς τὴν ὑπόστασιν τὴν ἑαυτῶν). Their role is highly important: they make their participants belong to them (αἱ δὲ ἑαυτῶν ποιοῦσι τὰ μετέχοντα). Proclus affirms that not only do they make the participants belong to themselves and establish them in themselves, but they *fill the participants with themselves* (τέλειαι γὰρ οὖσαι πληροῦσι μὲν ἑαυτῶν ἐκεῖνα, sc. τὰ μετέχοντα). Nevertheless, though there is a strong connection, they remain independent. The other type of entities generated by monads are the so-called *irradiations*. These need a substratum to exist in. This is the reason why they are called "*in*complete" (ἀτελεῖς γὰρ οὖσαι δέονται τῶν ὑποκειμένων εἰς τὴν ἑαυτῶν ὕπαρξιν). The complete existents do not need any such ὑποκειμένον. Failure to observe the distinction between the complete existents (αὐτοτελεῖς ὑποστάσεις) and the incomplete ones (ἀτελεῖς ὑποστάσεις) leads to serious confusion.

In the corollary of prop. 64 these complete existents are translated into Henads, which have being in themselves and are Gods, whereas other henads which are in need of substrata are not gods, but only manifestations (irradiations) of unity. Henads as Gods, then, are independent entities.

Nevertheless, it may be questioned whether the concept of Henads as αὐτοτελεῖς ὑποστάσεις can be explained consistently in terms of participation, as outlined sofar. They are not μετεχόμενος I, and do not possess a substratum.

---

[15] Guérard, 'La Théorie des Hénades et la Mystique de Proclus', 77, 78.

[16] Guérard's quotations ('La Théorie des Hénades et la Mystique de Proclus', 77, 78) from the *Elements* (props 119, 133) fail to prove that the Henads are pure participations.

[17] "Every divine being is subject to the Henads of the Gods" (*In Parm.* 1069, 3, 4).

Their relation to the One seems to have a special status, and perhaps cannot be accounted for in terms of participation.[18] For in *Theol. plat.* III 3, 14, 10 ff. Proclus says[19] that these Henads are different from the One, not in unity, but *only* in that they are participated (μετεχόμενος II). This agrees with the passage from *In Parm.* quoted earlier: a Henad is the One in so far as it is participated. This expression implies that there is participation in the One only via a Henad, which is participated itself by participants and is in this way the mediator. However this may be, we must allow for the presence, in Proclus' system, of these complete existents, which play an important role in that they prepare us for the independence of the Henads.

One comparable question remains with regard to the monads: what is the relation between the unparticipated monad and its lower monads? It is likely that this relation goes beyond the system of participation, just as the relation of the Henads to the One does. Proclus seems to use a special mechanism, or in any case a special term, to explain the production of monads: in the *In Parm.* 746, 10 ff. he uses the term ὑπόβασις for the generation of similar monads in one order and on the same level, whereas he uses πρόοδος for the production of vertical series of dissimilar monads (mind generating soul)[20]. The monads are lower than their leader, yet they are on the same level. We find the same configuration in the *Elements* and in *Theol. plat.* III.[21] Dodds speaks of "transversal series".[22] Here we no longer remain within the scheme of "regular" participation.

Generally speaking, however, the tripartite solution to the problem of participation is in accordance with the rules applied in *Theol. plat.* III, 1 - 6, which concern the Henads in particular. We hear about ἀμέθεκτος, μετεχόμενος and μετέχων. The One is said to be ἀμέθεκτον, whereas the Henads are called

---

[18] Although they can be said, as in prop. 114, to participate in the distinctive character of the One and the Good: (...) καὶ κατ' ἄμφω τῆς θείας ἰδιότητος μετέχει. In *In Parm.* 1069, 14, 15 the One is called "transcendent over the Henads" and "not collocated together with them", ἀσύντακτος. This word expresses the higher position of the One as compared to the Henads, but this does not imply a relation of participation. Morrow/Dillon (*Proclus' commentary on Plato's Parmenides*, 423) translate ἀσύντακτος by "unconnected", which is certainly wrong, since it does away with the intimate relationship of the Henads with the One.

[19] See below 75.

[20] The notion of weakening (ὕφεσις) is crucial for Proclus' mechanism of explanation of the procession. It is dominant in the process of generation in Proclus' *Theol. plat.* III, 1 - 6; see the note of S.W. on ὕφεσις on p.108 of *Theol. plat.* III.

[21] Σύστοιχος is the term, see *Elements,* prop. 21, Dodds, 24, 1 - 3, and 208; *Theol. plat.* III 2, 8, 1; 9, 2 where we read: Πλῆθος οὖν ὑφίσταται περὶ αὐτό (...). S.W. propose to interpret this αὐτό as τὸ ἕν or suggest αὐτήν, *sc.* τὴν μονάδα. If, however, one makes αὐτό to refer to τοῦ γεννῶντος of 8, 25, there are no problems.

[22] Dodds, *Proclus. The Elements of Theology*, 209. A.C. Lloyd, "Procession and division in Proclus", in: H.J. Blumenthal and A.C. Lloyd, ed., *Soul and the structure of Being in late Neoplatonism,* Liverpool 1982, 30 does not agree with the notion "transversal". See also S. Gersh, *From Iamblichus to Eriugena,* Leiden 1978, 151. The word ὑπόβασις is translated by Morrow/Dillon (*Proclus' commentary on Plato's Parmenides,* 118) by "declension", although it only denotes "being a step lower". Unfortunately in Proclus the term does not seem to be a fixed one, as Dodds observes.

and μετέχων. The One is said to be ἀμέθεκτον, whereas the Henads are called "participated". With regard to the monads an intriguing question emerges. One might wonder how Proclus could consistently refer to monads as μετεχόμεναι (11, 11 πρὸ τῶν μετεχομένων *sc.* μονάδων see also 11, 14 τὰς μεθεκτὰς.... μονάδας) whereas elsewhere he speaks of monads as being ἀμέθεκτοι (11, 11), which is the only qualification that monads are generally supposed to have.

3 Participation in Henads and monads in Theol. plat. III, 1 - 6

a) Henads and monads in Theol. plat. III, 2

In discussing *Theol. plat.* III, 1 - 6 one should be aware of Proclus' strategy. His attitude is defensive. Not all Neoplatonists, it appears, adhered to the doctrine of the Henads as Gods; this seems to have been a novelty, which is likely to have been introduced by Proclus' teacher, Syrianus.[23] In any case Proclus does his utmost to convince his readers in *Theol. plat.* III, as he had done in the *Elements*, that the doctrine is indispensable.

The theory about the Henads in *Theol. plat.* III is based upon four preliminary theses which we do not here need to expound in full. They are all meant to explain what can be elicited from Plato by a Neoplatonist about the production by the monads (ideas) of their dependents and the participation of the dependents (πρόοδος) in the monad (ἐπιστροφή). It is the similarity between the producing monad and its products that is stressed again and again (*cf. e.g. Theol. plat.* III 2, 7, 11 ff.). There is community and sympathy of the participants towards (συμπάθεια πρός) what is participated in (μετεχόμενα in sense II, see *Theol. plat.* III 2, 7, 12, 13, a point we shall return to below). Proclus' second thesis points to every monad being *productive, viz.* of similars (7, 29 ff.; 8, 9). These in their turn are monads, but *participated* monads. This theory is transmitted to the relation of the *One* (τὸ Ἕν) to its characteristic products, the *Ones* or Henads (Ἑνάδες), since the characteristic of the One is oneness. So the One is productive of similars, the Henads. The way of producing is appropriately denoted by the term ἑνιαίως.[24]

The monads in *Theol. plat.* III, 1 - 6 mostly behave as we would expect ideas or hypostases to behave. Thus they are described as ἀμέθεκτος, as in 11, 11. This passage belongs to the fourth thesis which, however, also speaks of μετεχόμεναι μονάδες (11, 11). In the opening section of this thesis (10, 16 - 26) the One emerges, for the first time in *Theol. plat.* III, as ἀμέθεκτος, and we also encounter the difficult term μετεχόμενος. I quote:

... ὡς ἄρα δεῖ πρὸ τῶν μετεχομένων αἰτίων πανταχοῦ τὰ ἀμέθεκτα προυπάρχειν ἐν τοῖς ὅλοις. Εἰ γὰρ δεῖ τὴν αἰτίαν τοῦτο εἶναι πρὸς τὰ ἑαυτῆς γεννήματα ὅπερ ἐστὶ πρὸς ἅπασαν τὴν τῶν ὄντων φύσιν τὸ ἕν, καὶ ταύτην εἰληχέναι τὴν τάξιν πρὸς τὰ δεύτερα κατὰ φύσιν, τὸ

---

23 Saffrey - Westerink, *Proclus, Théologie Platonicienne*, III, p. li.
24 See ch. 3, 11, 22 - 12, 14.

δὲ ἓν ἀμέθεκτόν ἐστιν, ἀπὸ πάντων ὁμοίως ἐξῃρημένον τῶν ὄντων ὡς πάντων ἑνιαίως παρακτικόν, προσήκει δήπου καὶ τῶν ἄλλων αἰτίων ἕκαστον τὴν τοῦ ἑνὸς ὑπεροχὴν πρὸς πάντα ἀπεικονιζόμενον ἐξῃρῆσθαι τῶν ἐν τοῖς δευτέροις ὄντων καὶ μετεχομένων ὑπο αὐτῶν.

(...) that it is necessary that everywhere in the wholes the unparticipated entities are present before the participated causes. For if it is necessary that the cause is to its own products that which the One is to the whole nature of beings, and has been allotted this rank in relation to the secondary beings according to nature, and if the One is unparticipated,[25] being equally transcendent in regard to all beings, as the producer of all things in the manner of oneness, then it is fitting that each of the other causes imitating the superiority of the One in regard to all things is transcendent in respect to what is in the secondary beings, and is participated by these.

A question may be raised as to the meaning of ἀμέθεκτα and μετεχόμενα in the first sentence (ὡς ἄρα δεῖ πρὸ τῶν μετεχομένων αἰτίων πανταχοῦ τὰ ἀμέθεκτα προυπάρχειν ἐν τοῖς ὅλοις). The ἀμέθεκτα are obviously causes like τῶν μετεχομένων αἰτίων, but what does μετεχομένων mean? Above I drew a distinction between μετεχόμενος I and μετεχόμενος II, the participatum and the entity participated in respectively.[26] It seems to me that μετεχόμενος II, not μετεχόμενος I, is at issue here: the unparticipated causes, then, are prior to those which are participated. It might be replied, however, that in this quality μετεχόμενος I here will do just as well. This is the opinion of De Rijk,[27] who recognizes only one signification of μετεχόμενος, equivalent to my μετεχόμενος I, *i.e.* the participatum which belongs to the participant, which as such could be applied to this sentence. This holds true also for the last sentence quoted, that each of the other causes imitating the superiority of the One in regard to all things is transcendent in respect to what is in the secondary beings, and *is participated by them* (sc. by the secondary beings): καὶ τῶν ἄλλων αἰτίων ἕκαστον τὴν τοῦ ἑνὸς ὑπεροχὴν πρὸς πάντα ἀπεικονιζόμενον ἐξῃρῆσθαι τῶν ἐν τοῖς δευτέροις ὄντων καὶ μετεχομένων ὑπὸ αὐτῶν. The decision depends on the status of the participated causes: are they independent entities which are participated or do they belong to their substrates and need them for their subsistence?

The issue is clarified, I think, by the sentence which follows. Here Proclus explains that each ἀμέθεκτον produces μετεχόμενα, which turn out to be monads.

Every unparticipated and original cause, in calling into subsistence from itself the participata, places the monads of the secondary entities similar to it before those which are dissimilar to it: I mean, *e.g.*, the one soul places the many souls before the natures, and the one mind places the participated minds before the many souls (10, 27 - 11, 5).[28]

---

25 At this point in *Theol. plat.* III the One is cautiously (εἰ ...) introduced as being unparticipated.

26 See above 67.

27 See above 16, 17.

28 (...) πᾶν τὸ ἀμέθεκτον καὶ πρωτουργὸν αἴτιον, ὑφιστάνον ἀφ᾽ ἑαυτοῦ τὰ μετεχόμενα, τοῖς ἀνομοίοις πρὸς αὐτὸ τῶν δευτέρων ἄνωθεν τὰς ὁμοίας προάττειν μονάδας, λέγω δὲ οἷον τὴν μὲν ψυχὴν τὴν μίαν ταῖς φύσεσι τὰς πολλὰς ψυχάς, τὸν δὲ ἕνα νοῦν ταῖς πολλαῖς ψυχαῖς τοὺς μετεχομένους νόας.

It is obvious that the participata here are to be identified with what is participated in, since it appears that the participata are monads. Proclus continues:

> For in this way the first transcendent class would everywhere occupy the rank analogous to the One, and the secondary (beings), participating in those which are akin to the cause, may be analogous to that, and through the likeness of these be connected with the "unparticipable" (ἀμέθεκτον) origin (11, 5 - 11, 9).[29]

Proclus states that the secondary beings *participate in* the entities which are cognate with the cause, which is the original unparticipated monad: καὶ τὰ δεύτερα μετέχοντα τῶν τῇ αἰτίᾳ συγγενῶν κτλ. This clearly implies that the monads as μετεχόμενα are participated by the secondary beings. For these cognate entities cannot be other than those monads which are participated, since the expression "akin" may be expected to qualify the monads which are produced by the original monad and are on the same level.[30] This is confirmed by what Proclus adds in the next sentences, where he restates the entire configuration:

> Before the forms, then, which are in other beings, there are those which are in themselves, and before the collocated causes are the transcendent ones, and before the participated monads there are the unparticipated monads (11, 9 - 12).[31]

Prior to the forms (εἰδῶν) which subsist in other beings we find the entities that are in themselves: τὰ ἐν αὑτοῖς ὄντα. In the expression τὰ ἐν αὑτοῖς ὄντα we recognize the αὐτοτελεῖς ὑποστάσεις (the counterparts of the ἀτελεῖς ὑποστάσεις) which are present here in the words πρὸ τῶν ἐν ἄλλοις ὄντων εἰδῶν. This confirms my suggestion that we are dealing with self-subsistent monads which do not require substrata for their existence. Secondly the rule of priority is applied to the transcendent causes which are above and prior to those causes which are collocated (τῶν συντεταγμένων) with the original cause. This rule holds also true for the ἀμέθεκτοι μονάδες which are above and prior to the μετεχόμεναι μονάδες (αὐτοτελεῖς ὑποστάσεις) as well. The expression "collocated causes" (τῶν συντεταγμένων) provides additional proof, for it can refer only to independent monads, which are on the same level as the unparticipated monad.[32] The passage therefore does not speak about μετεχόμενα as such, but as *qualified, i.e.* as the entities which are commanders[33] of series and are participated (μετεχόμενα) by lower entities. This is evident from the corollary as well:

> and — the corollary of what has been demonstrated — the transcendent causes are productive of the collocated ones (sc. monads) and the unparticipated entities (*sc.*monads) put the participated monads in charge of their offspring, and the

---

[29] Οὕτω γὰρ ἂν τό τε πρώτιστον γένος ἐξῃρημένον πανταχοῦ τὴν ἀνάλογον ἔχοι τῷ ἑνὶ τάξιν καὶ τὰ δεύτερα μέτεχοντα τῶν τῇ αἰτίᾳ συγγενῶν ἀναλογοῖ τε πρὸς αὐτὴν καὶ διὰ τῆς τούτων ὁμοιότητος συνάπτοιτο πρὸς τὴν ἀμέθεκτον ἀρχήν.

[30] See above 70.

[31] Ἔστιν ἄρα πρὸ τῶν ἐν ἄλλοις ὄντων εἰδῶν τὰ ἐν αὑτοῖς ὄντα καὶ πρὸ τῶν συντεταγμένων αἰτίων τὰ ἐξῃρημένα καὶ πρὸ τῶν μετεχομένων αἱ ἀμέθεκτοι μονάδες.

[32] See above 70.

[33] The name "commander" (ἄρχων) appears in *Theol. plat.* III, 19, 20.

entities which are of themselves produce the powers which are in other things (11, 12 - 11, 15).[34]

The corollary reaffirms that the transcendent entities are productive of the collocated entities (monads). The term "collocated"[35], as we have seen, denotes monads. Proclus speaks of μεθεκτὰς [36] μονάδας (*participated* monads), which seems to accord with our other observations to the effect that the whole passage is about monads, independent entities, which are participated in, and not about *participata* in the sense of μετεχομενος I.

The entire passage, then, makes it plausible that the μετεχόμενα of the first part of the fourth thesis (10, 26 and 11, 1) are monads, and that we may legitimately speak of participated monads: participated, it is implied, by lower entities (which presumably are often αὐτοτελεῖς ὑποστάσεις themselves). The phrase about the secondary beings as participating in the entities which are *cognate with the cause* (καὶ τὰ δεύτερα μετέχοντα τῶν τῇ αἰτίᾳ συγγενῶν) seems especially conclusive, and the same applies to the notion "collocated". These notions do not square with μετεχόμενος I. Here in the fourth thesis, then, we should interpret μετεχόμενος in the second sense.

b) *More evidence*

The participated monads reappear elsewhere. The verb μετέχεσθαι used in the sense of "to be participated in" recurs in 18, 1 - 2: "(...) it is absolutely necessary that with regard to the monads entities nearer to the One are participated in by things of simpler being; entities more remote, by things more composite": (...) πάντως ἀνάγκη καὶ ἐν ἐκείναις (*sc.* μονάσι) τὰ μὲν ἐγγυτέρω τοῦ ἑνὸς ὑπὸ τῶν ἁπλουστέρων τῇ οὐσίᾳ μετέχεσθαι, τὰ δὲ πορρώτερα ὑπὸ τῶν συνθετωτέρων. Proclus concludes: "Thus participation will be according to analogy, the first entities being always participated by the first, the secondary by the secondary (Οὕτω γὰρ ἔσται κατὰ τὸ ἀνάλογον ἡ μέθεξις, τῶν μὲν πρώτων ὑπὸ τῶν πρώτων, τῶν δὲ δευτέρων ὑπὸ τῶν δευτέρων ἀεὶ μετεχομένων)." One might conceivably interpret this sentence by an appeal to μετέχομενος I: "the first are the shares or *participata* of the first, the secondary the shares of the secondary." This translation, however, does not stand up against the objection that the passage is about monads (*cf.* 17, 24), whereas by applying μετέχομενος I in this case the

---

[34] καὶ τὸ τούτῳ συναποδεδειγμένον, τά τε ἐξῃρημένα γεννητικὰ τῶν συντεταγμένων ἐστὶν καὶ τὰ ἀμέθεκτα τὰς μεθεκτὰς ἐφίστησι τοῖς ἑαυτῶν ἐκγόνοις μονάδας καὶ τὰ ἑαυτῶν ὄντα τὰς ἐν ἄλλοις παράγει δυνάμεις.

[35] τῶν συντεταγμένων: the translation of S.W. "des subordonnées" neglects the preverb συν in συντεταγμένων, see note 22 on transversal participation.

[36] In connection with the meaning of μετεχόμενος it is worth noting that μεθεκτός, which as an *adjectivum verbale* could mean "participable", in this context can be rendered correctly only by "participated".

participatum would be the property of the *participans*, which would do away with the monad in its independence.

Not only monads can be participated, but also Henads. Briefly, it is this characteristic which separates them from the One, which remains unparticipated.[37] In ch. 4 (14, 11 - 15) Proclus inquires into their participability by beings, the crucial question in the whole argument of *Theol. plat.* III, 1 - 6.

Πότερον οὖν τὸ πλῆθος τοῦτο τῶν ἐνάδων ἀμέθεκτόν ἐστιν, ὥσπερ αὐτὸ τὸ ἕν, ἢ μετεχόμενον ὑπο τῶν ὄντων, καὶ ἐστιν ἐνὰς ἑκάστη τῶν ὄντων τινός, οἷον ἄνθος τοῦ ὄντος καὶ ἀκρότης καὶ κέντρον περὶ ὃ τὸ ὂν ἕκαστον ὑφέστηκεν;

Is this multitude of Henads *unparticipated*, as the One itself, or is it *participated by the beings* and is there a particular Henad of each of beings, as it were its flower and summit and the centre around which each particular being has taken its subsistence?

Obviously μετέχομενος cannot mean the share (*i.e.* unity) of the Henad belonging to the participant (μετέχομενος I), which according to prop. 23 is characteristic of μετέχομενος I, for it is suggested that the participated Henad remains what it is, since it is called the summit and centre *around* which the participant (a particular kind of being) exists. Therefore the Henad is what we may call a "complete Henad", which we discovered[38] to be existents in their own right not needing a substratum to be in, but filling their followers with themselves. In *Theol. plat.* III 3, 12, 14 Proclus himself speaks of αὐτοτελεῖς ἐνάδες. In the case of the Henads, then, μετεχόμενος may bear the meaning of μετεχόμενος II: "being participated by". A similar phrase τὸ πλῆθος τῶν θεῶν (*sc.* the Henads) μετεχόμενον ἀποφαίνειν ὑπο τῶν ὄντων is found in 16, 16 - 7 (*cf.* also 18, 10 - 1).

It is worth noting that Proclus applies to the Henads both the *passive* μετέχεται and the *active* μετέχειν in one context at 17, 14 - 16, from which it can be inferred that participants participate in the Henads, and that whenever Proclus says that Henads are participated, he indeed means that it is *they* that are participated and that they do not belong to their participants as their substrata; and moreover he implies that the unity of the participating entities derives from the Henad concerned.

In 17, 14 - 16 Proclus discusses the problem of whether the same number or a larger or a smaller number of participants participate in each of the Henads to which the participants belong. And if a different number, whether the larger number participates in the higher ones and a smaller number in the lower ones, or the reverse. The problem is not whether participants participate in Henads, which is presupposed, but about the number of participants in relation to the hierarchy of Henads.

---

37 In the *Elementatio* Proclus proves the participability of the Henads in a different and rather peculiar way, *cf.* Dodds, *Proclus. The Elements of Theology*, 102, prop. 116.
38 See above 69.

I quote this important sentence in full:

Ἐπειδὴ τοίνυν ἑνὰς μὲν ἐστι τῶν θεῶν ἕκαστος, μετέχεται δὲ ὑπὸ τῶν ὄντων τινός, πότερον ἑκάστου τὸ αὐτὸ μετέχειν φήσομεν ἢ τῶν μὲν πλείω, τῶν δὲ ἐλάττω τά μετέχοντα; καὶ εἰ τοῦτο, τῶν μὲν ἀνωτέρω πλείω, τῶν δὲ ὑφειμένων ἐλάττω, ἢ ἀνάπαλιν;

Saffrey - Westerink translate as follows:

Puis donc chacun des dieux est une hénade et qu' il est participé par quelque être, dirons-nous que chaque dieu a le même nombre de participants, ou bien que les uns en ont plus, les autres, moins? Et en ce cas, ce nombre est-il plus grand pour les élevés des dieux, et plus petit pour les moins élevés, ou inversément?[39]

In this translation the Gods are made the "owners", as it were, of the participants ("que chaque dieu *a* le meme nombre de participants; ou bien que les uns en *ont* plus etc"); regrettably, because a precious datum is thus lost sight of, which is the fact that Proclus not only can say that Gods *are participated* (μετέχεται δὲ ὑπὸ τῶν ὄντων τινός) but also that *participants can participate in the Gods* (μετέχοντα can μετέχειν in the Gods). When Proclus speaks about μετεχόμεναι ἑνάδες he clearly has in mind μετεχόμενος as referring to the entities (in this case the Gods) that are participated (μετεχόμενος II) and not as an expression of the participatum (μετεχόμενος I), as he does in prop. 23 of the *Elementatio*.

Since in *Theol. plat.* III, 1 - 6 Proclus invariably treats monads and Henads analogously, it is not too bold to claim that wherever he uses μετεχόμενος in connection with monads it has the same meaning. It may be inferred from this, then, that whereas the unparticipated monad cannot be participated, Proclus does assume a great number of *lower* monads (which depend on the unparticipated monad) which can be participated. This applies at the transcendent level, where many independent hypostases (αὐτοτελεῖς ὑποστάσεις) derive from the original monad.

The following outline, based on *Theol. plat.* III 2, 11, 1 - 5 may be helpful:

{ ἀμέθεκτος νοῦς

μετεχόμενος νοῦς (as hypostasized μονάς νοερά (see *Theol. plat.* III
↓   3, 13, 10) participated by)
ψυχαί.

The μετεχόμενος νοῦς in this scheme fulfils the function of a hypostasized monad (see 13, 10) and is participated (μετεχόμενος II) by other dependent entities (*i.e.* souls). With respect to μετέχομενος, then, we are not dealing with "what is

---

[39] My translation is: "Since each of the Gods, then, is a Henad, and is participated by one of the beings, shall we say that the same number participates in each, or that more participants participate in some Henads and fewer in others? And if so, do more participate in the higher ones and fewer in the lower ones, or the reverse?"

participated" as the immanent form (sense I), but with what is "participated" as μετέχομενος II, *i.e* causing immanent forms but remaining hypostasized. The reverse emerges in the corrolary of the rule (11, 12 - 15), as we have seen above.[40]

The upshot is that in many passages we find μετεχόμενος II, where μετέχειν means participation in the αὐτοτελεῖς ὑποστάσεις. This is very important, because a failure to distinguish μετεχόμενος II from μετεχόμενος I results in a distortion of perspective. Μετεχόμενος I refers to the formative principle, which belongs to the participant, whereas μετεχόμενος II concerns entities which are participated in and of a higher rank, and do not depend on their participants for their existence. Between an entity which is called μετεχόμενος II and the lower entities a connection of "regular" participation seems to be in operation: in Proclus' system one must assume that in this relation there is also a μετεχόμενον (I), *e.g.* the unity that is given to the participant; this, however, does not seem to bother him.[41]

We shall now return to our initial question of how monads may at the same time be called ἀμέθεκτος and μετεχόμενος. In my opinion monads are to be divided into *two kinds*: on the one hand the highest entity in a series, which has the privileged position of being unparticipated (ἀμέθεκτος), on the other hand its products, the lower monads, which may be and in fact are participated, without thereby losing their indepent position, and which appear as commanders of their own troops. The two kinds provide a neat analogy to the One as Henad which is ἀμέθεκτον, and the Henads which are participated.

In any case an entity which is ἀμέθεκτος can remain without participation because its lower representatives take care of participation. As to the Henads, Proclus believes he has found further indications in Plato to confirm his position. In order to demonstrate their participability (τὸ πλῆθος τῶν θεῶν (sc. the Henads) μετεχόμενον ἀποφαίνειν ὑπο τῶν ὄντων *Theol. plat.* III 4, 16, 15 ff.), Proclus also makes use of the notion of light as employed in Plato's *Republic* (508 d - 509 a).

4 *The role of light in connection with participation.*

The transcendent light that stems from the Good is a unifying force (*Theol. plat.* III 4, 16, 15 ff). Just as the things of our world are made sun-like by the light of the Sun, so the intelligible things are made like the Good by their participation in the (transcendent) light. Proclus affirms that if speaking about that light and speaking about unity (τὸ ἕν) do not differ from each other, and light stems from the One which holds the intelligibles together and makes them one, then what comes forward from the First as divine must be participated. In Proclus light and divinity have the same function. Consequently, if light stems

---

[40] See above 74.

from the One, divinity likewise originates with it, and if light unifies the intelligible things (τὸ ἐκ τοῦ ἀγαθοῦ προιὸν φῶς ἑνοποιὸν εἶναι) and holds them together, and their participation in light (διὰ τὴν τοῦ φωτὸς μετουσίαν) makes the intelligible things similar to the Good, then the intelligible things participate in that light. This implies that participation in light equals participation in divinity. Proclus repeats this in the conclusion he so eagerly sought to prove: "participated is the whole multitude of Gods": (... μεθεκτὴ μὲν ἐστιν ἡ ἀπὸ τοῦ πρώτου προιοῦσα θεότης), μεθεκτὸν δὲ πᾶν τὸ τῶν ἑνάδων πλῆθος. Having said that the Gods are above being (ὑπερούσιος) like the One, he repeats that the Gods are participated by essence and by what is (... μετέχονται δὲ ὑπο οὐσίας καὶ τοῦ ὄντος). His conclusion is important: "Thus according to this reasoning the Gods have turned out to be Henads, that is to say, participated Henads, binding all beings to themselves, and connecting through themselves all that comes after them with the One which transcends all equally" ('Ενάδες ἄρα ἡμῖν καὶ ἑνάδες μεθεκταὶ κατὰ τοῦτον τὸν λόγον οἱ θεοὶ πεφήνασιν, εἰς ἑαυτοὺς μὲν ἀναδησάμενοι τὰ ὄντα πάντα, δι᾽ ἑαυτῶν δὲ τῷ ἑνὶ τῷ πάντων ὁμοίως ἐκβεβηκότι τὰ μεθ᾽ ἑαυτοὺς συνάπτοντες, 17, 9 - 12). If, then, the Gods are *above being* (ὑπερούσιος) and bind all beings to themselves (thereby doing precisely what is expected of "complete existents"[42]), and through themselves connect to the One whatever specific beings they preside over, they cannot be mere *participata* belonging to those beings, but must remain independent entities which are participated (μετέχονται) by their followers (μετεχόμενος II).

5 *A problem of participation raised by the second hypothesis of Plato's Parmenides.*

Proclus defends the difference between the One and the Henads by indicating as a decisive distinction that Henads are participable (*Theol. plat.* III 4, 15, 6 ff.). He adduces two arguments: a) if they were not participable, it would be impossible to maintain the distinction between the One and the Henads, and b) we would not be convinced by the *Parmenides*, which in the second hypothesis affirms that there are as many portions of the one[43] as there are portions of being. The reference to Plato's *Parmenides* is important for Proclus. Thanks to Saffrey we now realize how pivotal the interpretation of the *Parmenides*, and especially of the second hypothesis, became for the Athenian School after Syrianus.[44] It was their claim to innovation. The second hypothesis is a source for determining the levels of the Gods, and its interpretation should be in harmony with the doctrine about the Henads. It is small wonder that Proclus is

---

[41] *Cf.* Dodds, *Proclus. The Elements of Theology,* 262.

[42] See above 69.

[43] I avoid capitalizing this "one", because Proclus is here not referring to the first One, but merely discussing the one of the second hypothesis.

[44] H.D. Saffrey, 'La théologie platonicienne de Proclus, fruit de l'exégèse du *Parménide*', *Revue de théologie et de philosophie,* 116 (1984), esp 8.

constantly occupied with interpreting the *Parmenides* and introducing it into the discussion as a source of proof, as he does in the passage just quoted. Here we are informed about the participation of beings in the one, and of the fact that the one coexists everywhere with being. Plato begins every article of his argument for the second hypothesis with "if the one is". In a word, by the second hypothesis Plato, as Proclus believes, indicates that the Henads exist and that they are participated by all layers of being. But now Proclus is stirring up a hornets' nest, for in the second hypothesis the very same *Parmenides* also teaches (in Proclus' own words (*Theol. plat.* III 4, 13, 14) "that generally the one of the second hypothesis *participates in being,* (which does not accord with orthodox Neoplatonist doctrine) and is participated by being[45] (which is unalarming)".

One may well inquire how it is possible for a One or one (as a Henad or henad) to participate in being: while the reverse is in accordance with the system, it cannot be accepted that the Henads *participate in being*, for Henads are "above being" (ὑπερούσιος).

Proclus is well aware of this problem, which disturbs a Neoplatonic confidence of being in harmony with Plato himself. He does not dodge it but tries to save his interpretation of the second hypothesis by introducing a special doctrine of participation. He declares that there are two kinds of participation. The kind that is involved here, i.e. participation of the one in being, is a καταλάμπειν: an illumination of what truly is by the one.[46] He repeats this position in his treatment of the first triad in *Theol. plat.* III 24, 85, 9 ff.[47]

The attempt to solve the problem by the notion of illumination (καταλάμπειν) in 15, 17 is an adroit move, because light acts as a form of communication between the illuminating and the illuminated, so that some sort of communication, and consequently participation, seems to have been salvaged. It seems to me, however, that Proclus' attempt (1) is in conflict with the tenor of Plato's claim that the One must participate in being *simply to be,* and (2) is fallacious in itself. Proclus is overstretching the elasticity of the system: the problem is that the orientation of καταλάμπειν is wrong. The explanation of participation as illumination breaks down on the one essential point that participation (μετέχειν) cannot but mean that a lower entity has a share in a higher, whereas καταλάμπειν as Proclus wishes us to understand it on this occasion, is meant to imply the reverse, which in itself would be a rather

---

45 *Parmenides*, 142 b: Ὅρα δὴ ἐξ ἀρχῆς ἓν εἰ ἔστιν, ἆρα οἷόν τε αὐτὸ εἶναι μὲν, οὐσίας δὲ μὴ μετέχειν; The answer is: this is impossible — οὐκ οἷόν τε.

46 S.W. rightly refer to prop. 162, p. 140, 28, where it is said of the Henads that they illuminate true being, τὸ καταλάμπον τὸ ὄντως ὄν; it is nearly the same expression which Proclus uses in *Theol. plat.* III 4, 15, 17, τὸ καταλάμπον τὴν ὄντως οὖσαν οὐσίαν: illuminating that being which truly is. However, there Proclus had not the problem he had in *Theol. plat.* III 4, 15, 14 ff.

strange use of καταλάμπειν and would invert the system. Perhaps there is an implicit appeal to the notion that μετέχεσθαι literally means "to have in common". But even if this speculation were true it would still not solve the problem, since it rests on a similar confusion between the roles of the two partners involved in an instance of participation. Within the bounds of Neoplatonism it cannot consistently be maintained that the participated participates in the participant. Proclus, as I have said, was aware of the problem and felt the need for a solution, and presented one (καταλάμπειν), but he immediately returns to more traditional views of the problem by adding "that being participates in the one as being held together by it and filled with divine unification and being directed towards the unparticipated One-self (lines 17 - 20)."

6 *Proclus' terminology*

If Proclus had any concern for consistency of terminology, the last thing he should have done was to mix up the terms monad and Henad. Yet Saffrey-Westerink in their introduction to part III of the *Theol. plat.* (xvii) mention two cases of "henad" allegedly being identical with "monad", both of them in the *In Timaeum*. In *Theol. plat.* III Proclus' henadic and monadic vocabulary seems perfectly consistent: (top)monads are said to be unparticipated and henads are participated, but at the opening of ch. 6 of *Theol. plat.* III at 20, 3 I find a summing up of the preceding argument (especially that of ch.4, see 17, 9 - 12), in which the Gods are called μονάδες αὐτοτελεῖς instead of the correct ἑνάδες αὐτοτελεῖς.[48] Sometimes Proclus can be charged with committing errors. A terminological inconsistency which invites comparison with the preceding one may be observed to exist between *Theol. plat.* II 7, 46, 18 and 50, 7, where Proclus first quite clearly defines the Good as τἀγαθόν, with the crasis form, and the Bonum Secundum as αὐτοαγαθόν, then a few pages later deflects from his own rule by calling the Bonum *primum* αὐτοαγαθόν.[49] In view of the consistent terminology in the earlier chapters of *Theol. plat.* III, however, it is perhaps justified to suspect a *scribal* error rather at 15, 20 than a mistake by Proclus himself. Therefore I would hesitantly propose to change μονάδες αὐτοτελεῖς into ἑνάδες αὐτοτελεῖς.

Another passage in which the terms seem to be confused is *Theol. plat.* III 4, 15, 20, where from a systematic point of view one expects to find Henads, but the transmitted text reads "monads". In the preceding sentence, as we saw at the end of our section 5, Proclus asserts "that being participates in the one

---

[47] Here it is less clear that this One is the Henad, see also *Theol. plat.* III 26, 89, 21, 22. In this passage participation of the one in being amounts to being connected to being (συνάπτειν).

[48] See also ch.3, 13, 14 and above 69.

[49] See Meijer, "Some Problems in Proclus' *Theologia Platonica* II, ch. 7", 192.

(the second one, i.e. that of the second hypothesis of the *Parmenides*) as being held together by it and filled with divine unification and being directed towards the unparticipated One-self". The Greek text reads: τὸ δὲ ὂν μετέχει τοῦ ἑνὸς ὡς συνεχόμενον ὑπ' αὐτοῦ καὶ πληρούμενον ἑνώσεως θείας καὶ πρὸς τὸ αὐτοὲν καὶ ἀμέθεκτον ἐπεστραμμένον. According to the transmitted text he goes on to argue that the participated *monads* connect beings with the All-transcendent (Αἱ γὰρ μετεχόμεναι μονάδες πρὸς τὸ τῶν ὅλων ἐξῃρημένον ἓν τὰ ὄντα συνάπτουσιν, κτλ.). This seems extremely unlikely. It is the Henads which are continually said to connect beings with the All-transcendent One, as e.g. at the end of ch. 4 (17, 9 - 12).[50] Here too at 15, 20 I suspect a scribal error and would tentatively propose to change μονάδες into ἑνάδες.

These vagaries, however, do not in my opinion invalidate the system, which, to go by what we have examined so far, seems coherent as a whole. So there are grounds, it seems to me, for defending Proclus against some of his critics.

7 In defence of Proclus: criticisms of his doctrine of participation rejected

a) Kremer. Can an ἀμέθεκτον and a μετεχόμενον be participated ?

Some scholars have objected to Proclus' doctrine of participation: thus Dodds, Festugière,[51] and Kremer[52] criticize Proclus for being "open to charges of inconsistency", as Dodds[53] puts it. In his excellent work on the *Elements* we repeatedly find somewhat irritable comments on Proclus' solutions to Neoplatonic problems. I shall turn to Kremer first, because his criticism particularly concerns the mutual relations of the ἀμέθεκτον, μετεχόμενον (in the sense of μετεχόμενος I), and μετέχον, whereas the criticisms of Festugière and Dodds have a more general character.

My point of departure will be Rosán, who is criticized by Kremer. Rosán offers a description of the system while abstaining from criticism of its substance, and confining himself to terminological questions. He[54] declines to speak of participation, preferring to talk of "unpossessed" and "possessed characteristic", and "possessor" in stead. Rosán gives two arguments: that 1) "each μετέχον does not share the μετεχόμενον with anything else since it is his own", and 2) "the μετεχόμενα cannot be said to share in the ἀμέθεκτον (...) because it is, literally, the 'Un-shared-in'". These arguments have some force, and as an interpretation of what Proclus means by participation, his proposal is

---

[50] See also *Theol. plat.* III 3, 13, 16 - 18.

[51] A.J. Festugière, *Proclus. Commentaire sur le Timée de Proclus.* Trad. et notes, Paris 1967, II, 52, following Dodds, see below 85.

[52] Kremer, *Die neuplatonische Seinsphilosophie und ihre Wirkung auf Thomas van Aquin,* 212, 213.

[53] Dodds, *Proclus. The Elements of Theology,* 211.

[54] Rosán, *The Philosophy of Proclus. The Final Phase of Ancient Thought,* 81, n. 54.

acceptable. What is against it is that Proclus, who is fully aware of the problems set by the introduction of the ἀμέθεκτον, does not therefore disavow the terms but incessantly uses forms of μετέχειν, which imply a closer connection than that expressed by "possess".

Kremer has objections to Rosán's proposal, which originate in Kremer's own misconceptions about Proclus' notion of participation. Kremer[55] wrongly maintains a) that in Proclus the μετεχόμενον itself is participated by a μετέχον, and b) that there is participation in the ἀμέθεκτον by the μετεχόμενα, so that there would allegedly be no need to choose a different set of terms, e.g. to render Proclus' terms in the way Rosán does. Kremer is convinced that Rosán's claims under (1) and (2) above contradict Proclus' express words.

Kremer's claim that the μετεχόμενον is participated by the μετέχον is based on what is said in prop. 23, line 27: the unparticipated generates the things that are capable of being participated: ἀμέθεκτα (....) ἀπογεννᾷ τὰ μετέχεσθαι δυνάμενα. In my view this does not mean that the μετεχόμενα can be participated as such, as if they were new entities to be shared in, but that the unparticipated, which has being of its own, transcends the participants, and generates what the μετέχοντα are allowed to have and do have as of their participation: the μετεχόμενον. This is the τι of line 28 of prop. 23, which is given to the participants and comes to exist μετεχομένως, "in the manner of being participated". So the μετέχομενον is a gift, something which can hardly be said of a thing an entity shares in.

A similar argument against Kremer applies to prop. 23, line 30. Here we are told that every participatum (μετέχομενον), becoming the property of something by which it is participated, is secondary to what is present in all, the ἀμέθεκτον (τὸ δὲ μετεχόμενον πᾶν, τινὸς γενόμενον, ὑφ' οὗ μετέχεται,[56] δεύτερόν ἐστιν τοῦ πᾶσιν ὁμοίως παρόντος). We should not conclude with Kremer that, again, we are taught that the μετέχομενον as such is participated, on the supposition that μετέχομενον is the subject of μετέχεται. Even if the subject of μετέχεται should be μετέχομενον, Proclus still does not intend to imply that the μετέχομενον as such is participated. The μετέχομενον is nothing but the content which is participated, i.e. what is possessed by the participant.

As to the so-called participation of the μετεχόμενον in the ἀμέθεκτον supposed by Kremer, he puts the rhetorical question "Proklos meidet nun den Ausdruck, die Mittelglieder partizipierten am ersten Glied, aber soll, wenn sie ihm ähnlich sind, keine Teilhabe statthaben?"[57]. In my view the anwer to this

---

[55] Kremer, *Die neuplatonische Seinsphilosophie und ihre Wirkung auf Thomas van Aquin*, 212 - 214.
[56] A similar phrase in prop. 53 ὁ δὲ μετεχόμενος ἐν ἐκείνοις μόνον, ὑφ' ὧν μετέχεται, has the same structure and offers similar problems to that discussed in the text as far as the subject is concerned; comparing it with that in prop. 23 (see note 12) is unfortunately no help.
[57] Kremer, *Die neuplatonische Seinsphilosophie und ihre Wirkung auf Thomas van Aquin*, 212.

must be negative. They do not share in the *imparticipabile*, but *are* what is participated by the participants. Kremer[58] draws a comparison with prop. 69, which, in his opinion, states of the μετέχομενον that it participates in the ἀμέθεκτον. Reading the proposition in question, one finds nothing of the kind. The rule that prior to every participatum there exist the unparticipated (πάντος τοῦ μετεχομένου προυφέστηκε τὸ ἀμέθεκτον) cannot serve as evidence for Kremer's case.

Kremer charges Proclus with insufficient insight into the problems of participation. It seems to me that it is Kremer who is open to this charge. In his opinion Proclus should have maintained in prop. 99 that "jedes Wesen an dem Ursprung, von dem es in die Existenz aufbricht, *teil hat*.. Gilt das nicht für die Dreierreihe Unpartiziertes, Partizipierbares und Partizipierendes? An der Teilhabe haltet Proklos fest; zweifel bekommt man allerdings bei der Frage, *ob Proklos das Teilhabeverhältnis immer ganz durchschaute*" (italics — P.A.M). From *In Rem. publ.* I, 260, 5, 6, however, it appears that Proclus is not so naive, but is in fact well aware of the problematic nature of participation, and that he is ready to admit that, in a sense, the unparticipated is participated: ἐπεὶ καὶ τὰ ἀμέθεκτα φαίης ἂν μετέχεσθαι πως ("since even the unparticipated might in a way be said to be participated"). However, the limitation expressed in the word πως (in a way) keeps everything within the bounds of the system. For what Proclus has in mind, is that the participants have a share and display similarity, and are called into existence by the ἀμέθεκτα. This is precisely what he brings up in his explanation of πως: τὰ ἀμέθεκτα are only participated *in as far as they give from themselves* (ἀλλ' ὡς μεταδιδόντα ἑαυτῶν). Now in Proclus giving is always a giving without being diminished. This is the only way one may take the unparticipated to be participated: it is seen from the point of view of the giver. This does not, however, mean that the recipient has a *part or share* of it. At best the recipient has the μετεχόμενον.

We find a comparable situation in *Elementatio* prop. 23. Of the two options: either (1) the ἀμέθεκτον remains sterile, or (2) it will give something of itself (ἢ δώσει τι ἀφ' ἑαυτοῦ), Proclus chooses the second one: the ἀμέθεκτον gives something of itself. This "something" (τι) is the μετεχόμενον (I). What it is that he is prepared to admit in the *In Rem publicam*, must be considered in its context. What forces Proclus to fathom here the similarities of the ἀμέθεκτον and the μετεχόμενον, is *his* reading of the passage involved in Plato's *Res publica*; it is within this limiting framework that he makes his apparent concession. We may say, then, that the ἀμέθεκτον and the μετεχόμενον have something in common: the ἀμέθεκτον may in a way be said to be participated like the μετεχόμενον, and the (transcendent) μετεχόμενον can be said to be eternally like the ἀμέθεκτον. I do not think that this concession is intended to

[58] Kremer, *Die neuplatonische Seinsphilosophie und ihre Wirkung auf Thomas van Aquin*, 212, n. 57.

make a difference to the system of ἀμέθεκτον, μετεχόμενον and μετέχον as given in props. 23 and 24 of the *Elementatio*. Ultimately it is the mystery of Platonic and Neoplatonic participation, how it is possible to have a "share" of something, while this something, the giver, remains undiminished.[59] Incidentally, Kremer could have quoted *In Rem publ..*, I, 260, 5, 6 in support of his view that the ἀμέθεκτον is participated. However, he neglects to do so.

Sofar we have not found Proclus to deviate fundamentally from his own doctrine. Fundamentally, then, there is no exception from the rule that the ἀμέθεκτον is not participated.

Kremer in his zeal to undermine the system adduces prop. 99. We must recognize, however, that this proposition expresses something which is completely at odds with what Kremer[60] makes Proclus claim: "Proklos sagt einmal, dass jedes Wesen an dem Ursprung, von dem es in die Existenz aufbricht, teil hat (ἀφ' ὧν γὰρ ὥρμηται, τούτων δήπου μετέχει, line 29). Gilt das nicht fur die Dreierreihe Unpartizipiertes, Partizipierbares und Partizipierendes?",[61] a sentence we quoted already above. According to Kremer's suggestion, ("Gilt das nicht fur die Dreierreihe Unpartizipiertes, Partizipierbares und Partizipierendes?") this line 29 of prop. 99 (ἀφ' ὧν γὰρ ὥρμηται, τούτων δήπου μετέχει) is an indication, that the ἀμέθεκτον and the μετεχόμενον (both as "jedes Wesen") are participated – something which would ruin the system, or would at least detract from its consistency.

Here we must come to Proclus' defence. For one thing Proclus does not say that "*jedes* Wesen an dem Ursprung teil hat." The subject of μετέχει is not "jedes Wesen", as Kremer has it, but an ἀμέθεκτον. In prop. 99 it is not participation in an origin in general which is at stake, but rather a very specific point: a qualified "Wesen", *viz.* the ἀμέθεκτον, participates in what it stems from *as springing from its origin*. Proclus is perfectly free, without any risk to his system, to affirm that an ἀμέθεκτον participates (μετέχει) in its origin (via a μετεχόμενον I [62], I may add) as a μετέχον. Proclus' point is that *only as to its own specific characteristic* an ἀμέθεκτον does not operate as a μετέχον. In that respect it does not participate in its origin, but is the first to have the characteristic, which is precisely the reason for its being ἀμέθεκτον. But that is not in Kremer's criticism the issue. Any charge of inconsistency based on an alleged assumption by Proclus of a direct participation in an ἀμέθεκτον or a μετεχόμενον is therefore unjustified.

---

[59] We already find in Plotinus the golden rule of the undiminished giver, *Ennead* 30 [III, 8], 10, see also 9[VI,9], 5,36.

[60] Kremer, *Die neuplatonische Seinsphilosophie und ihre Wirkung auf Thomas van Aquin*, 214.

[61] Then follows the sentence we discussed already: "An der Teilhabe halt Proklos fest; zweifel bekommt man allerdings bei der Frage, ob Proklos das Teilhabeverhältnis immer ganz durchschaute" *cf. Elem..* prop., 99, p. 88, line 29.

[62] In prop. 99 there was no need to bring up this point.

b) *Festugière and Dodds*

Festugière[63] ostensibly follows Dodds, but is more critical and draws certain consequences from Dodds' words which Dodds himself cannot be made responsible for. He glosses ἀμέθεκτος by "séparé", "transcendant" or "antérieur", though he does not wish to translate it by any of these terms. All these terms, however, have their equivalents in Greek[64], and therefore cannot properly express what ἀμέθεκτος *per se* means. The value of this term is the connection of a *specific* idea and its *special property* with its offspring. Besides, Festugière's arguments are inadequate. As proof for his suggestion he comes up with the (seeming) contradiction between utterances stating that the One or the Good are strictly ἀμέθεκτον, and those statements which indicate that they are nevertheless participated. Thus in prop. 1 of the *Elements* the One is said to be participated by every manifold in a certain way (πᾶν πλῆθος μετέχει πῇ τοῦ ἑνός), and in the *In Timaeum* the Good is participated by the Demiurge (Proclus, *In Tim.* II, 365, 11 μετέχει τῆς ἀγαθότητος, see also line 15). What Festugière does not seem to take into account is that within the framework of Proclus' "trinity" of participation it is always possible to say that the participant participates in a superior entity, which is not the same thing as stating of the ἀμέθεκτον that it is participated. Of course Proclus cannot drop the term μετέχει, and must be allowed to say in general that something participates in its origin, without thereby upsetting the system.

We must be aware that Festugière bases his suggestion on criticism by Dodds, who had claimed that Proclus' system of participation is open to inconsistency: "τὸ ἕν is ἀμέθεκτον, yet we have already been told (prop. 1) that πᾶν πλῆθος μετέχει πῃ τοῦ ἑνός." Festugière overlooks that Dodds himself gives a solution to the problem where he says: "the answer is that a term which is *proprie* ἀμέθεκτον is yet indirectly μεθεκτόν through the μετεχόμενα which it generates."[65] This might be a correct solution to the problem. Dodds could have strenghtened his case by pointing the little word πῃ: *in a way*. "Such a way" might contain the explanation required by Dodds, and thus no inconsistency would remain. In his explanation on p. 211, however, Dodds seems to assume that in prop. 1 τὸ ἕν should be thought of as the One. This is hardly consistent with his *translation* of πᾶν πλῆθος μετέχει πῃ τοῦ ἑνός by "Every manifold in some way participates *unity*" (3), correctly as I believe. If this rendering of τὸ ἕν by "unity" (judging from the contents of prop. 1 this concerns

---

[63] Festugière, *Proclus. Commentaire sur le Timeé* II, 51, n. 1.

[64] W. Beierwaltes, *Proklos. Grundzüge seiner Metaphysik*, Frankfurt am Main 1965, 352 gives a list of terms denoting transcendence. Beierwaltes wisely does not include ἀμέθεκτον.

[65] Dodds, *Proclus. The Elements of Theology*, 211. He quotes prop. 56, which cannot support his claims in any way. Presumably he means prop. 65, which does not, however, contribute much in favour of his solution either.

a unity belonging to each entity as its foundation⁶⁶) is correct, there is no inconsistency between τὸ ἕν is ἀμέθεκτον, and πᾶν πλῆθος μετέχει πῃ τοῦ ἑνός, for in this case τοῦ ἑνός in the sentence πᾶν πλῆθος μετέχει πῃ τοῦ ἑνός cannot be intended to refer to the One and means only "unity".

To continue the catalogue of objections to the doctrine of participation, Dodds is dissatisfied⁶⁷ with the fact that the Henads are said to be both above being (supra-essential, ὑπερούσιος) and participable. Here again Proclus is accused of inconsistency, because he at once assigns participability to all Gods and denies it to a special class, that of the supra-mundane Gods, in the *In Tim.* III, 204, 16 ff.⁶⁸. I do not think, however, that in the passage involved the reference is to Henads. If it is not, then Dodds' criticism misses the mark. In any case it seems to me rather unfair to accuse Proclus alone of inconsistencies concerning participation, since this is, first of all, a *common* Platonic problem. In his general theory of participation Proclus is not more inconsistent than Plato himself: the terminilogical oddity "imparticipated" (ἀμέθεκτος) neatly brings out Plato's problem.

I am aware of just one oddity which deviates from the Proclan system with regard to μετεχόμενος I and perhaps poses a real threat to its consistency. There is a remarkable systematic extension in the case of the lowest level of μετεχόμενα. This type of μετεχόμενον (the so-called χωριστῶς μετεχόμενον) can be detected in prop. 81, where Proclus discusses the problem of the relation between body and soul. The soul may not be affected by the bodily, and in fact it is not (*cf.* prop. 80, 32 τὸ δὲ ἀσώματον (*sc.* the soul) ἁπλοῦν ὄν, ἀπαθές ἐστι). If the χωριστῶς μετεχόμενον (which is actually the soul) must be considered as separate from the body, which possesses neither the χωριστῶς μετεχόμενον nor anything else of it, as Proclus asserts, how then can participation take place? Proclus' solution to this problem is very peculiar. There is a power (δύναμις⁶⁹) and irradiation (ἔλλαμψις) coming down to the participant, connecting the χωριστῶς μετεχόμενον (soul) and the participant. So there are three entities, viz. the power by means of which the participation operates (the "medium", as Dodds translates δύναμις), the participant, and the μετεχόμενον,⁷⁰ which remains

---

⁶⁶ For unity as the foundation of the being of a thing *cf.* Plotinus 9 [VI, 9], 1 ff. on which Meijer, 'Stoicism in Plotinus' Enneads VI,9,1', *Quaderni Urbinati di Cultura Classica,* 59 (1988), 63 ff.

⁶⁷ Dodds, *Proclus. The Elements of Theology,* 262.

⁶⁸ Dodds, *Proclus. The Elements of Theology,* 262; *In Tim.,* III, 204, 16 ff.

⁶⁹ On this interesting δύναμις see Dodds, *Proclus. The Elements of Theology,* 243, 244. It is the buffer between soul and body; a psychic entity, which is subjected to passions.

⁷⁰ Dodds' translation of καὶ τὸ μὲν ἔσται δι' οὗ μέθεξις, τὸ δὲ μετεχόμενον, τὸ δὲ μετέχον is remarkably free and loose: "and this medium of participation will be distinct from both", whereas Proclus himself does not talk here of distinction but stresses that this power (τὸ μὲν) is the instrument of participation. Τὸ δε is the μετεχόμενον, *participatum,* but this term has denaturated here, for it is expressly denied that it is participated; therefore the χωριστῶς μετεχόμενον must be meant. And finally (the second τὸ δὲ) one has the participant (body).

free from any bodily stain. Thus we have a kind of hypostasized[71] μετεχόμενον, which has something in common with the complete (αὐτοτελεῖς) ὑπόστασεις in that it is independent[72] in relation to its participant, and which as such is an exception to the rules which dominate μετεχόμενος I.

The incorporation of the Henads and monads into Proclus' system of participation, too, shows some accretions which overstep the bounds of the system, as we can see in the case both of the Henads and of the monads. As complete hypostases (αὐτοτελεῖς ὑποστάσεις), which do not belong to their particulars but are above them (μετεχόμενος II), the Henads have to play a role in participation by mediating between the One and what has to participate in it, but their own relation with their Origin, the One, is likely to fall outside the scope of participation. The same holds for the lower monads, whose relation to their leading monad seems to be a not strictly participational one[73].

In spite of these problems I conclude it may be maintained that on the foundation of his trinity of ἀμέθεκτον, μετεχόμενον and μετέχον Proclus has erected a well-organized system. Within the Neoplatonic framework it is to a great extent capable of systematizing in terms of participation the ontological hierarchy not only of ideas but also of such hypostases as mind and soul, both in the transcendent and in the sensible world.

---

[71] Proclus expressly calls the χωριστῶς μετεχόμενον hypostasized, "something which exists in itself" as Dodds translates ὡς τὴν ὑπόστασιν ἐν ἑαυτῷ κεκτημένον (referring to the χωριστῶς μετεχόμενον).

[72] See Dodds, *Proclus. The Elements of Theology*, 262.

[73] See above 70.

A. DE LIBERA

ALBERT LE GRAND ET LE PLATONISME.
DE LA DOCTRINE DES IDÉES
À LA THEORIE DES TROIS ÉTATS DE L'UNIVERSEL

Albert distingue trois écoles dans la philosophie antique.[1] Les Épicuriens: Thalès, Anaximène, Héraclite, Empédocle, "Démocrite et son collègue Leucippe", Cecinna, Attale, Hésiode, Homère, Épicure. Les Stoïciens: Pythagore, Hermès Trismégiste, Socrate,[2] Platon, Speusippe, les Académiciens et les Brahmanistes. Les Péripatéticiens: Anaxagore, Aristote, Alexandre, Théophraste, Porphyre, "Abubacher" et/ou al-Fârâbî,[3] Avicenne, Ghazâlî, Averroès.[4] Placé entre un épicurisme qui a donné son nom à Épicure ("épicurien" veut dire *super-curans* ou *supra cutem*, autrement dit: superflu, superficiel)[5] et un péripatétisme pour le moins éclectique, le platonisme d'Albert n'est qu'un "moment" du stoïcisme ou une *position* proche du stoïcisme.

Cette approche de l'histoire par l'intermédiaire des *positiones* n'est pas unique en son genre: on la retrouve, et pour cause, chez saint Thomas d'Aquin. La différence entre les deux auteurs, le maître et l'élève, est que Thomas définit

---

1 *Cf.* Albert le Grand, *De causis et processu universitatis* I, 1, 1, éd. A. Borgnet, *Opera omnia* X, Paris 1890, 361 b.

2 Dans certains textes Socrate est présenté comme le fondateur de l'école stoïcienne. *Cf.* Albert le Grand, *De anima* II, 1, 9, éd. Cl. Stroick, *Opera omnia* VII, pars I, 1968, 77, 1 - 18.

3 Trompé par les particularités des textes d'Averroès qu'il suit à la lettre, Albert ne sait pas toujours distinguer les deux personnages qui se cachent sous le mot latin "Abubacher" — Avempace (Abû Bakr, autrement dit: Ibn Bâgga) *et* Abubacer (Abû Nasr, autrement dit: al-Fârâbî) — il lui arrive donc de compter al-Fârâbî pour deux. Ailleurs il confond Abubacer et Haly.

4 Les néoalbertistes du XVe siècle, comme Jean de Maisonneuve, transposent ce cadre tripartite *ad usum proprium*: les péripatéticiens sont les albertistes, les épicuriens les nominalistes (*terministae, epicuri litterales*), les stoïciens les *formalizantes*. Sur ce point, *cf.* Z. Kaluza, 'Le *De universale reali* de Jean de Maisonneuve et les *epicuri litterales*', *Freiburger Zeitschrift für Philosophie und Theologie* 33 (1986), 486 - 489. Comme il arrive aussi chez Albert que les stoïciens, disciples de Socrate, soient distingués des académiciens, disciples de Platon, ce sont alors les académiciens qui représentent la théorie des Idées (donc les *formalizantes*), les stoïciens, trop stupides pour s'"arracher au sensible", n'ayant laissé ni doctrine ni descendance. Sur cette autre classification, *cf.* Z. Kaluza, *Les querelles doctrinales à Paris. Nominalistes et réalistes aux confins du XIVe et du XVe siècles* (Quodlibet 2), Bergame 1988, 17 - 18.

5 *Cf.* Albert le Grand, *De causis et processu universitatis* I, 1, 2, *Opera omnia* X, 1890, 365.

les platonismes *en philologue*, dans l'horizon herméneutique de Macrobe, d'Aristote, de Proclus et de Denys, là où Albert travaille une donne contradictoire avec les instruments de *l'histoire naturelle*.

Soit le thème de Proclus et de sa réception. Pour des raisons évidentes — la traduction Moerbeke date de 1268 —, Albert a lu tardivement les *Éléments de théologie*: il ne les utilise donc que dans sa seconde *Somme de théologie* rédigée à Cologne dans les années 1270.[6] Utilisation discrète, sinon frileuse: c'est que, même si son nom est quelquefois cité à côté des autorités que sont Denys et Boèce,[7] Proclus n'est pas à proprement parler un *auctor* et qu'il n'y a pas encore chez Albert une *position* platonico-proclienne de plein exercice, comme ce sera le cas chez Thomas, Dietrich de Freiberg et, surtout, Berthold de Moosburg.[8] Quelle est alors, pour lui, la norme du platonisme? La réponse est immédiate, mais complexe: ce n'est pas Proclus, c'est Platon, mais *Platon comme se le représentent le ou plutôt les péripatétismes*. Telle est en somme la place du platonisme dans l'exégèse philosophique albertinienne: entre un Platon lacunaire, quasi inconnu, et un Aristote syncrétique, quasi méconnaissable.

Le syncrétisme de l'aristotélisme d'Albert est particulièrement manifeste dans son interprétation des origines du *Liber de causis*.

Dans un bel article sur l'influence de Proclus au Moyen Age, L. Sturlese a récemment insisté sur la souveraine indifférence avec laquelle Albert traite la question du platonisme du *Livre des causes*. De cette indifférence, il offre deux explications: d'une part, "la réaction d'auto-défense instinctive d'un vieux professeur devant une découverte qui détruit" la pierre d'angle de toutes ses "convictions de commentateur", d'autre part, la mise en oeuvre d'une conception "concordataire et constructive" tendant à effacer la distinction des *textes* platoniciens et aristotéliciens dans l'aperception d'une "large convergence de vues entre les *auctores antiquissimi*."[9] Les deux explications sont bonnes, mais il faut – ce sera d'ailleurs notre conclusion – les nuancer.

---

[6] *Cf.* R. Kaiser, 'Die Benutzung proklischer Schriften durch Albert den Großen', *Archiv für Geschichte der Philosophie* 45/1 (1963), 1 - 22 (spécialement 14 *sqq.*).

[7] *Cf.* Albert le Grand, *Summa theologiae sive de mirabili scientia dei* I, 6, 26, 1, éd. D. Siedler, *Opera omnia* XXXIV, pars I, 1978, 183, 35 - 36; *ibid.*, I, 6, 26, 2; 192, 71 - 89.

[8] Sur Berthold et l'École dominicaine allemande, *cf.* L. Sturlese, 'Proclo ed Ermete in Germania da Alberto Magno a Bertoldo di Moosburg. Per una prospettiva di ricerca sulla cultura filosofica tedesca nel secolo delle sue origini (1250-1350)', dans: *Von Meister Dietrich zu Meister Eckhart*, hrsg. K. Flasch *(Corpus Philosophorum Teutonicorum Medii Aevi Beihefte 2)*, Hamburg 1984, 22 - 33; *id.*, '*Homo divinus*. Der Prokloskommentar Bertholds von Moosburg und die Probleme der nacheckhartschen Zeit', dans: *Abendländische Mystik im Mittelalter. Symposion Kloster Engelberg 1984*, hrsg. K. Ruh (Germanistische Symposien, Berichtsband 7), Stuttgart 1986, 145 - 161; *id.*, 'Tauler im Kontext. Die philosophischen Voraussetzungen des *Seelengrundes* in der Lehre des deutschen Neuplatonikers Berthold von Moosburg', *Beiträge zur Geschichte der deutschen Sprache und Literatur*, Band 109, Heft 3, Tübingen 1987, 390 - 426.

[9] *Cf.* L. Sturlese, 'Il dibattito sul Proclo latino nel medioevo fra l'università di Parigi e lo Studium di Colonia', dans: *Proclus et son influence. Actes du Colloque de Neuchâtel, juin 1985*, éds. G. Boss et G. Seel, Zürich 1987, 268 - 269.

Quand (dans les années 1265) Albert rédige le *De causis et processu universitatis*, il ignore la source véritable du *Liber* (qu'il paraphrase dans la seconde moitié de son ouvrage, après une première partie consacrée à l'exposé d'une théologie du Premier principe, largement influencée par la *Metaphysica* de Ghazâlî). Pour lui le *Livre* est un recueil de *dits* extraits d'une *Lettre d'Aristote sur le Principe de l'Univers – Epistola de principio universi esse –* auxquels un certain "David le juif", *alias* Avendauth,[10] a ajouté un commentaire "à la manière dont Euclide avait procédé pour la géométrie," "s'inspirant" de passages lus dans Avicenne et al-Fârâbî.[11] Bref, il ignore les origines procliennes, et secondairement plotiniennes, du Kalâm fî mahd al-khair traduit en latin par Gérard de Crémone.[12] En fait, le texte qu'il commente n'est pas même pour lui un livre: c'est un "montage" dont le niveau d'autorité est hétérogène — ce qui se reflète, d'ailleurs, dans la structure même de sa paraphrase, puisque si les *propositions* (supposées aristotéliciennes) ont droit à d'amples développements, le *commentum* (supposé non-aristotélicien) ne reçoit que quelques lignes et n'a manifestement d'autre fonction que celle d'un récapitulé (annoncé par une formule technique, telle que *capitulariter* ou *summatim restringendo dicendum quod*).[13]

---

[10] L'identification de "David Iudaeus" à Avendauth, c'est-à-dire au juif converti Abraham Ibn Daûd (Juan Ben David, *alias* Jean d'Espagne), avancée par Steinschneider, a fait l'objet de diverses critiques. En ce qui concerne Albert, il nous semble clair que les deux personnages ne pouvaient faire qu'un; en effet, les colophons du type Oxford, *Bodleian, Selden Sup.* 24 ou Paris, *Bibliothèque Nationale, latin* 14719, donnent indifféremment l'un ou l'autre: "*Explicit* Metaphysica *Avendauth*" ; "*Explicit* Liber de causis causarum *editus a David et cum commento ab eodem edito*," tout comme Albert le fait lui-même, attribuant tantôt le *Liber* à David, tantôt à "Avendaud". Pour ce dernier, *cf. De caelo et mundo* I, 3, 8, éd. P. Hoßfeld, *Opera omnia* X, pars I, 1971, 73, 30 - 31: "(...) secundum doctrinam Avendaud in *Libro de causis*." Reste qu'on pourrait aussi imaginer que les colophons du type *Bibliothèque Nationale, latin* 14719 aient dépendu d'Albert.

[11] *Cf.* Albert le Grand, *De causis et processu universitatis* II, 1, 1, *Opera omnia* X, 1890, 433; trad. H.D. Saffrey, 'Introduction' dans: *Sancti Thomae de Aquino Super* Librum de causis *expositio* (Textus Philosophici Friburgenses, 4/5), Fribourg-Louvain 1954, xxii.

[12] *Status quaestionis* dans R.C. Taylor, 'The Kalæm fî maḥ≈ al-khair (*Liber de causis*) in the islamic philosophical milieu', dans: *Pseudo-Aristotle in the Middle Ages. The Theology and other Texts* (Warburg Institute Surveys and Texts XI), Londres 1986, 37 - 52.

[13] En dehors du passage (*De causis et processu universitatis* II, 1, 1) où il prétend en établir l'origine, Albert ne mentionne jamais nommément le *Liber de causis*, que ce soit dans sa paraphrase elle-même — ce qui est conforme aux lois du genre —, ou lors d'une citation explicite et marquée — ce qui l'est beaucoup moins. Dans ce cas, le Colonais introduit les thèses qu'il utilise en les attribuant aux *Antiqui Peripatetici* (*De causis et processu universitatis* II, 1, 13, *Opera omnia* X, 1890, 456 a = *Liber de causis, propositio* 3a, comm., éd. H.D. Saffrey, 17), aux *Peripatetici* (à propos du *stramentum intelligentiae*: *De causis et processu universitatis* II, 1, 22, *Opera omnia* X, 1890, 471 a = *Liber de causis, propositio* 3, *ibidem*; repris en II, 3, 12, *Opera omnia* X, 1890, 561 b et 562 a - b, et II, 3, 16, *Opera omnia* X, 1890, 567 a - b), voire, à "certains philosophes", "*quibusdam philosophis*" (à propos du terme *hyleachim*: *De causis et processu universitatis* II, 2, 18, *Opera omnia* X, 1890, 505 b = *Liber de causis, propositio* 9a, éd. H.D. Saffrey, 57; repris en *De causis et processu universitatis* II, 2, 19, *Opera omnia* X, 1890, 507 b). Ce singulier effacement de l'*auctor* dans une sorte de pluralité de références anonymisantes correspond donc clairement à l'hypothèse de lecture d'Albert: le *Liber de causis* n'a pas d'*auteur*, car ce n'est pas *un* livre, mais un collage de textes tirés de plusieurs livres d'origines diverses.

On sait désormais que les grands philosophes de terre d'Islam n'ont pas fréquenté le *Livre du Bien pur* ou *Livre des causes*, puisque, comme l'a bien montré Taylor, ni al-Kindî, ni al-Fârâbî, ni Ibn Sînâ, ni Ibn Rusd n'ont utilisé le Kalâm fî mahd al-khair.[14] Comme toujours — ou presque — Albert est d'un autre avis que ses collègues arabisants. Dans le *De causis et processu universitatis* II, 1, 1, il va même jusqu'à énumérer tous ses lecteurs célèbres: al-Fârâbî, qui l'appelait *Tractatus de bonitate pura*, al-Ghazâlî, *Flos divinorum*, Avicenne *Liber de lumine luminum*, sans oublier d'obscurs "disciples d'Aristote", qui eux l'intitulaient *Liber de causis causarum*. Seuls Kindî et Ibn Rusd échappent à cet inventaire incohérent, voire incompréhensible. Comment, en effet, David le Juif, auteur andalou du XIIe siècle, pourrait-il être l'auteur d'un livre dont les premiers témoins connus seraient précisément ceux qu'il est censé avoir "déflorés" pour le composer! Mystère.

Les allégations d'Albert ont, cependant, un sens plus acceptable si l'on comprend que ces différents philosophes ont tous connu le texte d'Aristote à partir duquel David a confectionné son propre ouvrage, autrement dit si le *Liber de causis* ou *Metaphysica Avendauth* est bien l'adaptation d'une *Théologie*, la *Lettre sur le Principe de l'univers*, dont Ghazâlî aurait, notamment, donné une *autre* version dans le cinquième traité du livre I de sa *Philosophia*, intitulé *Flos divinorum*. Telle qu'elle la chose n'a rien d'impossible: Avicenne et Averroès ont, effectivement, cité la *Lettre*.

Une autre hypothèse, complémentaire, pourrait être qu'aux yeux d'Albert *tous* les péripatéticiens ont essayé de combler le *vide théologique* du livre *Lambda* de la *Métaphysique* et qu'ils ont défini ce que devrait être l'œuvre capable de boucler le savoir aristotélicien en une véritable sagesse, projet que seul David le Juif aurait mené à terme, synthétisant leurs différents apports à la lumière d'un texte fédérateur: la *Lettre sur le Principe de l'univers*.

Cette philologie-fiction est séduisante. Reste qu'elle repose sur une série d'erreurs.

Parmi ces erreurs, la plus décisive est évidemment l'attribution à Aristote d'une *Lettre sur le Principe de l'univers*. J'ai expliqué ailleurs l'histoire de cette méprise.[15] Trompé par un passage erratique de l'*Avicenna latinus*,[16] incapable d'en corriger l'effet pervers grâce aux indications qu'il aurait pourtant pu (dû?) lire dans un texte parallèle de Maïmonide,[17] Albert a attribué à Aristote une œuvre d'Alexandre d'Aphrodise, l'*Epître des principes du tout*

---

[14] *Cf*. Taylor, 'The Kalæm fî mahd al-khair (*Liber de causis*) in the islamic philosophical milieu', 40.

[15] *Cf*. mon livre *Albert le Grand et la philosophie*, Paris 1990, 55 - 72.

[16] *Cf*. Avicenne, *Metaphysica* IX, 2, éd. S. van Riet (*Avicenna Latinus*), Louvain-Leiden 1980, 463, 68 - 71.

[17] *Cf*. Maïmonide, *Dux neutrorum sive Perplexorum* II, 5, Paris 1520, f^o xlii.

selon l'opinion d'Aristote le Philosophe,[18] qu'il ne connaissait apparemment que de seconde main.

Il est inutile d'insister sur les conséquences philosophiques de cette bévue. On peut, en revanche, se demander s'il faut, comme certains arabisants — voire certains thomistes — accabler leur malheureux auteur. Assurément non. Allons au pire: même si, par extraordinaire, Albert a eu accès à une traduction latine — aujourd'hui perdue — de la *Lettre* d' "Aristote", il me semble qu'il ne pouvait qu'en être davantage enclin à persévérer dans ses hypothèses. Car, c'est vrai, à en juger par sa version arabe, le texte authentique de l'*Epistola*, autrement dit le Kitâb mabâdi' al-kull d'Alexandre d'Aphrodise, contient plusieurs passages qui évoquent bel et bien le *Livre des causes!*

Prenons un exemple. Même si la diversité des langues fait écran — l'ouvrage a été d'abord traduit du grec en syriaque par Abd Zaid Hunain ibn Ishâq, puis du syriaque en arabe par Ibrâhîm ibn 'Abd Allâh al-Nasrânî al-Kâtib, et nous n'avons aucun témoin latin — la *Lettre* éditée par A. Badawi,[19] contient au moins une thèse centrale du *Liber*, qui est aussi, naturellement, une thèse de Proclus. Il s'agit de l'axiome selon lequel "l'Intelligence se pense elle-même,"[20] thèse que l'on retrouve dans la proposition 12 du Kalâm fî mahd al-khair[21] (c'est-à-dire dans la proposition 13 du *Liber de causis*), dans la proposition 167 des *Éléments de théologie,*[22] sans parler, mais faut-il le rappeler?, de la *Métaphysique* d'Aristote. Ignorant Proclus, mais connaissant Aristote, Albert pouvait-il éviter de rapprocher, s'il les avaient tous trois sous les yeux, le *Liber*, Aristote et la *Lettre*? Disons que tout l'y incitait. Ce, d'autant plus que, telle que la paraphrase Maïmonide, la *Lettre* contient aussi

---

[18] Ce texte est traduit en français dans A. Badawi, *La transmission de la philosophie grecque au monde arabe* (cours professé à la Sorbonne en 1967) (Études de Philosophie Médiévale lvi), Paris 1987, 135 - 153.

[19] *Cf.* A. Badawi, Aristû ᶜinda 'l- ᶜArab, Le Caire 1947, 253 - 277.

[20] *Cf.* Badawi, *La transmission de la philosophie grecque au monde arabe,* 150.

[21] Proposition que Taylor, 'The Kalæm fî mahd al-khair (*Liber de causis*) in the islamic philosophical milieu', 52, traduit ainsi: "Every intelligence intellectually knows its essence." Le mot "intelligence" rend l'arabe "al-'aql".

[22] Selon la traduction anglaise de Taylor, 'The Kalâm fî mahd al-khair (*Liber de causis*) in the islamic philosophical milieu', 52, le texte du *Proclus arabus* dit: "Every knower knows its essence. But the *first knower* knows only its essence and it is only one in number: I say that it is knower and known because it is not one and another but rather it is one, knower and known at once." Le mot "knower" rend l'arabe al-'âlim, le "connaissant", que l'on retrouve sans doute dans le terme latin *cognitivum* employé par Albert dans le passage du *De intellectu et intelligibili* renvoyant explicitement à la *Lettre sur le Principe de l'univers.* Le mot *cognitivum* ne figure pas dans la traduction latine de la proposition 167 de Proclus, Moerbeke préférant *intellectus* ("*Omnis intellectus se ipsum intelligit,*" 1987, 181, 1). Il figure, en revanche, dans le texte latin de la proposition 102: "(...) *omnia cognitiva cognitionem participant propter intellectum primum,*" 1987, 52, 3 - 4), où, comme chez Albert, l'Intellect est défini comme *primum cognitivum*, une proposition dont Thomas d'Aquin se servira, quant à lui, pour opposer le point de vue des *Platonici* à la *Sententia Dionysi. Cf.* sur ce point, Thomas d'Aquin, *Super* Librum de causis *expositio, propositio* 18a, 1954, 103, 7 - 23.

une expression absolument typique du *Livre* (et de Proclus): *simplex in fine simplicitatis*.

Selon moi, il ne fait pas de doute qu'Albert a été troublé par ce phénomène. Exposant la théologie d'Aristote à partir de l'*Epistola de principio totius* (qu'il attribue correctement à Alexandre, ce qu'Albert n'a pas remarqué), Maïmonide pose que, pour Aristote, Dieu est le Premier Moteur, qui met en mouvement la sphère céleste au sens précis où "elle désire s'assimiler à l'objet de sa perception, c'est-à-dire à la chose conçue (par elle), laquelle est *au comble de la simplicité* (*in fine simplicitatis*), ne connaît aucun changement ni aucune situation nouvelle, et dont le Bien émane continuellement."[23]

Comme je l'ai dit ailleurs, cette définition de Dieu comme objet de désir existant "au comble de la simplicité" (*in fine simplicitatis*), se retrouve mot pour mot dans un passage du *commentum* de la proposition 21 du *Liber de causis:*

> Primum est dives propter seipsum et est dives magis. Et significatio eius est unitas eius, non quia unitas eius sit sparsa in ipso, immo est unitas eius pura, quoniam est *simplex in fine simplicitatis*.[24]

L'expression *simplex in fine simplicitatis* (*Liber*, prop. 21a, comm.) transpose, on le sait, le *prime et maxime simplex* de Proclus (*Éléments de théologie, propositio* 127a):

> Omne divinum simplex prime est et maxime, et propter hoc maxime per se sufficiens.

Dans le *Liber de causis*, comme dans une partie du néoplatonisme grec, le sens de cette assertion est clair: il s'agit de préciser le statut de la *sufficientia*, c'est-à-dire l'autosuffisance (αὐτάρκεια) ou autonomie des réalités divines. En ce sens, dire que le "Premier est riche par soi" signifie qu'il est au plus haut point "autosuffisant", αὐτάρκης.

Dans le *De causis et processu universitatis*, donc sans connaître encore Proclus, Albert, fournit une autre occurrence du syntagme *simplex in fine simplicitatis*. Il s'agit de la théorie du "Premier Agent" selon Avicebron:

> Talibus ergo inquisitionibus inventa prima materia et prima forma, studet ad inveniendum primum agens, dicens, quod et verum est, *primum agens simplicissimum esse in fine simplicitatis*.[25]

---

23 *Cf.* Maïmonide, *Dux neutrorum sive Perplexorum*, 1520, II, 5, *loco citato*.

24 *Cf. Liber de causis, propositio* 21a; Thomas d'Aquin, *Super* Librum de causis *expositio, propositio* 21a, 1954, 112.

25 *Cf.* Albert le Grand, *De causis et processu universitatis* I, 1, 5, *Opera omnia* X, 1890, 371 a. Dans le *De causis et processu universitatis* I, 2, 5, *Opera omnia* 1890, 395 a, en revanche, la notion de "comble de la simplicité" est fondue dans un texte de Ghazâlî! En ce qui concerne Avicebron, la position d'Albert est claire: c'est un faux péripatéticien, qui, en réalité, suit les thèses des stoïciens, surtout celles de Platon. *Cf.* Albert le Grand, *De XV problematibus* I, *Opera omnia* XVII, pars I, 1975, 34, 20 - 22: "*Quamvis enim Peripateticum se profitetur, tamen Stoicorum et praecipue Platonis dogma secutus est.*"

Dans la *Somme de théologie*,[26] en revanche, autrement dit dans la seule œuvre où il utilise les *Éléments de théologie* de Proclus, il ne renvoie ni à Proclus, ni d'ailleurs à Avicebron, mais bien à la *voie* qu'Aristote a empruntée dans son *Epistola de principio universitatis*:

> Et c'est [la thèse] d'Aristote dans une certaine *Lettre* qu'il fit *sur le Principe de l'Univers*. En effet, seule la Cause première simple, existant au comble de la simplicité (*in fine simplicitatis*), sans qu'aucune [autre chose] ne la détermine, peut, ramassée en vue d'une chose seconde, être la cause de l'être en tant qu'être.[27]

La conclusion s'impose: s'il ne connaissait pas la *Lettre*, Albert avait de bonnes raisons de l'attribuer à Aristote; qu'il la connût ou ne la connût pas, il avait de meilleures raisons encore de la rapprocher du *Liber*.

En plaçant le *Livre* dans l'orbite de la théologie d'Aristote, il a sans aucun doute grevé son aristotélisme de tous les corps étrangers dont le péripatétisme arabe avait, depuis le IXe siècle, lesté la pensée du Stagirite, mais il va de soi que cette surcharge a elle-même rejailli sur son interprétation du platonisme. Condamné à relativiser sinon à marginaliser Proclus, Albert a cherché chez deux pseudonymes, ce que nous trouvons dans le néoplatonisme: la *Lettre* du pseudo-Aristote, le *corpus* pseudo-aréopagitique. Cette fermeture initiale du champ des études procliennes a eu cependant chez lui une contrepartie: il a d'abord cherché le platonisme chez Platon.

Aussi choquante qu'elle soit pour un lecteur moderne, l'inscription de Platon dans la *positio Stoicorum* a une signification positive. Le platonisme d'Albert n'est pas celui de Thomas. Dans son commentaire du *Liber de causis*,

---

[26] *Cf.* Albert le Grand, *Summa theologiae sive de mirabili scientia Dei* I, 3, 18, 1, *Opera omnia* XXXIV, pars I, 1978, 88, 9 - 13.

[27] On notera qu'en *De causis et processu universitatis* II, 3, 3, *Opera omnia* X, 1890, 551 a - b, Albert expose la même théorie en s'appuyant exclusivement sur le passage du *De generatione et corruptione* (II, 10, 336 a 27 - 28) traditionnellement associé à un adage — "*ex uno non fit nisi unum*" —, qu'il prétend également trouver dans la *Lettre sur le Principe de l'univers*. Dans le même texte, il développe une théorie dionysienne de l'analogie de réception tout en utilisant l'expression "*unum punctum in fine simplicitatis*." Le même ensemble, articulant Denys, Aristote, et l'adage "*ex uno non fit nisi unum*," figure dans le *De causis et processu universitatis*, I, 1, 10, *Opera omnia* X, 1890, 382 b, où, exposant la *decima proprietas* de l'Être nécessaire (selon Ghazælî, *Metaphysica* I, II), Albert rapporte l'adage pseudo-aristotélicien au texte authentique d'Aristote, puis note le plein accord de Denys avec "le Péripatéticien," tout en soulignant le différend (à ses yeux non justifié) opposant les "théologiens" (modernes) aux "péripatéticiens" sur la question de l'unicité de l'effet immédiat de Dieu: "*Decima proprietas est, quod a primo quod est necesse esse,* immediate non potest esse nisi unum: *et in hoc quidem iam omnes consenserunt Peripatetici, licet hoc quidem non intelligentes* Theologi *negaverunt.* Idem enim eodem modo se habens, non est natum facere nisi unum et idem (...). *Nec hoc est contra Theologos: quia Dionysius dicit quod ab ea quae sunt, per distantiam ab ipso accipiunt differentiam: relata autem ad ipsum et in ipsum, unum sunt et idem. Similiter* Peripateticus *concedit, quod a primo per primum et immediate quod aliquo modo distat ab ipso, tota producitur rerum universitatis.*" Sur ce point, *cf.* A. de Libera, '*Ex uno non fit nisi unum. La Lettre sur le Principe de l'univers* et les condamnations parisiennes de 1277', dans: *Historia Philosophiae Medii Aevi*, éd. B. Mojsisch et O. Pluta (Bochumer Studien zur Philosophie), Amsterdam, sous presse.

l'Aquinate définit la *positio platonica* à partir de la hiérarchie proclienne: il identifie les Idées aux "dieux" de Proclus, et place cet *ordo deorum* en fonction d'intermédiaire situé entre l'Un, d'une part, les Intellects et les âmes d'autre part; bref, il aborde les Idées à partir de Proclus et, pour les critiquer, de Denys.[28] Dans sa lecture du platonisme, Albert discute la doctrine des Idées à partir d'autres sources, et épouse d'autres regards. Son platonisme n'est pas médié par Proclus, mais, plus simplement et, en un sens, plus authentiquement, par Aristote.

Cela dit, si le platonisme d'Albert est avant tout celui d'Aristote, son interprétation n'en reste pas moins conflictuelle et comme travaillée par une multiplicité de thèmes éxogènes, sinon parasitaires. Comme je l'ai écrit ailleurs,[29] c'est avec Berthold de Moosburg que la pensée de Proclus s'est vue distinguée pour la première fois de celle de Platon et du péripatétisme empreint de néoplatonisme proposé par Avicenne et par le *Livre des causes*. Philosophant dans la perspective doxographique du péripatétisme arabe, Albert a, au contraire, proposé un programme concordataire entre Platon et Aristote dont le point de vue "péripatéticien" qu'il adoptait était déjà en lui-même la réalisation concrète. Il ne faudrait pas croire pour autant qu'il n'a jamais tenté de clarifier (quitte à les harmoniser ensuite) les positions respectives de Platon, d'une part, d'Aristote et des *peripatetici,* de l'autre.

C'est cet effort qu'il nous faut essayer de restituer aujourd'hui. Trois questions donc:

1. Par quels canaux Albert connaissait-il le platonisme?

2. Comment et dans quelle perspective philosophique précise a-t-il articulé les matériaux qui lui étaient accessibles?

3. Jusqu'à quel point les conditions d'accessibilité des thèses dites "platoniciennes" ont-elles contribué à modeler sa propre conception du sens, c'est-à-dire de la fonction philosophico-théologique, du platonisme?

Ne pouvant traiter ici à fond chacune de ces questions, je me contenterai d'examiner de ce point de vue un thème qui caractérise assez fidèlement la lecture albertinienne du "platonisme": la théorie des trois états de l'universel. Pourquoi ce thème? D'abord, parce qu'il touche à la doctrine des Idées et à la sémantique philosophique, deux questions également chères à M. le Professeur L.M. de Rijk, historien des philosophies anciennes et médiévales; ensuite, parce que, comme je l'ai dit, Albert range Platon parmi les stoïciens et que les stoïciens désignent à ses yeux l'ensemble des philosophes qui ont admis la doctrine des Idées; enfin, parce que c'est là, sans doute, un terrain idéal pour

---

28 *Cf.* sur ce point A. de Libera, 'Albert le Grand et Thomas d'Aquin interprètes du *Liber de causis*', *Revue des Sciences Philosophiques et Théologiques* 74 (1990), 347 - 378.
29 *Cf.* A. de Libera, 'Philosophie et théologie chez Albert le Grand et dans l'École dominicaine allemande', dans: *Die Kölner Universität im Mittelalter* (Miscellanea Mediaevalia 20), Berlin - New York 1989, 49 - 67.

suivre dans le détail la pratique exégétique de l'histoire par laquelle Albert tente de surmonter le hasard des transmissions et l'incohérence des corpus.

La distinction des universels *ante rem, in re* et *post rem* est un *best-seller* de la scolastique. Sa source semble être la *Logica* d'Avicenne, même si le philosophe iranien la considère lui-même comme *usuelle* ou, à tout le moins, comme fondée sur une distinction *commune* entre trois façons de considérer les cinq prédicables, à savoir, comme entités naturelles, logiques, ou intellectuelles:[30]

> Usus fuit, ut, cum haec quinque distinguerentur, diceretur secundum hoc, quod uno respectu sunt *naturalia* et alio respectu *logicalia* et alio *intellectualia*, et fortassis etiam diceretur, quod uno respectu sunt absque multiplicitate et alio cum multiplicitate. (...) Sed quia omnium quae sunt comparatio ad deum et ad angelos est, sicut comparatio artificialium, quae sunt apud nos, ad animam artificem, ideo id quod est in sapientia creatoris et angelorum et de veritate cogniti et comprehensi ex rebus naturalibus, habet esse *ante multitudinem*; quidquid autem intelligitur de eis, est aliqua intentio; et deinde acquiritur esse eis, quod est *in multiplicitate*, et cum sunt in multiplicitate, non sunt unum ullo modo, in sensibilibus enim forinsecus non est aliquid commune nisi tantum discretio et dispositio; deinde iterum habentur intelligentiae apud nos, *postquam fuerint in multiplicitate*. Hoc autem, quod sunt ante multiplicitatem (...) noster tractatus non sufficit ad hoc, quia ad alium tractatum sapientiae pertinet.

La distinction avicennienne entre universaux *in multiplicitate (naturalia), postquam fuerint in multiplicitatem (logicalia)* et *ante multiplicitatem (ou intellectualia)*, et, davantage encore, la focalisation sur la distinction binaire des *logicalia* et des *intellectualia*, a servi de fondement à une des thèses les plus caractéristiques des élèves d'Albert:[31] la distinction entre universel "logique" abstrait (ou universel de prédication) et universel "théologique" séparé (ou universel de production), développée dans la ligne de la théorie néoplatonicienne-proclienne de la "précontenance" par Dietrich de Freiberg[32] et Berthold de Moosburg,[33] mais déjà esquissée par le Colonais sur une autre base documentaire que nous préciserons ici.[34] Cette distinction a également débordé le cadre allemand. Elle a été reprise par beaucoup de réalistes du *XIVe* siècle, tels que Wycliff († 1384), opposant universaux "logiques" et "métaphysiques".[35] La portée historique et doctrinale de la distinction

---

[30] *Cf.* Avicenne, *Logica,* éd. Venise, 1508, ff° 12 ra et 12 va. Pour une analyse de ces textes, *cf.* A. de Libera, 'Théorie des universaux et réalisme logique chez Albert le Grand', *Revue des Sciences Philosophiques et Théologiques* 65 (1981), 55 - 74.

[31] *Cf.* A. de Libera, *La philosophie médiévale,* (Que sais-je? 1044), Paris 1989, 118 - 119.

[32] *Cf.* Dietrich de Freiberg, *De cognitione entium separatorum* 10, 1 - 4, éd. H. Steffan, 176, 1 - 177, 33.

[33] *Cf.* Berthold de Moosburg, *Super Elementationem Theologicam Procli, propositio* Ia, éd. M.R. Pagnoni-Sturlese et L. Sturlese, 74, 99 - 102.

[34] *Cf.* Albert le Grand, *Metaphysica* XI, 2, 12, *Opera omnia* XVI, pars I, 1964, 499, 71 - 86.

[35] *Cf.* J. Wycliff, *Tractatus de universalibus* II, 2, éd. I.J. Mueller, Oxford 1985, 62 - 63.

d'Avicenne est donc indéniable. Ce n'est pourtant pas à Avicenne qu'Albert
l'attribue en général, mais à ... Platon.

Comment expliquer cette attribution? Albert n'a pas pu trouver cette
doctrine dans Platon.[36] Le seul texte que l'on puisse raisonnablement invoquer
à l'appui de sa thèse paraît, de fait, assez lointain. Il s'agit du passage célèbre
du *Timée* où Platon différencie "trois genres d'être": les "modèles
intelligibles", les "imitations" ou "empreintes de ces êtres éternels", et "cette
sorte d'être difficile et obscure" qu'est le "Réceptacle" (c'est-à-dire la matière):

> At vero nunc trinum genus animo sumendum est: quod gignitur, item aliud in
> quo gignitur, praeterea tertium ex quo similitudinem trahit mutuaturque quod
> gignitur.[37]

L'analogie existe. Plus exactement, le parallélisme joue entre les deux
premières variétés d' "êtres" et les deux première sortes d'universaux. Mais, il
ne joue plus pour la matière et l'universel abstrait (*post rem*). Le renvoi à
Platon ne saurait davantage s'expliquer par la *Logica* d'Avicenne, dont le
témoignage est d'autant plus vague que la distinction a déjà pour lui toutes les
allures d'un lieu commun. Il y a donc entre le *Timée* et Avicenne une source —
grecque ou arabe — que nous ne savons identifier.

Restent d'autres intermédiaires, situés entre Platon-Avicenne et Albert lui-
même. A défaut de pouvoir remonter aux origines, c'est sur ce second groupe
que nous allons nous concentrer.

Dans le chapitre 5 du *De intellectu et intelligibili*, livre I, traité 2, *De
confutatione erroris Platoni*, Albert écrit:

> Platon distingue trois sortes d'universel. Le premier est antérieur à la chose:
> c'est la cause formelle qui précontient virtuellement tout l'être de la chose et
> existe avant elle à titre séparé et perpétuel. En effet, puisqu'il est cause, il
> importe qu'il soit antérieur à la chose, et puisqu'il n'y a transmutation,
> génération et corruption que dans la matière qui leur sert de sujet, cet universel
> doit être antérieur à tous les processus de ce genre; c'est pourquoi il est
> inengendrable et perpétuel. Mais puisque c'est lui qui donne l'être à la matière,
> il est également l'être des individus, tout comme le sceau donne figure à la cire
> – je parle d'une figure qui possède d'avance tout l'être et toute la vertu de la
> chose. Cet universel donc, Platon dit qu'il est séparé et mathématique, existant
> selon lui-même, et qu'il est le principe de la science et la cause formelle de la
> génération dans tous les engendrés. Il dit aussi qu'il reste extérieur aux
> engendrés, tout comme le modèle de bois qui sert à faire les chaussures reste
> extérieur au cuir, même si chaque chaussure est formée d'après lui. Enfin,

---

36 On notera, toutefois, que chez Gilles de Rome, *In I Sententias,* dist.xix, pars ii, qu. i,
Venetiis 1521, l'universel *ante rem* est identifié à l' "universel de Platon" (*quia causat res),*
l'universel *in re* "à celui d'Aristote" (*quia idem est in essentia cum rebus),* le troisième étant
"ajouté aux autres" non comme "espèce prédiquée de plusieurs" mais comme "espèce
semblable à plusieurs". Le thème de l'universel *in re* entendu comme *forma communis
fundata in suis individuis*, est illustré par Robert Grosseteste, *In Analytica Posteriora* I, 7,
éd. P. Rossi, Florence 1981, 141, 131 - 141, et discuté jusque chez Ockham, *In I Sententias,
dist. ii, qu. vii, Opera omnia* II, éd. G. Gál - S. Brown, St. Bonaventure (N.Y.) 1967, 232, 8 -
21.

puisqu'il est perpétuel, il dit qu'il est le principe de la science, et puisqu'il est immatériel, il dit qu'il est toujours et partout identique en tous les vivants animés. Le deuxième universel, il dit qu'il est seulement dans la chose, et que c'est une forme imprimée aux choses à partir du premier universel, et que de ce premier universel sortent les formes des choses, comme d'un certain *etymagium,* c'est-à-dire un sceau. Et ce deuxième universel, dit-il, est sujet au mouvement et à la mutation, à cause de la matière où il est engagé. Quant au troisième, il dit qu'il est postérieur à la chose, parce qu'il est tiré des choses par une considération; et par lui, dit-il, non seulement la chose est connue, mais encore elle est connue dans sa nature propre et par application de la forme aux réalités qui la particularisent et l'individualisent.[38]

A l'évidence, ce texte est un mélange. Deux types de langages distincts — celui néoplatonicien de la "précontenance" et celui platonicien des Idées et des choses ou principes mathématiques — y convergent, articulés sur une trame aristotélicienne où l'on serait, toutefois, bien en peine de trouver une théorie des cinq prédicables!

La "précontenance", qui ne figure ni chez Platon ni chez Aristote, est d'Albert. Nous en verrons les sources. L'exemple du sceau, en revanche, est authentique, puisqu'on le retrouve à la fois dans le *Timée* et dans la *Métaphysique.* Cependant, c'est bien la *Métaphysique* qui filtre la lecture du *Timée,* comme le révèle l'utilisation même du mot *etymagium.*[39] En effet, si le terme ἐκμαγεῖον est bien employé par Platon, il n'est pas repris chez Calcidius[40] qui lui préfère le latin *signacula.* L'origine de l'*etymagium* est la *Métaphysique,* particulièrement la *Translatio anonyma* ou *Media,* texte de base d'Albert.[41] Si, en rédigeant le *De intellectu,* Albert pense au *Timée,* ce qui va de soi, il est non moins clair qu'il a aussi et déjà mis en place une grille de lecture. Son Platon n'est plus seulement celui de Calcidius, c'est davantage celui d'Aristote exposant la distinction des Idées, des choses mathématiques et des choses naturelles.

Quelle peut être alors l'origine de la théorie des trois états de l'universel? Il faut ici distinguer deux domaines de problèmes: l'analyse de la théorie platonicienne des trois sortes de formes, celle de la théorie pseudo-platonicienne des trois sortes d'universaux.

Albert s'attaque à la théorie des trois sortes de formes selon Platon dans le *Super Ethica,*[42] à propos d'*Ethica Nicomachea,* 1095 a 26 - 28:

---

[37] *Cf.* Platon, *Timée* 50 c - d, éd. J.H. Waszink (*Plato Latinus* IV), Londres - Leyden 1962, 48, 12 - 14; trad. J. Moreau, in *Platon. Oeuvres complètes* II, Paris ¹1950, 469.

[38] *Cf.* Albert le Grand, *De intellectu et intelligibili* I, 2, 5, éd. P. Jammy, 1651, 249 b.

[39] Sur l'*echmagium* ou *etymagium, cf.* Albert le Grand, *Metaphysica* I, 4, 13, *Opera omnia* XVI, pars I, 1964, 66, 10 - 63 et 71 - 77.

[40] *Cf.* Platon, *Timée,* 50 c - d, 1962, p. 48, 6 - 7; Calcidius, *Commentarius, ibid.,* p. 309, 10; 317, 8; 322, 10 - 11.

[41] La *Vetustissima translatio* a "ex quodam ejkmagei'on" (*Aristoteles Latinus* XXV 1/1a, p. 22, 14); la *Vetus* "ex quadam fantasia" (*Aristoteles Latinus* XXV 1/1a, p. 105, 15); la *Media* "ex aliquo echmagio" (*Aristoteles Latinus* XXV 2, p. 22, 26).

[42] *Cf.* Albert le Grand, *Super Ethica* I, 3, 17, *Opera omnia* XVI, pars I, 1968, 15, 55 - 16, 20. Le *Super Ethica,* commentaire *per modum scripti,* qui, aux dires de Guillaume de

Quidam autem existimaverunt praeter multa haec bona aliud quid esse secundum seipsum, quod et omnibus causa est essendi bonum.[43]

Dès l'amorce, on voit qu'il n'est pas seul, que sa lecture est *guidée*. C'est, en effet, sous l'autorité explicite d'Eustrate,[44] que le Colonais s'autorise à poser qu'Aristote traite ici de Platon *("Hoc de Platone videtur dixisse")*, "Platon qui, ajoute-t-il, parlait des mœurs non en termes de morale mais quasi mathématiquement." On sait que cette notation rappelle lointainement un fragment du livre *Sur le bien* d'Aristote, où le Stagirite raconte une célèbre leçon (orale) de Platon:

> On était venu dans l'espoir d'y entendre parler de ce que les hommes tiennent habituellement pour des biens: richesse, santé, vigueur, en un mot *bonheur* qu'on pût admirer! Mais lorsqu'on n'entendit discourir que de mathématiques, — arithmétique, géométrie, astronomie, — pour aboutir, en fin de compte, à proclamer que *le Bien, c'est l'Un*, cela sembla à tout le monde un paradoxe; les uns haussèrent les épaules et les autres se fâchèrent.[45]

Malgré les limites de son dossier, Albert ne semble guère plus réceptif que le jeune Aristote à la mathématique morale. Cependant, c'est sur un point particulier de la théorie platonicienne des Idées qu'il axe sa propre critique. "Nous autres", dit-il (par quoi il faut sans doute entendre *nous autres péripatéticiens*), "nous plaçons les Idées en tant que *rationes* dans la *mens* divine", tandis que, comme le montre Averroès,[46] "les platoniciens qui veulent dire cela avec leurs *formae* n'y arrivent pas parfaitement." C'est un premier déficit.

En évoquant les trois sortes de formes distinguées par Platon – les divines, les mathématiques, les sensibles –, Albert a évidemment aussi à l'esprit la théorie des trois sortes de substances exposée et critiquée par Aristote en *Métaphysique* III, 2, 987 b – Idées, Choses intermédiaires ou mathématiques,

---

Tocco, a été rédigé par Thomas d'Aquin *("studiose collegit, et redegit in scriptis opus")* étant quasiment contemporain du *Super Dionysium De divinis nominibus* (dont on possède une version également rédigée par Thomas), on peut le situer aux alentours de 1250-1252 (on sait que Thomas fut l'élève d'Albert à Cologne de 1248 à 1252), c'est-à-dire entre la *Lectura sur les Sentences* et la grande paraphrase des œuvres d'Aristote, qui durant les années 1254-1257, était arrivée jusqu'au *De anima*, alors qu'Albert était provincial de Teutonia. Il ne faut pas confondre le *Super Ethica* avec les *Ethicorum libri X* ou *Ethica* (éd. A. Borgnet, tome VII), exposés *per modum commenti*.

[43] *Cf.* Aristote, *Ethique à Nicomaque* I, 2, 1095 a 26 - 28; transl. Robertus Lincolniensis, éd. W. Kübel, *op. cit.* 14, 82 - 83; trad. J. Tricot, Paris, 1967, 41: "Certains, enfin, pensent qu'en dehors de tous ces biens multiples il y a un autre bien qui existe par soi et qui est pour tous ces biens-là cause de leur bonté."

[44] *Cf.* Eustrate, *In Primum Aristotelis Moralium ad Nicomachum* 1095 a 26 - 28, éd. H.P.F. Mercken (Corpus Latinum Commentariorum in Aristotelem Graecorum, VI/1), Leiden 1973, 49, 84.

[45] Texte cité et traduit par R.A. Gauthier et J.Y. Jolif dans: *L'Ethique à Nicomaque, Commentaire*, II, Louvain - Paris 1970, 28. Tricot renvoie à l'*Ethique à Eudème* I, 8, 1217 b 2 - 15, le souvenir personnel du passage d'Aristote à l'Académie.

[46] *Cf.* Averroès, *Metaphysica* XII, comm. 36, Venise 1562, f° 318 vM.

substances sensibles. Cela lui fournit une seconde perspective critique, d'ailleurs consonnante à la première.

Platon soutient qu'il y a des *species* de toutes choses, séparées et existant par soi, dont sont issues les formes matérielles.

Aux yeux d'Albert, cette théorie est inadmissible.

On ne saurait accepter l'existence de Formes séparées extérieures à la Pensée divine, si ces Formes sont pour elle des modèles, sur quoi se régler elle-même dans son activité poiétique. Ce péché originel du platonisme est l'erreur théologique que l'on retrouvera chez les *formalizantes* du XVe siècle: c'est pourtant sinon le platonisme même, du moins, compte tenu de la rareté des matériaux de première main au Moyen Age, un platonisme moins inauthentique que ne le serait l'attribution à Platon d'une doctrine des Idées divines. C'est, en tout cas, la seule variété de platonisme que condamne explicitement Albert d'un bout à l'autre de son œuvre. En effet, et c'est là l'important, le Colonais accepte certaines versions du platonisme: c'est ainsi que la théorie des Formes séparées a un droit de cité relatif, dès lors qu'elle s'insère dans un système de causalité émanative, dont la figure centrale, le *Dator formarum* d'Avicenne et de Ghazâlî, avatar médiéval de l'Ame du monde, porte une vision du platonisme comme théologie philosophique de l'*inductio formarum,* selon un ensemble articulé de thèses qui doit évidemment davantage au péripatétisme arabe et au néoplatonisme juif (Isaac Israeli) qu'à l'auteur du *Timée.* La *Metaphysica* d'Albert donne une description précise de cette *positio platonica* composite, où toutes les variétés de platonisme viennent s'amalgamer:[47] 1. Toutes choses ont été faites par les dieux secondaires auxquels le Dieu des dieux (le Démiurge) a confié la "semence de la génération";[48] 2. ces dieux secondaires sont les étoiles et les sphères célestes, qui "ont mis en mouvement la matière pour produire la totalité des réalités engendrables"; 3. la semence confiée aux dieux secondaires est une *forma formans* qui informe univoquement la matière *ad conveniens sibi in nomine*; 4. l'agent de la communication de la forme à la matière dernière est le "Donateur des formes" (*Dator formarum*);[49] 5. cette communication de la forme à la

---

[47] *Cf.* Albert le Grand, *Metaphysica* XI, 1, 8, *Opera omnia* XVI, pars II, 1964, 468, 62 - 469, 3.

[48] *Cf.* Platon, *Timée,* 41 c d, transl. Calcidius, 1962, 37, 9 - 12: "*Huius ergo universi generis sementem faciam vobisque tradam, vos cetera exsequi par est.*" Sur ce thème, *cf.* Macrobe, *In Somnium Scipionis* I, 12, éd. J. Willis, 47, 30 *sqq. Cf.* en outre, Albert le Grand, *De causis et processu universitatis* I, 2, 13, *Opera omnia* X, 1890, 630 b; *Metaphysica* I, 3, 4, *Opera omnia* XVI, pars I, 1960, 34, 70; *De fato* 5, 1, éd. P. Simon, *Opera omnia* XVII, pars I, 1975, 77, 1 - 18.

[49] Le *Liber de natura et origine animae* I, 2, *Opera omnia* XII, pars I, 1955, 5, 51 - 58 attribue explicitement la doctrine à Platon et à Pythagore, deux "stoïciens" (attribution reprise dans le *Super Dionysium De divinis nominibus* 2, n. 44, *Opera omnia* XXXVII, pars I, 1972, 73, 28 - 29): "*Et ideo dixerunt a datore primo dari formas et non esse in materia, sed tamen materiam mereri formam,* meritum materiae *vocantes id quod Aristoteles vocavit formae incohationem sive potentiam sive privationem.*" Le renvoi à Platon d'une doctrine typiquement avicennienne peut s'autoriser lointainement du *Timée,* 1962, 22, 19 - 20:

matière peut être appelée une "induction" (*inductio formarum*); 6. la forme induite, ou introduite, peut être appelée "image-copie" (*imago*), au sens où elle imite la forme extérieure à la matière, "écho" (*resultatio*) ou "ombre" (*umbra*), au sens où "elle s'obscurcit en entrant dans la matière"; 7. la forme-modèle, extérieure à la matière, est un "exemplaire" (*exemplar*); 8. la causalité *ad par* qui relie l'exemplaire à son ectype est une causalité univoque, par quoi "toute l'œuvre de la nature est celle d'une Intelligence".

Face à ce complexe la position d'Albert est évidemment nuancée. L'ensemble de la théorie est rejeté pour la causalité naturelle: l'induction des formes doit céder le pas à l'éduction des formes. Chaque thèse est en outre critiquable dans son contenu, sa formule ou son application. Reste que ce platonisme-là, qui combine Platon et Plotin, est tout de même moins nocif qu'une théorie des Formes sans théologie — que cette théologie soit ou non directement issue du *Timée*. L'intention théologique anime toute la philosophie d'Albert, qui fait du *Livre des causes* le couronnement de la *Métaphysique*. Tout en rejetant le *Dator formarum*, le Colonais n'a aucune raison de rejeter l'intégralité d'une doctrine — même imparfaite — de la création; une doctrine qui, faisant place à un Dieu des dieux et à une influence des étoiles et des sphères, laisse ouverte la possibilité d'une théologie des Intelligences qui, on le sait, reste, à ses yeux, la fine pointe du péripatétisme. Une fois amendé par l'*eductio formarum* le platonisme est une philosophie à peu près viable.

Reste qu'on ne voit pas qu'une théologie platonicienne des Formes, même rectifiée, conduise le moins du monde à une doctrine des trois états de l'universel. Pour expliquer l'attribution à Platon d'une théorie du *triplex universale*, il semble qu'il faille donc inéluctablement quitter le *Timée* et la critique aristotélicienne du platonisme, pour s'attacher à une tradition interprétative plus large, *platonicienne sans avoir Platon pour objet* : celle des commentateurs d'Aristote.

Il n'y a là nul paradoxe. Le Platon d'Albert n'est qu'un personnage théorique engagé dans une dramaturgie d'origine péripatéticienne. Pour reconstituer la trame de l'intrigue, il faut donc partir du corpus albertinien et chercher les principes de ce qu'on pourrait appeler sa logique d'attribution.

Sans prétendre à l'exhaustivité, on peut distinguer au moins six types d'assignation de la doctrine du *triplex universale:* la première en fait un simple lieu commun;[50] la deuxième l'attribue aux Antiqui;[51] la troisième, majoritaire,

---

"*Itaque consequenter cuncta sui similia, prout cuiusque natura* capax beatitudinis *esse poterat, effici voluit.*" La notion du "mérite de la matière" semble être un équivalent de celle d' "aptitude" *(secundum aptitudinem materiae),* comme en témoigne le passage parallèle de *Metaphysica* XI, 1, 11, *Opera omnia* XVI, pars II, 1964, 468, 68 - 70: "*Hanc etiam et huiusmodi formam dicit <Plato> communicari materiae per datorem formarum et ipsam materiam formae aptari recipienda.*" Sur le *Dator formarum* et Platon, *cf.* Averroès, *Metaphysica* XII, comm. 18, Venise 1562, ff° 304 rA - B, 304 vG.

[50] *Cf.* Albert le Grand, *De sex principiis* I, 2, *Opera omnia* X, 1890, t. I, p. 308 a.

à Platon;[52] la quatrième à "Platon selon le Commentateur";[53] la cinquième au "Commentateur";[54] la sixième à Eustrate.[55]

Nous ne pouvons examiner ici la totalité du corpus. Nous voudrions, en revanche, revenir sur certains textes dont nous avons tenté une première analyse dans notre livre, *Albert le Grand et la philosophie*: *Super Ethica* I, 5, 28-29; *Super Ethica* I, 2, 9; *Super Dionysium De divinis nominibus* 2, 83-84.

Le *Super Ethica*, livre I, leçon 5, §§ 28 - 29, est à nouveau consacré à un passage de l'*Ethique* où Aristote critique la théorie platonicienne du Bien.

> Ferentes autem opinionem hanc non faciebant ideas, in quibus prius et posterius dicebant; propter quod neque numerum ideam constituebant.[56]

Selon Aristote, la thèse la plus générale de Platon est qu'il ne peut y avoir de genre commun, de quiddité commune, pour les essences hiérarchisées dans lesquelles il existe de l'avant et de l'après. Pour un platonicien, il ne peut donc y avoir idées des choses admettant une subordination hiérarchique, autrement dit des nombres, qu'il s'agisse des nombres mathématiques ou plutôt des nombres idéaux. Aux yeux d'Aristote, cette thèse, mathématique, peut être aisément retournée contre Platon métaphysicien.

Le principal argument du Stagirite est fondé sur la notion de priorité de la substance. Puisque le Bien s'affirme et dans l' "essence" ou substance (*in eo quod quid*) et dans la qualité (*in quali*) et dans la relation (*in ad aliquid*), puis, en outre, que la substance (*substantia*) possède une antériorité naturelle sur les autres catégories, il ne saurait y avoir Idée du Bien aux yeux d'un platonicien conséquent.

Commentant l'*Éthique*, Albert suit pied à pied l'argumentation d'Aristote, mais sa lecture est tout sauf servile.

Aristote, dit-il, "impose à Platon" (*imponit Platoni*) une certaine doctrine: l'univocité de l'Etre. Avant de se demander si cette prosopopée a le moindre fondement, le Colonais met en scène une discussion sur la pertinence même de la doctrine rapportée. Cette discussion prend la forme d'une question – peut-

---

[51] *Cf.* Albert le Grand, *De praedicabilibus* II, 3, éd. A. Borgnet, *Opera omnia* X, 1890, t. 1, p. 24 b.

[52] *Cf.* Albert le Grand, *Physica* I, 1, 6, *Opera omnia* IV, pars I, 1987, 10, 53 - 78; *De anima* I, 1, 4, *Opera omnia* VII, pars I, 1968, 8, 81 - 89, 10; *De intellectu et intelligibili* I, 1, 5, éd. P. Jammy, 1651, 249 a - b; *Liber de natura et origine animae* I, 2, *Opera omnia* XII, 1955, 4, 51 - 92; *Super Ethica* I, 3, 17, *Opera omnia* XIV, pars I, 1968 - 1972, 15, 55 - 16, 20.

[53] *Cf.* Albert le Grand, *Super Ethica* I, 5, 29, *Opera omnia* XIV, pars I, 1968 - 1972, 25, 1 - 34.

[54] *Cf.* Albert le Grand, *Super Ethica* I, 2, 9, *Opera omnia* XIV, pars I, 1968 - 1972, I, 2, 9; 7, 26 - 41; *Super Dionysium De divinis nominibus* 2, n. 84, *Opera omnia* XXVII, pars I, 1972, 97, 49 - 50.

[55] *Cf.* Albert le Grand, *Summa theologiae sive de mirabili scientia dei* I, 6, 26, 1; *Opera omnia* XXXIV, pars I, 1978, 183, 1 - 5.

[56] *Cf.* Aristote, *Éthique à Nicomaque* I, 4, 1096 a 17 - 19.

être directement issue d'une *disputatio in scolis* (on sait que le *Super Ethica* étant le compte-rendu de l'enseignement d'Albert, il fait normalement alterner gloses et questions).

Telle que la restitue Albert (à moins qu'il ne faille dire Albert-Thomas, si l'on compte la part du rédacteur), la question s'organise autour de cinq arguments destinés à montrer que "Platon ne pouvait faire autrement" que de poser la doctrine que lui impose Aristote (*quod hoc erat necessarium Platoni dicere*). C'est donc une défense de l'univocité en même temps que de la théorie des Idées:

1 – Ce qui convient dans un principe est univoque, car il n'y a d'autre alternative à l'univocité que l'équivocité *a casu* — (ἀπὸ τύχης), par opposition à l'homonymie, volontaire, *a consilio* (ἀπὸ διανοίας)[57]—, or ce qui a une Idée une convient nécessairement dans un unique principe.

2 – On ne peut invoquer ici l'analogie, car si les équivoques se ramènent aux univoques, cela vaut à plus forte raison des termes analogiques. Cet argument s'appuie sur un adage, *omnia aequivoca reducuntur ad univoca,* généralement attribué par les médiévaux à Aristote ou à Averroès.

3 – L'idée une de différents "idéats" (*ideatorum*) ne peut se rapporter à eux que de deux manières: identique ou non-identique. Si le rapport est non-identique, elle n'est pas leur principe; si le rapport est identique, elle ne peut être qu'univoque.

4 – On ne peut dire qu'une diversité dans la participation vient seulement des participants. En effet, pareille diversité ne peut être que matérielle. Elle ne change donc rien à l'espèce, puisqu'elle ne fait pas varier son unité. Donc, la même nature est bien participée par toutes les réalités appartenant à une même espèce.

5 – Tout ce qui a similitude de nature est de même espèce. Or "toutes les choses désirent un certain principe unique" (*unum principium*), et "toute chose ne désire que son semblable"; donc si l'on pose un premier dans une certaine nature, tout ce qui possède cette nature sera de même espèce; donc tout ce dont il y a une idée sera univoque. Cet argument repose doublement sur Boèce: *De Consolatione Philosophiae* III, prose 11 (744 b): "*Omnia igitur, inquit, unum desiderant*"; *De hebdomadibus* 1311 D - 1312 A: "*Omne tendit ad simile*".

Après l'exposé des *rationes*, Albert expose sa solution:

> *Dicendum secundum Commentatorem* quod hoc falso imponit Aristoteles Platoni ("selon le Commentateur, Aristote a eu tort d'attribuer ou d'imposer cette doctrine à Platon").

---

[57] Sur ces distinctions d'origine porphyrienne, *cf.* A. de Libera, 'Les sources gréco-arabes de la théorie médiévale de l'analogie de l'être', *Les études philosophiques* 3 - 4 (1989), 319 - 345.

La stratégie est donc claire. Elle consiste à épouser, contre Aristote, le point de vue d'Eustrate, métropolite de Nicée, dont, en 1247-1248, Robert Grosseteste a publié de larges extraits, annexés à sa propre version de l'*Ethica*.

On sait que la doctrine *platonicienne* invoquée par Eustrate pour contrer l'interprétation aristotélicienne de Platon est précisément la doctrine des trois sortes d'universaux, *triplex universale*.

En *Super Ethica* I, 5, Albert admet donc que la doctrine platonicienne des universaux vue par Eustrate peut légitimement rectifier la doctrine platonicienne des Idées vue par Aristote. Naturellement, cette rectification ne va pas sans une certaine "réécriture", typique du style de travail philosophique albertinien.

Il y a, dit-il, trois sortes d'universaux selon Eustrate:

– l'universel *ante rem* précontient et possède d'avance (*praehabet*) la chose ou nature dont il est le principe formel et producteur. Étant l'Idée de cette nature, il réside à ce titre même dans le Premier moteur, car "de même que toutes les formes sont en puissance dans la matière première, elles sont en acte dans le Premier moteur." C'est de telles formes que viennent celles qui sont dans la matière, de même que "tout ce qui est en puissance est tiré *(trahitur)* et mené à l'acte par ce qui est en acte."

– l'universel *in re* est la nature participée en tant qu'elle est distribuée ou distribuable en acte dans plusieurs.

– l'universel *post rem* est ce que l'âme "abstrait" de la chose. C'est de lui qu'Aristote dit qu'il est un accident quant à l'être,[58] c'est-à-dire l'être d'abstraction, qui est le sien.

Ainsi donc: étant donné que la temporalité, le multiple et l'unité, donc aussi l'ordre de l'avant et de l'après, suivent (*consequuntur*) la nature en tant que participée, et puisqu'on ne peut abstraire d'une chose que ce qui est en elle, on ne peut abstraire quelque chose d'un et de raison une des choses où une certaine nature réside selon l'avant et l'après; mais, justement, si on la considère dans le Premier principe, une nature reste extérieure à toutes ces dispositions accidentelles; c'est pourquoi Platon "a soutenu que l'universel qui est Idée en Dieu n'a dans le Premier ni ordre de l'avant et de l'après *ni nombre*."

Le résultat de cette démonstration est sans ambiguïté aucune: Aristote n'a rien compris à Platon, car *il a confondu logique et théologie*. "Il lui a fait dire" (*imposuit*) que l'universel en tant que nature participée était un et univoque et non pas un selon l'analogie (*per prius et posterius*). Or ce qui est logiquement vrai est métaphysiquement — ou plutôt théologiquement — faux. L'universel logique est univoque, l'universel théologique n'est pas univoque.[59] Soutenir

---

[58] *Cf.* Aristote, *Metaphysica* VII, 13 - 14, 1038 b 1 - 1039 b 19.

[59] La "précontenance" ou "précompréhension" *(praecomprehensivitas)* qui caractérise l'universalité de la Cause première dans sa "primauté" (*primitas*) et sa "noblesse" (*nobilitas*) n'est pas l'univocité du concept logique. Sur ce point *cf.* Berthold de Moosburg, *Super*

une telle univocité est donc bien une erreur, mais précisément ce n'est pas la
thèse de Platon.

Plus d'un lecteur restera sans voix devant cette reconstruction. N'est-ce
pas, en effet, Albert lui-même qui, tantôt, reprochait aux platoniciens de ne pas
poser les Idées dans la *mens divina*? Comment peut-il à quelques pages de
distance se séparer ainsi d'Averroès et troquer la doctrine des Formes séparées
pour celle des Idées divines? L'explication est simple: Albert expose le Platon
d'Eustrate.[60] Exposé provisoire ou provisionnel, pour ne pas dire heuristique,
puisque, dans la suite du texte, une fois réfutés les arguments avancés en faveur
de l'univocité, il ne craint pas de conclure:

> Et hoc dictum sit secundum opinionem Commentatoris. Si tamen verum est,
> quod Aristoteles imponit Platoni, ut dictum est supra, absolute male dixit.

Il est clair que ce qu'Aristote "impose" à Platon correspond davantage à son
enseignement authentique qu'une doctrine des Idées divines: ailleurs Albert
suit donc le plus souvent Aristote contre Platon, ou plutôt, il adopte en général
l'interprétation aristotélicienne plutôt que celle d'Eustrate. On peut se demander pourquoi il prend ici le parti d'Eustrate. La raison la plus immédiate est
que, exposant l'*Ethique*, il épouse quasi naturellement les perspectives de son
"Commentateur". Reste à se demander si sa lecture d'Eustrate est elle-même
fidèle. On va voir qu'elle est, pour le moins, "enrichie".

Albert utilise souvent Eustrate.

En psychologie, il lui doit une notion d'*intellectus possessus*, qui lui
permet de rendre plus crédible le caractère aristotélicien d'une notion,
essentiellement farabienne, d'*intellectus adeptus*, qui commande toute sa
doctrine philosophique de la "conjonction" de l'homme à l'Intellect séparé.[61]

Elementationem Theologicam Procli, propositio 26a, éd. L. Sturlese - M.R. Pagnoni-
Sturlese - B. Mojsisch (Corpus Philosophorum Teutonicorum Medii Aevi VI/2), p. 154, 63 -
65: "*Et sic etiam dicitur universalis universalitate actus et separationis, non logica:
Praecomprehendit enim omnia et extendit se ad simpliciter omnia suae intentioni subiecta.*"

[60] Eustrate présente explicitement Platon et les platoniciens comme partisans des Idées
divines *(in conditoris Dei mente existentes)*, "présubsistantes" aux formes *(species)* existant
dans les corps, Cf. Eustrate, *In Primum Aristotelis Moralium ad Nicomachum*, 1096 a 10 -
14; 1973, 70, 30 - 71, 45. Sur la doctrine des Idées chez Eustrate, *cf.* K. Giocarinis,
'Eustratius of Nicaea's Defense of the Doctrine of Ideas', *Franciscan Studies* 12 (1964), 159
- 204. On peut aussi invoquer Augustin, dont la célèbre *Quaestio de Ideis (Quaestiones
LXXXIII*, qu. 46; Bibliothèque Augustinienne 10, Paris 1952, 123), est souvent interprétée
comme tendant à enrôler Platon sous la bannière des Idées divines. Mais il s'agit déjà là
d'une interprétation, dont le principal promoteur est précisément le traducteur d'Eustrate,
Robert Grosseteste. Sur Grosseteste, *cf.* Kaluza, 'Le *De universale reali* de Jean de
Maisonneuve', 485.

[61] *Cf.* Albert le Grand, *De XV problematibus, Opera omnia* I, 1975, 32, 62 - 71. *Cf.*
également, *De causis et processu universitatis* I, 2, 25, *Opera omnia* X, 1890, 510 a: "*Taliter
ergo dictus intellectus dictis rationibus* possessus *vel* adeptus *vocatur (...) propter quod dicit
Eustratius, quod possessus intellectus numquam potest tantum depurari et perfici, quod per
essentiam intellectus efficiatur, vel illi similis, nisi per analogiam suae possibilitatis*"*;*
même doctrine en *De causis et processu universitatis* II, 2, 32, *Opera omnia* X, 527 b - 528
a. Sur ce point *cf.* Eustrate, *Ethica Nicomachea* VI, 5, éd. Heylbut 314, 9 - 10; *transl. ant.,*

Hoc igitur omnium Peripateticorum antiqua est positio, secundum quod eam Alfarabium determinavit. Ex qua sequitur intellectum possibilem intelligibilium omnium esse speciem et non omnino potentiam esse materialem ad ipsa. Post hoc Graeci sapientes, Porphyrius scilicet et Eustratius, Aspasius et Michael Ephesius et quam plures alii venerunt praeter Alexandrum, qui Epicuro consentit, qui omnes intellectum hominis intellectum possessum et non de natura intelligentiae existentem esse dixerunt. Et quem Graeci sapientes possessum, eundem Arabum philosophi Avicenna, Averroes, Abubacher et quidam alii adeptum esse dicebant, quia id quod possessum est, aliud est alterius naturae a possidente.

Dans le même sens, il lui attribue, ainsi qu'à Michel d'Éphèse, une véritable doctrine de la félicité mentale – autre thème farabien qui lui permet de placer l'union à l'Intellect au sommet de la vie philosophique, réalisation de l'essence pensante de l'homme où est censée culminer la "sagesse théorétique" louée par Aristote dans l'*Éthique à Nicomaque*.[62]

On peut discuter cette démarche, qui "(f)arabise" sans doute à l'excès l'enseignement pseudo-"philosophal" d'un chrétien byzantin. Reste que la lecture d'ensemble est assez fidèle, et qu'Albert n'a d'autre moyen de comprendre le singulier "aristotélisme" d'Eustrate qu'à le rapprocher d'autres concordats philosophiques, dont Fârâbî lui offre à la fois le modèle et la tentation.

S'agissant des Idées, Albert fait deux emprunts au "Commentateur":

– l'un est indirect, puisqu'il ne concerne pas *prima facie* la doctrine des Idées: il s'agit de la notion de "précontenance", qu'il trouve *aussi* chez Denys (c'est le προέχειν des *Noms divins*),[63] mais dont il lit la *même* figuration dite *platonicienne* dans l'analyse eustratienne du Bien[64] comme "principe unique de tous les êtres", "possédant tout être de façon éminente" — *superhabens*:

Vat. lat. 2171, f° 110 va: "(...) *sed non substantialiter existere in ipsa intellectum ponit, sed* possessum *et ut habitum* supervenientem." Cf., enfin, Albert le Grand, *Ethica* VI, 2, 13, éd. A. Borgnet, p. 423 et VI, 2, 18, éd. A. Borgnet, p. 433. Sur la distinction entre Abubacher et al-Færæbî, *cf. supra*, note 3.

[62] *Cf.* Albert le Grand, *De anima* III, 3, 11, *Opera omnia* VII, pars I, 1968, 222, 4 - 14, qui renvoie aux "péripatéticiens", c'est-à-dire Aristote, *Éthique à Nicomaque* X, 7, 1175 b 5 - 1178 a 9, mais aussi "Eustrate et Michel d'Ephèse", commentateurs de l'*Éthique*, expressément cités.

[63] *Cf. e.g.* Denys le Pseudo-Aréopagite, *De divinis nominibus* 13, n. 2, *PG* 3, 977 D; *cf.* dans Albert le Grand, *Super Dionysium De divinis nominibus*, *Opera omnia* XXXVII, pars I, 1972, 432, 70 - 73 ("(...) *sicut omnia in seipso praehabens et supermanans secundum unam impausabilem et eandem et superplenam et imminorabilem largitionem (...)*").

[64] Je remercie ici vivement M. le prof. H.P.F. Mercken, éditeur d'Eustrate, qui, lors des discussions, a bien voulu clarifier ce point. J'ajouterai que dans son texte plus tardif des *Ethicorum libri X*, Albert reconnaît explicitement l'existence d'une théorie *platonicienne* de la "précontenance" en réunissant lui même, comme ils le sont de fait, les deux passages d'Eustrate *ici* distingués: le premier qui porte sur le Bien comme tel, le second sur les Idées platoniciennes. *Cf.* Albert le Grand, *Ethica* X, I, 5, 12, 23, *Opera omnia* VII, 1891, 72: "(...) *oportet nos positionem Platonis exponere. Ad hoc autem sex notanda sunt, quorum primum est, quod Plato posuit unum et universale principium, quod est omnia praehabens (...).*" Sur Albert et Eustrate, *cf.* l'excellente analyse de M.J.F.M. Hoenen, *Marsilius van Inghen († 1396) over het goddelijke weten. Zijn plaats in de ontwikkeling van de opvattingen over het goddelijke weten ca. 1255-1396*, I, Nijmegen 1989, 358 - 359.

"surpossédant tout" — et *praehabens*: "précontenant tout" — "en lui-même de façon surintellectuelle (*superintelligibiliter*) et suressentielle (*supersubstantialiter*)."[65]

– l'autre est immédiat: il s'agit d'une théorie *de universali et toto circa Platonem* distinguant trois sortes de "tout" où, par-delà un recours aux notions aristotéliciennes d'homéomères et d'anoméomères utilisées pour définir l'universel *ex partibus* (= *in re*), est clairement posée l'équivalence entre universel *in partibus* (= *post rem*) et intelligible logique:[66]

> Tripliciter enim aiunt dici totum: ante partes, ex partibus, in partibus. *Ante partes* quidem illas species, quoniam ante multa quae ad illas, simplicissimas existentes et immateriales, facta sunt unaquaeque illarum subsistit. *Ex partibus* autem composita et in multa partita, sive homoiomera (id est similium partium), ut lapis in lapides, totum existens ad partes in quas divisibilis est, quarum unaquaeque et nomen et rationem totius recipit, sive anhomoiomera (id est dissimilium partium), ut homo in manus, pedes, caput. Nulla enim partium hominis similis est toti, ut neque nomen neque rationem totius recipiens. *In partibus* autem, ut *intelligibilia*, quae et de multis et posteriora generatione dicuntur.

L'assimilation albertinienne du platonisme grâce à la rencontre, historiquement et philologiquement fondée, entre Eustrate et Denys, est une nouveauté importante, qui a eu une fortune indéniable. On la retrouve encore, en plein XIVe siècle, chez le nominaliste Marsile d'Inghen, quand, contre toute attente, il expose une doctrine des Idées de Platon *secundum mentem beati Dionysii – opinio antiqua*, qui, comme l'a bien montré M. Hoenen, est entièrement tirée d'Eustrate et d'Albert *lecteur d'Eustrate*.[67]

Pourtant, et c'est là l'autre aspect décisif de la lecture albertinienne, deux thèses argumentant sa présentation de la doctrine "platonicienne" de l'universel *ante rem* ne sont ni chez Platon, ni chez Denys, ni chez Eustrate!

En premier lieu, l'adage selon lequel "les formes sont en acte dans le Premier moteur", fait partie des autorités d'Averroès dans le recueil des *Auctoritates Aristotelis*[68] et il est vraisemblablement tiré de *Metaphysica* XII, comm. 18, *in fine*. Albert ne l'ignore pas, puisqu'il le cite lui-même sous ce patronage dans le *Super Dionysium De divinis nominibus* :

> Unde dicit Commentator in XI *Metaphysicae*, quod omnes formae sunt in actu in primo motore et in potentia in prima materia.[69]

---

[65] *Cf.* Eustrate, *In Primum Aristotelis Moralium ad Nicomachum*, 1096 a 10 - 14, éd. 1973, 68, 69 - 71.

[66] *Cf. ibid.*, 1096 a 10 - 14; 1973, 69, 4 - 70, 14.

[67] *Cf.* M.J.F.M. Hoenen, *Marsilius van Inghen († 1396)* ..., 360 - 361, et le texte des *Quaestiones super quattuor libros Sententiarum*, liber I, qu. 1, art. 1, ff° 2 rb - va de Marsile, cité à la note 217.

[68] *Cf. Auctoritates Aristotelis* 1, n. 283, éd. J. Hamesse, 1974, 139, 87 - 88: "*Quicquid est in materia prima potentia passiva, in primo motore est potentia activa.*"

[69] *Cf.* Albert le Grand, *Super Dionysium De divinis nominibus* 2, n. 45, *Opera omnia* XXXVII, pars I, 1972, 73, 60 - 62.

En second lieu, l'adage selon quoi "tout ce qui est en puissance est mené à l'acte par ce qui est en acte" est d'Aristote,[70] pour qui "d'un être en puissance un être en acte est toujours engendré par un autre être en acte."[71]

Albert incorpore donc dans sa restitution de la doctrine de "Platon selon Eustrate" deux théorèmes étrangers à l'un comme à l'autre, le premier emprunté à Averroès, le second à Aristote! Ce montage nous a d'abord surpris. Il y va pourtant de la doctrine même d'Albert, laquelle ne réclame pas seulement un Platon possible contre le Platon réel, ni un platonisme filtré par Aristote et ses commentateurs byzantins ou arabes, mais aussi, et jusqu'à un certain point, un Aristote lui-même platonisé en retour, et avec les mêmes ingrédients.

Le *Super Ethica*, livre I, leçon 2, § 9 est l'illustration parfaite de cette "replatonisation" d'Aristote[72] à laquelle Albert sacrifie souvent — et sacrifie volontiers. Le support textuel se prête d'ailleurs à merveille à l'opération, puisqu'il s'agit du début de l'*Ethique*, 1094 a 1 *sqq.*: *ideo bene enuntiaverunt bonum, quod omnia appetunt,*[73] texte dont l'aspect concordataire est évident.

La question posée au § 9 est: "Toutes choses peuvent-elles désirer un seul et même Bien?"

Un aristotélicien dur attendrait une homonymie pure et simple, chaque chose recherchant son propre bien. Mais ce n'est pas la réponse d'Albert. Et pour cause, puisque, de nouveau, il adopte le point de vue d'Eustrate. En bref: les choses ne cherchent pas un même bien selon le sujet *(subiecto),* mais quelque chose d'"un exemplairement" *(exemplariter).* Ce qui autorise cette distinction entre unité subjective et unité exemplaire ne saurait, désormais, nous surprendre. C'est la distinction — ici clairement attribuée à Eustrate — entre trois universels: l'universel *cum re* ou *forma rei,* l'universel *post rem,* qui est *abstractum a re,* et l'universel *ante rem.*

L'universel *ante rem* n'est pas prédicable des choses, c'est "ce en quoi une certaine nature est *primo,* à titre premier, et ce dont elle descend exemplairement en tout ce qui l'imite en cette nature", *secundum suam proportionem,* selon sa proportion, c'est-à-dire son analogie. En effet, précise Albert, "ce qui est premier est cause de tout ce qui est postérieur", tel le feu qui cause la chaleur en tout ce qui est chaud.

On a vu que la tripartition de l'universel pouvait être légitimement tirée d'Eustrate, l'exégèse albertinienne est donc, sur ce point, fondée. Il n'en va pas de même, en revanche, du principe qui fonde la théorie de la causalité

---

[70] *Cf.* Aristote, *Metaphysica* IX, 8, 1049 b 24 - 25.
[71] *Cf.* Aristote, *ibid.*, 1049 b 24 - 25, trad. Tricot, Paris 1966, 508.
[72] *Cf.* Albert le Grand, *Super Ethica* I, 2, 9, *Opera omnia* XIV, pars I, 1968 - 1972, 7.
[73] *Cf.* Aristote, *Ethique à Nicomaque* I, 1, 1094 a 1 *sqq.*, trad. J. Tricot, p. 32: "(...) ainsi a-t-on déclaré avec raison que le Bien est ce à quoi toutes choses tendent." *Cf.* dans le même sens, *Topiques* III, 1, 116 a 19 - 20.

exemplaire ou analogique de l'universel *ante rem*: l'unité d'action dans une même série ou ordre causal. Quelle est sa source? Albert la précise lui-même: Aristote, *Metaphysica* II, 1.[74] Il va de soi qu'on ne trouve ni théorie de l'"exemplarité" ni notion d'un ordre causal — au sens néoplatonicien du terme — dans l'original aristotélicien.

Que signifie ce nouveau collage? Il faut souligner qu'Aristote sert ici une tentative philosophique ailleurs placée — plus naturellement — sous le signe de Platon: la définition conceptuelle d'une causalité formelle prise dans le sens de la cause formelle-exemplaire et non pas formelle-univoque. Or, paradoxalement, c'est bien contre le Platon d'Aristote, partisan de l'univocité, que se risque, toujours à travers Aristote, cette synonymie nouvelle, une synonymie qu'Albert lui-même explore tantôt sous le titre de causalité exemplaire, tantôt sous celui, plus déconcertant, d'univocité d'analogie (*univocitas quae est analogia*).

Ne pouvant analyser en détail cette notion cardinale de la philosophie albertinienne qu'est l'univocité selon l'analogie, nous nous contenterons d'en noter les principaux traits. Telle que nous la comprenons, l'univocité d'analogie est d'abord une refonte de la notion aristotélicienne de paronymie où la ci-devant *denominatio*, intermédiaire entre synonymie et homonymie pures, acquiert le statut d'un opérateur causal. Ensuite et surtout, c'est ce qui assume dans le langage de l'être le mouvement par lequel le Bien descend, s'épanche exemplairement dans tous les biens. Pour Albert, qui parle en *philosophus theologizans*, tous les biens désirent un seul et même Bien, mais l'unité de ce Bien n'est pas celle d'un concept univoque. L'Un-et-Bien est *un par mode d'exemplarité*, et non pas *un logiquement*, c'est-à-dire "un en raison", selon l'espèce ou le genre. La "Bonté que toutes choses désirent" n'est pas selon une raison unique. Les partisans de l'univocité stricte, de l'univocité générique, bref les platoniciens selon la *Métaphysique* d'Aristote, ont donc tort. Mais qu'est-ce qui bloque l'univocité au sens strict du terme? Qu'est-ce qui rend légitime le recours à l'analogie? On attendrait, parallélisme oblige, cette polysémie de l'être et du bon qui est traditionnellement assumée dans la théorie aristotélicienne de la "signification focale (*focal meaning*) de l'" "être". Albert ne recourt pas à cette notion — et pour cause. L'analogie qu'il oppose à l'univocité n'est pas l'*analogia* des "philosophes", mais, dit-il, l'"analogie des théologiens".

D'une formule: si "la Bonté que toutes choses désirent", ne peut être prise selon une unique raison dans tous les biens, c'est à cause de la diversité de leur

---

[74] *Cf*. Aristote, *Metaphysica* II, 1, 993 b 25 - 26, trad. J. Tricot, p. 109. Sur le même thème *cf*. Albert le Grand, *Summa theologiae sive de mirabili scientia Dei* I, 6, 26, 1, 3, *Opera omnia* XXXIV, pars I, 1978, 181, 44 - 45; Thomas d'Aquin, *In Posteriora Analytica* I, c. 2, lect. iv, n° 16 (155b): *"Primum in unoquoque genere et maximum est causa omnium eorum quae sunt post";* Ulrich de Strasbourg, *De summo bono* II, 3, 1, 4 - 5, éd. A. de Libera, p. 43, 71 - 80. D'après Averroès, *Metaphysica* II, comm. 4, éd. G. Darms (Thomistische Studien 11) Fribourg, 1966, 58, 22 - 26.

proportio, de cette analogie constitutive qui détermine pour chaque étant et chaque bien un rapport particulier à la Bonté suprême, conforme à leur place dans la Hiérarchie, place à partir de laquelle ils peuvent répondre à l'*advocatio* d'un Bien les *appelant* à monter vers Lui autant qu'ils le peuvent.[75] La chose est claire: l'analogie qu'invoque ici Albert est celle de Denys,[76] non celle d' "Aristote", plus exactement, c'est l'analogie de réception des commentateurs néoplatoniciens d'Aristote[77] — non l'analogie dite "aristotélicienne" de l'être —, *analogia recipientium* inséparable d'une notion de la causalité divine comme "causalité d'appel" qu'Albert prétend trouver à la fois dans la notion dionysienne du Bien et dans celle, proprement aristotélicienne, de l'éduction des formes.

L'interprétation exemplariste de l'adage aristotélicien sur la causalité formelle a donc une fonction précise et une portée théorique capitale: Albert rejette l'univocité stricte de "Platon", mais c'est pour lui substituer une univocité d'analogie, fondée sur une théorie causale qu'il dit retrouver chez Aristote grâce à sa propre lecture de l'*eductio formarum*. L'analogie néoplatonicienne peut ainsi venir à la place de l'univocité platonicienne, grâce à un progrès décisif dans la conception de la causalité univoque, accompli par

---

[75] On sait qu'Albert se plait à citer l'étymologie rapportant le mot "bonum" à *boo, boas. Cf.* notamment *De causis et processu universitatis* II, 3, 15, *Opera omnia* X, 1890, 565a. Le thème, relayé par le *Commentator In De divinis nominibus* 4 (ms. Paris, *Bibliothèque Nationale, latin* 17341, ff° 222 rb - 222 va), est emprunté à Jean Scot Ériugène, *Periphyseon (De divisione naturae)* II, n. 24, *PL* 122, 580C - D, éd. I.P. Sheldon-Williams, 1968, 124, 5 - 13 et à Denys, *De divinis nominibus* 4, 7, *PG* 3, 701 C. Sur cet axiome, *cf.* Albert le Grand, *Super Dionysium De divinis nominibus* 4, n. 3, 1972, 114, 36 - 39 et n. 77, p. 186, 22 - 31. *Cf.* également Ulrich de Strasbourg, *De summo bono* II, 2, 1, 2, éd. A. de Libera, p. 28, 25 - 30: "*Bonum* enim in Latino dicitur a *boo, boas,* id est *voco, vocas,* et *kalos,* quod est nomen boni in Graeco, dicitur a *kalo, kalas,* id est *clamo, clamas*". Sur le *Commentator,* voir H.F. Dondaine, *Le Corpus dionysien de l'université de Paris au XIIIe siècle,* Rome 1953, 84 - 89. Sur son utilisation chez Albert et Ulrich, voir A. de Libera, 'Ulrich de Strasbourg lecteur d'Albert le Grand', *Freiburger Zeitschrift für Philosophie und Theologie* 32/1-2 (1985), 122 - 124.

[76] Sur l'analogie selon Denys, *cf.* Vl. Lossky, 'La notion des *analogies* chez Denys le Pseudo-Aréopagite', *Archives d'histoire doctinale et littéraire du Moyen Age* 5 (1931), 279 - 309.

[77] La doctrine de l'analogie de réception est attestée chez des auteurs aussi différents qu'Alexandre d'Aphrodise (commentateur de la *Métaphysique*), Asclépius et Jean Philopon — *cf.* sur ce point J.-F. Courtine, 'Différence ontologique et analogie de l'être: le tournant suarézien', *Bulletin de la Société française de Philosophie,* 83e année, n° 2 (Séance du 28 janvier 1989), Avril-Juin 1989, 59 - 61 (Alexandre), 62 (Asclépius) et 63 (Philopon) — cependant, Albert ne pouvait connaître directement toutes ces doctrines. Reste donc, en dehors de Boèce et d'Averroès, la piste de la *Lettre* d'Alexandre *De principio universitatis*; de fait, le kitæb mabædi' al-kull soutient explicitement que: "Toutes les choses font ce qu'elles font (...) selon leur nature propre, par désir d'imiter cet être qui les a formées selon la première intention et *ce que chacune reçoit selon sa capacité.*" Sur ce point, cf. Alexandre d'Aphrodise, *Épître des principes du tout selon l'opinion d'Aristote le Philosophe,* trad. Badawi, in '*La Transmission ...*', 137 - 138. Texte parallèle dans Albert, *De causis et processu universitatis* II, 2, 16, ed. 1891, 502 b : "*Natura (...) movet generata et corrupta, ut ad formam primam unumquodque quantum possibile est secundum analogiam terminetur. Et hoc est quod dicit Aristoteles, quod omnia appetunt esse divinum, et propter illud agunt quidquid agunt.*"

Aristote lui-même. On voit que malgré les déficits empiriques de sa doxographie, Albert retrouve à son insu une certaine vérité de l'histoire du péripatétisme, c'est-à-dire de l'aristotélisme néoplatonisant.

Les origines de la théorie platonicienne des trois états de l'universel se révèlent ainsi non seulement postérieures à Platon, ce qui était attendu, mais étroitement liées à un complexe où circulent le Platon historique, le néoplatonisme des commentateurs byzantins d'Aristote, le péripatétisme empreint de néoplatonisme des commentateurs arabes et le néoplatonisme dionysien. Cet entrecroisement des lieux et des doctrines est sans doute ce qui définit le mieux l'horizon philosophique d'Albert.

Reste un dernier geste théorique, qui terminera notre parcours.

Jusqu'ici la doctrine platonicienne nous est apparue à travers le commentaire de textes d'Aristote. Cette démarche nous a conduits à Denys. Notre nouveau témoin va nous en faire repartir et retraverser en sens inverse les étapes mêmes que nous avons parcourues.

Dans le *Super Dionysium De divinis nominibus* 2, §§ 83-84, Albert traite le thème dionysien de la procession de la "divine discrétion" par laquelle tous les biens sont dits "procéder d'un Bien unique". Menée sous forme de question, l'opération consiste à mettre le texte de Denys en crise au nom d'Aristote.[78]

Le premier argument du *quod non*, fondé sur le thème aristotélicien de la multiplicité des fins (*Éthique,* 1094 a 5 - 7) met en contradiction la thèse dionysienne de la procession formelle *ab uno bono* avec la thèse aristotélicienne de l'homonymie du bien. Tel quel, ce *contra* nous ramène donc aux discussions du *Super Ethica* §§ 9 et 28 - 29, mais Denys a remplacé Platon. Disciple de Denys, Albert le défend contre Aristote comme il avait tantôt défendu le philosophe athénien, en recourant à la notion de causalité exemplaire.

Il y a, dit-il, deux sortes de formes. L'une, exemplaire, n'est pas commune par communauté de prédication, mais "de par la procession des réalités exemplifiées à partir de ladite forme", *sicut forma calcificis omnibus calceis*: une telle forme n'est pas participée de manière univoque par tous ses participes, mais analogiquement, c'est-à-dire par chacun *secundum suam possibilitatem*. La seconde sorte de forme, en revanche, est commune à plusieurs par la seule prédication, c'est la forme au sens logique.

Comme dans le *Super Ethica*, la première étape de la conclusion consiste ainsi à substituer la causalité formelle-exemplaire du théologien philosophe à la causalité formelle-univoque du philosophe logicien: les biens procèdent formellement d'un seul et même bien, non au sens d'une forme générique ou spécifique, mais au sens d'un exemplaire unique. Platon est certes réfuté —

---

[78] *Cf.* Albert le Grand, *Super Dionysium De divinis nominibus* 2, n. 83 - 84, *Opera omnia* XXXVII, pars I, 1972, 96, 46 *sqq.*

tous les biens ne sont pas d'un même genre ou d'une même espèce —, mais les droits du (néo)platonisme sont saufs et les deux positions bien distinguées.

Toutefois, le problème rejaillit. Aristote a rejeté la théorie platonicienne de l'univocité. Mais il aurait aussi bien refusé l'idée d'unité exemplaire.

Pour sauver Denys des griffes du Stagirite, Albert n'a qu'une solution: distinguer deux sortes d' "exemplarisme". Aristote a certes refusé la thèse proprement platonicienne de l'existence d'un exemplaire unique de tous les biens, mais un "exemplaire" pris au sens limité de *forme* séparée. Il n'a pas condamné d'avance la notion d'un exemplaire de tous les biens, où "exemplaire" signifierait quelque chose comme *une idée dans l'esprit d'un artisan*. N'est-ce pas lui, en effet, qui, dans la *Métaphysique*, livre VII, écrit que:

> la santé du corps qui est dans l'équilibre du froid et du chaud vient de la santé qui est dans l'âme du médecin, <de même que> la maison <vient> de la maison <qui est dans l'esprit de l'architecte>.[79]

Muni de cette référence, où s'exprime une tendance de fond de la pensée aristotélicienne — ce que Le Blond a appelé d'un terme heureux un "schème artificialiste"[80] — Albert ajoute, pour notre plus grande surprise: "C'est bien pourquoi le Commentateur distingue à cet endroit un triple universel."

Ainsi nous voilà ramenés une fois de plus à la théorie des trois états de l'universel. Il n'est plus question de Platon. Il est encore question du "Commentateur". Qui est visé ici? Si le texte commenté est bien, comme le suggère le mot *ibidem,* la *Metaphysica* VII, 1032 b 5 - 30, le *Commentator* ne peut être qu'Averroès, "commentateur" de la *Métaphysique* par excellence. Averroès aurait donc, lui aussi, proposé une doctrine des trois états de l'universel? C'est ce que comprend P. Simon, l'éditeur du *Super Dionysium De divinis nominibus,* qui dans sa note propose un texte qui, sans être absolument littéral, semble incontestablement véhiculer cette distinction:

> Tria considerantur in unoquoque eorum, scilicet forma sine materia, et forma quae est in materia, idest in concreto, et forma quae est in anima (...) unum est in anima medici et aliud est corpus animatum et tertia est forma sanitatis nuda ab omni subiecto.[81]

Nous avons dit ailleurs que cette référence ne nous paraissait pas entièrement convaincante. De fait, au moins dans l'édition de 1562 — la seule source que j'aie pu consulter —, Averroès semble tracer une simple distinction binaire entre les formes mentales (*in anima*) et les réalités qui en découlent *extra animam,* distinction qu'il rattache ensuite, vraisemblablement sur les pas du *Timée,* aux trois facteurs nécessaires de tout engendrement:

---

[79] *Cf.* Aristote, *Metaphysica* VII, 7, 1032 b 5 - 30.
[80] *Cf.* J.M. Le Blond, *Logique et méthode chez Aristote*, Paris 1939, 326 - 346.
[81] *Cf.* Albert le Grand, *Super Dionysium De divinis nominibus* 2, n. 84, *Opera omnia* XXXVII, pars I, 1972, 97, n. 49.

D.d. *Ars enim medicinae,* etc. id est et causa eius est, quoniam ars medicinae, quae est in anima, est eadem cum forma medicinae, quae est extra animam et similiter de arte aedificatoria cum formis aedificatorum. *D. d. et dico substantiam* et forte intendit: et dico substantiam id est formam sine materia, formam quae est in anima: et formam quae est in materia, formam quae est extra animam. Deinde cum hoc copulatur hoc, quod dicit: *et hoc est tale* etc. et in sanitate inveniuntur tria, quae inveniuntur in omnibus generabilibus. Est enim aliquid, et ex aliquo in potentia, et per aliquid in actu: et est illud quod assimilatur principio motionis.[82]

On peut donc se demander si le *Unde Commentator ibidem distinguit* d'Albert renvoie au commentaire sur le livre VII de la *Métaphysique* ou s'il ne reprend pas plutôt le commentaire sur le livre I de l'*Ethique*, qui, on l'a vu, encadre toute la discussion sur les universaux, ce qui alors nous ramènerait à Eustrate. Une chose est claire: qu'il s'appuie sur Averroès ou sur Aristote lu à travers Eustrate, c'est le "schème artificialiste" de la cause formelle aristotélico-averroïste qui porte ici l'analyse de l'exemplarité. En effet, en déployant l'habituelle distinction des trois universels, l'universel *ante rem,* cause de la chose, l'universel *in re,* qui a son être dans les singuliers, l'universel *consequens,* qui a son être dans l'abstraction, autrement dit, dans l'âme, Albert insiste avant tout sur ce que l'universel *ante rem* "précontient" le particulier qui en dérive, comme la *forma operis* dans l'esprit de l'artisan cause ce qui est dans les choses et se produit, s'extériorise (*producit se*) en elles par mode d'exemplification. Si donc l'expression *universale ante rem* n'est pas tirée d'Averroès — où quel que soit le texte allégué elle ne figure pas —, le "schème de métier" (médical ou architectural) qui vient lui donner sens reste typiquement averroïste. Ainsi, c'est sous un triple patronage — Aristote, Eustrate, Averroès — que s'organise la théorie albertinienne de l'exemplarisme.

Le temps vient alors d'une dernière surprise qui nous ramène à l'intitulé général de ces journées: *Proclus and the Reception of his Thought in the Middle Ages.*

Confronté aux *Éléments de théologie* à la fin de sa carrière, Albert ne renonce pas, c'est vrai, à ses "convictions de commentateur". Proclus est disponible; il en dispose. C'est même à lui qu'il confie le soin de patronner le collage de Denys et d'Averroès qui boucle définitivement sa théorie de l'universel. Proclus trouve ainsi une fonction, tardive, mais qui laisse l'essentiel intact. Cela donne une des pages les plus curieuses de la *Summa theologiae,* exposant au nom du Diadoque une doctrine de l'analogie englobant rétrospectivement toutes les voies et tous les discours précédemment essayés; cela donne une distinction entre quatre types de "prédication commune", une selon l'univocité stricte, trois selon l'analogie;[83] bref, cela donne un ultime

---

[82] *Cf.* Averroès, *Metaphysica* VII, comm. 23; Venise 1562, f° 174 rA - B.
[83] *Cf.* Albert le Grand, *Summa theologiae sive de mirabili scientia Dei, Opera omnia* XXXI, pars I, I, 6, 26, 1, éd. D. Siedler, 1978, 169, 60 - 68.

montage qui, à partir de certaines expressions proclusiennes sur le caractère salvifique et unitif du bien ("le bien est ce qui sauve tous les êtres et devient ainsi le terme de leur tendance"),[84] permet de retrouver tacitement l'interprétation averroïste de la triade porphyrienne des homonymes ἀπὸ διανοίας· ἀφ' ἑνός πρὸς ἕν, κατ' ἀναλογίαν. Voilà comment Proclus l'absent gagne enfin sa place: en achevant son Odyssée dans une doctrine de l'*analogia* que toute la scolastique tardive s'appliquera à trouver chez Aristote.

Au terme de cette série de renversements, on est en droit de se demander quelle est la véritable position d'Albert à l'égard de la théorie platonicienne des Idées. La réponse est simple. Si les Idées sont conçues dans le sens que leur donneront plus tard les *formalizantes* — celui d'entités existant *in re extra Deum*: Albert les rejette avec la dernière énergie.[85] Reste une autre possibilité: celle du concordat Platon-Aristote.

Dans le *De intellectu et intelligibili*, fidèle lecteur de la *Métaphysique* d'Aristote, Albert critique la théorie platonicienne des Formes séparées, autrement dit: la future doctrine des *formalizantes*. Dans le *Super Ethica*, en revanche, il adopte plus ou moins le point de vue d'Eustrate, critiquant la lecture aristotélicienne de Platon, pour rabattre, comme lui, la notion des Formes séparées sur celle des Idées divines. Dans le *Super Dionysium De divinis nominibus*, il défend la théorie dionysienne de la procession contre un aristotélisme qui ignorerait les acquis d'une doctrine de l'analogie précisément issue de l'interprétation néoplatonicienne d'Aristote.

La diversité de ces points de vue est liée en partie au contenu des textes commentés, en partie aux objectifs de leur commentateur. Elle a néanmoins sa cohérence — Albert soutient sans le savoir le néoplatonisme contre le platonisme —, et, en toute hypothèse, elle n'implique aucune évolution de la part de l'auteur: on peut défendre Denys contre Aristote en 1249-1250 puis soutenir Eustrate contre Aristote en 1252, tout en continuant de rejeter un certain platonisme (celui des Formes séparées) aux alentours de 1255-1257. Les enjeux sont différents, les problèmes distincts.

Il est, en revanche, permis de se demander si l'interprétation albertinienne de Platon n'a pas profondément évolué après ses premières années d'enseignement à Cologne. A lire l'analyse qu'il donne du platonisme dans ses œuvres les plus tardives, l'impression dominante est qu'il a tiré une conséquence globale de ses pondérations successives. Tel qu'il se présente dans le *De causis et processu universitatis* (postérieur à 1263), le Platon d'Albert est devenu sinon plotinien, du moins, ce qui sur le point précis revient à peu près au même, quasi albertinien.

Trois textes s'imposent ici à l'attention.

---

[84] *Cf.* Proclus, *Eléments de théologie, propositio* 13a, comm., trad. J. Trouillard (Paris 1965), p. 69; éd. H. Boese (De Wulf-Mansion Series 1), Leuven 1987, 10, 3 - 4.
[85] Sur les *formalizantes*, *cf.* Z. Kaluza, 'Le Chancelier Gerson et Jérôme de Prague', *Archives d'histoire doctinale et littéraire du Moyen -Age* 51 (1984), 81 - 126.

Dans le *De causis et processu universitatis* II, 1, 20,[86] Albert paraphrase la prop. 4 du *Liber de causis* et, comme le soulignera d'ailleurs après lui Thomas (pour l'opposer sur ce point à Proclus), il montre — sans toutefois imputer cette thèse au *Liber de causis* (qui n'est jamais cité, mais toujours fondu dans sa propre paraphrase) — qu'il y a, en bon péripatétisme, un seul et même Agent incréé de l'être et de la vie: le Premier Principe ou Intellect. C'est dans ce contexte, celui de la supposée "théologie" d'Aristote, qu'il expose la *voie platonicienne*, autrement dit: la théorie de la création selon Platon.[87] Reprenant la notion de *sigillum*, dont il avait auparavant montré l'inanité lorsque, dans le *De intellectu et intelligibili*, elle instrumentait une théorie de l'impression des Formes séparées dans la matière, il l'inscrit désormais dans une perspective péripatéticienne, c'est-à-dire émanatiste, celle de la procession des Formes à partir d'un Premier Intellect agent, identifié au Premier Agent universel de tout l'être. Dans ce nouveau cadre doctrinal, le platonisme apparaît alors comme une doctrine de l'effusion lumineuse, vraisemblablement reliée au thème porphyrien de l'Intellect paternel.[88] Les Formes ont toujours trois modes d'être, mais il y a, désormais, un *medium* qui prolonge l'existence de l'Idée-cause, dans une manière de chaîne causale: la lumière.

> Formae autem (…) tripliciter accipi possunt, scilicet ut in principio processionis (…), et sic omnes accipiuntur in unum. Et ut in lumine extenso a primo procedentes, et sic differentes sunt ratione. Et tertio ut in lumine terminato ad res, et sic accipiuntur secundum esse diversae.

La caractéristique du platonisme est d'avoir privilégié l'existence des Formes *in luminis processu*, autrement dit: leur état second.[89] La voie platonicienne n'est donc pas incompatible avec la théologie péripatéticienne, elle n'en est

---

86 *Cf.* Albert le Grand, *De causis et processu universitatis, Opera omnia* X, 1890, 467 b - 468 a.

87 *Cf.* Albert le Grand, *Metaphysica* XI, 2, 3, *Opera omnia* XVI, pars II, 1964, 486, 63 - 65: "*Plato et sui sequaces distinxerunt causam efficientem primam a prima causa movente*"; Ulrich de Strasbourg, *De summo bono* IV, 1, 8, 3, éd. Pieperhoff, p. 45, 51 - 46, 58; et II, 2, 2, 2, éd. de Libera, p. 31, 23 - 32, 44. Sur la théorie porphyro-avicennienne du Premier Agent (*Primum Agens*, par opposition au *Primum Movens* aristotélicien), et son attribution au "Vieillard Grec" (al-shaykh al-yᵉnânî), *cf.* A. de Libera, 'Ulrich de Strasbourg lecteur d'Albert le Grand', *loc. cit.*

88 *Cf.* Albert le Grand, *Metaphysica* I, 4, 12, *Opera omnia* XVI, pars II, 1960, 64, 80-65, 42, d'après Augustin, *Cité de Dieu* X, XXIII, Bibliothèque Augustinienne 34, éd. 1959, 504; Macrobe, *In Somnium. Scipionis* I, 14, 6 - 7, éd. J. Willis, p. 56, 9 *sqq. Cf.* également Albert le Grand, *Ethica* X, 1, 1, *Opera omnia*, 1890, 601 b ("(...) in fine *Timaei*"), d'après Platon, *Timée* 41 a, 1962, 35, 10. Selon Albert, *De XV problematibus* I, *Opera omnia* XVII, pars I, 1975, 34, 22 - 23, la théorie de Platon est (mal) reprise par Avicebron.

89 Cette présentation est plus fidèle à Platon que celle qui consiste à lui attribuer une doctrine des Idées divines. Dans cet "état second" les Formes sont bien, en effet, distinctes à la fois des singuliers et extérieures à l'Intellect divin, donc plus proches de la notion "authentique" des Formes séparées. Toutefois, il va de soi que considérées dans la "Procession lumineuse" ou la "lumière émanée" lesdites Formes s'apparentent davantage aux formes dont sont remplies les Intelligences du *Liber de causis* (prop. 10) – elles sont donc "péripatétisées". C'est l'*esse intellectuale tantum et formale* des Néoalbertistes (d'après Albert, *Metaphysica* V, 6, 7, *Opera omnia* XVI, pars I, 1960, 285, 56 - 76), autrement dit (..) l'être formel causé-causal des péripatéticiens.

qu'un cas particulier. Sans avoir à proprement parler professé l'existence des Idées divines, Platon en a recueilli la première manifestation — ce qu'on pourrait appeler leur état rayonnant (*sicut radii ab uno solis puncto procedentes*) —, et en a fait l'objet principal de ses analyses. Cela explique certaines de ses erreurs, mais cela permet aussi, une fois sa doctrine replacée dans le cadre qu'elle réclame en quelque sorte d'elle-même, d'en rectifier la portée jusqu'à lui donner un sens acceptable. Il suffit d'identifier les Idées platoniciennes aux *formae simplices in lumine Intelligentiae acceptae* du *Liber de causis*.[90] Pour effectuer un tel rapprochement il faut un moyen terme: la notion farabienne de "Formes du monde" (*formae mundi*) — opposées au "Formes de la matière" — y pourvoie,[91] et à bon droit: les *Formae quae sunt in mundo* dont parle le *De intellectu* de Fârâbî[92] ne sont-elles pas, de fait, la version "péripatétisée" des Idées de Platon?

Dans le *De causis et processu universitatis* II, 2, 21,[93] où Albert paraphrase la proposition 10 du *Liber de causis* — *omnis intelligentia est plena formis* —, la théorie platonicienne de l' ἐκμαγεῖον, est mise au service d'une analyse du pouvoir formateur des formes dont les Intelligences sont dotées, donc d'une analyse de la procession comme *formatio*, causalité univoque placée sous le double patronage d'Aristote ("(…) unde dicit Aristoteles quod domus est ex domo, et sanitas ex sanitate") et de Platon ("Propter quod Plato dicebat, quod causaliter prima formantia formae separatae esse dicuntur. Quae autem sunt in rebus producta, non formae, sed imagines formarum sunt"). Platon se voit ainsi encore plus explicitement enrôlé sous la bannière des partisans de l'Intelligence agente. Le Démiurge a désormais un statut franchement péripatéticien, celui de l'*Intelligentia agens, les dieux secondaires étant, quant à eux, assimilés aux Intelligences subalternes* du *Liber de causis*:

Sicut enim dicit Plato, forma ex hoc forma vocatur, quia extra res manens format et imaginem suam imprimit in formata: *extra res autem manens non est nisi substantiale lumen agentis intelligentiae*. Sic ergo forma est et in agente quidem unum est: procedendo autem ab agente diversificatur et igitur in pluralitatem. Et Plato de hoc ponebat simile in sigillo et sigillatis. Sigillum enim essentialiter forma est in se manens immutabiliter formans omne cui imprimitur: et sic dicebat res naturales omnes de intelligentia agente sicut de quodam etyvagio sive sigillo procedere: et *talia lumina intelligentiarum* rebus comparata et ad res ordinata formas sive ideas separatas esse dicebat.

---

[90] *Cf.* Albert le Grand, *De causis et processu universitatis* II, 1, 19, 1890, 466 b.

[91] *Cf.* Albert le Grand, *De intellectu et intelligibili* II, 2, *Opera omnia* V, éd. P. Jammy, 1651, 254 a.

[92] *Cf.* Al-Fârâbî, *De intellectu et intellecto*, éd. É. Gilson, *Archives d'histoire doctrinale et littéraire du Moyen Age* 4 (1929), 120, 201 - 121, 232.

[93] *Cf.* Albert le Grand, *De causis et processu universitatis* I, *Opera omnia* X, 1890, 510 b - 511 a

Le *De causis et processu universitatis* II, 2, 22[94] achève cette réappropriation péripatéticienne du platonisme. La distinction des trois états de l'universel est définitivement inscrite dans une théorie générale de la Procession:

> Et propter hoc distinxit Plato triplex universale (...). Et primum quidem universale in lumine agentis constitutivum est. Secundum autem esse et ratio rei est. Tertium autem re posterius est, et a separatione a re causatum. Primum ergo est causativum. Secundum causa et causatum. Tertium autem causatum tantum. Adhuc primum est formans et forma, secundum imago formae, tertium resultatio imaginis ad similitudinem formae formantis. Sic ergo patet, quod formae quae in superioribus sunt universales et universaliter, in inferioribus sunt particulares et particulariter.

En reformulant la théorie platonicienne des formes dans les triades causales, qu'il a ailleurs généralisées aux quatre causes à partir des remarques d'Aristote sur la structure causale du mouvement (réclamant un *tantum movens*, un *movens et motum* et un *tantum motum*),[95] Albert nous livre la clef de cette singulière exégèse: si le vrai sens du platonisme est la Procession, le platonisme ne s'oppose pas au péripatétisme, car:

> Ce que les Grecs appellent procession, les arabes l'appellent flux.

En faisant de Platon le Père fondateur de la métaphysique du flux, Albert l'identifie à la théologie d'Aristote, autrement dit: à la doctrine du *Liber de causis*. Les déficits du platonisme demeurent — Platon n'a pas su véritablement maîtriser les modalités de l'activité causale des Formes séparées — la doctrine d'ensemble n'en est pas moins amendable, et, sous cette réserve, intégrable à une théologie de l'émanation. Au vrai, le sens même des critiques d'Aristote, dont il s'était fait abondamment l'écho dans le *De intellectu et intelligibili*, a, semble-t-il, changé aux yeux d'Albert, perdant toute radicalité. Aristote n'a pas rejeté la théorie platonicienne de la *formatio*, il en a seulement critiqué l'instrumentation conceptuelle:

> Si quis autem objiciat, quod hanc positionem impugnavit Aristoteles, et maxime in XII et in XIII *primae philosophiae*. Dicimus, quod non hoc modo impugnavit eam, sed in hoc impugnavit, quod formae separatae transmutarent et formarent res: hoc enim esse non potest: quia quod non tangit, non agit: et quod non agit, huius actionem non sequitur generatio vel alteratio: sed quando formae quae sunt ante rem, per motum corporis et actione calidi et frigidi et humidi et sicci, quae sunt informata forma intellectus agentis, materiae conjunguntur, et materiam tangunt, nihili prohibet quin sequatur generatio vel alteratio.

S'il avait correctement apprécié le rôle du Corps divin — la *sphère* d'Aristote, c'est-à-dire la *nature* (on sait que sous ce titre relayé par Isaac Israeli se cache

---

[94] *Cf.* Albert le Grand, *De causis et processu universitatis* I, *Opera omnia* X, 1890, 512 b - 513 a.
[95] *Cf.* Albert le Grand, *De causis et processu universitatis* I, 1, 7, *Opera omnia* X, 1890, 376 a - b.

l'Ame inférieure du monde selon Plotin)[96] — et plus généralement celui des Corps célestes, s'il avait su penser l'apport des qualités élementales, bref, s'il avait adopté la théorie de l'éduction des formes naturelles et su fondre le tout dans un véritable système de causalité universelle, Platon aurait abouti aux mêmes résultats que le péripatétisme. Rapporté à l'intention philosophique, le platonisme est une bonne philosophie: ses limites sont, avant tout, instrumentales. C'est ici le lieu de rappeler le mot d'Averroès, complaisamment repris par Albert: "Les platoniciens veulent dire comme nous avec leurs *formae*, mais ils n'y arrivent pas parfaitement".

Que dire de ce diagnostic aussi surprenant que tardif? D'une part, qu'il n'est pas contradictoire avec les thèses antérieures: Albert a toujours cherché à acclimater Platon sous le soleil du paripatétisme. D'autre part, qu'il suppose une absorbtion progressive du Platon "historique" — pour Albert celui du Timée —, dans un platonisme qui doit tout, ou presque, aux sources arabes et juives de l'exégèse philosophique albertinienne. En ce sens, il est donc ultimement faux de parler d'une "souveraine indifférence d'Albert à la question du platonisme du *Liber de causis*".

Si Albert ne s'est pas soucié de rattacher le *Livre* au platonisme de Proclus, c'est parce qu'il avait déjà rattaché Platon au péripatétisme du *Liber*.

---

[96] *Cf.* Albert le Grand, *De causis et processu universitatis* II, 2, 15, *Opera omnia* X, 1890, 501 b; *De causis et processu universitatis* II, 2, 16, *Opera omnia* X, 1890, 502 b - 503 a. Sur l'identification *nature* (plotinienne) — *sphère* (aristotélicienne) chez Isaac, *cf.* A. Altmann et S. M. Stern, *Isaac Israeli. A Neoplatonic Philosopher of the Early Tenth Century* (Scripta Judaica I), Oxford 1958, 51.

JAN A. AERTSEN

ONTOLOGY AND HENOLOGY IN MEDIEVAL PHILOSOPHY
(THOMAS AQUINAS, MASTER ECKHART AND BERTHOLD OF MOOSBURG)

1. *Introduction*

"Metaphysics of Being or philosophy of the One?" With this question commences an article by J. Trouillard, well-known for his studies of Neoplatonism.[1] But the writer himself immediately wonders if the question he has raised is not purely academic. Even experienced philosophers, so he says, regard the option with skepticism. Does a philosophy of the One still have philosophical relevance and is the question not in effect passé? Trouillard mentions no names, but I should not be surprised if by "experienced philosophers" he had in mind especially É. Gilson, the great expert on medieval philosophy.[2]

One of Gilson's most important works is *Being and Some Philosophers*, in which he presents a problem-historical survey of the question of being.[3] In the first chapter ("Being and the One") Gilson traces the development in Greek philosophy that results in the metaphysics of the One in Plotinus and Proclus, a doctrine for which he introduces the term "henology."[4] Over against Neoplatonic metaphysics he sets the "metaphysics of being," more precisely: the "Christian" metaphysics of being. He elucidates this opposition by pointing to the famous 4th proposition of the *Liber de causis*: *Prima rerum creatarum est esse*. Gilson comments:

> This is straight Neoplatonism: the first principle is the One, and being comes next as the first of its creatures. Now this is, though self-consistent, yet absolutely inconsistent with the mental universe of Christian thinkers, in which being cannot be the first of all creatures for the good reason that it has to be the Creator Himself, namely, God.[5]

---

1 J. Trouillard, 'Un et être', *Les études philosophiques* 15 (1960), 185 - 196.
2 *Cf.* the reference to a "thomiste existentiel" on p. 186.
3 Toronto, 21952. The English version is based on, but not identical with the French original *L'être et l'essence*, Paris 1948.
4 The term is introduced in *L'être et l'essence*, 42. *Cf.* E.A. Wyller, 'Henologie', in: *Historisches Wörterbuch der Philosophie* III, Darmstadt 1974, col. 1059. W. Beierwaltes, *Denken des Einen. Studien zur neuplatonischen Philosophie und ihrer Wirkungsgeschichte*, Frankfurt am Main 1985, 11.
5 *Being and Some Philosophers*, 30 - 31.

Gilson's conclusion is: "One cannot think, at one and the same time, as a Neoplatonist and as a Christian." This thesis is provocative. His statement seems more doctrinal than historical in character, that is, seems primarily inspired by Gilson's own systematic concerns. For he has a very definite view of what "the mental universe of Christian thinkers" is, a view he has summed up in the expression: "metaphysics of Exodus." Constitutive for Christian thought is the passage of Exodus 3, 14, where the Lord says: "I am who I am." "If the Christian God is first, and if He is Being, then Being is first, and no Christian philosophy can posit anything above Being."[6]

Yet Gilson presents his statement about the incompatibility of a metaphysics of being with a henology as a historical thesis. He sees his view confirmed as it were *e contrario* by the thought of Master Eckhart, for this shows the paradox to which the connection of Neoplatonism with Christian thought can lead. In his first Parisian question Eckhart says, referring to the fourth proposition of the *Book of causes,* that as soon as we come to being, we come to a creature. Since being belongs to creatures, it cannot be in God, except as in its cause. Thus in God, there is no being, but *puritas essendi,* a formula which, according to Gilson, obviously means not the purity of being, but the purity from being — an interpretation to which we shall return. In Gilson's view it is paradoxical to define Him Who is as a God in Whom no trace of being can be found. This paradox arises from Eckhart's connection with the henological tradition. No wonder then that the text on which Eckhart would never tire of preaching or of writing is Deuteronomy 6, 4: "Listen Israel, the Lord our God, the Lord is one." Gilson concludes: "In his whole commentary on these words two lines seem to me more precious than all the rest: '*Deus est unus:* God is one; this is confirmed by the fact that Proclus, too, and the *Liber de causis* frequently call God the One or Unity.'"[7]

For Gilson the choice between a "metaphysics of Being" and a "philosophy of the One" has been philosophically and historically settled. Since Gilson's book, however, a certain shift in the discussion seems to have occurred.[8] Two factors, I believe, are responsible for this. A first factor has been that we have witnessed in the last decades a revival of Neoplatonic studies. Thus the thought of Proclus has been made accessible by translations of the *Elementatio theologica* and the monographs of W. Beierwaltes and J. Trouillard.[9] In the latter we find an explicit justification of the henological

---

[6] *Ibid.*, 30.

[7] *Ibid.*, 38 - 39. The exposition on Eckhart is absent in the French version.

[8] *Cf.* W. Hankey, 'Aquinas' First Principle: Being or Unity?', *Dionysius* 4 (1980), 135 - 139.

[9] Proclus, *The Elements of Theology, A revised Text with Translation, Introduction and Commentary* by E.R. Dodds, Oxford, 21963; French translation by J. Trouillard, Paris 1965; W. Beierwaltes, *Proklos. Grundzüge seiner Metaphysik, Frankfurt am Main* 1965, 21979; J. Trouillard, *L'un et l'âme selon Proclos,* Paris 1972; J. Trouillard, *La mystagogie de Proclos,* Paris 1982.

position. The superiority of the One to being is for him a metaphysical option which is warranted for spiritual reasons — the motive of negative theology — and for philosophical reasons.[10]

A second factor has been that recent studies have made clear how strongly Neoplatonism, via the *Liber De causis* and the *Proclus latinus*, permeated medieval philosophy.[11] I have in mind, for example, the work of W. Beierwaltes, *Denken des Einen;*[12] the study by K. Kremer, in which it is argued, clearly in reaction against Gilson, that Aquinas's philosophy of being must be understood primarily from Neoplatonic influences;[13] the work of A. de Libera on mysticism in the Rhineland;[14] and the broadly conceived study by K. Flasch on "The Metaphysics of the One in Nicolaus of Cues."[15] Historically speaking, the answer to the question: "metaphysics of Being" or "philosophy of the One"? seems to have been less univocal than Gilson suggested.

In this contribution I would like to investigate whether and in which way the opposition between ontology and henology took shape in medieval thinkers and was a subject of discussion. I will focus my inquiry on three Dominicans of different generations, namely, Thomas Aquinas, Master Eckhart and Berthold of Moosburg. The last one is the least well known of the three. Yet I want to begin with him, since we find in his work not only a justification but also a philosophical deepening of our question.

2. *Berthold of Moosburg*

(1) Berthold of Moosburg is the last representative of the German Dominican school. One of the very few things we know about his life is that he became Eckhart's successor as head of the Studium generale of the Dominicans in Cologne. He wrote, sometime between 1327 and 1361, an extensive commentary on the *Elementatio theologica* of Proclus. The critical edition of this writing, which is in the process of being published, constitutes a new contribution to our insight into the influence of Neoplatonism on medieval philo-

---

10 A good summary of his justification of the henological position can be found in J. Trouillard, 'Un (Philosophies de l')', in: *Encyclopaedia universalis*, Paris 21988, 427 - 429. *Cf. La mystagogie de Proclos*, ch. 5, 93 - 108. See also S. Breton, 'Le théorème de l'Un dans les *Eléments de théologie* de Proclos', *Revue des sciences philosophiques et théologiques* 58 (1974), 561 - 583.
11 *Cf.* R. Imbach, 'Le (néo-)platonisme médiéval, Proclus latin et l'école dominicaine allemande', *Revue de théologie et de philosophie* 110 (1978), 427 - 448.
12 See note 3.
13 Kl. Kremer, *Die neuplatonische Seinsphilosophie und ihre Wirkung auf Thomas von Aquin*, Leiden 1966, 21971.
14 A. de Libera, *Introduction à la mystique rhénane d'Albert le Grand à Maître Eckhart*, Paris 1984.
15 K. Flasch, *Die Metaphysik des Einen bei Nikolaus von Cues. Problemgeschichtliche Stellung und systematische Bedeutung*, Leiden 1973. See also of the same author 'Eine (das), Einheit II', in: *Historisches Wörterbuch der Philosophie* II, Darmstadt 1972, 367 - 377.

sophy.[16] Berthold's commentary is an indication that reception of Proclus' thought was not simply considered inconsistent with the mental universe of a Christian thinker.

In still another respect Berthold's commentary is of importance. The commentary is so constructed that what is presupposed (*suppositum*) in Proclus' theses is always exposited first. Berthold's analysis of the assumptions of Proclus' systematics reflects an awareness that two fundamentally different options are to be found in the philosophical tradition. On the basis of a broad historical erudition he works this opposition out. It is this aspect of Berthold's commentary that is now of special interest to us.

In his exposition of the *suppositum* of the 11th proposition of the *Elementatio theologica* ("All that exists proceeds from a single first cause") Berthold points out that Plato and Aristotle held different views of being, the one and the good (*"ens, unum, bonum aliter accipiuntur ab Aristotele et aliter a Platone"*).[17] From the way in which he elaborates this divergence, it is clear that "Plato and Aristotle" here stand for the traditions of thought they inspired.

Aristotle, according to Berthold, posited some *communia*, which he called *transcendentia* because these terms are not restricted to one category but go through all predicaments (*circumeunt*). To these transcendentals belong "being," "one," "true," and "good." "Being" is the first of them; it is the most formal of all concepts, because by it each thing is distinguished from nothing. The other *transcendentia* add something in concept to "being." "Being" is in itself the most general (*communissimum*), on account of the universality of the abstraction effected by the intellect. From this Berthold draws the conclusion that "being" has no existence in reality (*in rerum natura*) other than in the soul alone. Plato, on the other hand, was of the opinion that being and the good, taken in their generalness, also exist in reality. For Plato based this generalness not on the *universalitas logica seu praedicationis*, but on the *universalitas theologica sive separationis*. On the basis of this theological universality, something is the more actual according as it is the more universal. The most universal is therefore the most actual. This is the good, for according to the Platonists, the relation between being and good is such that "good" is prior, more universal and more absolute than "being," because the good is the most universal cause of all things. For this priority of the good to being, Berthold refers to, among others, Dionysius the Areopagite, in whose *De divinis nominibus* Good is the primary divine name. The most universal being is in

---

[16] Berthold von Moosburg, *Expositio super Elementationem theologicam Procli: Prologus. Propositiones* 1-13 (Corpus Philosophorum Teutonicorum Medii Aevi VI, 1), ed. by M.R. Pagnoni-Sturlese and L. Sturlese, Hamburg 1984. The first volume contains a valuable 'Einleitung' by K. Flasch (xi - xxviii). See also A. de Libera, *Introduction à la mystique rhénane*, 317 - 442.
[17] *Expositio, propositio* 11A, ed. Pagnoni-Sturlese 185, 22.

contrast the first caused, as is expressed in the fourth proposition of the *Liber de causis*.[18]

Earlier in his commentary Berthold had already pointed to the radical difference between the way of thought of the Aristotelians and that of the Platonists, namely, in his analysis of the *suppositum* of the first proposition of the *Elementatio theologica* ("Every manifold in some way participates unity"). In this analysis, focussed on the relation between being and the one, Berthold introduces the opposition between the *universalitas praedicationis* and the *universalitas separationis*. The Aristotelian universality of predication implies that the more general is the more potential, that is determined and distinguished by the act. But this universality applies according to Plato only to material things, not to the immaterial. What holds for the latter is the universality of separation, according to which the more general is the more actual, that is determined only by a potency.[19]

The metaphysical consequences of these two forms of generalness become apparent in the Aristotelian and Neoplatonist concepts of unity. For the Aristotelians the one, like being, is a transcendental that has no being in extramental reality. The one follows directly after being in the order of the *transcendentia*; it adds to being the negation of "division." For Platonism, the One is the reality of which any determination by a potency is excluded. It is beyond being and is the cause of all things. Pseudo-Dionysius and Proclus function in Berthold as the preeminent witnesses for the Platonic view.[20]

(2) What is interesting about Berthold's commentary is the philosophical deepening he gives to the opposition between ontology and henology. Berthold is aware that in this opposition something more fundamental is at issue than the question of whether being or the one has priority. The divergence should be traced back to the different approaches of the Aristotelians and of the Platonists to reality. Ontological thought and henological thought do not move on the same level. The two have in common that they intend a transcending movement towards the first and most general, but they part ways with respect to the nature and direction of this transcending.

Characteristic of the Aristotelian position is in the first place what we might call the transcendentality of the first. Berthold himself uses the term *transcendentia*, which had acquired a new, technical sense in medieval philosophy. Berthold spells it out: *transcendentia* transcend the special modes of being which Aristotle called the "categories." "Being" and "one" transcend the categories, not because they refer to a reality beyond the categories but because they are not limited to one category. Transcendentals are *communia*.

---

[18] *Ibid.* 185, 23 - 188, 98.
[19] *Expositio, propositio* 1A, ed. Pagnoni-Sturlese 72, 48 - 74, 105.
[20] *Ibid.*, 74, 106 - 125; *Expositio, propositio* 1D, ed. Pagnoni-Sturlese 77, 214 - 78, 244.

They belong to a way of thought oriented to what Berthold calls "predicative universality."

In Aristotle one cannot yet speak of a doctrine of the *transcendentia*. The doctrine was formed in the thirteenth century.[21] Historically, its starting point was a statement by Aristotle in the fourth book of the *Metaphysics:* "Being and one are the same and are a single nature in the sense that they follow upon each other (...), not however in the sense that they are expressed by a single concept (*logos*)."[22] Aristotle emphasizes, perhaps in reaction against the second hypothesis in Plato's *Parmenides*, the real identity of "being" and "one": they are convertible. Yet "being" and "one" are not synonyms. The *logos* of the one expresses something which is not expressed by the term "being," namely, the undividedness (*indivisio*) of that which is. The second characteristic of the Aristotelian position is that the first, from a transcendental point of view, is "being." The most general is "being" which Berthold interprets — an interpretation which at the same time contains a critique — as an *universale logicum* having no being in extramental reality.[23]

The primary characteristic of the Platonic position, in contrast, is the transcendence of the first, a term suggested by Berthold's expression *universalitas separationis*. The first is indeed the most general, yet this generalness is not predicative in nature. In a way of thought which is oriented to "theological universality" the most general is the most actual, which is as such the cause of all the rest. The generalness of the first results from its causality. The first itself remains "separated" from what is caused. The first is beyond being — "being" is rather the first of created things. The second mark of the Platonic position is that the absolute first is the One that is identical with the Good.[24] Berthold identifies himself with this position which to him is superior to a metaphysics of being. "Our divine superwisdom," so he says, excels Aristotle's first philosophy because it deals not only with being as being but also with principles which are above being.[25]

Berthold in his commentary traces the opposition between ontology and henology to the different structures of thought in Aristotelianism and Platonism: transcendentality of the first versus transcendence of the first. He

---

[21] *Cf.* J.A. Aertsen, 'Die Transzendentalienlehre bei Thomas von Aquin in ihren historischen Hintergründen und philosophischen Motiven', in: *Thomas von Aquin* (Miscellanea Mediaevalia 19), ed. A. Zimmermann, Berlin-New York 1988, 82 - 102.

[22] *Metaphysica* IV 2, 1003 b 22 - 25.

[23] *Expositio, propositio* 1A, ed. Pagnoni-Sturlese, 74, 100.

[24] Flasch, 'Einleitung', xvi, holds that Berthold places unity under the good in the series of the most general determinations. He refers to *Expositio, propositio* 11A *prol.*, ed. Pagnoni-Sturlese, 185, 4: "(...). *in prima et absolutissima intentione, scilicet boni.*" But this view seems to me to be incorrect. Other texts suggest an identity between the "good" and the "one". See, *e.g., Expos. prop.* 7A, ed. Pagnoni-Sturlese p. 140, 3 7: "(...) *in prima et absolutissima intentione boni sive unius, quod idem est"; Expositio, propositio* 131A (221, 15 - 16).

[25] *Expositio praeambula* C., ed. Pagnoni-Sturlese, 65, 454 - 66, 458; 66, 482 - 485.

thereby provides us with a scheme, a model which we shall use to interpret and place the thought of Thomas Aquinas and Master Eckhart.

3. *Thomas Aquinas*

(1) To Thomas Aquinas goes the credit for having been the first in the Middle Ages to have recognized the true *auctoritas* of the *Liber de causis*. Although in his early writings he still regards Aristotle as the author of this book,[26] he discerns in his commentary on the *De causis* that this work is an excerpt from the *Elementatio theologica* of Proclus.[27] Thomas was able to arrive at this insight because he was the first to dispose over a copy of the Latin translation of the *Elementatio,* completed in 1268 by William of Moerbeke.[28] Thomas must have made a thorough study of Proclus' work, for in his commentary he refers again and again to the propositions from the *Elementatio* drawn upon by the writer of the *De causis*. Thus Thomas's commentary on the *De causis* can likewise be considered a commentary on Proclus.

In his exposition of the *ratio* of the 4th proposition ("The first of created things is being") Thomas goes extensively into the Neoplatonic background of this thesis. He observes that according to the views of the Platonists *(secundum positiones platonicas)* the more general *(communius)* something is, the more separate *(separatum)* it is. This more general is the prior *(prius)* that is participated in by the later, it is the cause of the later *(posteriorum causa)*. The Platonists hold further that the one and good are the most general *(communissimum);* they are even more general than "being." Thomas also advances a reason for this greater generalness. According to the Platonists, "one" and "good" are predicated of something of which "being" is not predicated, namely, primary matter. From this it follows that the separated one (and good) is the highest and first principle of things. After the one there is nothing so general as being. Hence in the Platonic view separated being itself *(ipsum ens separatum)* is created: it is the first among created things.[29]

We can establish that in his characterization of the Platonic position Thomas employs the same notions as Berthold of Moosburg: the first is the most general, is separated and is cause. Moreover, the order of the communia is determined by both writers in the same way. The one or the good surpasses

---

[26] See, *e.g.*, *In I Sententiarum* 8, 1, 3 *sed contra.*

[27] *Sancti Thomae de Aquino super librum de causis expositio*, ed. H.D. Saffrey, Fribourg-Louvain 1954, 3, 7 - 9: "*Unde videtur (hic* Liber de Causis) *ab aliquo philosophorum arabum ex praedicto libro Procli excerptus.*" For Thomas's commentary see W. Beierwaltes, 'Der Kommentar zum *Liber de causis* als neuplatonisches Element in der Philosophie des Thomas von Aquin', *Philosophische Rundschau* 11 (1963), 192 - 215.

[28] *Cf.* Proclus, *Elementatio theologica* translata a Guillelmo de Morbecca, ed. H. Boese, Leuven 1987.

[29] *In De causis propositio* 4a, ed. H.D. Saffrey, 27, 14 - 28, 9.

being, because it is more general. Typical of Neoplatonic thought is the transcendence of the first.

There is, however, a difference to be noticed between Thomas's commentary on the *De causis* and Berthold's commentary on Proclus. The Plato of whom Berthold speaks is — as De Libera has observed — a being with a double face: it is Proclus-Dionysius.[30] The comparison between the position of Proclus and that of pseudo-Dionysius is also one of Thomas's constant concerns in his commentary. Yet, in contrast to Berthold, he puts more emphasis on the differences between their views. Dionysius, so Thomas says, rejects an order of separated principles; being is to him not something "separated." But he does maintain, in *De divinis nominibus*, the Neoplatonic order of perfections in which the other things participate. For to Dionysius Good is the primary divine name, and participation in the good is more comprehensive than participation in being. To Thomas's mind the author of the *Liber De causis* thinks in the same line as Dionysius.[31] Thomas is more alive than Berthold to the complexity of the Neoplatonic tradition.

In his commentary Thomas explains the philosophical backgrounds of the fourth proposition but does not engage in a discussion with the henological tradition. That discussion he carries on elsewhere in his work.

(2) Thomas's thought too is directed towards the first and most general. But for him the generalness of the first is transcendental in character. What is first is the *transcendentia*, which transcend the categories because they go through all the predicaments. On this point Thomas's critique of the Neoplatonic position begins.

The first and most general are "being," "one" and "good."[32] They are the first not because they are the cause of the other things but because they are the first in the order of the knowledge of things. The doctrine of transcendentals functions in this respect as a critique of knowledge. Thomas makes a sharp distinction between the first in commonness *(primum in communitate)* and the first in causality *(primum in causalitate)*. The latter, because of its transcendence, is not directly accessible to human knowledge. The former, because of its predicative generalness, is the first that is apprehended by the intellect.[33] Transcendentals are the *prima intelligibilia* because they are implicit in every concept.

Transcendentals are *communia*. The essential mark of that which is general is that it is predicated of many things *(de multis praedicetur)* and exists in many things *(in multis existat)*. Now if the one, as the Platonists claim, were a

---

[30] De Libera, *Introduction à la mystique rhénane*, 388 - 389.
[31] *In De causis propositio* 4a, ed. H.D. Saffrey, 28, 10 - 25.
[32] *In Boethii De hebdomadibus*, lect. 2, 20: *"Ea autem quae in omni intellectu cadunt, sunt maxime communia quae sunt: ens, unum et bonum."*
[33] *De veritate* qu. 10, art. 11 ad 10.

"separated," subsisting principle, then it could not be found in many things at the same time, that is, be general. The generalness of the one is not compatible with its substantiality.[34] Transcendentals are not *subsistentia*. A recurring reproach to the Platonists in Thomas's work is that they simply project our abstract and general mode of knowing onto the mode of being of things.[35] They hold incorrectly that what is abstracted in the intellect is also "separate" in reality.[36]

Berthold of Moosburg drew the conclusion in his analysis of the Aristotelian position that *transcendentia* have no extramental reality, but exist in the soul alone. "Being" is an *universale logicum*. Thomas would have objected to this interpretation. It would be correct to say that transcendentals do not have the being that the Platonists ascribed to the most general. But from this it does not follow that they have purely a logical character. Thomas's definition of the general indicates as much: it contains not only the moment of predicative universality but also an existential moment *(in multis existat)*. In discussing the difference between the philosophical positions of Plato and Aristotle, Thomas observes that this divergence has no bearing on the question whether knowledge refers to reality. For both philosophers hold that the thing that is known has being outside the soul. They differ, however, in their views on the mode of being of the thing that is known.[37]

The most decisive argument for the onto-logical character of transcendentals is Thomas's concept of metaphysics. The proper subject of metaphysics is being in general *(ens commune)*. Because of the generalness of its subject metaphysics has a similarity — Thomas speaks of *affinitas* — with logic.[38] The radical difference, however, is that metaphysics deals with things themselves while logic treats of the intentions which reason forms of things.[39] That the subject of metaphysics is "being in general" means that it deals with being *as being* and with the properties belonging to being as such. Against this background the importance of the doctrine of transcendentals becomes understandable. For they are the general properties of being.[40]

Thomas criticizes the Neoplatonic position not only with respect to the transcendence of the most general determinations but also with respect to their order. About the one as prior to being Thomas does not speak explicitly, but he

---

[34] *In VII Metaphysic.* lect. 16, n. 1641.

[35] *Cf.* R.J. Henle, *Saint Thomas and Platonism*, The Hague 1956, 323 ff.

[36] *In De sensu et sensato*, lect. 6: *"Et quia Platonici ponebant communia, sicut sunt separata secundum rationem, ita etiam separata esse secundum esse"; De spiritualibus creaturis*, art. 3: *"Existimaverunt etiam quod quidquid est abstractum in intellectu, sit abstractum in re."*

[37] *De spiritualibus creaturis* art. 9 ad 6.

[38] *In VII Metaph.* lect. 3, nr. 1308: *"Haec scientia (metaphysica) habet quamdam affinitatem cum logica propter utriusque communitatem."*

[39] *In I Posteriora Analytica* lect. 20, n. 171.

[40] *Cf.* J.A. Aertsen, 'Die Lehre der Transzendentalien und die Metaphysik', *Freiburger Zeitschrift für Philosophie und Theologie* 35 (1988), 293 - 316.

does discuss the primacy of the good. In *Summa theologiae* I, q. 5, art. 2 he poses the question "Whether the good is prior in concept *(secundum rationem)* to being?" Thomas first advances a number of arguments which suggest the priority of the good and which are taken in part from pseudo-Dionysius. The second argument develops an idea which Thomas mentions but does not discuss in his commentary on *De causis:* the good is more extensive than being, because participation in the good also extends to non-being, namely, first matter. In the *Summa,* however, Thomas rejects this idea. First matter is not pure nothing, is no mere privation of being; it is being in potency. The good is therefore not more extensive than being.[41] Being and the good have the same *ambitum praedicationis;*[42] they are convertible. The question of the priority of one of the two is for Thomas not a question of *metaphysical* priority, but of priority *in concept.*

Next he presents as the *sed-contra* argument the fourth proposition from the *De causis:* "the first of created things is being." It is somewhat surprising that this proposition functions as a counterargument, since the original sense of the thesis implies the real priority of the good above being. I think the place of the proposition in the argumentation is to be accounted for from Thomas's cognitive approach to the question of priority. In his view the discussion concerns what is first in the order of human knowledge. Considered from this perspective, it is not forced to connect the 4th proposition from *De causis* with another thesis that had a great impact on medieval philosophy, namely Avicenna's idea that "being" is the first known.[43] This connection remains unexpressed in Thomas, but in his response to the question "Whether the good is prior in concept to being?" the influence of Avicenna is clear.

Thomas argues that "that is prior in concept which is first conceived by the intellect. Now the first thing conceived by the intellect is being." He also advances an argument for this priority: "For everything is knowable only insofar as it is in act." Hence, being is the first intelligible and is prior in concept to the good.[44] Thomas bases the priority of being on its actuality. His argumentation qualifies Berthold's analysis, in which the thesis that the more general something is, the more potential it is was considered to be characteristic for the Aristotelian position.

"Being" is the first and most general. The other transcendentals make explicit what belongs to every being. In the order of transcendentals, "the one"

---

[41] *Summa theologiae* I, q. 5, art. 2 ad 1 and 2.

[42] *In I Sententiarum* 8, 1, 3 ad 2.

[43] Avicenna Latinus, *Liber de philosophia prima,* tractatus I, c. 5 (ed. S. van Riet, Louvain-Leiden, 1973, 32 - 33).

[44] *Summa theologiae* I, 5, 2: *"Illud ergo est prius secundum rationem quod prius cadit in conceptione intellectus. Primo autem in conceptione intellectus cadit ens, quia secundum hoc unumquodque cognoscibile est quod est actu (...). Unde ens est proprium objectum intellectus, et sic est primum intelligibile (...). Ita ergo secundum rationem prius est ens quam bonum"* .

comes immediately after "being." It expresses that that which is is not divided. Insofar as something is, it is one.[45] The thesis that "being" and "one" are convertible indicates the place of the one in Thomas's way of thought.

The result of our analysis thus far seems to be that — with the provisos I have made — Thomas's own position roughly coincides with Berthold's description of the Aristotelian approach: transcendentality of the first, and this first is "being." Yet this is not the complete picture of Thomas.

(3) It is notable that Thomas also integrates in his thought structural elements of the Platonic position which he had described in his commentary on the *De causis*: the transcendence of the first on grounds of its generalness, the first is that which is participated in by the later, and it is the cause of the later. The best access to this side of Thomas's thought is afforded by the prologue to his commentary on Dionysius's *De divinis nominibus*.

In the prologue Thomas wants to justify Dionysius's Platonic way of speaking of God as "the Good itself" and "the *per se* Good." He describes the Platonists as wanting to reduce all that is composed to simple and abstract *(abstracta)* principles. Thus they posit the existence of separate Forms of things. They apply this "abstract" approach not only to the species of natural things but also to that which is most common *(maxime communia)*, namely, "good," "one," and "being." They hold that there is a first, which is the essence of goodness, of unity, and of being, a principle that we, Thomas says, call "God." The other things are called "good," "one" and "being" because of their derivation from the first, because of their participation in that which is essentially.

In the continuation of the prologue Thomas rejects the first application of the Platonic method, subscribing to Aristotle's criticism: there are no separate, subsisting Forms of natural things. But with regard to the first principle of things, Thomas recognizes the legitimacy of the Platonic approach.[46] It is this point that deserves further attention.

Thomas advances no argument for the validity of the Platonic method, but this can lie in nothing else than its application to that which is most common. For Thomas the Platonic reduction to "abstract" principles is only justified at the level of the *maxime communia*, that is, at the transcendental level. In this way he establishes a connection between the two traditions which Berthold of Moosburg places in sharp opposition: the transcendental approach of the Aristotelians and the transcendent approach of the Platonists. Thomas connects the Platonic type of generalness, which Berthold calls the *universalitas theologica sive separationis*, with the predicative generalness of transcend-

---

45 *Ibid.*, I, 11, 1.
46 *In De divinis nominibus, prooemium*: "*Sed quantum ad id quod dicebant de primo rerum principio, verissima est eorum opinio et fidei christianae consona*".

entals. This connection is possible because there is a causal relation between the first "separated" principle and the transcendentals. The *maxime communia* have to be reduced to what "is general through causality," namely, to God as the most universal cause.[47]

This connection is implied in Thomas's concept of metaphysics: the proper subject of this science is being in general *(ens commune)*. God is dealt with in metaphysics insofar as He is the cause of this subject.[48] Proper to the first principle is that its causality extends to being as being. One could therefore call this causality "transcendental." This transcendental causality, speaking in Christian terms, is a creating causality. For the essence of creation is the production of being in an absolute sense. It is in this way that Thomas interprets the 4th proposition from the *De causis* in his treatise on creation:

> When it is said that "the first of created things is being," "being" ... means the proper nature of the object of creation. For something is called created because it is a being *(ens)*, not because it is this being *(hoc ens)*.[49]

K. Kremer has undertaken to render plausible the thesis that under the influence of Neoplatonic philosophy Thomas has identified God with *esse commune*.[50] Now it is true that Thomas knows of a *communitas* of causality, but Kremer's view is hardly convincing. He himself must acknowledge that there is not a single text in which Thomas actually identifies God with *esse commune*. A weighty argument against Kremer's interpretation in my view is that such an identification does not fit in Thomas's concept of metaphysics. *Communia* are for Thomas, in keeping with the Aristotelian notion of generalness, *transcendentia*. They are the subject of metaphysics. God is dealt with in metaphysics insofar as He is the cause of this subject. Indeed, in several places in his work Thomas states that the *ens commune* is the proper effect of the highest cause, which is God.[51] God is for Thomas not *esse commune*, but *ipsum esse per se subsistens*. That is the expression he uses by preference to indicate the transcendence of the first principle.

"The One", too, is a divine name, but it plays no special role in Thomas's reflection. An important difference with the Neoplatonic position continues to be that for him the primary name of God is "Being." One of the arguments Thomas advances for this is typical of his approach. For this argument is based on the universality of being, that is, on its transcendental character. Being is the

---

[47] Cf. *In Boethii De trinitate* qu. 5, art. 4: "*Quae quidem principia possunt dici communia dupliciter (...) uno modo per praedicationem (...); alio modo per causalitatem (...). Huiusmodi ergo res divinae (...) sunt principia communia omnium entium*". Thomas makes a distinction between *communitas universalis* and *communitas causae* in *In X Metaph.* lect. 3, 1964.

[48] *In Metaphys., prooemium.*

[49] *Summa theologiae* I, 45, 4 ad 1.

[50] Kremer, *Die neuplatonische Seinsphilosophie,* 310; 356 ff.

[51] *Summa theologiae* I - II, 66, 5 ad 4: "*Ens commune est proprius effectus causae altissimae, scilicet Dei*" ; *De veritate* 10, 12 ad 10 *(in contrarium)*.

most general: it determines no mode of being. Because of its generalness and indeterminateness this name can be applied most properly to God. "All other names are either less universal, or, if convertible with it, add something above it at least in concept; hence in a certain way they inform and determine it."[52] "Being" is from a transcendental perspective the first and is therefore the most suitable name for expressing the transcendence of the divine being.

In *lectio* 6 of the *De causis* Thomas engages in a discussion with Proclus which is telling for the similarities and differences between the two thinkers. He discusses the 123d proposition of Proclus: "All that is divine is itself ineffable and unknowable" and points to the backgrounds of this thesis. The thesis presupposes that something is intelligible insofar as it is and is further based on the Platonic view that the first cause, which is essentially goodness and unity, is beyond being. With Proclus, Thomas recognizes the negative character of our knowledge of God. God's essence remains hidden from man. He also endorses the premise that something is intelligible insofar as it is. That in which the *ratio entis* is not found is not attainable by the intellect. He criticizes, however, the way in which Proclus understands the transcendence of the first cause.

> In truth, the first cause is beyond being insofar as it is infinite being *(esse)*. "Being" *(ens)*, however, is called that which participates in being *(esse)* in a finite way; and this is proportionate to our intellect (...) Therefore that alone is attainable by our intellect, which has an essence that participates in being. God's essence, however, is being itself *(ipsum esse)*. Therefore it is beyond the intellect.[53]

In this text it becomes apparent that Thomas expresses the transcendence of the divine being by means of the Platonic model of predication "essentially/by participation". Thomas adopts this model which was so fiercely criticized by Aristotle, but once again not without qualification. This Platonic model too is valid only when what is predicated has a transcendental character.[54] By applying the notion of participation to being it is possible for Thomas to conceive transcendence and transcendentality together. God alone is being *per essentiam*. All the rest is being through participation; in its being it is dependent upon the first principle. Only this created being is proportionate to our intellect. It is the first "in commonness."

4. *Master Eckhart*

In the Introduction we saw that Gilson presents the philosophy of Master Eckhart as a historical confirmation of the thesis that linking Neoplatonic henology with Christian thought leads necessarily to paradoxes. For Eckhart

---

[52] *Summa theologiae* I, 13, 11.
[53] *In De causis, propositio* 6a, ed. H.D. Saffrey, 47, 11 - 18.
[54] *Cf.* Thomas's adoption of the Platonic model of predication in *Quodlibeta* II, 2, 1.

teaches that in God there is the purity from being. Yet is the picture of Eckhart which is evoked here correct? First, I want to make clear that his thought is more complex than Gilson's account seems to indicate. Next, I shall undertake to determine Eckhart's philosophical position more precisely. Once again the two different models of thought sketched by Berthold of Moosburg will be useful to us.

(1) The starting point of my analysis is one of Eckhart's Latin sermons, which is of interest just because it deals with a Bible text which, as Gilson correctly observes, was precious to Eckhart, namely, Deuteronomy 6, 4: "Listen, Israel, the Lord our God, the Lord is one"[55] *(Deus unus est).* Eckhart's exposition begins with a *notandum,* which is typical of his handling of texts. The statement *"Deus unus est",* so he notes, has two senses. The text can be read in the first instance as "God, the one, is." It can also be understood as "nothing other than God is truly one."[56] The text can be interpreted onto-logically and henologically.

The first sense of *"Deus unus est"* is: God alone is.[57] "For by the very fact that he is one, being belongs to him, which is to say he is his being, he is pure being *(purum esse),* the being of all things."[58] Why does being belong to him because of his unity? The meaning of the one *(unum)* which Eckhart had given earlier in his sermon needs to be taken into account: "the one is that which is indistinct *(indistinctum)* from all." In this way he introduces a definition of unity that differs from Thomas's. For Thomas, following Aristotle, the "one" means "undivided" *(indivisum).* Insofar as a thing is, it is one, that is, is undivided in itself. From this it does not yet follow, however, that it is indistinct from something else. Eckhart defines the one as *indistinctum* — a definition to which we shall return — and infers from it: "Therefore, because of indistinctness or unity, all things and the fullness of being are in Him (God)."[59]

Deus unus means first of all that God is pure being. This terminology recalls the expression *"puritas essendi",* which Eckhart had earlier used in the first Parisian question and which Gilson interprets as the "purity from being." The subject in this question is: "Whether being and understanding are the same in God?"[60] Eckhart develops a series of arguments supporting the priority of understanding to being in God, arguments which can be read as a critique of

---

[55] *Sermo* 29: *"Deus unus est"* (*LW* IV, 263 - 270).

[56] *Ibid.,* n. 301 (*LW* IV, 267).

[57] *Cf. Expositio libri Exodi* n. 22 (*LW* II, 29): *"'Deus noster deus unus est', id est solus est".*

[58] *Sermo* 29 n. 301 (*LW* IV, 267).

[59] *Ibid.,* n. 298 (*LW* IV, 265).

[60] *Quaestiones Parisienses* qu. 1: *"Utrum in Deo sit idem esse et intelligere"* (*LW* V, 37 - 48).

medieval theo-ontology.[61] "Being" means to be caused, to be limited, "being" is the mark of creatureliness. Therefore God is not *esse* but *intelligere*.[62] Yet it is notable that in the Parisian question Eckhart leaves room for another semantics and another meaning of being. It is in this context that he introduces the expression *"puritas essendi"*. Even more striking is the fact that Eckhart sees this purity voiced in the text from Exodus which according to Gilson is normative for Christian thought.

> So the Lord, wishing to show that he possesses the *puritas essendi*, said 'I am who I am'. He did not say simply 'I am', but added 'who I am'. Therefore being does not befit God, unless you call this purity being *(nisi talem puritatem voces esse)*.[63]

Puritas essendi in this context cannot mean purity from being, but must mean the purity of being, that is, the *purum esse* of the sermon on *Deus unus*, the fullness of being. Eckhart clearly does not intend his different statements about the identity of being and understanding in God in the Parisian question as mutually exclusive alternatives.[64]

This interpretation is confirmed by Eckhart's sermon on the text from Deuteronomy. That God alone is is not the only possible explanation of *Deus unus est*. The text can also be understood as expressing God's unity. In elaborating this unity Eckhart adopts central ideas from the Parisian question. For he connects unity with intellectuality. "Unity or the one appears to be a property of the intellect alone."[65] All things are composed. Only God is completely simple and one: he is entirely intellect. The second meaning of *Deus unus est* is that God alone is pure understanding *(purum intelligere)*. Nothing that is created is entirely intellect, for in that case it would no longer be creatible *(creabile)*. The mark of the creature is that it has being different from understanding. "Being" is the *ratio creabilitatis*; Eckhart refers for this to the 4th proposition from the *De causis*.[66]

This sermon makes especially clear the complex character of Eckhart's thought. His first account of *Deus unus* moves within an ontological perspective: God is pure being. The other account moves within a henological perspective, which Eckhart elaborates in a new way: God is pure under-

---

[61] *Cf.* R. Imbach, *"Deus est intelligere". Das Verhältnis von Sein und Denken in seiner Bedeutung für das Gottesverständnis bei Thomas von Aquin und in den Pariser Quaestionen Meister Eckharts*, Freiburg (Switserl.) 1976, 144 ff.; E. zum Brunn *et al.*, *Maître Eckhart à Paris. Une critique médiévale de l'ontothéologie*, Paris 1984.

[62] *Quaestiones Parisienses* qu. 1, n. 10 (*LW* V, 46): "(...) *est de ratione entis quod sit causatum"*; n. 4 (*LW* V, p. 41): *"Et ideo Deus, qui est creator et non creabilis, est intellectus et intelligere et non ens vel esse"*.

[63] *Ibid.*, n. 9 (*LW* V, 45).

[64] *Cf.* W. Beierwaltes, *'Deus est esse — Esse est Deus*. Die onto-theologische Grundfrage als aristotelisch-neuplatonische Denkstruktur', in: *Platonismus und Idealismus*, Frankfurt am Main 1972, 51 - 54.

[65] *Sermo* 29, n. 300 (*LW* IV, 266).

[66] *Ibid.*, n. 301 (*LW* IV, 267 - 268). *Cf. Expositio libri Sapientiae* n. 24 (*LW* II, 344 - 345): *"Ratio creabilitatis est esse, secundum illud: 'Prima rerum creatarum est esse.'"*

standing. The two approaches have also something in common. Eckhart is always intent upon thinking through the transcendence of the first principle with respect to the creature. God alone is. Only God is truly one. Does Eckhart attain a philosophical integration of the different approaches?

(2) In Eckhart as in Thomas we find the thesis: "being and one are convertible."[67] The thesis of the convertibility belongs to the doctrine of *transcendentia*. I know of no medieval writing in which this doctrine comes so prominently to the fore as in Eckhart's *Opus tripartitum*. The general prologue to this work begins with some observations about the proper nature of "general terms" *(termini generales)* like being, unity, truth and goodness. Being itself and that which is convertible with it are not added to things as though posterior to them; on the contrary they are prior to every aspect of things. Moreover, the prior and superior *(superiora)* affects the inferior and posterior, and descends into it with its own properties.[68] *Transcendentia* are for Eckhart the basic words of thought, for they indicate the primary, from which things are to be understood.[69] In his grand project of the *Opus tripartitum* the transcendentals form the basis of the first part, the *Opus propositionum*. This part was to consist of fourteen treatises, the first four of them dealing with "being," "unity," "truth," and "goodness."

Eckhart's doctrine of transcendentals differs from Thomas's. In fact, this difference already becomes apparent in the observations on general terms just cited. It is striking that he calls the transcendentals not just the "prior" but also the "superior." Distinctive of Eckhart's doctrine is his identification of transcendentals with God. A text particularly illustrative of this identification is his commentary on John 1, 11: "He came unto his own *(in propria venit)*." What are the *propria* to which God came? Eckhart explains: these *propria* are being *(esse sive ens)*, the one, the true, and the good. These four God has as his own, because he is "the first" that, according to prop. 21 of the *De causis*, is "rich through itself" *(dives per se)*. He has these because he is "rich"; he has them as his own, because he is "through himself." For the four transcendentals in question are for all other things "strangers and foreigners," but for God they are "of the household" — Eckhart borrows these terms from Ephesians 2, 19.[70]

---

[67] See, *e.g., Expositio libri Genesis* II n. 17 (*LW* I, p. 487); *Expositio libri Exodi* n. 134 (*LW* II, 123); *Expositio libri Sapientiae* n. 5 (*LW* II, p. 326); *Sermo* 30, 2, n. 317 (*LW* IV, 279).

[68] *Prologus generalis* n. 8 (*LW* I, 152 - 153); n. 10 (*LW* I, 154).

[69] For the doctrine of the *transcendentia* in Eckhart see K. Albert, *Meister Eckharts These vom Sein. Untersuchungen zur Metaphysik des Opus tripartitum*, Saarbrücken-Kastellaun 1976, 109 - 189.

[70] *Expositio libri Iohannis* n. 97 (*LW* III, 83).

In the prologue to the *Opus propositionum* Eckhart's first *notandum* is that "God alone is properly being, one, true and good."[71] He justifies this identification, with respect to each transcendental separately, by appealing to the authority of Scripture and of the philosophers. We restrict ourselves here to "being" and "one." That God alone is properly being, is evident from Exodus 3: "I am who I am." In support of this is the fact that Parmenides and Melissus, the first philosophers, held that there is only one being. Also confirming this is the text of Deuteronomy 6 and Galatians 3: *deus unus est* — a text which clearly must be read here as "God, the one, is," in keeping with the first, ontological exposition Eckhart presents in his sermon.[72] The case is the same with respect to the one: God alone in the proper sense is the One, or is one. Again Eckhart cites Deuteronomy 6, this time to be read as "God is one." In support of this is the fact that Proclus and the *Book of Causes* often call God by the name of One or Unity.[73] Gilson quotes these last lines in his *Being and some Philosophers* and calls them "more precious than all the rest," apparently because he regards them as typical of Eckhart's henological position. But Gilson's statement completely disregards the context of these lines. Eckhart's intention in the prologue is to show that every transcendental, not just the one, must be equated with God. God alone in the proper sense is the One, just as also he alone is Being, Truth and Goodness.

The first result of our analysis, based on Eckhart's sermon on *Deus unus est,* was the differentiated character of his thought. We have now seen that his two interpretations of the Deuteronomy text are incorporated in his reflection on the *transcendentia*. This doctrine is the place where the ontological and henological approaches are brought together. That is possible because Eckhart gives the doctrine of transcendentals a new elaboration by identifying them with God. This identification is the key to determining what is distinctive in his philosophical position.

Eckhart's thought must be regarded as an original synthesis of the two approaches to reality that Berthold of Moosburg opposes to each other. What is special in this synthesis is Eckhart's uniting of the transcending movements of Aristotelianism and Platonism: the transcendentality of the first, namely, being with which one is convertible, and the transcendence of the first, namely, the one, are integrated. The transcendentals are proper to God, they are of his "household." God alone is being, he is the *puritas essendi*. All the rest is

---

[71] *Prologus in opus propositionum* n. 4 (*LW* I, 167): "*Solus Deus proprie est ens, unum, verum et bonum*".

[72] A.A. Maurer, in his English translation (*Master Eckhart — Parisian Questions and Prologues,* Toronto 1974, 95), reads "God is one". But this translation obscures the difference with the second reference to this text in the continuation of Eckhart's prologue.

[73] *Prologus in opus propositionum,* n. 5 - 6 (*LW* I, 168 - 169).

determined and limited: it is this or that being. To God unity is proper; what is created falls away from unity.[74]

(3) From Eckhart's synthesis the distinctive features of his philosophy can be accounted for. For the synthesis entails a number of consequences. The first of these bears upon the character of transcendentals: they are *communia*. The consequence of the identification of transcendentals with God must be that God is "general." Indeed, says Eckhart: *Deus communis est*. But in his thought this statement has by no means a pantheistic connotation. For Eckhart himself points out that it is precisely this communality that constitutes the transcendence of the first.

> Notice that all that is general, insofar as it is general, is God, and that all that is not general, insofar as it is not general, is not God but is created. For every creature is something finite, something limited, something distinct and something proper.[75]

God is not something distinct; what is proper to him is the *indistinctum*.[76] Earlier we observed, in Eckhart's exposition of *Deus unus est,* that he defines the "one" as "that which is indistinct from all." From our analysis it has now become clear why Eckhart can define the one in this way. The one, as that which is indistinct, expresses what has become characteristic for all transcendentals, now that they have become identified with the transcendent, namely, the generalness of God, who is not determined to a genus or species.[77]

Another consequence of Eckhart's synthesis of the transcendental approach with the transcendence of the first is that the One as divine name has a much more fundamental place in his thought than in Thomas's. Eckhart's reflection on the one contains elements adopted from Scholastic tradition. Like Thomas he teaches that, in the order of the transcendentals, one comes directly after being. For one does not add a positive content to "being," but just a negation.[78] Yet Eckhart says more: he calls the one the negation of negation *(negatio negationis)*. The concept "one" contains a double negation, for one is the denial of many, a concept which contains a negation in its own turn in the

---

[74] *Expositio libri Genesis* I, n. 26 *(LW* I, 205): *"Hoc ipso quod aliquid creatur et creatum est, cadit ab unitate et simplicitate. Deo enim proprium est et eius proprietas est unitas et simplicitas, sicut notavi diffuse super illo: 'deus unus est'"* (a clear reference to *Sermo* 29).

[75] *Sermo* 6, 1, n. 53 *(LW* IV, 51 - 52). Cf. *Expositio libri Iohannis* n. 103 *(LW* III, 88 - 89).

[76] *Expositio libri Exodi* n. 104 *(LW* II, 106): *"Indistinctum proprie deo competit, distinctio vero creaturis"; Sermo* 37, n. 375 *(LW* IV, 320).

[77] *Expositio libri Genesis* II, n. 86 *(LW* I, 548): *"Deus necessario est quid commune omnibus. Hoc autem est solum esse et quae cum ente convertuntur, puta unum, verum, bonum"*. Cf. *Expositio libri Sapientiae* n. 144 - 45 *(LW* II, 481 - 483).

[78] *Expositio libri Sapientiae* n. 148 *(LW* II, 486).

sense that "this being" is not "that being."[79] From this it follows that the one, although negatively expressed, means in reality a pure affirmation.[80]

It has been suggested that Eckhart borrowed the expression *negatio negationis* from Thomas,[81] but the basis for this suggestion seems rather weak to me. The phrase plays a marginal role in Thomas. It is actually found in just one place where it has, moreover, a different sense. For Thomas argues that in the concept "one" not only a negation of negation is implied but at the same time a real negation *(negatio negationis et rei simul)*. "The one" expresses that something is not divided. The most fundamental division is that by means of affirmation and negation. If in the concept "one" this division is denied, then this means that one contains a denial of both affirmation and negation. This conception excludes that "one" means a pure affirmation for Thomas.[82]

It has also been suggested that Eckhart's *negatio negationis* goes back to the influence of Proclus. But Beierwaltes has pointed to the important differences in this regard between the two thinkers[83] In Proclus the negation of negation leads, in the exceeding of the negative dialectic, to silence before the unknowable One. For Eckhart, however, as we have established, the negation of negation means a pure affirmation, is even, so he says, the marrow *(medulla)* and the summit *(apex)* of the purest affirmation.[84] But what is then affirmed in the negativity of the one?

In pursuing this question we return to the prologue of the *Opus propositionum* where Eckhart asserts that "God alone is properly being, one, true and good." We saw earlier that he justifies this thesis by appealing to the authority of Scripture and the philosophers. Notable, however — a point to which we have not yet called attention — is the fact that only with respect to the transcendental "one" Eckhart adds an argument. It is as follows:

> Moreover, "one" is the negation of negation. Hence it applies solely to the primary and complete being *(pleno esse)*, which is God, of whom nothing can be denied because he at once precontains and includes all being.[85]

"One", taken as *negatio negationis*, can be identified with God, for what is affirmed in this negation is the purity and fullness of being. Only God is the

---

[79] *Cf. Expositio libri Iohannis* n. 611 (*LW* III, 533). The places where Eckhart speaks on the *negatio negationis* are mentioned in *Deutsche Werke* I, 361, n. 4.

[80] *Expositio libri Sapientiae* n. 147 (*LW* II, 485): "*Li unum primo est voce quidem negativum, sed re ipsa affirmativum*"; *In Eccli.* n. 63 (*LW* II, 292 - 293): "*Unum transcendens in voce quidem negatio est, sed in significato, cum sit negatio negationis, est mera affirmatio*"; *Sermo* 111 (*LW* IV, 104).

[81] Imbach, *Deus est intelligere*, 190.

[82] *Quodlibeta* X, qu. 1, art. 1 ad 3.

[83] Beierwaltes, *Proklos*, 395 - 398.

[84] *Expositio libri Iohannis* n. 207 (*LW* III, 175): "*Negatio negationis, quae est medulla et apex purissimae affirmationis*".

[85] *Prologus in opus propositionum*, n. 6 (*LW* I, 169).

fullness of being.[86] Eckhart at several places accordingly connects the definition of the one as the negation of negation with the Exodus text: "I am who I am." In his commentary on this text he says: "The repetition of 'I am' in the statement 'I am who I am' points out the purity of the affirmation, which excludes every negation from God."[87]

In his study of Master Eckhart, B. Mojsisch contends that in his doctrine of the one as the negation of negation, Eckhart breaks through "the transcendental level" of being. The negativity implicit in one expresses the marrow, the purity and the summit of being. In its relation to being, the one surpasses being and gives being its ground. God as the One is the ground of transcendental being.[88]

It seems to me that this interpretation is incorrect. "Transcendental" in the sense in which Eckhart takes this term is not surpassable, because the *transcendentia* are identified with the Transcendent. Eckhart's doctrine of the one as *negatio negationis* must be considered an elaboration of this identification. Being and one are convertible because of their transcendentality. They are at the same time the *propria* of God. The transcendental "one" adds something in concept to "being." In Eckhart's reflection on this matter, the Neoplatonic transcendent approach to the first is given its place. Specific to the one, so he says, is that it makes explicit something which is not yet expressed by the term "being" itself, namely, the purity and fullness of being.[89]

5. Conclusion

In my paper I first presented a medieval version of the question: "Metaphysics of Being or philosophy of the One?" — namely, the interpretation of Berthold of Moosburg. In his commentary on Proclus he traces the opposition between ontology and henology to the different structures of thought associated with Aristotelianism and Platonism, which we have indicated with the keywords "transcendentality" and "transcendence" of the first. I then proceeded to use Berthold's model to elucidate the thought of Thomas Aquinas and Master Eckhart. To this analysis I would add three concluding observations.

First, we can ascertain that for Thomas and Eckhart the transcendental and transcendent approaches do not form an absolute opposition. Thomas posits a causal relation between God and the *maxime communia*. Transcendentals are to be traced to God as their cause. Eckhart identifies God and the *transcendentia*. That which is most general is God.

---

[86] *Expositio libri Iohannis* n. 692 (*LW* III, 608 - 609): "*Est in ea (divina natura) omnis negationis negatio, consequenter nulla prorsus imperfectio, defectus, sed plenitudo esse, vertitatis et bonitatis*".

[87] *Expositio libri Exodi* n. 16 (*LW* II, 21). Cf. n. 74 (*LW* II, p. 77); *Expositio libri Iohannis* n. 556 (*LW* III, 485); *In Eccli.* n. 63 (*LW* II, 292 - 293).

[88] B. Mojsisch, *Meister Eckhart. Analogie, Univozität und Einheit*, Hamburg 1983, 82 - 86.

[89] Cf. *Expositio libri Sapientiae* n. 148 (*LW* II, 486).

Secondly, both in Thomas and in Eckhart the doctrine of transcendentals is found to have an integrating function. That is notable, because Berthold regards this doctrine as typical of the Aristotelian position. Now this theory certainly contains anti-Platonic elements, as we observed in Thomas, such as the emphasis on predicative generalness. But transcendentals have yet another aspect, which Berthold does not mention, an aspect which played an essential role in the development of the doctrine. Generally, the *Summa de bono* of Philip the Chancellor, written about 1230, is regarded as the first treatise on transcendentals. In the prologue of this work Philip observes that "being," "one," "true" and "good" are not only that which is most common but are sometimes also "appropriated," that is, treated as "proper" to something. For in Scripture these names are attributed pre-eminently to God, they are also divine names.[90] The attention given this second kind of naming is undoubtedly influenced by pseudo-Dionysius, who functions in Berthold as an eminent witness for the Platonic view. Thus we see that in the context of the doctrine of *transcendentia* themselves the question must arise concerning the relation between the most general which goes through all categories, and the divine which surpasses all categories.

Thirdly, the medieval doctrine of transcendentals is pluriform. The solutions of Thomas and Eckhart diverge. Philosophically more important, however, is that in which they agree. Characteristic of philosophy is a transcending movement. It surpasses the concrete things of experience in quest of a first, from which reality can be understood. The answer to the question of what this first is can be sought in different directions. Berthold sketches two options: the first is the most general, which is the precondition for man's intellectual knowledge; or the first is the cause of the being of things but is not itself of the nature of the caused. Thomas and Eckhart represent a type of philosophical thought in which the two options in question are connected. That is their contribution to the debate about what philosophy should be: ontology or henology.

---

[90] Philippi Cancellarii Parisiensis *Summa de bono* (ed. N. Wicki), Bern 1985, 4 - 5. *Cf.* H. Pouillon, 'Le premier traité des propriétés transcendantales. La *Summa de bono* du Chancellier Philippe', *Revue néoscolastique de philosophie* 42 (1939), 40 - 77.

WERNER BEIERWALTES

PRIMUM EST DIVES PER SE
MEISTER ECKHART UND DER *LIBER DE CAUSIS*

I. GESCHICHTLICHE VORAUSSETZUNGEN DER FRAGE

"Die pseudo-aristotelische Schrift *Über das reine Gute,* bekannt unter dem Namen *Liber de causis,*"[1] von Meister Eckhart auch als Traktat vom "Licht der Lichter" zitiert, gehört zu denjenigen Texten, die der mittelalterlichen Philosophie und Theologie — anfangs durch die Autorität des Aristoteles noch in besonderem Maße motiviert — neuplatonisches Denken in genuiner und veränderter Form vermittelt haben.[2] In ihm hat die *Elementatio theologica* des Proklos zum einen eine empfindliche Reduktion erfahren, zum anderen aber ist sie durch die Einführung eines Schöpfungsbegriffes mit christlichem Denken kompatibler geworden, ohne daß der Begriff des verursachenden *"influxus"* verdrängt worden wäre. Neuplatonisch in ihm ist immerhin der das Ganze bestimmende Grundgedanke, daß das Sein jeder Ursache und jedes Verursachten im Sein und Wirken einer ersten Ursache gegründet sei, "die durch ihre Gegenwart in Ursache und Verursachtem" die Gesamtheit von Seiendem als ontologische Relation stiftet. Diese Relation vollzieht sich als creativer Hervorgang aus der alle anderen Ursachen bestimmenden ersten

---

[1] so der Titel der Ausgabe von Otto Bardenhewer, die (neben einer großen Einleitung) den arabischen Text mit einer deutschen Übersetzung, ferner den lateinischen Text samt einer Abhandlung zur Geschichte der lateinischen Übersetzung enthält (Freiburg 1882, Nachdruck Frankfurt, o. J.). Im Folgenden zitiere ich nach der neuen kritischen Ausgabe: *Liber de causis.* Édition établi à l'aide de 90 manuscrits avec introduction et notes par Adriaan Pattin, Louvain 1966 (innerhalb der *Tijdschrift voor Filosofie, 28).* Zur Problematik des *Liber de causis* insgesamt vgl. H.D. Saffrey, 'Der gegenwärtige Stand der Forschung zum *Liber de causis* als einer Quelle der Metaphysik des Mittelalters', in: *Platonismus in der Philosophie des Mittelalters,* hrsg. von W. Beierwaltes, Wege der Forschung, Bd. 197, Darmstadt 1969, 462 - 483; C.J. de Vogel, 'Some reflections on the *Liber de causis*', *Vivarium* IV (1966) 67 - 82; R.C. Taylor, 'St. Thomas and the *Liber de causis* on the hylomorphic composition of separate substances', *Mediaeval Studies* 41 (1979), 506 - 513. Vgl. auch J. Barnes, 'Immaterial causes', *Oxford Studies in Ancient Philosophy* 1 (1983), 169 - 192 (primär zu Proklos). Eine ausfürliche Untersuchung, die den *philosophischen* Gehalt des *Liber de causis* auf seine innere Konsistenz und seine Nähe oder Ferne zu seinen neuplatonischen Quellen analysiert, fehlt bislang. Auch die Kommentartradition des Mittelalters verdiente über eine rhapsodische Behandlung hinaus eine größere Aufmerksamkeit.

[2] Bardenhewer, *Die pseudo-aristotelische Schrift,* 11 ff.; 270 ff. H.D. Saffrey in seiner Ausgabe von Thomas' Kommentar zum *Liber de causis: Sancti Thomae de Aquino super Librum de causis expositio,* Fribourg/Louvain 1954, xv ff.

Ursache und als Rückkehr des Geschaffenen in das Erste: "Hervorgang" (neuplatonisch πρόοδος) als In-Sein der ersten Ursache in allen Ursachen, "Rückkehr" (neuplatonisch: ἐπιστροφή) als bewegtes Verbundensein des Verursachten mit seiner eigenen und damit mit der umfassenden ersten Ursache.[3]

Der Weg vom griechischen Vorbild über eine resümierende und verändernde Form ins Arabische und ins Lateinische des Gerhard von Cremona am Ende des 12. Jahrhunderts hat auf die Feinstruktur des Gedankens sicher nicht gerade klärend gewirkt. Dennoch hat Thomas von Aquin die *Elementatio theologica* des Proklos als neuplatonische Quelle und als Gedankenfundament des *Liber de causis* erkannt und sie in seiner Auslegung umsichtig und für diese Denkform sensibel ausgewertet.[4] Eine lateinische Übersetzung der *Elementatio theologica,* die einen kritischen Vergleich ermöglichte, wurde von Wilhelm von Moerbeke am 18. Mai 1268 in Viterbo abgeschlossen.[5] "Es war dies die erste von seinen Proklos-Übersetzungen, aber zugleich diejenige, die den größten Erfolg hatte, weite Verbreitung fand und recht eigentlich den Ruf des Proklos bei den lateinisch sprechenden Gelehrten des 13. bis 15. Jahrhundert begründete[6] und "der erste, der von der neuen Übersetzung ein Exemplar bekam, ist gewiß Thomas von Aquino gewesen."[7] Im *Prooemium* seiner *Expositio super librum de causis* charakterisiert Thomas das Verhältnis des *Liber* zu seiner arabischen Vorlage und zur *Elementatio theologica* folgendermaßen: "Im Griechischen findet sich ein Buch des Platonikers Proklos, das 211 Propositionen umfaßt und den Titel 'Theologische Grund-lehre' führt; im Arabischen aber findet sich das Buch, das bei den Lateinern 'De causis' heißt, von dem feststeht, daß es aus dem Arabischen übersetzt ist und im Griechischen gar nicht vorhanden ist: daher scheint es von einem arabischen Philosophen aus dem vorgenannten Buch des Proklos exzerpiert zu

---

[3] W. Beierwaltes, 'Der Kommentar zum *Liber de causis* als neuplatonisches Element in der Philosophie des Thomas von Aquin', *Philosophische Rundschau* 11 (1964), 192 - 215, hier: 193, 200 ff. zu Saffreys Ausgabe.

[4] Die unbesonnene Behauptung Bardenhewers, *Die pseudo-aristotelische Schrift,* 257, daß "von irgendeiner entscheidenden Beeinflussung seines <Thomas'> Lehrbegriffes durch dieses Buch <*Liber de causis*> auch nicht 'im entferntesten die Rede sein' könne", ist durch die neuere Forschung längst und gründlich widerlegt. Außer dem in Anm. 1 Genannten vgl. die Sammlung derjenigen Stellen aus dem Werk des Thomas von Aquin insgesamt, an denen der *Liber de causis* zitiert wird, die zugleich die Bedeutung des *Liber de causis* für zentrale Aspekte von Thomas' Lehre evident machen: C. Vansteenkiste, 'Il *Liber de causis* negli scritti di San Tommaso', *Angelicum* 35 (1958), 325 - 374.

[5] H. Boese, *Wilhelm von Moerbeke als Übersetzer der* Stoicheosis theologike *des Proclus,* Abhandlungen der Heidelberger Akademie der Wissenschaften, phil.-hist. Klasse, Jg. 1985, 5. Abhandlung, Heidelberg 1985, 11. Hierin dokumentiert Boese seinen langjährigen, höchst kundigen Umgang mit der handschriftlichen Tradition der *Elementatio theologica,* dem wir glücklicherweise nun auch einen kritischen Text verdanken: Proclus, *Elementatio theologica, translata a Guillelmo de Morbecca,* hrsg. von H. Boese, Leuven 1987 (Ancient and Medieval Philosophy, De Wulf-Mansion Centre, series 1,V).

[6] Boese, *Wilhelm von Moerbeke,* 11.

[7] Boese, *ibid.,* 48.

sein, zumal da alles, was in diesem Buch enthalten ist, viel reicher und ausführlicher in jenem (Proklos) enthalten ist", "(...) *multo plenius et diffusius continentur in illo*".[8] In Thomas' aus seiner späten Zeit (um 1272) stammenden Interpretation dieses Textes zeigen sich — analog zu seiner Dionysius-Rezeption[9] — Grundgedanken, die sich als neuplatonische Leitlinien oder Implikationen in seinem eigenen Denken wiederfinden oder dieses in bestimmter Weise differenzieren und entfalten.[10] Der *Liber de causis*-Kommentar des Thomas ist ein bedeutendes Dokument dafür, daß in Thomas "Platonismus" mit "Aristotelismus" auf eine produktive Weise konkurrieren.

Meister Eckhart hat sich mit dem *Liber de causis* bei weitem nicht so intensiv auseinandergesetzt wie Thomas oder Albertus Magnus,[11] dennoch ist für die Methode und die Sache seines Denkens aufschlußreich, daß er an zahlreichen Stellen seines Werkes zentrale Sätze aus dem *Liber de causis* in seine eigene Argumentation, eigens oder im Ensemble mit anderen Texten, aufnimmt und dadurch genuinen neuplatonischen Denkfiguren in ihr einen systematischen Ort gibt.

Daß Meister Eckhart vom *Liber de causis* eine unmittelbare Kenntnis hatte, ist anzunehmen.[12] Als sicher kann es auch gelten, daß er den Kommentar des Thomas benutzt hat.[13] Aus dem Umgang mit diesem war ihm wohl auch bekannt geworden, daß der *Liber de causis* und Proklos voneinander zu

---

[8] Thomas von Aquino, *Super Librum de causis expositio* III, 3 - 10 (hrsg. von H.D. Saffrey).

[9] Von Francis O' Rourke wird hoffentlich in absehbarer Zeit eine philosophische Dissertation publiziert werden, die in einer Interpretation des Dionysius-Kommentars des Thomas von Aquin u.a. dessen neuplatonische Implikationen herausarbeitet.

[10] Ich habe in der Anm. 3 zitierten Abhandlung vier Gedankenkomplexe skizziert, die als metaphysische Implikationen neuplatonischer Herkunft für das Denken des Thomas als konstitutiv gelten können: 1. Selbstreflexion des Denkens; 2. der Ternar *esse—vivere—intelligere*; 3. das Problem der Ursächlichkeit; 4. Schöpfung und Teilhabe.

[11] *Liber de causis et processu universitatis*, in: *Alberti Magni Opera omnia*, hrsg. von A. Borgnet, Paris 1891, tomus 10, *Parva naturalia*, pars II, 361 - 619; das zweite Buch *(De terminatione causarum primariarum)* enthält eine Paraphrase einer Reihe von Sätzen aus dem *Liber de causis*. Der Text der Borgnet'schen Ausgabe ist fehlerhaft und bedarf einer kritischen Erneuerung.

[12] Meine Hinweise auf wörtliche und verdeckte Zitate aus dem *Liber de causis* bei Meister Eckhart, die ich im Folgenden geben werde, erstreben keine Vollständigkeit. Zur Orientierung über Meister Eckhart im ganzen vgl. Kurt Ruh, *Meister Eckhart. Theologe, Prediger, Mystiker,* München 1985 (²1989); Alois M. Haas, *Sermo Mysticus,* Freibrug (Schweiz) 1984, passim. Die *Texte* Eckharts zitiere ich nach der — leider immer noch nicht vollendeten — kritischen Ausgabe: *Die deutschen Werke,* hrsg. im Auftrag der Deutschen Forschungsgemeinschaft von Josef Quint, Stuttgart 1936 ff. *(DW); die lateinischen Werke,* hrsg. von Josef Koch u.a., Stuttgart 1936 ff. *(LW).* 1987 hat *L.* Sturlese die *Prologi in opus tripartitum et Expositio Libri Genesis* nach einer von ihm in der Bodleian Library Oxford entdeckten Handschrift publiziert, die die bisherigen Textzeugen in *LW* 1 an Authentizität übertrifft. In Sturleses Ausgabe ist der neue Text dem der Urfassung in der Amplonianischen Handschrift (E) und der sog. "CT-Rezension" (Codex *Cusanus* 21 et *Treverensis* 72/1056) gegenübergestellt, so daß dessen Abweichungen von der Edition in *LW* 1 leicht zu verifizieren sind.

[13] In den deutschen Werken zitiert er den *Liber de causis* durch folgende Hinweise: "ein meister" (Nû sprichet ein meister von der êrsten sache (...)): *DW* 1, 329,1 f., "ein heiden" oder ein "heidenischer meister", *DW* 1, 56, 8 f.; ebd., 346, 3 f.

unterscheiden sind, daß sie aber in der Sache auch miteinander über-
einstimmen; er zeigt dies gelegentlich durch die Formulierung "(...) *de causis
et Proclus*" an.[14] Ob Meister Eckhart allerdings die proklische *Elementatio*
direkt aus einem Kölner oder dem Pariser Exemplar von Moerbekes Übersetzung kennen lernte, bedarf immer noch einer genaueren Klärung. Josef Koch
hielt es für "zweifelhaft" und bekräftigte dies noch 1948 in seiner
"Akademischen Festrede zur Universitäts-Gründungsfeier" in Köln über
"Platonismus im Mittelalter" mit der Behauptung: "Die Art und Weise, wie
Eckhart Proklos zitiert, spricht mehr dafür, daß er dessen Schrift nur aus dem
Kommentar des Thomas zum Buch von den Ursachen kennt."[15] Ich neige zu
einer positiven Antwort auf die gestellte Frage, weil es bei Eckhart mindestens
zwei Zitate aus der *Elementatio theologica* gibt, die *nicht* bei Thomas von
Aquin vorkommen und aus dem Kommentar des Albertus Magnus ohnehin
nicht gewonnen werden konnten.[16]

Die Gedanken, zu deren Erläuterung, Klärung und autoritativer Stützung
Meister Eckhart den *Liber de causis* heranzieht, sind für sein Denken durchaus
leitend und bestimmend: sie betreffen seine Lehre von Gottes Sein und Einheit
in sich, nicht minder dessen creatives Wirken nach außen, das Sein und Wirken
des göttlichen Grundes und Ursprungs *im* Sein des Geschaffenen, weiterhin die
Stufung der Wirklichkeit insgesamt in ihr selbst und die Struktur des Intellekts
oder der Seele als einer sich selbst reflexiv erfassenden Bewegung.

Am häufigsten zitiert Meister Eckhart die *propositio* XX des *Liber de
causis:* "*Primum est dives per seipsum*" in der Form: "*Primum est dives per
se,*"[17] weiterhin solche Sätze, die das Sein-konstituierende, in ihm anwesende

---

14 Die Formulierung, die im Kontext des Hinweises auf die erste *propositio* des *Liber
de causis* steht, stammt aus Thomas' Interpretation eben dieser *propositio*: "Primo (...)
advenit et ultimo recedit": Thomas 8, 11; Eckhart, *LW* 2, 511, 8 f. Ähnlich 1, 173, 12 f.; 3,
81, 1 f. ist die zitierte Stelle mit dem Hinweis verbunden: "*ut ait propositio prima de causis
et eius commentator,*" mit dem sicher Thomas gemeint ist. "*Commentator*" ist zu
unterscheiden von dem Hinweis "*in commento*" (z. B. *LW* 3, 28, 6), der wohl auf die
Erläuterung der These im *Liber de causis* selbst hindeutet.

15 "*Proclus et Liber de causis*": *LW* 1, 169, 4 f.; "*Ex libro Procli et De causis*": *LW* 3,
488, 2.

16 J. Koch, 'Meister Eckhart. Versuch eines Gesamtbildes', in: *Kleine Schriften,* Roma
1973, I, 212; Ders., *Platonismus im Mittelalter,* Krefeld 1948, 29. Koch erläutert allerdings
nicht die von ihm apostrophierte "Art und Weise", in der Eckhart Proklos zitiert, die nach
seiner Meinung ein Ausweis dafür sein soll, daß Eckhart den Text der *Elementatio nicht*
direkt gekannt habe. — Ein Exemplar der *Elementatio theologica* war Eckhart in Paris oder
in Köln durchaus erreichbar gewesen. Die Anregung zu einer mehr oder weniger
ausführlichen Lektüre dieser Texte mag von seiner Kenntnis des Thomas-Kommentars
ausgegangen sein.— Die Propositionen, die Eckhart zitiert und die sich *nicht* bei Thomas
finden, sind die erste und zwanzigste in der *Expositio Libri Genesis* 4 (*LW* 1, 197, 8 f.), bzw.
im *Liber parabolarum Genesis* 209 (*LW* 1, 684, 3 - 5). — Weder Albertus' *Liber de causis*
noch seine *Metaphysica* können seine Quelle für Zitate aus der proklischen *Elementatio
theologica* gewesen sein, da beide weder direkte noch indirekte Proklos-Zitate enthalten.

17 Der *Liber de causis*-Text bei Thomas lautet: "*Primum est dives* propter *seipsum et
est dives magis*" (112). Außer im Kontext seines Kommentars zum *Liber de causis* erläutert
oder zitiert Thomas diesen Satz nicht, obgleich er das damit eng verbundene Philosophem
"*bonum est diffusivum sui*" nicht nur kennt, sondern zustimmend in seinen *creatio*-Begriff

und es erhaltende Wirken der ersten Ursache beschreiben, so vor allem die *propositio* IV: *"Prima rerum creatarum est esse"*. In Form und Intention gleichen die aus dem *Liber de causis* genommenen *propositiones* den Sätzen aus dem *Liber XXIV Philosophorum,* die Meister Eckhart ebenfalls für Grundzüge seines Gottesbegriffs heranzieht.[18]

In meinen Überlegungen konzentriere ich mich auf diejenigen Bereiche des Eckhartschen Denkens, auf die die beiden zitierten Sätze ein besonderes Licht werfen. Ich werde dabei jeweils die neuplatonische Problemlage kurz erörtern, um so deutlich zu machen, welche neuplatonischen Elemente — genuine und durch den *Liber de causis* veränderte — durch die Vermittlung eben dieses komplexen, aber dennoch autoritativen Textes im Denken Meister Eckharts prägend wirksam geworden sind. Was Eckhart aus dem *Liber de causis* zitiert, zitiert er mit Zustimmung. — Für den unmittelbar folgenden Zusammenhang sollte bewußt gehalten werden, daß Eckhart das als *"primum"* oder *"causa prima"* benannte erste Prinzip der Wirklichkeit insgesamt mit *"Deus"* ineins setzt.

II. GOTT: DAS SICH ENTÄUßERENDE EINE UND GUTE — DIE ANTWORT DES MENSCHEN

"Primum est dives per se." ("Das Erste (Gott) ist reich durch sich selbst"); im Sinne des Folgenden kann die These auch in der Form verstanden werden, wie sie bei Thomas steht — *"propter seipsum"*: ("das Erste ist reich *aufgrund* seiner selbst"). Die Erläuterung dieses Satzes im *Liber de causis* sieht den Grund des Reich-Seins des Ersten in dessen *Einheit*; es ist nicht in sich selbst "zerstreut", es hat also keine Unterschiedenheit in ihm selbst, ist deshalb *"reine"* Einheit oder Einfachheit (*simplicitas*). Diese Begründung des Reich-Seins vollzieht auch Meister Eckhart nach; sie führt uns später zu dem zweiten Aspekt dieser Frage.

1. Das Moment des *creativen Sich-Verströmens* ist durch die Identifikation der Einheit oder Einfachheit mit der Gutheit (*bonitas*) angezeigt. Das durch sich selbst oder aufgrund seiner selbst "Reiche" ist zugleich das "zuhöchst Reiche", das Reichste schlechthin (*dives maius* oder *magis*), welches durch keinerlei "Einfluß über oder aufs es selbst" (*influxio super ipsam per aliquem modorum*) begründet wird; als erste Ursache ist es vielmehr Grund in ihm selbst oder durch sich selbst, es bedarf deshalb keiner Grundlegung "von anders woher", oder: eine solche ist durch die absolute Selbstbestimmtheit des

---

einbezieht, vgl. z.B. *In De divinis nominibus* 501 (hrsg. Pera): *"Bonitas divina (...) se extendit diffundendo per bonitatem, usque ad infimas substantias." Summa contra gentiles* I 37: *"dicitur bonum esse diffusivum sui esse. Haec autem diffusio deo competit"* — Der Text von *propositio* XX bei Albertus: *"Primum est dives per seipsum"*, a.a.O. (Anm.11), 576 f., 579.

[18] Zum *Liber XXIV Philosophorum,* vgl. *Die deutsche Literatur des Mittelalters,* Verfasserlexikon V, 767 - 770.

Ersten gar nicht möglich; alles Andere jedoch, was ihm entspringt, "bedarf" (*indiget*) als ein in seinem Eins-Sein "Zusammengefügtes" eines Anderen, eines verursachenden Grundes. — Ganz im Sinne des *Liber de causis* und seines genialen Interpreten Thomas versteht Meister Eckhart das Reich-Sein Gottes durch sich selbst als ein herausgehobenes, ihm einzig zukommendes Sein: als das Sein eines grund-losen, alles Seiende grund-los (*gratia*) gründenden Grundes, der sich als solcher selbst in diesem seinem eigenen Sein genügt (*sufficientia*), zugleich im Blick auf das, was aus ihm oder "unter ihm" (*inferiora*) ist, das Ganze der Wirklichkeit im vorhinein *ist*, oder alles Andere in der *ihm* eigentümlichen Existenzweise *vor* diesem als Ganzes *hat* (*praehabere*),[19] so daß er als die "Fülle" oder "Überfülle" (*plenitudo, abundantia*) des Seins gedacht werden müß: "Fülle des Seins" in dem doppelten Sinne eines genitivus subiectivus und genitivus obiectivus zugleich: alles Sein als Es selbst — das Erste und Reichste — *in sich* umfassend, indem es dieses vor aller creativen Entfaltung als subiectum und Grund seiner selbst *ist*, und zum anderen *begründende* Fülle des Seins, die an ihm selbst teilgibt, indem sie dieses allererst konstituiert, d.h. als Seiendes, Einzeln-Existierendes im Kontext eines Ganzen (*universum*) hervorbringt. Die "Fruchtbarkeit" (*fecunditas*) des durch sich selbst Reichen "entfaltet sich" (*diffunditur, diffusio*); gemäß der Terminologie des *Liber de causis* und in der Auslegung des zitierten Satzes "fließt" das Erste in das Andere aus oder in dieses hinein, *indem* es dieses in seinem Sein begründet. "Ausfluß" oder "Einfluß" des Ersten meint creative Teil-Gabe an seinen eigenen "Eigenschaften", neben anderem an seiner Einheit und Ungeteiltheit; im Akt des creativen Aus- oder Einfließens bleibt es selbst "ungeteilt" in ihm selbst und *wirkt* gerade dadurch in dem geschaffenen Sein von in sich "geteilter", zusammengesetzter Einheit als das sammelnde und einende Prinzip.[20]

Im Kontext des "*dives*-Satzes" aus dem *Liber de causis* verweist Meister Eckhart auf eine Bestimmung des Reichen, wie sie Aristoteles in seiner *Politik* gegeben hat: "Zum Wesen des Reichen gehört es, zu geben, nicht zu empfangen"; zugleich erinnert er an die Bestimmung des Guten oder Zuhöchst-Guten, wie sie Platon im *Timaios* voraussetzt: daß von ihm — dem Guten — Neid oder Mißgunst "weit entfernt" sei — ein Gedanke, der in der neuplatonischen Tradition durchweg als Grundzug des Guten gedacht wurde:[21] dieses gibt neidlos an ihm selbst teil, es verströmt sich ("*bonum est diffusivum sui*"), es gibt sich selbst *als* Anderes und *im* Anderen. Mit diesem Konzept als einer

---

[19] *In Johannem* 1, *LW* 3, 462, 4 ff.
[20] *Prologus generalis in opus tripartitum* 10, *LW* 1, 155, 1 ff. *Prologus in opus propositionum* 21, *LW* 1, 178, 10 ff.; *Sermo* 29, 299, *LW* 4, 266, 7 ff.
[21] Vgl. hierzu K. Kremer, 'Bonum est diffusivum sui. Ein Beitrag zum Verhältnis von Neuplatonismus und Christentum', in: *Aufstieg und Niedergang der römischen Welt*, Teil II: Principat. Band 36, 2, Berlin-New York 1987, 994 - 1032.

"*ratio philosophorum*"[22] ist für Eckhart ohne Bruch der für die Botschaft des Neuen Testamentes grundlegende Gedanke verbindbar: Gott *gibt* Alles Allen "im Überfluß", als die Selbstgenügsamkeit in sich gibt er sich selbst und wird so zu unserem eigenen Genügen: "*sufficientia nostra ex deo est* (2 Cor. 3, 5), *id est per hoc et ex hoc quod sumus ex deo et cum deo*";[23] als das durch sich selbst Reiche, das nichts "empfängt", auf das nichts "einfließt", "gibt" es Allem und dem Einzelnen sich ganz und Alles, was ihm selbst als solchem gehört. Dieses Sich-selbst-im-Anderen-Geben meint zuerst, daß es als "*causa prima et universalis omnium*" das Sein im Sinne von Existent-Sein erwirkt,[24] d. h. es schafft (*creat*) das Sein im Ganzen und als Ganzes *und* in seiner jeweiligen Einzelnheit (*hoc aut hoc*). Es ist *ganz* aus ihm: als Existenz *und* als Wesen. In einem relativen Sinne vermögen einzelne aktive Seins-Gestalten (*formae*) oder Seins-Prinzipien ein "*hoc aut hoc*" hervorzubringen, jedoch nur im Bezug auf dessen jeweilige Form oder Einzelnheit, nicht aber im Bezug auf dessen Existenz als solche.[25] Wieder im Kontext des *dives*-Satzes gesagt: *prima enim causa necessario dat omnibus omnia; aut enim omnibus aut nulli, omnia vel nihil, secundum illud Rom. 4:* "*vocat ea quae non sunt, tamquam ea quae sunt.*"[26] Oder: "*dives per se*", *quia dat omnibus, dat omnia, dat omnibus omnia,* "*dives per se*" *propter sufficientiam et abundantiam,* "*et est dives maius*" *sive* "*magis*" *propter copiam, superabundantiam et redundantiam sive effluxum.*[27] — Am Ende einer eigenständigen Auslegung der Aussage: "In gleicher Weise sind Gott, der Gottlose und seine Gottlosigkeit verhaßt" aus dem 14. Kap. des *Liber Sapientiae*, ausgehend von dem im *Liber de causis* sich zeigenden Grundgedanken, daß Gott als das "Erste" im Seienden und die erste Ursache von Allem das reine Sein ("*esse purum*") ist, und daß dieser Gott "sich selbst in Allem und Alles in sich selbst liebt",[28] steht der das Wirklich-Sein des Geschaffenen verteidigende Satze Eckharts: "Wenn wir (dies) sagen" d.h. daß Gott in Allem einzig das Sein und sich selbst, der selbst das Sein *ist,* erkenne und liebe "zerstören wir nicht das Sein der Dinge, sondern (*be*)gründen es".[29]

Diesen Akt des freien Gebens oder Gründens von in sich als Einzelnes seiendem Sein durch die erste Ursache, die das "Reiche durch sich selbst" ist,

---

[22] Über den methodischen und sachlichen Leitgedanken, auch in der Auslegung der Bibel philosophisch verfahren zu wollen —"*naturali ratione clare exponuntur*" (*LW* 1, 165, 11 f.) — vgl. K. Flasch, 'Die Intention Meister Eckharts', in: *Sprache und Begriff, Festschrift für Bruno Liebrucks*, hrsg. von H. Röttges, B. Scheer, J. Simon, Meisenheim 1974, 292 - 318.

[23] Zuvor: "*Quia primum est dives per se, dat omnibus affluenter*" (Jac. 1, 5): *Sermo* 27, 2, 270 f.; *LW* 4, 247, 1 ff.; *Sermones et Lectiones super Ecclesiastici* 12, *LW* 2, 242, 1 ff.

[24] *Prologus in opus propositionum* 20 f., *LW* 1, 178, 3 ff.; *Sermo* 54, 2, 533, *LW* 4, 149, 5 ff.

[25] *Prologus in opus propositionum, loc. cit.* 178, 11 ff.

[26] *Super Eccli., loc. cit.* 242, 5 - 7.

[27] *Sermo* 34, 3, 348, *LW* 4, 302, 13 ff.

[28] *In Sap.* 255, *LW* 2, 587, 3 ff.; 588, 5.

[29] "(...) *hoc* (...) *dicendo non destruimus esse rerum, sed constituimus*": *ibid., LW* 2, 260; 591, 12 f.

charakterisiert Eckhart mit eben diesem Satz und drei anderen *propositiones*
aus dem *Liber de causis* — eine zentrale, auf Gott als den Ursprung ver-
weisende Aussage des Römerbriefs umschließend — durch: "fest fügen", eine
klare, in sich stehende Gestalt geben (*figere*), einen (bewahrenden) "Grund
legen", eine Grundlage für jedes Einzeln-Seiende im Sein setzen (*fundare*), es
als Seiendes im Sein, "beständig" halten (*stabilire*).[30] Sein-Geben, Einzelnes
als in sich Seiendes in seinem Sein Gründen schließt also das *Bewahren* eben
dieses Seins unmittelbar ein: indem Gott "Alles stärkt und ihm Bestand gibt"
— Er, der von "keinem als von sich selbst und durch sich selbst in sich selbst
bestärkt und beständigt ist,"[31] — *wirkt* selbst in allem Seienden, damit dieses
sich als *es* selbst in seiner Eigentümlichkeit bewahren könne. Die
propositiones, die im Kontext des *dives*-Satzes diesen Gedanken bestätigen
sollen, beziehen sich exemplarisch auf die "*fixio et essentia*", auf den "festen
(Be-)stand und das Sein" der denkenden Wesenheit, weiterhin auf die
Abhängigkeit aller "Kräfte" (*virtutes*) von dem unbegrenzten (un-endlichen)
Ersten, welches "Kraft" oder Mächtigkeit schlechthin ist (*virtus virtutum*), und
auf die ursächliche Herkunft des *Seins* jeglicher essentia vom ersten Sein, des
Lebens vom ersten Leben, und des Wissens oder der Fähigkeit *und* des Aktes
des *Denkens* und Wissens vom ersten Denken her — auf eine in sich gestufte
Wirklichkeit also von "Sein-Leben-Denken", deren Elemente sich voneinander
unterscheiden und zugleich im Unterschied aufeinander bezogen sind.[32]

Dieses freie Geben des Seins als des Daseins, das Gründen und Gestalten
von Einzeln-Seienden und das Bewahren jeglicher existierender Gestalt wird
von Meister Eckhart in einer Konvergenz von Sätzen aus dem *Liber de causis,*
die aus dem *dives*-Satz sich ableiten, mit der für den christlichen Gedanken
charakteristischen Bestimmung dieses Gebens unmittelbar und intensiv
verbunden: das Erste oder Gott, weil reich durch sich selbst, "gibt Allem Alles
umsonst", ("*gratis dat omnibus omnia*").[33] Daß Gott das Sein frei gibt, es sein
läßt, gründet und bewahrt — dies ist ein Akt seiner *Gnade,* ein Ausdruck also
der freien und ungeschuldeten, aktiven Zuwendung Gottes zum Geschaffenen,
in dem er sich selbst erkennt und liebt, oder dieses liebt *wie* sich selbst.[34]
Dadurch bewegt er das Geschaffene auch wieder zu sich selbst als dessen Ziel
im Ursprung *hin.*

2. Das Reich-Sein des Ersten oder Gottes durch sich selbst und das Sich-
Verströmen dieses Reichtums ist in seiner *Einheit* oder in seinem *Eines-Sein*

---

[30] *Ibid.*, 591, 14 ff.
[31] *Ibid.*, 591, 14 ff.
[32] *Ibid.*, 592, 3 ff.
[33] *In Sap.* 272, *LW* 2, 602, 7 f.; 603, 3 ff.; *Sermo* 34, 3, 348, *LW* 4, 302, 5 ff.; 13 ff.;
DW 2, 297, J. Quints Anm. 1.- Im Kontext des christlichen Gedankens einer "frei
schenkenden Gnade" sei immerhin an Plotin, *Enneaden* IV 8, 6, 23 erinnert, wo er von dem
Einen Guten sagt: ἐν χάριτι δόντος.
[34] *In Sap.* 590, 11 ff.

begründet: "*deus eo dives profusivus est, quia* unus."[35] Nach einer landläufigen
Vorstellung könnte man erwarten, daß "Reichtum" als Prädikat des göttlichen
Absoluten und Ersten gerade durch die Fülle des Vielen in ihm, durch das
Aufgefächert- und Umfassend-Ganze und nicht durch das Prädikat "Einheit"
oder "Sein als Einheit" beschrieben würde. Für ein durch neuplatonische
Konzeptionen geleitetes Denken indes ist es nicht nur nicht befremdlich,
sondern geradezu gefordert, die Fülle oder das Ganze des ersten und creativ
begründenden Seins als eine Einheit zu fassen.[36] Eine derartige Einheit des
göttlichen Seins ist in ihr selbst "differenziert", ohne jedoch eine *trennende*
Andersheit in sich selbst wirksam werden zu lassen; der Begriff des Einen als
"*indivisum esse*" schließt schon von sich her eine das Sein selbst "teilende"
Andersheit aus. Das Eine ist selbst "Negation der Negation" (*negatio negationis*, "versagen des versagennes"):[37] weil es *Alles* schon im *Vorgriff* auf die
creativ gesetzte, reale Andersheit des Seienden *ist*, kann von ihm "nichts
negiert werden";[38] durch sein Sein und durch den dieses Sein vollziehenden
Akt der Reflexion schließt es alles begrenzende, einschränkende, teilende
Andere aus ihm selbst aus ("*in deo enim non est aliud*");[39] insofern negiert es
als "*negatio negationis*" alles möglicherweise Nichtige in ihm selbst und
erweist sich *in* der Negation als reine Selbstaffirmation (*puritas
affirmationis*).[40] Trotz oder gerade wegen des negierenden Ausschlusses aller
realen Andersheit aus dem göttlichen Sein ist es in seinen ihm wesentlichen
Momenten — den trinitarischen Personen und dem Sein des "Zu-Schaffenden"
in der Vorhabe oder im Vorblick auf dessen reale Andersheit und Einzelnheit
— in der intensivst denkbaren Weise in sich aufeinander bezogen. Dieser
Bezug *ist* als eine "*reflexiva conversio in se ipsum et super se ipsum*", als eine
ihr eigenes Sein denkende Spiegelung und Selbstdurchdringung und — in einer
absoluten Metapher gesagt als einer Selbst-Durch*lichtung* (*in lucem se toto se
totum penetrans*).[41] Diese in sich bewegte Beziehung oder Reflexivität, —

---

[35] *Sermo* 29, 299, *LW* 4, 266, 7.
[36] *Ibid.*, 266, 5 f. Die Konzeption einer in sich differenzierten Einheit bei Meister
Eckhart werde ich in einer eigenen Abhandlung darstellen.— Für eine Typologie der
griechisch-metaphysischen und christlich-theologischen Einheitsbegriffe verweise ich auf
mein *Denken des Einen. Studien zur neuplatonischen Philosophie und ihrer Wirkungsgeschichte,* Frankfurt 1985, ferner: 'Einheit und Identität als Weg des Denkens', in: *L'uno e
i Molti,* a cura di V. Melchiorre, Milano 1990, 3 - 47.
[37] *Prologus in opus propositionum* 6, *LW* 1, 169, 6 und die dort in Anm. 5 und 6
gegebenen Hinweise. Zu den neuplatonischen Voraussetzungen dieser Konzeption vgl.
Exkurs IV, "*Negatio negationis*", in: W. Beierwaltes, *Proklos, Grundzüge seiner Metaphysik,* Frankfurt am Main 2 1979, 395 - 398; Ders., *Identität und Differenz,* Frankfurt am
Main 1980, 100, 166, 264 f. K. Hedwig, 'Negatio Negationis. Problemgeschichtliche
Aspekte einer Denkstruktur', *Archiv für Begriffsgeschichte* 24 (1980), 7 - 33.
[38] *LW* 1, 169, 7.
[39] *Sermo* 29, 304, *LW* 4, 270, 7 f. Dies ist einer der Bezugspunkte für Cusanus' Begriff
des "*non -aliud*".
[40] *Expositio Libri Exodi* 16, *LW* 2, 21, 7. Hierzu auch W. Beierwaltes, *Platonismus
und Idealismus,* Frankfurt am Main 1972, 38 ff.
[41] *Ibid.*, 21, 9, 12.

Ausdruck auch des intensivsten Lebens und des liebenden Zusammengehörens
— ist die Weise der trinitarischen Selbstentfaltung, des sich selbst denkenden,
sich selbst aussprechenden und sich selbst liebenden Seins des trinitarischen
Gottes. Dieser innertrinitarische Selbstbezug in Denken, Sprechen und Lieben
vollzieht sich als ein Kreis, in dem der Anfang der Bewegung sich auf sich
selbst wieder zurückführt — dies ausgedrückt in dem Satz aus Exodus 3, 14:
"ego sum qui sum" ("Ich bin der Ich bin"), sofern er als eine *Bewegung* vom
ersten "Ich bin" in das zweite "Ich bin" gedacht wird — durch die Vermittlung
des die Relation anzeigenden *"qui"*; in dieser Bewegung zeigt sich das "Ich
bin" im Vollzug des göttlichen Seins — in seinem Selbst-Bezug — als das
Selbe: Die Bewegung, die vom ersten "Ich bin" ausgeht, kehrt im zweiten "Ich
bin" in sich selbst zurück. Einheit in ihrer intensivsten Form der Selbst-
bezüglichkeit des Absoluten aber ist *Identität* (*identitas est unitas*).[42]

Diese Einheit als trinitarisch bewegte Selbstidentität *ist* der göttliche
"Reichtum", den Gott durch sich selbst hat, weil und indem er ihn *ist* (*"dives
per se"*). Die Erläuterung dieses Satzes[43] — die ausführlichste im gesamten
Eckhartschen Werk — bringt Eckhart mit seiner Interpretation der im Exodus
gegebenen Selbstaussage Gottes zusammen: die "Selbstgenügsamkeit" (*suf-
ficientia*) oder die Bestimmtheit einer jeden Wesenheit durch sich selbst kommt
Gott im höchsten Sinne zu; die göttliche Wesenheit *ist* ihr eigenes Sein, ihre
Washeit (*quidditas*) ist mit ihrer Existenz (*Obheit, anitas*) identisch und genügt
so sich selbst, weil sie frei ist von den möglichen Differenzen, die eine solche
zwischen Wirklichkeit und Möglichkeit, von Sein und Wirken einschließen.
Die im *"ego sum qui sum"* gegebene Selbstaussage Gottes könnte somit als
Ausdruck der Selbstgenügsamkeit des göttlichen Seins, als Aussage der Selbst-
identität Gottes auf *ein* "Ich bin" zurückgeführt werden: das Subjekt *"sum"* im
Satze *"ego sum qui sum"* bedürfte als Aussage über Gott oder als dessen
Selbstaussage keines zweiten *"sum"* als des Prädikats zu diesem Subjekt —
"sum" genügte sich selbst, weil es mit seinem eigenen Prädikat identisch ist,
sofern man in dem *einen* "sum" die trinitarische Kreisbewegung, den inneren
Selbstbezug mitdenkt; die *"repetitio"* des Subjekts im Prädikat zeigt nur dessen
in sich bewegte Identität nach außen, d.h. in unserer Sprache an. *"Ego sum qui
sum"* ist dadurch ein Identitätssatz im reinen Sinne; das Subjekt *ist* das
Prädikat. Im Prädikat *"sum"* reflektiert sich das Subjekt *"sum"* in einem
doppelten Sinne: es *spiegelt* sich in seiner eigenen Identität ohne reale
Differenz, es *denkt* oder durchdringt sich als Subjekt reflexiv im Prädikat
selbst. Diese reflexive Selbstdurchdringung ist identisch mit der Selbst-
Aussage eben dieses absoluten Subjektes.

Der Identitätssatz, reduziert auf das *eine* "Ich-bin", ist also Index der
Einzigkeit, Einheit und zugleich des inneren sich selbst aufschließenden und

---

[42] *Sermo* 29, 303, *LW* 4, 269, 12 f.
[43] *Expositio Libri Exodi* 20, *LW* 2, 26, 2 ff.

gerade dadurch sich mit sich selbst wieder zusammenschließenden "*Reichtums*": "*sufficientia*" schlechthin. — Meister Eckhart bestärkt in einem zweiten Gang diesen Gedanken aus dem dialektischen Verhältnis von Reichtum und Entbehrung (oder Armut) heraus. Dabei geht er von der Annahme aus, daß "*ego sum qui sum*" auch als Äquivalent zu dem Satz gedacht werden könne: Gott ist sein Sein selbst, dies aber impliziere, daß eine so gedachte Wesenheit sich selbst gar nicht "*verlassen*" *könne*, also im Sinne seiner Selbstidentität sein eigenes Sein gar nicht *nicht* sein könne und insofern "*notwendiges Sein*" (*necesse esse*) sein müsse (dies soll freilich nicht den Ausschluß von Freiheit bedeuten!). Der absoluten Selbstgenügsamkeit Gottes setzt er die "Bedürftigkeit" des Geschaffenen entgegen: im Gegensatz zu allen Formen der Defizienz und Nicht-Identität und damit der Bedürftigkeit "außerhalb" Gottes *bedarf* dieser als "das Sein selbst nichts, weil ihm nichts mangelt (…) Nichts zu entbehren (daß nichts mangelt) ist das Wesen höchster Vollkommenheit, ist vollstes und lauterstes (reinstes) Sein. Und wenn es volles Sein ist, dann ist es auch Leben und Weise-Sein (intelligere, Denken) (…) Wie er selbst sich und Allem [der Grund] ist, so genügt er auch sich selbst und Allem, er ist selbst seine und Aller Genügen, 2 Cor. 3, 5: 'Unser Genügen ist aus Gott.'"[44]

"Reichtum", Gottes Reich-Sein durch sich selbst, ist also identisch mit seiner sich selbst entfaltenden und sich in sich haltenden trinitarischen Einheit; als solche, d.h. sich selbst als die Einheit des eigenen Seins und Denkens vollziehende Identität, ist er die sich selbst genügende Vorbedingung seines eigenen Wirkens "nach außen" — die Entfaltung des "inneren" Reichtums als Grund für dessen creative Entäußerung: "*hinc est quod emanatio personarum in divinis ratio est et praevia creationis.*"[45] Damit ist der Satz bestätigt und begründet, von dem die Überlegung ausging: "*deus eo dives profusivus est, quia unus.*"[46]

3. Durch die Auslegungen des Satzes "*primum est dives per se*" im Blick auf die absolute Selbstgenügsamkeit der ersten Ursache oder des Gottes, sowie auf die in sich bewegte Seins-Fülle als Voraussetzung und Begründung des Sich-selbst-Verströmens des mit der ersten Ursache identischen Guten schlechthin ist bei Meister Eckhart, analog zu Thomas, eine genuin *neuplatonische* Denkfigur wirksam geworden.[47]

Eindeutig ist dieser Gedanke bei *Plotin* grundgelegt und für die spätere Entwicklung des Neuplatonismus maßgebend geblieben: das Eine, mit dem

---

[44] *Ibid., LW* 2, 27, 3 ff.; 11 ff.: "*Ipsum autem esse nullo indiget, quia nullo eget. Sed ipso indigent omnia, quia extra ipsum nihil. Nihil autem eget esse, sicut infirmus eget sanitate, egenus est. Sanitas non eget infirmo. Egere infirmo, non habere infirmitatem perfecta sanitas est.*"

[45] *Ibid.*, 16; 22, 7 f.

[46] *Sermo* 29, 299, *LW* 4, 266, 7.

[47] Was ich hier nur vergewissernd und erinnernd skizzieren kann, habe ich in anderen Publikationen des öfteren entwickelt und ausführlich belegt; ich verweise deshalb gelegentlich darauf zur Entlastung dieses Textes und für genauere Information.

Guten identisch, bedarf für sein eigenes Sein und Wirken keines Anderen —
dies aufgrund seiner Einheit im Sinne der Einfachheit, die durch jede Form von
Vielheit und damit Differenz gestört, d.h. in ihrer Absolutheit negiert und
aufgehoben würde. So benennt Plotin, im Kontext seiner Bestimmung des
Einen als des Un-Endlichen aufgrund seiner "unumgreiflichen Fülle der
Macht", im Blick auf es selbst und auf das ihm entspringende Andere: als das
"Hinreichendste von Allem und das Selbstgenügsamste und das Unbe-
dürftigste," demgegenüber alles Andere, d.h. das nicht reine Eine oder Viele,
eines Anderen als seines Grundes "bedürftig" ist ("ἐνδεές"). Die Bestimmung
des ersten gründenden Prinzips, des Einen selbst, kann deshalb heißen: "Als
Ursprung von Allem ist es all dessen unbedürftig."[48] Alles Andere jedoch, was
als Entsprungenes des Ursprungs bedarf, strebt aufgrund dieser seiner
ontologischen Verfaßtheit zum einen Ursprung hin. Für die Entfaltung des
Einen qua Gründung des Vielen als des zum Einen hin Anderen und in sich
vielfältig Differenten benutzt Plotin, wie auch die späteren Neuplatoniker (den
für das christliche Denken besonders maßgebenden Dionysius eingeschlossen),
neben den Metaphern des Samens, des Zeugens, der Wurzel und des Lichtes
vor allem die der *Quelle*.[49] Diese Metapher trifft den Sachverhalt genau, daß
das Eine oder Gute als Ursprung sich selbst "verströmt", in diesem "Strömen"
bis in den äußersten Bereich der Wirklichkeit wirksam ist, und daß es selbst
gerade *als* dieser ständig wirkende und erhaltende Ursprung *in ihm selbst
bleiben* muß. Dieser Gedanke lebt aus dem anderen, ebenfalls metaphorisch
auftretenden: das Eine als das Gute schlechthin bestimmt sich gerade dadurch,

---

[48] Plotin, *Enneaden* VI 9, 6, 15 ff.: ἐφ' ἑαυτοῦ γάρ ἐστιν οὐδενὸς αὐτῷ συμβεβηκότος.
Τῷ αὐτάρκει δ' ἄν τις καὶ τὸ ἓν αὐτοῦ ἐνθυμηθείη. Δεῖ μὲν γὰρ ἱκανώτατον ⟨ὂν⟩ ἁπάντων καὶ
αὐταρκέστατον, καὶ ἀνενδεέστατον εἶναι. πᾶν δὲ πολὺ καὶ μὴ ἓν ἐνδεές; 34 ff.: Ἀρχὴ δὲ οὐκ
ἐνδεὲς τῶν μετ' αὐτό. ἡ δ' ἁπάντων ἀρχὴ ἀνενδεὲς ἁπάντων. V 4, 1, 12 ff.: αὐταρκέστατόν τε
τῷ ἁπλοῦν εἶναι καὶ πρῶτον ἁπάντων. VI 7, 23, 7 f.: (…) τὴν τοῦ ἀγαθοῦ φύσιν
αὐταρκεστάτην τε εἶναι αὐτῇ καὶ ἀνενδεᾶ ἄλλου ὁτουοῦν παντός.
[49] Vgl. hierzu W. Beierwaltes, *Plotin, Über Ewigkeit und Zeit*, Frankfurt am Main
31981, 13 f.; in *Denken des Einen* das Kapitel über die "Entfaltung der Einheit", 155 ff.;
Weiterhin die in Anm. 21 genannte Abhandlung von K. Kremer über "*bonum est diffusivum
sui.*" Die Verwendung des Begriffes "Emanation" für die hier zitierte Konzeption ist
irreführend, da er seit dem 17. und 18. Jahrhundert zunehmend als Characteristicum eines
"Pantheismus" gesehen wird. Dem steht die Bedeutung von "*emanatio*", "*influxus*",
"*influentia*" o. ä. durchaus entgegen: Eine philosophisch scharf umgrenzte Bedeutung hat
"*emanatio*" (zusammen mit "*fluere*" und "*influxus*") mindestens schon in der Schöpfungs-
lehre des Albertus Magnus bekommen, vgl. z.B. *De causis et processu universitatis* (vgl.
Anm. 11), 411 a: "*fluxus est emanatio formae a primo fonte, qui omnium formarum est fons
et origo.*" Vom ursprunghaften, göttlichen Licht (*lumen luminum*): *fluit in centrum
cuiuslibet entis* (421 a). Thomas von Aquino, *Super Librum de causis expositio* 5, 14; 8, 28
ff.: "*unde et hic ponitur verbum influendi et Proclus (Elem. theol. 56) utitur verbo
productionis [παράγειν] quae exprimit causalitatem causae efficientis*". Idem, *II Sent.*, dist.
i, qu. 1, art. 2 "*influentia causae*" ; *De substantiis separatis* 9 (hrsg. von R.M. Spiazzi, n. 98
ff.) "*influentia*", "*influxus*", "*emanatio.*" *II Sent.*, dist.. viii, qu. 1, art. 2 c: "*emanatio
creaturarum a Deo*"; *Summa theol. I*, qu. 45, art. 1 c.: "*creatio, quae est emanatio totius
esse, est ex non ente quod est nihil*".

daß es an seiner eigenen "Fülle" ohne Mißgunst teilgibt:[50] ὃν γὰρ τέλειον τῷ μηδέν ζητεῖν μηδὲ ἔχειν μηδὲ δεῖσθαι οἷον ὑπερερρύη καὶ τὸ ὑπερπλῆρες αὐτοῦ πεποίηκε ἄλλο.[51] "Überfülle" meint jedoch weder bei Plotin noch bei einem späteren Neuplatoniker, daß das erste Prinzip in sich selbst in der intensivsten Form von Relationalität Alles in sich *denkend umfasse*, was es creativ aus sich entläßt — dies entspricht eher einem dem trinitarischen Gedanken verpflichteten christlichen Denken, wie es sich exemplarisch bei Meister Eckhart gezeigt hat. "Überfülle" kann für Plotin nur dies heißen: daß dasjenige, was aus dem Einen-Guten als Wirkliches und Mögliches entspringt, in ihm in einer *nur* dem Einen selbst entsprechenden, also "über-seienden" Form gegenwärtig ist, frei von differenzierender Relationalität. Was die neuplatonische Entfaltung dieses Gedankens anlangt, so ist zwar seine Grundstruktur die selbe geblieben, der Begriff der "Selbstgenügsamkeit" (αὐτάρκεια) jedoch wurde vor allem von *Proklos* für die unterschiedlichen Bereiche der dem Einen entstammenden Wirklichkeit — der Götter und der Welt — differenziert, so daß "selbstgenügsam" oder das schlechthin "Selbstgenügsame" nicht primär und ausschließlich dem ersten Prinzip vorbehalten und dadurch in gewissem Sinne relativiert wurde. Diese Differenzierung und Relativierung des Begriffes "αὔταρκες" und "αὐταρκέστατον" wurde weder vom Autor des *Liber de causis* in seine Auslegung des *dives*-Satzes noch von den Kommentatoren des Liber de causis, die die proklische *Elementatio theologica* kannten, in ihre eigenen Überlegungen aufgenommen. Dennoch sei der proklische Gebrauch dieser Begriffe hier wenigstens angedeutet. Während Syrian, der Lehrer des Proklos, das Erste oder Eine gerade aufgrund seiner Einfachheit und Einheit seines Wesens (ἁπλότης καὶ ἑνότης τῆς ὑπὸ στάσεως) als das "Selbstgenügsamste" benannte und es mit dem autarken Guten selbst identifizierte,[52] ist Proklos offensichtlich — anders als Plotin[53] und Syrian — zurückhaltend in der Vergabe des Prädikats "αὔταρκες" oder "αὐταρκέστατον" für das Eine selbst. Zumindest legt dies zunächst einmal die Bestimmung des Begriffs αὔταρκες in der *Elementatio theologica* nahe:[54] "Was ist das Selbstgenügsame anders als dasjenige, welches von ihm selbst her und in ihm selbst das Gute (erworben)

---

[50] Beierwaltes, *Denken des Einen*, 411 f. Proclus, *Elem. theol.* 122; 108, 10 ff., 15 f., 19 - 21: über die ἀγαθοῦ μετάδοσις des Göttlichen, die in seinem Sein begründet ist (αὐτῷ τῷ εἶναι).
[51] Plotinus, *Enneaden* V 2 1, 7 - 9 f.
[52] Syrian, *In Metaphysica commentaria* 183, 10 ff. hrsg. G. Kroll).
[53] Neben den in Anm. 48 genannten Texten gibt es allerdings auch bei Plotin eine Andeutung dieser Entwicklung, wenn er in Enneaden V 3, 17, 10 sagt: "Wenn dieses (das Eine selbst, ßn) jedem Einzelnen das Sein gibt und die Vielheit des Einzelnen selbst lediglich durch die Gegenwart des Einen sich selbst genug ist, so ist klar, daß jenes nur deshalb Sein und Selbstgenugsamkeit hervorzubringen vermag, weil es selber nicht 'Sein', sondern jenseits von Sein und jenseits von 'Selbstgenügsamkeit' ist." Damit wird herausgehoben, daß das Gründende oder an ihm selbst Teilgebende sich in der Seinsweise oder in der Intensität dessen, was im Gegründeten oder Gegebenen mit ihm verbunden ist, ebensosehr von ihm *unterscheidet*.
[54] *Propositio* X, 10, 31 ff. (hrsg. von E. R. Dodds).

hat (oder besitzt)? Dies aber meint, daß es voll ist (πλῆρες) des Guten und an ihm teilhat, jedoch nicht das schlechthin Gute selbst ist. Jenes nämlich steht *über* der Teilhabe und dem Voll-Sein (...) Wenn sich also das Selbst-genügsame selbst mit dem Guten erfüllt hat, dann wäre dasjenige, von dem her es sich selbst erfüllt hat, höher als das Selbstgenügsame und über der Selbstgenugsamkeit". Zwar setzt Proklos, wie Plotin, das schlechthin Gute mit dem "Unbedürftigen" oder Nichts-Bedürfenden gleich. Der Gedanke des Sichselbst-erfüllt-Habens, sich selbst und in sich selbst das Gute erworben zu haben und es so in Fülle zu besitzen, müßte im Sinne des Proklos mit der Bestimmung des Guten (oder Einen) kollidieren, die extrem auf deren relations-lose Einfachheit achtet: Daß es nichts anderes als es selbst ist, daß also der Akt des Sich-selbst-mit-Gutheit-Erfüllens eine Hinzufügung und eine Verminderung des eigenen Wesens wäre.[55] Um also für das Gute oder Eine schlechthin noch nicht einmal einen Anschein von Vielheit in der Weise des Sprechens über es zu suggerieren, sollte der Begriff des Selbstgenügsamen für das erste Prinzip besser gemieden werden. Nicht irreführend hingegen und deshalb immer wieder in verschiedenen Aspekten sinnvoll angewandt, ist dieser Begriff im Sinne des Proklos gültig einmal für den Bereich der sich denkenden Einheit, des κόσμος νοητός, oder — im Sinne der *zweiten Hypothesis* des platonischen Parmenides gesprochen — für die Dimension des *seienden* Einen, zum anderen für die Bestimmung des Göttlichen überhaupt und seiner unterschiedlichen Individuierungen.[56] Diesem nämlich, jedem einzelnen der Götter, konzediert Proklos eine "Gutheit schlechthin" und damit auch (im Widerspruch zu *propositio* X der *Elementatio theologica*?) eine Selbst-genügsamkeit, die ihr weder durch "Teilhabe", noch durch "Einstrahlung" oder durch "Ahnlichkeit" zukommt, sondern "durch das Sein selbst, das sie (selbst) ist". Die Götter sind also "durch sich selbst und von ihnen selbst her selbstgenügsam, sie haben sich selbst erfüllt (mit Gutheit), ja, sie sind als die Fülle des Guten insgesamt da": αὐτοὶ δὲ οἱ θεοὶ δι' ἑαυτοὺς καὶ παρῳ ἑαυτῶν αὐτάρκεις, ἑαυτοὺς πεπληρωκότες, μᾶλλον δὲ πληρώματα τῶν ὅλων ἀγαθῶν ὑπάρχοντες.[57] In dieser Bestimmung der Götter als selbstgenügsamer Wesen-heiten ist die frühgriechische Vorstellung im philosophischen Begriff eingelöst, daß es das Zeichen des Gottes ist, nichts zu bedürfen. Der Mensch kommt dem Göttlichen dann am nächsten, wenn er den Gott durch eine konsequente Einschränkung seiner eigenen Bedürfnisse nachahmt.[58]

---

55 *Ibid.*, 10, 9 ff.
56 *Ibid.*, 127; 112, 25 f.: πᾶν τὸ θεῖον ἁπλοῦν πρώτως ἐστι καὶ μάλιστα, καὶ διὰ τοῦτο αὐταρκέστατον. 31 - 33: τὸ δὲ ἁπλούστατον καὶ ἑνιαῖον καὶ τὸ ἓν τῷ ἀγαθῷ ταὐτὸν προ-στησάμενον αὐταρκέστατον. τοιοῦτον δὲ τὸ θεῖον πᾶν. *Theol. Plat.* I 19; 90, 14 ff. (hrsg. von H.D. Saffrey und L.G. Westerink).
57 *Theol. Plat.* I 19, 91; 18 - 20.
58 Außer den von Dodds in seinem Kommentar zur *propositio* IX und X (*The Elements of Theology*, Oxford ²1963, 197) angegebenen Stellen, vgl. Euripides, *Hercules Furens*

"Fülle der *Gutheit*" als Bestimmung des Göttlichen oder der einzelnen Götter kommt dem Prädikat *"dives per se"* für die erste göttliche Ursache auch sprachlich am nächsten; der Sache nach freilich ist der neuplatonische Gedanke mit dieser Bestimmung eng verbunden: daß das Erste als Eines und Gutes zugleich der in Allem gründend und erhaltend wirksame Ursprung von Allem ist. Indes blieb die spezifische Bezeichnung dieser "Fülle" als *Reichtum* oder "Reichtum durch sich selbst" dem Christentum vorbehalten: Paulus nennt so — hymnisch — die Fülle des Segens, der vom Handeln Gottes für das Geschick Israels und der Heiden ausgeht: *"O altitudo divitiarum et sapientiae et scientiae dei! (...) Ex ipso et per ipsum et in ipsum omnia."*[59]

4. Die ontologische Verschiedenheit der Bereiche, der dialektische Bezug des selbstgenügsamen "Reich-Seins durch-sich-selbst" zur Dimension des grundsätzlich "Bedürftigen" hat für Meister Eckhart auch einen anthropologischen Aspekt.

Daß der Mensch das Ziel seines bewußten Lebens, die Einung mit Gott als den "Durchbruch" in die Gottheit erreiche, dies hängt zunächst an der realistischen, nicht die Welt abwertenden Erkenntnis, daß das Geschaffen-Seiende im Vergleich zur Fülle oder dem "Reichtum" des "göttlichen Seins" ein reines *"Nichts"* ist. Mit ihm kann sich der Mensch um seines Zieles willen nicht innig verbinden, sich nicht mit ihm "erfüllen": Vorbedingung des Durchbruchs in die Gottheit durch die Gottesgeburt im Menschen ist deshalb die *Befreiung* vom Geschaffenen, vom Vielen, von dem durch Differenz Bestimmten, das Sich-Frei-Machen von den dieses Seiende charakterisierenden und das Denken bestimmenden *modi* der Zeit und der Zahl, das Ledig-Werden von "Bildern" in einem Akt universaler *"Entbildung"* — um durch die Gottheit "überbildet" zu werden;[60] die dem derart Seienden gegenüber geläufigen (objektivierenden) Einstellungen: das Wollen, das Wissen und das Haben, muß der Mensch *lassen* zugunsten einer radikalen *"Abgeschiedenheit"* und freien, d.h. frei machenden *"Gelassenheit"*; auch *seiner selbst* als des auf das Geschaffene bezogenen, egoistischen oder egoman in es verstrickten und von Gott "abständigen" Ichs muß der Mensch ledig werden. Entbildung, Abgeschiedenheit und Gelassenheit charakterisieren den Stand und das Bewußtsein der *Armut*. Nur sie vermag das Reich-Sein Gottes selbst in sich aufzunehmen, kann sich selbst in es verwandeln lassen. "Und dû solt wizzen: laere sîn aller crêatûre ist gotes vol sîn, und vol sîn aller crêatûre ist gotes laere sîn."[61]

1345 f.: δεῖται γὰρ ὁ θεός, εἴπερ ἔστῳ ὀρθῶς θεός, οὐδενός. Xenophon, *Memorabilia*: I 6, 10: ἐγὼ δὲ νομίζω τὸ μὲν μηδενὸς δέεσθαι θεῖον εἶναι, τὸ δῷὡς ἐλαχίστων ἐγγυτάτω τοῦ θείου.

[59] Rom. 11, 33; 36. Heinrich Schlier, *Der Römerbrief*, Freiburg 1977, 344 ff.

[60] Zur Begründung dieses Gedankens bei Meister Eckhart vgl. die Dissertation von W. Wackernagel, *Imagine denundari. Éthique de la désimagination et métaphysique de l'image chez Maître Eckhart*, Paris 1991.

[61] Von abegescheidenheit: *DW* 5, 413, 3 f. *Predigt* 52 *"Beati pauperes spiritu"*, *DW* 2, 504, 4 ff.; 8 - 505, 5: "ich bin, daz ich was und daz ich blîben sol nû und iemermê. Dâ

Das Suchen und Finden des "Reiches Gottes" vollzieht sich im und aus dem Bereich des Bedürftigen und Kontingenten als Armuts-Bewegung: in der universalen Ent-Bildung aller Dinge ledig zu werden, ist mit der Bildung zum oder in den Reichtum Gottes identisch. Die im Deutschen schon von der Sprache her mögliche Assoziation von "rîche" (= regnum dei) und "gotes rîchtuome" oder Gott als "rîche in im selber" nutzt Eckhart in den Predigten "Quaerite ergo primum regnum dei", "Homo quidam erat dives" oder "Scitote, quia prope est regnum dei", um auch die Gleichheit in der Sache zu demonstrieren: "'gotes rîche' daz ist got selbe mit allem sînem richtuome" — oder: "hie ist got rîche, und daz ist gotes rîche".[62]

In diesen Reflexionen über die Einheit von "Reich Gottes" und "Reichtum" spielt der dives-Satz des Liber de causis eine bedeutsame Rolle — in dem Sermo 34, 3 z.B. als Einsatz — und End-Punkt des Gedankens, der ihn nicht nur zur autoritativen Stützung "heranzieht", sondern auch dessen (zuvor beschriebenen) Gehalt ganz im Sinne von "De causis" und der ihm kompatiblen Texte bewußt macht.[63] Dies zu "wissen", soll — davon sind wir ausgegangen — im Menschen die Einsicht zeitigen, daß er in der Bewegung auf dieses Ziel hin: reich zu werden durch den Reichtum von Gottes Reich, zuvor selbst arm werden muß, indem er die ihn in einem grundlosen Ich verfangenen "Eigenschaften" oder die vielheitlichen, vom "unum necessarium" wegführenden Modi und damit sich selbst als sein vermeintliches "Eigentum" aufgibt, um in der Einung mit seinem Grund wahrhaft er selbst zu werden: "Du solt alzemal entzinken diner dinisheit und solt zer fliesen in sine sinesheit und sol din din und sin sin éin min werden als genzlich, das du mit ime verstandest ewiklich sin ungewordene istikeit und sin ungenanten nitheit." Durch den Vollzug dieser Armuts-Bewegung — "es muos alles abe!"— wird "Er" und "Ich" ein IST, in dem beide ein "Werk wirken."[64]

---

enphâhe ich einen îndruk, der mich bringen sol über alle engel. In disem îndrucke enphâhe ich sôgetâne rîcheit, daz mir niht genuoc enmac gesîn got nâch allem dem, daz er 'got' ist, und nâch allen siinen götlîchen werken; wan ich enpfâhe in disem durchbrechen daz ich und got einz sîn. Dâ bin ich, daz ich was (...)."

[62] Die genannten Predigten: Sermo 34, 3, LW 4, 302, 3 ff.; Predigt 80, DW 3, 378, 2 ff.; Predigt 68, DW 3, 140, 2 ff. Die beiten Zitate: DW 3, 143, 2; Predigt 38, DW 2, 232, 3 f.

[63] Sermo 34, 3, LW 4, 302, 3 ff.; Predigt 80, DW 3, 382, 8 - 383, 5: (eine Erläuterung des "dives per se"): "Alsô ist got rîche in im selber und in allen dingen. Nû merket! Diu rîcheit gotes diu liget an vünf dingen. Daz êrste: daz er diu êrste sache (causa prima) ist, her umbe ist er ûzgiezende sich in alliu dinc.- Daz ander: daz er einvaltic ist an sînem wesene, her umbe ist er diu innerkeit aller dinge.- Daz dritte: daz er ursprunclich ist, her umbe ist er gemeinende sich allen dingen. — Daz vierde: daz er unwandelhaftic ist, her umbe ist er daz behaldelîcheste ("Beständigste") — Daz vünfte: daz er volkomen ist, her umbe ist er daz begerlîcheste." — Vgl. auch Predigt 47, DW 2, 398, 6 ff.

[64] Predigt 83 ("Renovamini spiritu"); DW 3, 443, 5 - 7.; 447, 5 f.; 448, 6. Die rede der underscheidunge, DW 5, 297, 6 ff.; 300, 1 ff. — Zum asketisch-mystischen Aspekt der "Armut" vgl. A. M. Haas, Sermo mysticus 199 - 201; ders., Meister Eckhart als normative Gestalt geistigen Lebens, Einsiedeln 1971, 91 ff.; K. Ruh, Meister Eckhart, 157 ff. Über die franziskanische "speculatio pauperis in deserto" und ihre neuplatonischen Implikationen, siehe Beierwaltes, Denken des Einen, 421 ff.

Dem Eckhartschen Impuls zur Ent-Bildung, der Bewegung der Armut in die Fülle des "Einig-Einen" entspricht im neuplatonischen Denken die Forderung nach einer universalen *"aphairesis "* alles Vielen und Anderen, d.h. dem Einen selbst und dem Ziel des Menschen Fremden (ἄφελε πάντα),[65] nach einer umfassenden Ent-Differenzierung und Ent-Zeitlichung des Denkens, um eine zumindest punktuelle, augenblickhafte Einung mit dem Einen selbst zu erreichen, die freilich das weitere Leben des Menschen im Sinne eben dieser Befreiung von der Differenz spürbar formen sollte.[66] Analog ist auch derjenige Bereich charakterisiert, in dem sich diese Abstraktionsbewegung ereignet: seine Pole sind, proklisch gesprochen, das göttlich Selbstgenügsamste, das es noch übergreifende Eine selbst *und* das in sich unterschiedliche Bedürftig-Sein des dem Einen entsprungenen Vielen und Anderen.[67] Die das Denken und die Emotionen einigende Abstraktionsbewegung setzt sich zum Ziel, diese dialektische Spannung zwischen Fülle und relativer oder äußerster Bedürftigkeit zu erkennen und sie im Vollzug des eigenen Einheitspotentials denkend aufzuheben. Die Einung selbst markiert den Selbst-Überstieg dieses Denkens in seinen eigenen Grund.

III SEIN ALS ERST-GESCHAFFENES. — DENK- UND AUSSAGBARKEIT DER *causa prima*

1. Das erste Wirken der ersten Ursache in der Entfaltung eines ursächlich zusammenhängenden "Systems" der Wirklichkeit trifft der vierte Satz des *Liber de causis:* "Das erste der geschaffenen Dinge ist das *Sein* und vor diesem selbst ist nichts Anderes geschaffen (gibt es kein anderes Geschaffenes)," (*prima rerum creatarum est esse et non est ante ipsum creatum aliud*). Dieser Satz ist von Philosophen des Mittelalters häufig zitiert worden. Er benennt das Sein (oder Sein als Existieren) als ein Geschaffenes und provoziert so eine Analogie oder den Gedanken der Differenz des geschaffenen zu einem ungeschaffenen, absoluten Sein, welches der creative Ursprung des Geschaffenen ist. In enger Verbindung zu der von Proklos entwickelten Stufung der Wirklichkeit insgesamt begreift der *Liber de causis* das aus Grenze und Unbegrenztem "zusammengesetzte" Sein dennoch als "einiger" (*vehe-*

---

[65] Plotinus, *Enneaden* V 3, 17, 38.

[66] Zur Bedeutung von *"aphairesis":* siehe Beierwaltes, *Denken des Einen*, 129 ff. Vgl. auch den Index unter *"Abstraktion"*.— Für die neuplatonische Konzeption des Verhältnisses der Dimension des Entsprungenen — und daher "Bedürftigen" — zur "Selbstgenügsamkeit" des Göttlichen oder des ersten Prinzips überhaupt ist von Platon, mythologisch, metaphorisch, aber auch sachlich mit der Ideentheorie übereinstimmend, die Beziehung von Poros und Penia thematisiert worden: ihre Verbindung bringt genau jene Fähigkeit im Menschen hervor, in einer denkenden Erfahrung des Bedürftigen dieses auf seinen erfüllenden, "reichen" Grund hin zu überwinden.

[67] Proclus, *Elem. theol.* 9; 10, 21: §nde°w. Für Plotin vgl. Anm. 48. *Liber de causis* XX; 164, 58: "(...) *omne compositum diminutum, indigens (...) alio*"; 165, 65 f.: "(...) *indigent uno vero influente.*"

mentius unitum) als alles andere Geschaffene; dies kommt ihm durch seine im wörtlichen Sinne zu nehmende unmittelbare Nähe zum reinen oder wahren Einen zu. Während Proklos dem Sein Leben und Geist (Denken) *ohne* Vermittlungsstufen, also in intensiver Verbundenheit mit dem Sein, folgen läßt, spart der *Liber de causis "vita"* hier aus und schließt *"intelligentia"* an das Sein an, er nimmt offenbar die zuerst festgestellte "Folge" so wenig als Differenz, daß er noch im Kommentar zu Satz IV eine Identität von *esse* und *intelligentia* behauptet oder es zumindest zuläßt, daß Sein unmittelbar auch Denken sein kann: *"et esse quidem creatum primum est intelligentia totum, verumtamen intelligentia in ipso est diversa per modum quem diximus"*.[68]

Der Satz über Sein als das Erst-Geschaffene ist als ein wahrer Satz für Eckharts eigene Konzeption von Sein wesentlich. An denjenigen Stellen, an denen er eben diesen Satz nicht nur im Ensemble von ungleichen oder weiterführenden Zitaten nennt, lassen seine kargen Erläuterungen folgende Gedankenkonstellationen erkennen: In der Auslegung der Aussage *"creavit deus, ut essent omnia"* ("er schuf Alles, daß (damit) es *sei*") aus dem "Buche der Weisheit", deutet der Satz über Sein als das Erst-Geschaffene ganz allgemein auf die *"ratio creabilitatis"*;[69] Sein ist nicht nur der Grund dafür, daß etwas erschaff*bar* ist, sondern ebensosehr die Anzeige dafür, daß etwas geschaffen *ist*. Sein kommt einem Geschaffenen nicht als etwas Nachträgliches hinzu, es geht vielmehr allen anderen Modi des Geschaffenseins als die grundlegende, reale Möglichkeit aller Differenzierung und Konkretisierung in die vielfältigsten Gestalten von Seiendem *voraus*: *"praevenit et prius est omnium"*. Im Sinne des *Liber de causis* liegt der Grund darin, daß *"esse omnium est* immediate *a causa prima et a causa universali omnium."*[70] Sein als *ratio creabilitatis* schließt den Gedanken ein, daß ein Lebendes oder Denkendes *dieses* nur sein kann, weil es *ist*. Sein also ist als ein Geschaffenes nicht in sich isoliert oder hypostasiert nur es selbst, sondern es ist für jede individuelle Gestalt der Wirklichkeit insgesamt der reale, alle möglichen Möglichkeiten eröffnende, innerlich umfassende Grund oder die jede einzelne Gestalt der Wirklichkeit ermöglichende und "realisierende" Grundstruktur. Die Annahme dieses Satzes über Sein als das Erst-Geschaffene bedingt eine differenzierte Denk- und Sprechweise über "Sein" insgesamt: Sein als ein Geschaffenes, unter dem Aspekt der *ratio creabilitatis* betrachtet, ist zu unterscheiden von dem ungeschaffenen und daher auch nicht unter der *ratio creabilitatis* stehenden Sein Gottes selbst — dem reinen, absoluten, selbst-

---

[68] IV; 44, 64 f. — Zur *propositio* IV in anderen mittelalterlichen Kontexten: R. Schönberger, *Die Transformation des klassischen Seinsverständnisses. Studien zur Vorgeschichte des neuzeitlichen Seinsbegriffes im Mittelalter,* Berlin 1986, 270 ff.; 317.

[69] *In Sap.* 24, *LW* 2, 344, 5; 5, 41, 11; dort 41, 7 ist *"esse"* als ein Geschaffenes zu verstehen: *"unde statim cum venimus ad esse, venimus ad creaturam."*

[70] *Prologus generalis in opus tripartitum* 8, *LW* 1, 153, 4 f. Zu *"immediate"*: Heinrich Ebeling, *Meister Eckharts Mystik. Studien zu den Geisteskämpfen um die Wende des 13. Jahrhunderts,* Stuttgart 1941, 56 ff.

bezüglichen und durch sich selbst reichen Sein. Dieser Selbstbezug des reinen Seins als *intelligere* oder *sapientia* aber ist der Grund für das geschaffene Sein; ihm geht das gründende "*intelligere*" des creativen Seins voraus, *in* ihm selbst jedoch als dem Unerschaffbaren ist es mit ihm identisch. Durch diese intensive, mit seinem "*intelligere*" identische Weise des Seins *wirkt* Gott in den Kreaturen. "*Deus autem se toto est esse et operatur in creaturis per ipsum esse et sub ratione esse*" — ("als das Sein selbst wirkt er in den Geschöpfen durch das Sein und insofern er das Sein ist").[71] Man kann von hierher gesehen den Zusammenhang der beiden Weisen von Sein *in* ihrem Unterschied deutlich machen: *Weil* Gott das Sein selbst ist *durch* sein, *in* seinem oder *als* sein Denken, und *weil* er im Geschaffenen "durch das Sein selbst" und in der Weise des mit seinem Denken identischen Seins wirkt, ist dasjenige, was für ihn selbst das Erste, seine eigene Wesenheit ist, auch das erste "Resultat" seines creativen Wirkens nach außen: *prima rerum creatarum est esse*. Diesen *finalen* Aspekt in der Aussage des Buches der Weisheit: "*creavit, ut essent omnia*", hebt Meister Eckhart eigens hervor, indem er "*ens sive esse*" als "*primus terminus creationis*", "den ersten Zielpunkt des Schaffens" benennt[72] oder mit "*finis*" identifiziert.[73] Danach realisiert sich durch das Sein-verursachende Schaffen Gottes *in* eben diesem Sein des Geschaffenen die "erste (immanente) Ursache der geschaffenen Dinge und der Schöpfung" überhaupt. "Erste" immanente, d.h. neben den drei übrigen Modi der Ursachen wirkende Ursache aber ist das "Ziel", "*prima causa causarum finis est*."[74] Mit der Setzung des *Seins* als der ersten Realisierung ursächlichen Wirkens — Sein demnach bestimmt als verursachtes Ziel oder Ziel-Ursache der Schöpfungsbewegung — ist es *als* "*ratio creabilitatis*" zugleich das Fundament für alle weitere creative Vereinzelung. Wenn dies — "*esse*" als "Ziel" der Schöpfungs bewegung — *eine* Verstehensmöglichkeit ("*unus intellectus*")[75] des Satzes aus dem *Liber de causis* ist, dann wäre eine andere Auslegung unter dem Aspekt der "*causa efficiens*" denkbar.[76] Sachlich gesehen schließt das herausgehobene "Ziel" den Aspekt der "*causa efficiens*" durchaus ein: Gott als die erste Ursache erwirkt in seinem Schöpfungsakt das Sein als das Ziel eben dieser Bewegung, so daß der "Effekt" mit dem Ziel identisch ist; oder: die "*causa efficiens*" realisiert sich als das Ziel ihrer eigenen Bewegung.

Die Grundlinien des Verständnisses der *propositio* IV, wie sie bei Meister Eckhart sichtbar werden, sind in der wesentlich differenzierteren Interpretation eben dieses Satzes in Thomas' Kommentar angelegt. In ständigem Rückgriff auf Proklos erörtert dieses die Dialektik von Einfachheit (Allgemeinheit) und

---

[71] *In Sap.* 23, *LW* 2, 343, 9 f.
[72] *In Joh.* 65, *LW* 3, 54, 5.
[73] *In Sap.* 26, *LW* 2, 346, 7. *Expositio libri Genesis* 141, *LW* 1, 295, 2.
[74] *LW* 1, 295, 2; 2, 346, 7 f.
[75] *LW* 1, 295, 1.
[76] "*Utrum in deo sit idem esse et intelligere*" 4, *LW* 5, 41, 9 f.; *In Joh.* 66, *LW* 3, 54, 6 ff.

Mannigfaltigkeit im geschaffenen Sein selbst; er schließt aus, daß das Sein als
erstes Geschaffenes ein einzelnes, bestimmt-seiendes Etwas meinen könne,
welches geschaffen ist (*subiectum creatum*); es bedeutet vielmehr "das
eigentliche Wesen eines Gegenstandes der Schöpfung" (*propria ratio obiecti
creationis*). Das *Wesen* des Geschaffenen aber ist ihm nicht das Dies- oder
Das-Sein (*hoc ens*), sondern das in jedem Einzelnen sich aspektreich
verwirklichende Sein selbst. Als das Formalste und "Einfachste" ist aber das
Sein der vierten *propositio* — das Erst-Geschaffene — nicht der leere
Begriff, eine indifferente Bestimmungslosigkeit in sich, ein für sich seiendes,
hypostasiertes, reines Existieren. Allgemeinheit, Einfachheit und schlecht-
hinnige "Formalität" des Seins ist vielmehr der ermöglichende Grund jeder
Besonderung, Vielfalt und Wesensbestimmung von Anderem, d.h. individuell
Seiendem. Sein als der allgemeine Grund befaßt die Besonderung (Konkre-
tisierung, Individuierung) als *seiende* Möglichkeit immer schon in sich. Diese
im Sein befaßte mögliche Wirklichkeit aber kommt im Horizont der
unendlichen Vielfalt von Möglichkeiten in der bestimmten Wesensform eines
Seienden zur Ruhe: *esse est aliquid fixum et quietum in ente*. In der
Vervielfältigung (*multiplicari, diversificari*) seiner ursprunghaft gesetzten
Einheit erweist sich das als Ziel des Schöpfungsaktes vermittelte Sein so als
der ermöglichende und zugleich bewahrende Grund in jedem Seienden. Auch
von daher wird der Satz verstehbar: "Sein aber ist jenes, was Jeglichem das
Innerste ist und was tiefer in Allem ist."[77] — Dem enspricht genau der von
Meister Eckhart auf die erste These des *Liber de Causis* zurückgeführte
Gedanke: "Nichts ist so Eines, nichts so übereinstimmend, nichts so innerlich
und mit seiner Wirkung und mit jedem beliebigen Ding verbunden wie das
Sein selbst und seine erste Ursache;"[78] im Sein als dem Erst-Geschaffenen
bekundet sich das erste Wirken des göttlichen Ursprungs und hat in ihm als
dem ersten und innerlichsten Constitutivum jedes Seienden die Basis für die
Entfaltung seines weiteren Wirkens.

    Zur Festigung und Differenzierung dieses Gedankens zieht Meister
Eckhart des öfteren drei andere Sätze aus dem *Liber de causis* heran. Sie
stellen zumindest wesentliche Elemente innerhalb eines möglichen Gesamt-
entwurfs einer Theorie dar, welche die Weise und Intensität des Wirkens der
ersten Ursache, des schaffenden Gottes, also dessen In-Sein im Geschaffenen
darstellt, zugleich aber bewußt macht und bewußt hält, daß der göttliche
Ursprung *im* Wirken und *als* im Geschaffenen Seiender er selbst oder *der selbe*
bleibt. Die erste *propositio* des *Liber de causis* stellt das intensive, bis in den

---

77 *Summa theologiae* I, qu. 8, art. 1 c: "*esse autem est illud quod est magis intimum
cuilibet et quod profundius omnibus inest.*" Zum Vorhergehenden siehe meine in Anm. 3
zitierte Abhandlung 212 f.
    78 *In Sap.* 194, *LW* 2, 529, 7 - 9: "*nihil autem tam unum, nihil tam conveniens, nihil
tam intimum et coniunctum effectui et rei cuilibet quam esse ipsum et causa sua prima, ut
ait propositio prima de causis*", *In Joh.* 34, *LW* 3, 28, 5 f.

äußersten Bereich des Wirklichen reichende Wirken der ersten Ursache heraus: diese "nimmt ihre Kraft nicht von der zweiten Ursache (oder den zweiten Ursachen) weg"; während diese sich von ihr unterscheidet und in bestimmter Weise von ihr wegbewegt, trennt sich die erste nicht von ihr, hebt ihren "Einfluß" nicht auf; vielmehr "hilft" die erste Ursache durchweg allem Zweiten, sie "hängt ihm mit heftiger Anhänglichkeit an und bewahrt es," sie "bleibt" in ihm.[79] Auch im Blick auf diese Gedankensequenz verficht Meister Eckhart mit Nachdruck die These, daß jedes Seiende und jedes Einzelne sein Sein nicht nur von Gott *hat*, sondern daß es dies "ohne jegliche Vermittlung", "*unmittelbar*" (*immediate*) hat: weil Gott "ganz und gar Sein ist, einfachin Einer oder Eines," ist er auch "notwendigerweise durch sich ganz unmittelbar jedem Einzelnen gegenwärtig, dies also nicht einem Teil nach dem anderen, auch nicht einem Teil durch den anderen."[80]

Weil das Seiende insgesamt nicht nur sein Sein, sondern auch seine Einheit, Wahrheit und Gutheit dem göttlichen Sein verdankt, welches die genannten Grundstrukturen in absoluter Weise, d.h. als selbstbezügliche Identität *ist*, ist auch der Satz konsequent verstehbar: "*esse autem deus est*" — ("das Sein aber ist Gott").[81] Zur Verwahrung dagegen, daß dieser Satz "pantheistisch" mißverstanden würde: das von Gott geschaffene Sein sei mit ihm selbst *identisch*, Gott *ist* das von ihm Geschaffene in gleicher Wesenheit, Welt *ist* Gott, — dafür dient wiederum eine These aus dem *Liber de causis:* "*Causa prima regit res (creatas) omnes praeter quod commisceatur cum eis*", ("die erste Ursache beherrscht alle (geschaffenen) Dinge, ohne sich mit ihnen zu vermischen").[82] Das — im Sinne des Johannes-Evangeliums — in der Finsternis, d.h. im Geschaffenen, wirkende göttliche Licht ist in diese "nicht eingeschlossen, nicht mit ihm vermischt", nicht von ihm [als Ganzes] umfaßt,[83] Gott ist, paradox antipantheistisch gesagt, derart als Ganzer *im* Einzelnen daß er als Ganzer *außerhalb* ist und bleibt, "*quia ipse sic totus est in rebus singulis, quod totus est extra.*"[84] Diese an Bonaventuras *Itinerarium*[85] erinnernde

---

[79] *Liber de causis, prop.* I: "*Non separatur (...) non removetur (...) adiuvat, adhaeret, servat, influit virtutem suam, remanet in ea.*"
[80] *Prologus in opus propositionum* 14, *LW* 1, 173, 14 - 16: "*(...) quia deus, se toto esse, simpliciter est unus sive unum est, necesse est, ut se toto immediate toti assit singulo, quod non parti post partem nec parti per partem*" ; zuvor wird die erste *propositio* des *Liber de causis* zitiert.
[81] *Ibid.*, 173, 4. Vgl. zu diesem Satz auch Beierwaltes, *Platonismus und Idealismus*, aus dem Kapitel "*Deus est esse, esse est deus*" den 4. Abschnitt, 37 ff. A. de Libera, 'Le problème de l'être chez Maître Eckhart: Logique et métaphysique de l'analogie', *Cahiers de la Revue de Théologie et de Philosophie* 4, 1980.
[82] *Propositio* XIX.
[83] *In Joh.* 12, *LW* 3, 12, 6 ff.
[84] *Expositio libri Genesis* 166, *LW* 1, 312, 11. Vgl. auch — ebenso im Anschluß an *De causis .*— *ebd.*, 69; 233, 2 ff. *In Sap.* 135, *LW* 2, 473, 8: "*Deus sic totus est in quolibet, quod totus est extra quodlibet*". *Predigt* 71, *DW* 3, 217, 6 f.: "*Got vliuzet in alle creâtûren, und blîbet er doch unberüeret von in allen. Er enbedarf ir niht*".

paradoxe Formulierung ist von Meister Eckhart als ein spekulativ höchst subtiler Gedankenzusammenhang entwickelt worden, der das dialektische Verhältnis von In- und Über-Sein Gottes einsichtig zu machen versucht. Er geht dabei in seinem *Sapientia*-Kommentar von einem Satz aus, der die Divergenz *und* die Einheit von Unterschied und Un-Unterschiedenheit ineins fügt: *"Deus indistinctum quoddam est quod sua indistinctione distinguitur"* ("Gott ist ein Un-Unterschiedenes, das sich durch seine Un-Unterschiedenheit (von allem Geschaffenen) unterscheidet"). Der Satz impliziert einen doppelten Aspekt von Un-Unterschiedenheit: 1) Un-Unterschiedenheit Gottes in ihm selbst als trinitarische Einheit, die keine reale Andersheit in sich hat. Durch diese Un-Unterschiedenheit *in sich* unterscheidet sich die reine Einheit vom in sich und voneinander Unterschiedenen. 2) meint das *indistinctum-esse* Gottes in Bezug auf das durch ihn Geschaffene: es ist der dem Seienden als *dessen* Sein innerliche Grund, unmittelbar und "ohne Unterschied" mit ihm verbunden. Gerade durch dieses *"intimum esse cuilibet"* aber — das selbe Sein in Allem in je unterschiedlicher, individueller Ausprägung — *unterscheidet* es sich von allem Einzelnem. Aufgrund *seiner indistinctio* in Allem unterscheidet es aktiv eben dieses Einzelne voneinander und zugleich von sich.[86]

Neuplatonisch ist an diesem Gedanken einer intensiven Verbindung von *In-* und *Über-*Sein des Ursprungs eine allen anderen Aussagen über das Eine bestimmende Grundansicht: Das Eine selbst ist als Grund von Allem *in* Allem und *zugleich über* Allem. Dies heißt: als der selbst grund-lose, aber gerade dadurch universal gründende Grund ist das Eine durch sein Wirken dergestalt in jedem Einzelnen, daß es zwar dessen Wesen konstituiert, jedoch nicht in diesem aufgeht, also nicht zum einzelnen Etwas selbst *wird* und sich dadurch mit einem durch es selbst Begrenzten identifizierte. Es ist gerade nicht Etwas von dem, was es selbst als Etwas begründet: *"vor"* jedem Etwas das *"Nichts*

---

85 V 8: *"Ideo est intra omnia, non inclusum, extra omnia, non exclusum, supra omnia, non elatum, infra omnia, non prostratum."* Hierzu Beierwaltes, *Denken des Einen*, 410 f.; auch 424 f.

86 Ausführlicher habe ich dieses Philosophem dargestellt in *Identität und Differenz*, 97 ff. ("Unterschied durch Ununterschiedenheit"). Den universalen Wirkzusammenhang der ersten Ursache hat Meister Eckhart mit einer Formulierung präzisiert, die offensichtlich aus dem Kommentar des Thomas zur ersten *propositio* entnommen ist. Das den Dingen ganz unmittelbar verbundene Wirken Gottes (in ihnen) —*"actio dei immediatissima est rebus"* — wird durch den auf die "Kraft der ersten Ursache" bezogenen Satz des Thomas erläutert: *"Primo advenit et ultimo recedit": In Sap.* 176, *LW* 2, 511, 7 ff; *In Joh.* 93, *LW* 3, 81, 1 f. *("primo adest (...) postremo abest")*. Vgl. Thomas 8, 10 f.: *"impressio causae primae primo advenit et ultimo recedit,"* die Wirkung oder das aktive Sich-Einprägen der ersten Ursache "kommt zuerst an und zieht sich zuletzt zurück." Im Zusammenhang mit Isaias 41, 4: *"ego sum primus et novissimus"* im *Prologus in opus propositionum* 13, *LW* 1, 173, 13 f: *"adest primo, quia prima (causa), abest ultimo, quia novissima"*. Genauso wenig wie *über* das "Der Erste *und* der Letzte-Sein Gottes" hinaus etwas gedacht werden kann, so auch nicht bei der ersten Ursache. Wenn die Rede davon ist, daß sie sich "zuletzt zurückziehe", zo kann damit nicht gemeint sein, daß "nach" diesem Rückzug noch etwas bliebe, was ihrer bedürfte, es ist vielmehr mit dieser Formulierung ihre *Alles* umfassende Wirksamkeit ausgesagt.

von Allem". Darin zeigt sich seine absolute Transzendenz oder Differenz zu Allem. Die beiden Extreme: die radikale Andersheit des Einen als alles Andere *und* sein In-Sein in Allem sind als Pole einer dialektischen Bewegung paradox ineins zu denken. In seiner universalen Selbstentfaltung bleibt das Eine durchaus *es selbst*: es ist Alles und Nichts zugleich.[87]

Den Gedanken, daß das In-Sein oder das konstitutive und immanent-bewahrende Wirken der ersten Ursache im Geschaffen-Seienden die Differenz beider Bereiche nicht in eine Identität aufhebt, soll im Sinne Eckharts analog dem eben Erläuterten auch der Satz XXIII aus dem *Liber de causis* bestärken: "*Causa prima existit in rebus omnibus secundum* unam *dispositionem, sed res omnes non existunt in prima causa secundum unam dispositionem*", ("die erste Ursache ist (existiert, wirkt) in allen Dingen gemäß (aufgrund) einer einzigen Anlage ("*dispositio*" oder "*modus*", Art und Weise), alle Dinge jedoch sind (existieren) in der ersten Ursache *nicht* gemäß einer einzigen Anlage (oder einer einzigen Weise)"). Dies heißt im Sinne des *Liber de causis*: Der "Einfluß" der ersten Ursache ereignet sich in der von ihr geschaffenen Wirklichkeit insgesamt, ohne Unterschied, als *eine* Intensität des Wirkens, das Geschaffene aber ist von der Art, daß es aufgrund der Unterschiedenheit des Einzelnen die Eine Wirkung der ersten Ursache auch nur verschieden *aufnehmen*, d.h. in sich als Einzelnes realisieren kann. Die geschaffenen Dinge selbst also sind durch ihre unterschiedliche "Rezeptionsfähigkeit" der Grund für die unterschiedliche Konkretisierung der universalen Dynamis der ersten Ursache: "*diversitas (...) receptionis non fit ex causa prima sed propter recipiens*."[88] Thomas hat diesen Gedanken genau entwickelt, um die unterschiedliche Form und Intensität der Teilhabe und des Empfangens der Einen Wirkung des göttlichen Ursprungs im einzelnen Seienden deutlich zu machen. Für Meister Eckhart zeigt die zitierte *propositio* (analog zu Thomas) die Differenz des göttlichen Seins und Wirkens zum Geschaffenen, gibt aber auch einen Wink für die rechte, d.h. gottförmige Weise des Lebens: der Mensch müsse, um "einförmig" und/oder "gottförmig" zu werden, wie Gott selbst "in Allem gemäß einer einzigen Weise" sein; dies aber bedeutet, daß er sich nicht in das viele Einzelne verliere, sich in einzelne Seins-*Weisen* verfestige, er muß sich vielmehr in einer uni-versio von ihnen befreien. Nur so ist er *wie* der Gott "überall" und zugleich "nirgends";[89] er überwindet die das Geschaffene bestimmende Differenz ("*diversitas receptionis!*") auf deren selbst differenz-losen Grund hin in einer Denk- und Lebensform der Gelassenheit und Abgeschiedenheit. Die in einem langwierigen Bewußtseinsprozeß vollzogene Umkehr realisiert im Menschen selbst die von Gott *ausgehende* "una

---

[87] Vgl. zu diesem Gedankenkomplex W. Beierwaltes, *Denken des Einen*, 38 ff. und den Index unter "Transzendenz-Immanenz".

[88] *Propositio* XXIII; 179, 35 f.

[89] *In Joh.* 112, *LW* 3, 97, 7 ff. Im Kontext derselben *propositio* aus dem *Liber de causis: ibid.*, 79; 68, 4 - 7; 368; 313, 4 - 7.

dispositio" — einen Status des Menschen, der in Eckharts Predigten als die Gottesgeburt im Menschen eindringlich beschrieben wird. Die Befreiung von den Bildern und Weisen (*modi*) im Sinne einer Entdifferenzierung und eines immer intensiveren Einswerdens mit sich selbst und mit seinem Grunde ("*quanto quis elongatur a multo et unum intendit, tanto est perfectior et divinior*"),[90] der bewußt vollzogene Auszug aus der eigenen Entbehrung *(egestas)*, in der der Mensch am Vielen und Einzelnen festhält, führt — wieder paradox gesagt — gerade in die Fülle oder in den Reichtum, den das göttliche Eine durch sich selbst ist.[91] "Du sorgst Dich um Vieles, das Eine ist not" (Lukas 10, 41)[92] — das Eine als das durch sich selbst Reiche ist das einzig Notwendige zu einem erfüllten, glückenden Leben.

2. Dem Gedanken, daß die erste Ursache trotz der freien, creativen Teilgabe an ihrer eigenen Seinsfülle sich von allem Anderen durch ihre Transzendenz oder Andersheit unterscheidet, entsprechen ganz konsequent zwei Sätze des *Liber de causis,* die sich auf die Denkbarkeit und Aussagbarkeit der *causa prima* beziehen: "*Causa prima superior est omni narratione*", ("die erste Ursache ist höher als jegliche Aussage"),[93] d.h. sie geht über jegliche Möglichkeit der Aussage im Sinne einer Wesensaussage der präzise erfassenden Bezeichnung oder Benennung hinaus ("*narratio*" = "*significatio*"). Aussagen über die erste Ursache treffen nicht ihr Sein im eigentlichen Sinne ("*esse ipsius*"), sondern stellen sich lediglich als sekundäre, durch's Zweite vermittelte, daher eingeschränkte und letztlich inadäquate Aussageweisen dar ("*non narratur <causa prima> nisi per causas secundas*"; "*ipsa (...) non significatur nisi ex causa secunda*").[94] Der zweite Satz der denselben Gedankenbereich betrifft, lautet: "*Causa prima est super omne nomen quo nominatur*", ("die erste Ursache ist über jeglicher Benennung (Namen), durch die sie benannt wird").[95] Beide Sätze haben ihren Grund im *neuplatonischen* Denken, insofern dieses durch die gemeinsame Überzeugung geprägt ist, daß das Eine selbst als ein über dem Sein, vor jedem "Etwas", vor jeder in sich bestimmten und abgegrenzten Gestalt und Form "Seiendes" in seinem An-sich- oder In-sich-Sein, d.h. in seiner radikalen Andersheit weder durch ein diskursiv verfahrendes Denken adäquat begreifbar, noch durch die immer nur "Etwas" benennende Sprache ausgesagt werden könne.[96] Beide Sätze, in ihrer Intention

---

90 *In Joh.* 113, 97, 14 f.
91 *Sermo* 22 ("*Homo quidam erat dives*") 209, *LW* 4, 194, 4 ff.
92 *Ibid.,* 194, 9. Vgl. dort auch die Anm. 2.
93 *Propositio* V.
94 *Propositio* V; 57, 25 f.; 63, 59 f.
95 *Propositio* XXI. Dem Gedanken entsprechend müßte das Prädikat heißen: "(...) durch die sie benannt werden *könnte.*"
96 Zum neuplatonisch gedachten Verhältnis von Sprache zum "unaussprechbaren" Grund der Wirklichkeit vgl. Beierwaltes, *Denken des Einen,* 102 ff. Zur Relativierung der menschlichen Rede gegenüber dem Einen: Plotin, *Enneaden* V 3, 13, 4 ff., zurückgehend (wie später auch Proclus, *In Parm.* VII 46, 19 ff. (hrsg. von R. Klibansky) auf Platons Aussage am Ende der ersten Hypothesis des Parmenides (142 a 3): οὐδ' ἄρα ὄνομα ἔστιν

zusammengenommen, gebraucht auch Meister Eckhart für die Frage einer angemessenen Benennung des göttlichen Seins. Er verbindet sie jeweils mit Psalm 137, 2 und dem Philipperbrief 2, 9: *"magnificasti super omne nomen sanctum tuum"*. *"Donavit illi nomen, quod est super omne nomen"*. In seiner *Expositio libri Exodi*[97] stellt er sie in einen aufschlußreichen Zusammenhang: der Satz aus dem *Liber de causis*, die erste Ursache sei *"superior omni narratione"*, lasse sich verstehen *"secundum illud Psalmi"*, gemäß "jenem Wort des Psalms" und dem Philipperbrief, so daß der theologische Gedanke mit dem philosophischen als konvergent oder gar von ihm bestimmt erscheint.

Im Kontext der Exodus-Auslegung Meister Eckharts, besonders im Blick auf die Selbstaussage Gottes im *"ego sum qui sum"*, in der Gott seinen "Namen" selbst nennt, ist zu bedenken, daß *"narratio"* und *"nomen"* nicht nur "Aussage" oder "Bezeichnung" meinen, die sich auf Gott beziehen, sondern auch "Name", in dem sich Gott selbst nennt und durch den wir ihn nennen können, Name also als der nur Ihm zukommende *"Eigen*name".[98] In einer differenzierten Beweissequenz versucht Meister Eckhart "Sein" (*esse*) oder "der ist" ("der IST", *"qui est"*) als den "ersten" und unter allen anderen Namen (oder Benennungen) Gottes "eigentümlichsten", im höchsten Sinne angemessenen Namen zu erweisen (*"hoc nomen esse est primum et magis*

αὐτῷ (scil. τῷ ἑνί). Konsequenterweise grenzt Proklos das Eine selbst von einem begreifenden Zugriff der Sprache ab und nennt es "ultra nomen omne" (*In Parm.* VII 60, 17). *Nennbar* ist es nur als das "Eine in uns", als "unser" Begriff des Einen: *"intrinseca unius intelligentia"* (*In Parm.* VII 54, 12; 3 ff. Beierwaltes, *Proklos*, 367 ff.).— Die diskursive Rede, auch die das An-sich-Sein des Einen *ausgrenzenden* Negationen, gehen über in den "Hymnus", der die Einsicht in die *begrifflich* adäquate *Un*aussprechlichkeit des göttlichen Grundes in den Preis dessen wendet, was sich uns als Erscheinung oder Wirkung des Wesens des Einen oder des Gottes zeigt. Vgl. hierzu meine Interpretation des Hymnus Ὦ πάντων ἐπέκεινα in *Denken des Einen*, 309 ff. Die Aussage im Kommentar zu V. *propositio* des *Liber de causis*: *"ipsa (causa prima) non significatur nisi ex causa secunda (...) et non nominatur per nomen causati primi nisi per modum altiorem et meliorem,"* entspricht sowohl der plotinischen Konzeption als auch der proklischen These in *Elem. theol.* 123 (108, 25 ff.), daß "alles Göttliche selbst aufgrund seiner überseienden Einheit unaussprechlich und für alles Zweite unerkennbar ist, faßbar und erkennbar jedoch von dem Teil-Habenden (= dem Zweiten, 'Abhängigen' (110, 4)) her."
Der Gedanke Plotins (VI 9, 3, 49 ff.), daß wir im Sprechen über das Eine mehr "uns selbst" sagen als dessen Wesen, erscheint bei Meister Eckhart zusammen mit seinem expliziten Anknüpfungspunkt im *Liber de causis (propositio* V) in dem Satz: "Nu merkent! Got ist namlôz, wan von ime kan niemant nit gesprechen noch verstan. Har umb spricht ein heidens meister: Swas wir verstant oder sprechent von der ersten sachen, das sin wir me selber, dan es die êrste sache ist, wan si ist über allis sprechen und verstan." (*Predigt* 83, *DW* 3, 441, 1 - 4). — So bleibt, wenn dennoch über Gott gesprochen wird, jede Aussage über ihn im Uneigentlichen: "Nû spricht ein meister von der iersten sache, daz si sî oben (supra) wort. Der gebretse ist an der zungen. Daz kumet von dem überswanke der lûterkeit sînes wesens" (*Predigt* 20a, *DW* 1, 329, 1 - 3); und noch einmal unter Berufung auf die *propositio* V des *Liber de causis*: "Ein heidenischer meister sprichet, daz kein zunge enkan ein eigen wort geleisten von gote durch die hôheit und die lûterkeit sînes wesens" (*Predigt* 20b, *DW* 346, 3 - 5).
[97] *LW* 2, 35; 41, 11 ff.
[98] Analog hierzu die Überlegungen Eckharts zum menschlichen Eigennamen "Martinus": *Expositio Libri Exodi* 165; *LW* 2, 144, 18 ff. Zu einer "Theorie des Namens" bei Eckhart, vgl. A. de Libera (Anm. 81), *Le problème de l'être*, 20 - 27.

proprium inter omnia nomina dei (...) esse est proprium nomen solius *dei*").[99]
Am angemessensten ist dieser Name, weil er das Fundament aller anderen
möglichen Benennungen ist; diese können nicht nur auf ihn zurückgeführt
werden, sondern stellen die innere Differenzierung einer relationalen Identität
mit ihm dar. Vor allem hat Gott sich in diesem Namen als der zentralen und
zugleich umfassendsten Anzeige seines Wesens selbst ausgesprochen: "*Ego
sum qui sum*".[100] Aus diesem Grunde — als der so verstandene "erste Name"
— ist er "über jeglichem Namen", d. h. "über" oder "vor" allen anderen
möglichen Namen oder Benennungen.[101] Die V. *propositio* des *Liber de
causis:* "Die erste Ursache ist höher als jegliche Aussage", versteht Meister
Eckhart von der XXI. *propositio* her: "*causa prima est super omne nomen*"; er
behauptet, damit sei nicht schlechthin die "Unaussagbarkeit Gottes" ("*deus non
innarrabilis*")[102] gemeint, sondern der entschiedene Hinweis auf eben diesen
Ur-Namen SEIN, der dadurch "exklusiv" ist, daß er alle Namen oder
Benennungen — übersteigend — in sich einschließt.[103] So könne der "Name
über allen Namen" — statt als ein unnennbarer ("*innominabile*") zu gelten —
gerade als der "allesnennende" ("*omninominabile*") aufgefaßt werden: Gott
durch seinen einen und eigensten Namen SEIN zugleich der "Allnamige".[104]
Einschluß aller "Namen" im SEIN heißt freilich nicht, daß der Gedanke Gott
damit auf einen begrenzten Begriff gebracht worden sei, der neben anderen
Begriffen gleichrangig gedacht werden könnte, die Emphase des einen Namens
SEIN bedeutet aber auch keine *einschränkende Reduktion* aller anderen
Namen auf diesen hin — "nichts ist reicher als diese Armut"[105] —, er ist
vielmehr die Benennung des einen umfassenden Identitäts-Grundes der in Gott

---

99 *Ibid., Expositio libri Exodi* 163; *LW* 2, 142, 13 f. 164; 144, 5. 165; 145, 8. 168;
147, 6.
100 Über die Auslegung von Exodus 3, 14 "*Ego sum qui sum*" im Kontext von dessen
Interpretationsgeschichte und mit Blick auf die neuplatonische Grundlegung des Seins-
Begriffs vgl. W. Beierwaltes, *Platonismus und Idealismus,* 5 - 28. K. Albert, *Meister
Eckharts These vom Sein. Untersuchungen zur Metaphysik des Opus tripartitum,*
Kastellaun-Saarbrücken 1976.
101 *Expositio Libri Exodi* 166, *LW* 2, 146, 3 ff. 168; 147, 8 f.
102 *Ibid.,* 35; 41, 11.
103 *Ibid.,* 166; 146, 4.
104 41, 15. 42, 1.— Außer dem in Anm. 1 von *LW* 2, 42 (ed. K. Weiß) genannten
Asclepius wäre auf *Dionysius* zu verweisen, den den göttlichen Grund einmal als
polu≈numow, dann als ἄn≈numow und als Ῐper≈numow bezeichnet (vgl. hierzu, in einer
neuen Interpretation des Hymnus Ὦ πάντων ἐπέκεινα (vgl. oben Anm. 96), M. Sicherl, 'Ein
neuplatonischer Hymnus unter den Gedichten Gregors von Nazianz', in: *Gonimos,
Neoplatonic and Byzantine Studies, presented to L. G. Westerink at 75,* Buffalo, New York
1988, 61 - 83; 77 f.) — Auch im Zusammenhang mit Dionysius sieht Vl. Lossky diesen
Gedanken Eckharts, der die ersten beiden Kapitel seiner sich auf die Negation und auf den
Seins-Begriff konzentrierenden Eckhart-Interpretation unter die beiden Titel stellt: "*Nomen
innominabile*" und "*Nomen omninominabile*" in: *Théologie négative et Connaissance de
Dieu chez Maître Eckhart,* Paris 1960, 13 ff. Dieses Kapitel entwickelt die Komplexität des
Gedankens, die hier nur angedeutet werden konnte. Vgl. auch S. 42 f., 60 f.
105 Eckhart zitiert diesen Satz aus Augustins Johannes-Kommentar.

als *er selbst* real seienden Möglichkeiten, Fundament seines creativen Wirkens: *dives per se*.

3. Die bisherigen Überlegungen haben sich auf die innere Struktur und Bewegung des göttlichen Ursprungs und auf dessen Erwirken *von* und Wirken *in* Anderem konzentriert. Für beide Gedankenbereiche hat sich der Begriff der *Relationalität* als leitend und bestimmend erwiesen. Sie differenziert sich gemäß den Bereichen als eine "ständig" in sich bewegte und als eine gesetzte und in zeitlicher Bewegung sich je verschieden vollziehende Relationalität.

Im Sinne eines *Corollariums de relatione* soll beim Antworten auf die Frage nach dem Bezug Meister Eckharts zum *Liber de causis* diejenige These nicht außer Acht bleiben, die ein konstitutives In-Sein oder Inne-Sein eigens nennt und zudem noch in einem neuen Welt-Konzept (Cusanus) weiterwirkt.

Mit der *propositio* XI des *Liber de causis*: "*Primorum omnium quaedam sunt in quibusdam per modum quo licet ut sit unum eorum in alio*", ("Alles Erste ist ineinander in der Weise, in der es möglich ist, daß Eines von ihnen im Anderen sei"), verbindet Eckhart die ansonsten als "Satz des Anaxagoras" überlieferte These "*quodlibet in quolibet*";[106] von Thomas wird er auf die *propositio* 103 der *Elementatio theologica* des Proklos zurückgeführt: "*omnia in omnibus, proprie autem in unoquoque*". Thematisiert ist in beiden Satzen die Frage nach der Art und Weise des gegenseitigen In-Seins, der inneren Relationalität und Durchdringung von geistigen Wesenheiten, vor allem aber das trinitarische Ineinander-Sein oder Identisch-Sein der göttlichen Personen. Was für die Ursache (*causa*) gilt, daß sie "ganz in das Verursachte hinabsteigt", dies ist in noch intensiverer Weise für den Ursprung (*principium*) zu denken — Meister Eckhart differenziert hier ausdrücklich zwischen diesen beiden Begriffen, er nennt "*principium*" für diesen Bereich des göttlichen Seins als den angemesseneren Namen im Vergleich zu "*causa*": die seienden Momente der trinitarischen Selbstbewegung begreift Eckhart als Relation zwischen den "ursprunghaften oder ursprünglichen allerersten Ursachen" zu dem Verursachten oder "vom Ursprung zum (zeitfrei) Entsprungenen". "(...) Der Ursprung steigt ganz und gar (durch sich ganz) und mit allen seinen Eigentümlichkeiten in das aus ihm Entsprungene herab. Ich wage zu sagen, (daß er) auch mit seinem Eigenen niedersteigt — "Ich bin im Vater und der Vater ist in mir" (Joh. 14, 10) — so daß nicht nur Dieses *in* Jenem ist, sondern Dieses Jenes, *Jedes Jedes* ist: "Ich und der Vater sind eins" (Joh. 10, 30)".[107] Die trinitarisch bewegte Einheit wird also durch die spezifische Interpretation des Satzes "*quodlibet in quolibet*" als relationale Identität verstanden — ein

---

[106] Zur Verbindung von *propositio* XI mit dem "Satz des Anaxagoras" bei Eckhart: *In Joh.* 320, *LW* 3, 269, 8 f.; *Sermo* 2, 1, 6, *LW* 4, 8, 5 f.

[107] *Ibid., LW* 4, 8, 4 - 11: "*In causis autem primordialibus sive originalibus primoprimis, ubi magis proprie nomen est principii quam causae, principium se toto et cum omnibus suis proprietatibus descendit in principiatum. Audeo dicere quod etiam cum suis propriis — Ioh. 14: 'ego in patre et pater in me est'- ut non solum hoc sit in illo, quodlibet in quolibet, sed hoc sit illud, quodlibet quodlibet, Ioh. 10: 'ego et pater unum sumus'.*"

Beispiel mehr für den Versuch Eckharts, theologische "Sachverhalte" durch philosophische Argumentation oder Begrifflichkeit zu durchdringen und darzustellen.

Für *Nicolaus Cusanus*, der diesen Text kannte — er hat ihn in seinem Eckhart-Manuskript korrigiert und durch eine nota hervorgehoben, — wurde "*quodlibet in quolibet*" zum Leitmotiv, das *Universum* als einen Relations- oder Funktions-Zusammenhang des Einzelnen zu einem Ganzen hin darzustellen. Im Blick auf seinen Ursprung führt er das gegenseitige Innesein des Einzelnen im Universum auf das In-Sein Gottes in Allem zurück. Aufgrund der creativen Selbst-Explikation des Absoluten, die die Dimension der Andersheit allererst setzt, wird das Universum — auch als Ganzes betrachtet — zu einer alles Einzelne in ihm selbst umfassenden *quidditas contracta*, zu einer "eingeschränkten Wesenheit". Gemäß dem Prinzip der *contractio* ist diese universale Wesenheit, als die das Universum zu denken ist, "anders in der Sonne und anders im Mond eingeschränkt". So verhindert der Gedanke der *contractio* die Gefahr einer alles Einzelne aufs Ganze hin einebnenden Identifizierung: ebensowenig wie man sinnvoll annehmen kann, daß Gott sich mit dem Ganzen der Welt in seiner eigenen *explicatio* identisch setze, sofern er in der Selbstexplikation er selbst bleibt, ebensowenig ist zu denken, daß das Universum in dem jeweils Einzelnen als Ganzes *dieses selbst* sei. Das In-Sein des Universums in dem von ihm umfaßten Einzelnen ist *analog* der Immanenz des göttlichen Prinzips in der Welt im Sinne einer Selbst-Differenzierung des Universums zu sehen. Diese erst macht das Einzelne zu dem, was *es* selbst ist.

Cusanus' eigentümlicher Gedanke über das Verhältnis von Gott und Welt, d.h. über das In-Sein Gottes in Allem oder im Einzelnen, welches sich zu Allem zusammenschließt, hängt an der spezifischen Bestimmung des Universums: Dieses ist, wie gesagt, im Gegensatz zu *Deus ipse sive esse absolutum* als eine "*quidditas* contracta" zu verstehen. Wenn *contractio* eine Einschränkung auf Etwas hin, auf ein Dieses oder Jenes, bedeutet, so ist das All oder Universum als die individuierende Einschränkung auf jedes Einzelne in und zugleich als das Bewahrend-Umfassende eben dieses Einzelnen zu begreifen. Gerade um eine pantheistische Deutung des biblischen Satzes, Gott sei "Alles in Allem" zu vermeiden, führt Cusanus den Begriff des Universums als eine differenzierende *Vermittlung* ("*mediante universo*") eben dieses göttlichen In-Seins in Allem ein: "Gott, der Einer ist, ist im Einen Universum. Das Universum jedoch ist in allen Dingen in eingeschränkter Weise". Dies meint: das Universum ist das Einzelne dadurch, daß *es* sich *selbst* auf dessen Wesen hin einschränkt.

Aus dem Gedanken des durch das Universum vermittelten Inneseins *Gottes* entwickelt Cusanus auch das *gegenseitige* In-sein des *Einzelnen* im Universum selbst, wofür eben dieses Universum das dem göttlichen Prinzip analoge Prinzip ist: Im Un-Endlichen ist das Einzelne, auch das Gegensätzliche und Widersprüchliche, so ineinander, daß es als eine die Vielheit absolut aufhebende Einheit in ihm selbst verstanden werden kann. Im Universum hingegen, als dem explicativen Bild des Un-Endlichen, ist das In-sein des Einzelnen ineinander als jeweils *unterschiedlich* zu bestimmende *Relationalität* gedacht. Durch sie als eine Wirkung dieses analogen Prinzips "*Universum*" ist das Einzelne als eine je verschiedene Konkretion des Ganzen mit jedem anderen Einzelnen im Universum auf bestimmte Weise verbunden, so daß das Universum zu einem in sich bewegten Relationsgeflecht oder zu einem Funktionszusammenhang wird. Das Universum als der Zusammenhalt dieses Ganzen ist in jedem Einzelnen *eben dieses* selbst, ohne aufgrund seiner Ganzheit und Universalität sich mit diesem von ihm selbst her identifizieren zu müssen. Darin besteht seine Analogie zum Wirken des Göttlich-Un-Endlichen. Jedes Einzelne aber repräsentiert oder spiegelt das Universum oder das Ganze in je verschiedener Weise: "*quodlibet in quolibet.*"[108]

Abgesehen von der skizzierten Frage, worin der cusanische Entwurf einer relationalen Welt mit Eckharts Rezeption des "Anaxagoras-Satzes" verbunden sein könnte, konnte Cusanus zudem in der Art und Weise, wie Meister Eckhart "*quodlibet in quolibet*" für die Seinsweise Gottes in seinem Sapientia- und Ecclesiasticus-Kommentar gebrauchte, eine Anregung oder Bestätigung seiner Gotteskonzeption als Coincidenz der Gegensätze erhalten: "(...) *in minimo habetur maximum, 'quodlibet in quolibet', unde ibi maius et minus, multum et paucum locum non habent. — In divinis 'quodlibet est in quolibet.' et maximum in minimo.*"[109]

---

108 Nicolaus Cusanus, *De docta ignorantia* II 5; 76, 5 - 10 (hrsg. von E. Hoffmann und R. Klibansky): "*Nam cum manifestum sit ex primo libro Deum ita esse in omnibus, quod omnia sunt in ipso, et nunc constet Deum* quasi mediante universo *esse in omnibus,* hinc omnia in omnibus esse constat et quodlibet in quolibet. *Universum enim quasi ordine naturae ut perfectissimum praecessit omnia, ut quodlibet in quolibet esse posset.*"
109 *In Sap.* 271, *LW* 2, 601, 6 f. Sermones et Lectiones super Ecclesiastici 20, *LW* 2, 248, 1 f. Dazu die Anm. 2 mit der Marginalie des Cusanus: "in divinis quodlibet in quolibet, maximum in minimo."

E.P. BOS

WILLIAM OF OCKHAM'S INTERPRETATION OF THE FIRST PROPOSITION OF THE *LIBER DE CAUSIS*[1]

(William of Ockham, *Quaestiones in librum secundum Sententiarum (reportatio)*, quaestiones iii - iv, edited by G. Gál and R. Wood (*Opera Theologica* V, St. Bonaventure, N.Y. 1981), 71, lines 4 - 6 (*dubium*) and 75, lines 11 - 23 *(solutio)*))

I. INTRODUCTION

Even after his own works had been translated into Latin, the fifth-century non-Christian philosopher Proclus continued to influence the Christian West through the *Liber de causis* ("Book of causes"), a Latin translation of an anonymous Arab version of Proclus' *Elementatio theologica*. Among those who commented on the *Liber* were many well-known philosophers. In the thirteenth century these include Albert the Great, Roger Bacon, Thomas Aquinas, Siger of Brabant, Giles of Rome and the author of a commentary ascribed to Henry of Ghent. In the fourteenth century there is one commentary by Walter Burley, as well as Guillelmus de Levibus[2] and many anonymous commentators.[3] The fifteenth century is represented by Johannes Wenck von Herrenberg,[4] and the early sixteenth century by Chrysostomus Javellus.[5]

The *Liber de causis* stimulated authors to discuss the problem of the relation between higher (or first, or primary) and lower (or second, or secondary) causes through its first *propositio*[6] which reads:[7] *omnis causa*

---

[1] I wish to thank dr. Jennifer Ashworth (Waterloo, Canada) for the correction of my English.

[2] According to A. Pelzer, 'Guillelmus de Leus (de Levibus), Frère Prêcheur de Toulouse', in: *Aus der Geisteswelt des Mittelalters. Studien und Texte Martin Grabmann zur Vollendung des 60. Lebensjahres von Freunden und Schülern gewidmet* (Series: Beiträge zur Geschichte der Philosophie und Theologie des Mittelalters, Supplementband III), Münster in Westfahlen, 1935, 1068, this William composed his *Liber causarum* between 1305 and 1309.

[3] See C.H. Lohr, 'Medieval Latin Aristotle Commentaries', *Traditio, Studies in Ancient and Mediaeval History, Thought and Religion* 23 (1967) - 30 (1974), *passim*.

[4] He died 1460; see R. Taylor, 'The *Liber de causis*: A Preliminary List of Extant Manuscripts', *Bulletin de Philosophie Médiévale* 25 (1983), 81 - 84.

[5] He died circa 1538.

[6] I shall translate *propositio* as "proposition".

[7] The first *propositio* of the *Liber de causis* corresponds to *propositio* 56 in Proclus' *Elementatio theologica* (for the Latin text, see the edition: Proclus, *Procli Elementatio theologica translata a Guillelmo de Moerbeke*, ed. C. Vansteenkiste, *Tijdschrift voor Filosofie* 13 (1951), 263 - 302; 491 - 531. *Cf.* the Greek text Proclus, *The Elements of Theology. A Revised Text with Translation, Introduction and Commentary* by E.R. Dodds, Oxford ²1963, 54).

*primaria plus est influens super causatum suum quam causa universalis
secunda*[8] ("every primary cause exercizes more influence upon its effect than
does a universal second cause").[9] The idea of a hierarchy of causes was
important to Christian medieval phiosophers, because it affected the relation
between God as the first cause among primary causes,[10] and the things created
by God as second causes. According to Christian doctrine, God was the first
and principle cause, since He had created heaven and earth and everything in it.
However, a kind of causality of their own could be ascribed to both natural
agents, such as fire, and free agents, such as man. Fire could be said to be the
cause of heat; a man could be said to be the cause of his deeds. Indeed, one of
the main reasons for assigning causality to created things was man's moral
responsibility, which seemed evident to medieval philosophers.[11]

In this contribution I shall discuss the interpretation of the first proposition of
the *Liber de causis* offered by the fourteenth century philosopher William of
Ockham (ca. 1285 - 1347). Ockham did not write a separate treatise on the
Liber s a whole, it seems; neither did John Duns Scotus (ca. 1265 - 1308/9),
whose theory of the relation between first and second causes should also be
taken into account here, since he is the object of Ockam's criticism. Both
philosophers were acquainted with at least some theses of the *Liber*,[12] though I
cannot determine how they came to know them, whether through an anthology,
or in some other form.

   A discussion of Ockham's interpretation of the first proposition may have
some interest, I hope, because Ockham's view on the priority of a cause with
respect to its effect, and his conclusion that sometimes a cause may be *after* its
effect, not only reveals the core of his conception of causation, but also shows
an important difference between his view and those of John Duns Scotus and
thirteenth century philosophers on the problem of the relation between first and
second causes. Ockham's view is also intriguing, because in modern analyses
of causality a cause is usually said to exist *before* its effect, or to be

---

[8] Edition A. Pattin: Le *Liber de causis*, Édition établie à l'aide de 90 manuscrits avec
introduction et notes par A. Pattin, O.M.I., *Tijdschrift voor Filosofie* 28 (1966), 46.

[9] I have used the English translation by D. J. Brand, The *Book of Causes*, Translated
from the Latin with an Introduction by D.J. Brand, Milwaukee, Wisconsin [2]1984 (revised),
18.

[10] Another example of a primary cause is the sun, which can not be *the* first cause, of
course (see below, § IV. 2. 1).

[11] See e.g. John Duns Scotus, *Lectura* I, 39 in Johannes Duns Scotus, *Lectura in
primum librum Sententiarum, a distinctione octava ad quadragesimam quintam, Opera
Omnia* XVII, Civitas Vaticana 1966, 491 [n. 40], 17 - 24, where Scotus refers to Aristotle's
De interpretatione. For William of Ockham's view, see below § IV. 3. 1.

[12] See below § IV. 3. 1. and IV. 4. 1.

contemporaneous with it, as when motion of a hand is said to be the contemporaneous cause of the motion of the pen that is held by the hand.[13]

The core of Ockham's solution is as follows: 1) he gives a new interpretation of the priority of a first cause. As first cause God is first in perfection and limitlessness, he says, but not necessarily in time. 2) God is an immediate cause of creatures, not an indirect cause, as Duns Scotus had claimed. 3) A first cause need not to be more perfect than a second cause: the sun is less limited than a man, but not more noble. 4) God can create different creatures, not only with the help of second causes, — which is done by God *de facto* — but also on his own, because he is completely free. In general, both a free cause (like the will) and a natural cause (like the sun) can have more than one effect, which is an frequently recurring thesis in Ockham's works. 5) A corollary to 4) is that God creates many things, but, according to Ockham, this does not imply a change in God, and one need not postulate that God can only have *one* determinate effect. With this Ockham rejects Avicennean determinism, albeit in a different way from his predecessor Duns Scotus.

Three modern scholars have paid specific attention to the *background* of the text, *i.e.* to the relation between first and second causes. G. Leff, *William of Ockham and the metamorphosis of scholastic discourse* (1975) succinctly summarizes the problem. Kl. Bannach discusses it in his *Die Lehre von der doppelten Macht Gottes bei Wilhelm von Ockham*, 1975.[14] The problem is also treated by Marilyn McCord Adams in her *William Ockham*, 1987[15] in a chapter on efficient causality. None of these scholars discuss Ockham's conclusion that a cause may be later than its effect.

II. THE TEXT

In his commentary *(reportatio)*[16] on the second book of the *Sentences* Ockham interlaces two *quaestiones*, of which the contents are closely related. The title of *quaestio* iii runs:[17] *Utrum Deus sit agens naturale vel liberum* ("whether

---

[13] See e.g. R. Taylor, 'Causation', *The Encyclopedia of Philosophy,* ed. by P. Edwards, vol. II, New York, London 1967, 56 - 66, esp. 65 - 66. In his article Taylor refers to other literature.

[14] Chapter III, 1, esp. p. 276 - 314. Though in general very stimulating, the book is not always as accurate as one might wish; e.g. on p. 294, Bannach says that the particular cause (as opposed to the universal cause, the sun) is "das Verfaulende" ('that which spoils') instead of any particular cause, *e.g.* a father; "*secundum veritatem*" refers to a certainty of belief, *viz.* that in his omnipotence God can act without a second cause; on p. 295 Bannach misses the point that according to Ockham the definition is correct, because otherwise any knowledge of causes would be impossible. When, *e.g.* on p. 296, Bannach suggests (by using quotationmarks) that he is quoting texts, in fact he is giving paraphrases.

[15] Part II, chapter 18, esp. p. 772 - 784. McCord Adams mentions both Leff's and Bannach's book only once in a note and does not discuss their general theses and interpretations. Her study is excellent, though I sometimes missed examples to illustrate the difficult theory.

[16] *I.e.* not a version that was authorized by Ockham himself, which would be an *ordinatio* ("authorized version").

[17] William of Ockham, *Quaestiones in librum secundum Sententiarum (reportatio)* ediderunt G. Gál et R. Wood (*Opera Theologica* V), St. Bonaventure, N.Y., 1981, 50.

God is the first and immediate cause of everything"); that of *quaestio* iv:[18]
Utrum Deus sit agens naturale vel liberum ("whether God is a natural or a free
agent").

In his solution to the quaestions Ockham cites the story found in Daniel[19]
of the miracle of the three youths in the fiery furnace: the fire did not hurt them
because God did not immediately co-operate with the fire to produce heat.
Therefore, Ockham says, God is an immediate cause.

God is the first cause *primitate perfectionis* ("in primacy of perfection")
and *primitate illimitationis* ("in primacy of limitlessness"), but not *primitate
durationis* ("in primacy of duration"). The reason is, Ockham continues, that
when God acts as cause, the same moment (i.e. not necessarily later) a second
cause can act:[20] in this case God co-operates and at the same moment with a
second cause. It follows that God, in this case and, generally, in the present
circumstances of creation, is a *partial* cause.

Some *dubia* ("doubts") are raised that purport to deny that God is a free
agent. One of them is:[21]

> *Item, contra hoc quod dicitur quod Deus non potest esse causa cuiuslibet prima
> prioritate durationis, quia causa prima plus influit et prius quam causa
> secunda, igitur etc.*
>
> "Further, against the thesis that God cannot be the first cause of anything with
> the priority of duration: because the first cause is more influential than and prior
> to a second cause; therefore and so on."
>
> (...)

<Ockham replies>:[22]

> *Ad aliud dico quod illa prioritas sufficit in causa quod causa non existente non
> existit effectus, et ideo sicut si causa secunda causaret cum Deo, non existente
> causa secunda non est effectus, sic si causa secunda conservaret effectum cum
> Deo, non existente causa secunda non est effectus. Et ideo licet effectus
> producatur a causa prima, si post conservaretur a causa secunda, secunda
> potest dici causa illius effectus sicut prima.*
>
> *Si dicas quod conservare et creare differunt, dico quod quantum ad nullum
> positivum differunt sed quantum ad negationes connotatas, quia "creare"
> connotat negationem immediate praecedentem esse, "conservare" connotat
> negationem interruptionis esse, sicut prius dictum est. Et ideo accipiendo
> causam prout causat esse post non esse immediate praecedens, sic causa
> praecedit effectum; sed accipiendo pro illo quod continuat effectum sine
> interruptione, sic potest esse posterior.*
>
> "To the other doubt I reply that this priority is sufficient incausation, that if
> the cause does not exist, the effect does not exist. Thus, just as, if a second cause
> causes together with God, then, if the second cause does not exist, there is no
> effect, in this sense: if a second cause conserves an effect together with God,
> there is no effect, if the cause does not exist. Hence, even if an effect is produced

---

[18] *Ibid.*, 51.

[19] Daniel 3, 46 - 50.

[20] *Ibid.* (see note 18), 62, 20 - 24 (this is in fact a version of Ockham's metholological
principle of parsimony, the so-called "razor").

[21] *Ibid.*, 71, 4 - 6.

[22] *Ibid.*, 75, 11 - 76, line 2.

by a first cause, if it is later conserved by a second cause, the second cause may be called, just like the first cause, a cause of the effect.

If the objection is raised that there is a difference between conservation and creation, my solution is: there is no difference in any positive respect, but <only> as regards the connoted negations. For 'to create' connotes a negation that immediately precedes being, 'to preserve' connotes a negation that being is interrupted, as has been said before.[23] If, therefore, one accepts 'cause' as far as it causes being after that immediately preceding non-being, in that sense the cause precedes its effect; but if one interprets <'cause'> for that which continues its effect without interruption <'of being'>, in that sense it can be later."

Ockham's opponent quotes the first proposition of the *Liber de causis*. It is not the text, however, that can be found in the modern edition by Pattin;[24] in the text of Ockham's *reportatio* the words *et prius* have been added to *plus influit*. This is relevant, because in his solution of the doubt Ockham's discussion is about priority in time.

III. SUMMARY OF THE TEXT

As has been said, the background of the *dubium* about priority in causation is the problem of the relation between first and second causes. The *disputant* in Ockham's text says that a first cause is more influential than and prior to a second cause. He apparently means that the first cause influences the effect that is caused by a second cause, and that this first cause exercizes a stronger influence on the effect than does the second cause. This implies, it seems to me, that the first cause acts with the same form, *i.e.* with the same formal causality, as the second cause; in this way, the first cause is also immediately linked with the effect.

Ockham replies that a first cause's priority in causation of a first cause with respect to a second cause need not be temporal. Both first and second cause can be contemporaneous with the effect, indeed, a second cause can be later than its effect and still be called "cause". Ockham defines cause in this way: it is sufficient for something to be a cause that if it does not exist, the effect does not exist. In the following chain of first and second causes: God — sun — man, in which God is the first cause, the sun the second cause and a man the effect of causation, both God and the sun can be called causes, though God is here the creating cause, the sun a conserving cause. This is true not only if God acts simultaneously with a second cause, but also if the second cause acts later, as when if a man is produced by God and the sun later conserves the man. In joint causation, God and the sun are partial[25] causes.

Someone objects that "to conserve" and "to create" have different meanings. This opponent suggests, it seems to me, that God first creates the

---

[23] *Ibid.*, 65, 15.
[24] *Liber de causis* I, 1, ed. A. Pattin, 1966, 46, 1 - 2.
[25] See the *apparatus criticus*, in which MS Giessen, *University Library 732* adds *partialiter* to *conservetur*, which is logically correct.

sun, and afterwards a man, and that although God and the sun both conserve man, the sun functions man only as a sort of attribute to God on a secondary level, when it conserves man. Ockham apparently takes this objection to mean that "to create" and "to conserve" have totally different meanings.

Ockham denies this objection. "To create" and "to conserve" do have the same meaning in that both terms refer to a creature related to some other thing, *i.e.* God and the sun respectively. However, the two words differ in meaning in that their connotations *(i.e.* secondary significations) are different: "to create" connotes the negation that existence immediately precedes, whereas "to conserve" connotes the negation that existence is interrupted. According to Ockham, both God and the sun fulfill the requirements of the definition of cause. Ockham imagines that the action of the sun was suspended by God during the creation of the man, but he claims that the sun conserves the effect in existence, and that therefore it can be called a later cause.[26]

IV. COMMENTARY

I shall try to elucidate Ockham's view on the relation between first and second causes by, first, making some observations about Ancient and Medieval views up to the XIIIth century (§ IV. 1). Then (§ IV. 2) I shall discuss some distinctions used in the XIIIth century about first and second causes (§ IV. 2. 1), as well as about "essentially" and "accidentally ordered causes" (§ IV. 2. 2). Then I treat of some aspects of thirteenth century thought on the problem (§ IV. 2. 3). In § IV. 3 John Duns Scotus' view will be considered; and I shall end (§ IV. 4) my commentary by systematizing Ockham's view, and by contrasting it with that of his predecessors, especially Duns Scotus.

IV. 1 *Some observations about Ancient and Early Medieval views on the relation between first and second causes*

One might say that the Medieval philosophers inherited from Antiquity a hierarchical metaphysics according to which different levels of reality were distinguished. A reality of a higher level was superior to a reality of a lower level in many respects; realities of a higher level have the property of unity and they are prior in time; realities of a lower plurality are characterized by potency, they are potential as regards the realities of the higher level, they are later in time and so on. This hierarchy is also reflected in Ancient theories of causation.

As is well known, Medieval philosophers often used texts from Antiquity, especially texts by Plato and Aristotle, as starting-points for their investi-

---

26 *Cf.* William of Ockham, *Scriptum in librum primum Sententiarum, Ordinatio* dist. xix - xlviii, ediderunt G.I. Etzkorn et F.E. Kelley (*Opera theologica* IV), St. Bonaventure, N.Y., liber I, dist. xlv, qu. unica, p. 668, 8 - 20 and 669, 4 - 9, where Ockham says that the existence of a cause after its effect is seldom or never the case.

gations. For the problem of the relation between first and second causes, however, they did not regard the texts cited as being authoritative,[27] i.e. containing truth. Sometimes, *e.g.* Aristotle's *Metaphysics* V, xi, 1018 b 37 - 1019 a 4, is referred to, in which the Philosopher says: "Some things are called prior and posterior in this sense; again, attributes of prior subjects are called prior, e.g. straightness is prior to smoothness because the former is an attribute of the line in itself, and the latter of a surface; others according to nature and substance, *viz.* so many as can exist without other things, whereas those other things can not exist without them; this distinction was used by Plato."

According to many Medieval philosophers Aristotle did not allow for *direct* causation by the first cause on things caused by second causes, but only for *indirect* causation, *i.e.* by way of realities somewhere midway in the hierarchy between the first cause and effects of second causes.[28] One of the condemnations (proposition 43) of 1277 explicitly criticizes theories of mediate causation.[29]

Centuries later, the Christian Augustine (354 - 432) developed a view on the problem of the relation between first and second causes, which is found, for instance, in his *De Genesi ad litteram*,[30] in his *De Trinitate*,[31] and in his *De diversis Quaestionibus LXXXIII*.[32] In his *De Genesi ad litteram* (book VI, xiv,

---

[27] They referred to e.g. *Physics* VIII, vi, 259 b 32 - 260 a 19, *Metaphysics* XII, vi, 1072 a 9 - 17 (so did Siger of Brabant, in Siger of Brabant, Les *Quaestiones super Librum de causis* de Siger de Brabant, édition par A. Marlasca, Louvain-Paris (Philosophes Médiévaux xii), 1972, 36); *Metaphysics* V, xi, 1018 b 27 - 29 or somewhat below in the text to 1019 a 1 - 4 (so does an anonymous commentary on the *Liber de causis* written by a *frater Simo*, which commentary is preserved in ms. Vienna, Österreichische Nationalbibliothek, V.P.L. 2330, f. 160 va - vb. See A. Dondaine et L.J. Bataillon, 'Le manuscrit *Vindobonensis lat.* 2330 et Siger de Brabant', *Archivum Fratrum Praedicatorum* (1966), 153 - 261; C.H. Lohr, 'Medieval Latin Aristotle Commentaries, authors Robertus - Wilgelmus', *Traditio* 29 (1973), 93 - 197. The manuscript contains Siger's commentary on the *Liber de causis* as well).
[28] Among these medieval philosophers was William of Ockham. I shall return below to his comments on what he viewed as Aristotle's theory (see below, § IV. 3. 3).
[29] See *Chartularium Universitatis Parisiensis* I, ab anno MCC usque ad annum MCCLXXXV, édité par H. Denifle et A. Chatelain, Paris 1889, 546.
[30] Augustine, *De Genesi ad litteram*, ed. J. Zycha (CSEL 28), Vienna-Leipzig 1894, IV, iii, 2; VI, xiv, 25; IX, xvii, 32 (*cf.* R.A. Markus, 'Marius Victorinus and Augustine', *The Cambridge History of Later Greek and Early Medieval Philosophy*, Cambridge 1970, 327 - 419, esp. 400).
[31] Augustine, *De Trinitate libri XV*, cura ac studio W.J. Mountain auxiliante Fr. Glorie, 2 vols., Turnhout 1968, ch. III, viii (9. 16), 143; also *De Trinitate* II, according to manuscript G (= Giessen, *University Library* 732) of Ockham's *Reportatio*, liber II, qq. iii - iv, in *Opera Theologica* V, 61, critical note to line 17: "*Augustinus, II De Trinitate, verius attribuit Deo causalitatem istorum inferiorum quam causis secundis. Potest etiam illa conclusio persuaderi sic*" ("In book II of his *De Trinitate*, Augustine assigns God as cause of the things in our created world rather than secondary causes. A persuasive argument can be given to this thesis as follows"). In this part of the text, Ockham tries to prove that each effect is more dependent on a first cause and a universal cause that is unlimited without qualification. According to this text, Ockham thinks he can give persuasive arguments for Augustine's thesis. I have not found the exact reference in Augustine's work.
[32] Augustine, *De diversis quaestionibus LXXXIII*, ed. A. Mutzenbacher, Turnhout, 1975, 70 - 75.

25). Augustine says that "causal natures (*rationes causales*) are capable of being in two ways, *i.e.* either in the way according to which temporal things most usually develop, or in the way unusual and extraordinary things arise owing to God's will, which creates what is convenient to each moment of time". Augustine apparently means that causal natures have been instituted by God to be subject to a double causation: one is according to the natural process of development, the other according to a miraculous causation by God. Augustine does not seem to imply that an explanation in terms of God's causality contradicts the explanation in terms of natural laws. God's miraculous causality is not *against* nature, on the contrary, it perfects it.[33] What man calls "miraculous" is in fact the perfection of nature.[34]

The main text, however, that led Medieval philosophers to discuss the problem of the relation between first and second causes, was, as has been said above, the *Liber de causis*, notably the first proposition.

IV. 2 *The thirteenth century*

IV. 2. 1. *Causa prima, causa primaria, causa secunda*
("first cause, primary cause, secondary cause")

In the thirteenth century, a distinction was common between *causa prima* and *causa primaria* ("first cause" and "primary cause"), in contradistinction to *causa secunda* or *secundaria* ("second cause" or "secondary cause"). This distinction was also used in the fourteenth century.

According to, for instance, Albert the Great[35] primary causes are God, the intelligences, the noble soul, *i.e.* the *anima orbium*, that is: the soul that moves the spheres; and nature, *i.e. natura naturans* the general informing principle of the natural universe, or, in other words, nature as far as it imparts motion. The latter is a kind of immanent moving principle. Each of these primary causes influences what follows from them in virtue of their own causality and in virtue of the causality of an even higher primary cause. The lower the cause, the less powerful its causality. The first cause is God.[36] In his Commentary *(expositio)* on the *Book of Causes*[37] Thomas says that (1) the first cause helps the second

---

33 *Cf.* R.A. Markus, 'Marius Victorinus and Augustine', 401.
34 *Cf.* Augustine, *De Trinitate* III, 8, qu. 16, ed. 1968, 143.
35 See Albert the Great, *Liber de causis et processu universitatis* (= Parva naturalia I), ed. A. Borgnet, Paris (Vivès, vol. X) 1890, 316 - 619, book II, *De terminatione causarum primariarum*, tractatus I, *De potentiis et virtutibus earum*, caput II, *De numero causarum primariarum*, 436 a - 437 b.
36 Giles of Rome (Aegidius Romanus) (1247 - 1316) follows this lead: Aegidius Romanus, *Opus super Authorem de causis, Alpharabium*, ed. Venetiis, 1550, f. 1r. Giles adds that "nature" is in a certain sense an instrument of the other causes.
37 Thomas Aquinas, *Super Librum de causis expositio*, ed. H.D. Saffrey, Fribourg (Sw.)-Louvain, 1954, 6, 22 - 28, esp. line 11.

cause to act, that (2) the first cause arrives at the effect before the second cause and that (3) the first cause leaves its effect later that the second cause.[38]

Duns Scotus and Ockham do not use, it seems, the term "primary cause" in contradistinction to "first cause". "First cause" can refer not only to God, but also to the sun and the intelligences. "Second cause" refers to causes that are created by a first cause, or stand below a first cause, and that are lower in rank, or range.[39]

IV. 2. 2. *Causae essentialiter vel accidentaliter ordinatae*
("essentially or accidentally ordered causes").

A second distinction commonly used by thirteenth century and later by fourteenth century philosophers was between *essentially and accidentally ordered causes*. They probably felt that this distinction was not clearly made in the *Book of Causes*, since this neo-platonic source seems only to have essential and formal causality in mind.

Thomas Aquinas[40] (1224 - 1274) illustrates the case of *essentially ordered causes* with the example of a craftsman moving his shoulders, the shoulders moving the arms, the arms the hands, the hands a hammer, the hammer a helmet. The causality of the hammer was brought about essentially by that of the hand, the causality of the hand by that of the arm and so on, up to the action of the carpenter himself. Hand and hammer and so on were instrumental to the causal action of the carpenter. The carpenter is the cause of the causal action of the hammer. As another example the causal chain God — sun — creatures can be given.[41]

An example given by Thomas Aquinas[42] of *accidentally ordered causes* was that of a grandfather, a father and a son. The grandfather is *not* the cause of the causal action of the father begetting a son. The grandfather's role is confined to producing the existence of the father, and he is not essential to the father's own exercise of causation in the act of begetting.

Thomas Aquinas[43] and Siger of Brabant[44] say that in *essentially ordered causes* the primary cause *intends* the effect of the secondary cause (thus the carpenter *intends* his shoulders to move his arms and so on), which is not the

---

[38] So already in Plato, *Philebus* 27 a 5 - 6; see e.g. Albertus Magnus, *Summa theologiae sive de mirabili scientia Dei*, ed. D. Siedler P.A. collaborantibus W. Kübel et H.G. Vogels, *Opera omnia* XXXI, pars I, Münster in Westfahlen 1978, liber I, pars I, tr. 4, qu. 19, cap. 3, ed. 1978, 94 b - 95 b.

[39] For Ockham's definition, see William of Ockham, *Scriptum in librum primum Sententiarum, Ordinatio*. dist. xix - xlviii, ediderunt G.I. Etzkorn et F.E. Kelley (*Opera theologica* IV), liber I, dist. xlv, qu. unica, St. Bonaventure, N.Y. 1979, 667, 19 - 668, 7.

[40] Thomas Aquinas, *Super Librum de causis expositio*, ed. 1954, 9, line 26 - 10, line 3.

[41] *Ibid.*, 10, 9 - 15.

[42] *Ibid.*, 10, 3 - 8.

[43] *Ibid.*, 9, 26 - 10, 15.

[44] And an anonymous commentator whose commentary was written by brother Simo; see also above, note 27.

case in *accidentally ordered causes*. Thomas emphasizes[45] that God does create the intelligences but does not create other things by way of the intelligences in an essentially ordered causation,[46] so God is in direct contact with the effects of second causes.

IV. 3. *John Duns Scotus*

For a proper understanding of Ockham's theory some texts of John Duns Scotus have to be analysed, because Ockham criticizes Duns Scotus' approach to the problem under consideration.

IV. 3. 1. *The texts*

The texts in which Duns Scotus' view on the relation between first and second causes can be found, are his *Reportatio Parisiensis* liber II, dist. i, qu. iii, n. 6 (*ed. Wadding* VI, 244), his *Ordinatio*, liber I, dist. ii, pars 1, qq. i - ii, nn. 43 - 53, *ed. Vaticana* II, nn. 151 - 159) and his *De primo principio* I, 4. These works were have written between approximately 1304 and 1308, the *De primo principio* probably being the latest of the three.[47]

As has been said,[48] Duns Scotus probably did not write a separate commentary on the *Liber de causis*. Unlike e.g. Ockham, who only quotes three propositions of the *Liber* (three different propositions, each quoted once[49]), Duns Scotus often cites propositions from the *Liber*.[50] However, he considers their *auctoritas* not *authentica* ("not authentic", *i.e.* not containing truth), because, in his view, the *Liber* is based on the thought of the Arab philosopher Avicenna. For Duns Scotus, this means that it is based on an *radix erronea* ("erroneous root").[51] As regards the problem of the relation between first and second causes, Duns Scotus rejects the view suggested by the first *propositio* of the *Liber*, that in essentially ordered causes the first cause is predominant while the second cause has no causality of its own.[52]

---

45 Thomas Aquinas, *Super Librum de causis expositio, propositio* III, ed. 1954, 21, 21 - 22, 8.
46 According to É. Gilson, Thomas' interpretation is a background for the interpretation of Descartes (see Descartes, René, *Discours de la méthode*. Texte et commentaire par É. Gilson, Paris 1925, 325).
47 See W. Kluxen, in: Johannes Duns Scotus, *Abhandlung über das erste Prinzip*, herausgegeben und übersetzt von Wolfgang Kluxen, Darmstadt 1974, xvi-xvii.
48 See above, § I.
49 See below, § IV. 4. 1.
50 See the *Opera omnia*: in the *editio Vaticana:* vol. III: 2 quotations; vol. IV: 1; vol. V: 2; vol. VII: 3; vol. XVI: 5; vol. XVII: 2, vol. XVIII: 4 (see the indexes).
51 See John Duns Scotus, *Ordinatio, liber secundus, a distinctione prima ad tertiam, Opera omnia* VII, Civitas Vaticana, 1973, 238; Johannes Duns Scotus, *Lectura in librum secundum Sententiarum, a distinctione prima ad sextam, Opera Omnia* XVIII, editio Vaticana, 1982, 152 [n. 163].
52 See John Duns Scotus, *Opera omnia, ed. Vaticana* IV, 315, line 9. *Cf.* É. Gilson, *Jean Duns Scot, Introduction à ses positions fondamentales*, Paris 1952, 273.

IV. 3. 2. *Duns Scotus on the relation between first and second causes*

Duns Scotus distinguishes between problems of causality and problems of concausality.[53] Some *concausae* (i.e. causes jointly operating), Duns Scotus says, are on an equal level *(ex aequo),* as when two men draw a ship; but others are *not* on an equal level *(non ex aequo).* Of the latter, there are two principal relations. Some *concausae* are accidentally ordered, as in the traditional example of the grandfather, the father and the son,[54] other *concausae* are essentially ordered.[55] There are three types of essential ordering. (a) Sometimes the lower cause acts because it is moved by the higher cause, as when a stick hits a ball because it is moved by an arm which holds the stick.[56] Here the hand and the stick are *partial* causes, and together they are the *total* cause of the movement of the ball. (b) Sometimes, the lower cause receives a power *(virtus)*[57] from the higher cause,[58] as when God gives power to created causes. (c) Sometimes, the lower cause receives its form from something else, while it merely receives its actual movement from the higher cause. In the text of the *Ordinatio*, Scotus does not give an example to illustrate this member of the division, but he probably means the case of intellection, where two causes, *i.e.* the intellect and the object known, cause the act of intellection.[59] I shall concentrate on causal chain (b), which occupies Ockham's attention.

In his *De primo principio*[60] Duns Scotus says that in this essential order: God — created cause — effect, there is an *indirect* causality. God is the *remote* cause, the created cause (*i.e.* the sun) is the *proximate* cause. The effect depends essentially, Scotus says, on the *proximate* cause (*i.e.* the sun), and that for three reasons. 1) The effect can not exist if this proximate cause does not exist. 2) The causality of the cause is related to the effects in a well-determined order, and conversely, the effect and the proximate cause are essentially related to each other insofar as far as both are related to their common cause, *i.e.* the remote cause. Hence, the order between second cause and effect is also well-

---

[53] Just like Thomas Aquinas: *cf.* L. Schütz, *Thomaslexikon.* Sammlung, Übersetzung und Erklärung der in sämtlichen Werken des h. Thomas von Aquin vorkommenden Kunstausdrücke und wissenschaftlichen Aussprüche, Paderborn 1895, 143, *sub voce.*

[54] See above § IV. 2. 2.

[55] See also *De primo principio* I, 4.

[56] Duns Scotus, *Ordinatio* II, dist. xxxvii, qu. 2, n. 7, ed. Vivès, vol. xiii, 1893, 373 a - b; *Reportatio* III, 4, qu. 2, n. 8, ed. Vivès, vol. xxiii, 1894, 275 a.

[57] According to the modern edition *(Ordinatio* I, dist. iii, pars 3, qu. 2, *Opera omnia,* ed. *Vaticana* III, p. 293, l. 10) Duns Scotus later added: *"seu forma"* ("or form").

[58] *Reportatio* III, 4, qu. 2, n. 8, ed. Vivès, 1894, 275 a.

[59] In this essential order, no movement, or virtue is imparted: instead, the higher cause possesses in itself a more perfect power than the lower cause. The example, Scotus gives, is of a father (in himself the higher cause) and a mother (in herself a lower cause) in begetting a child *(Reportatio* III, 4). The father and the mother are two partial causes in a special order. Both are necessary causes; separately, each is not a sufficient condition for the generation of a child. Other examples are: the sun (a higher cause) and a created cause (a lower cause) as regards a created object, e.g. a man *(Reportatio* II, 1).

[60] *De primo principio* I, 4, ed. W. Kluxen, 1974, 6.

ordered. 3) God is the proximate cause of the second cause. The effect of the second cause is not produced by the remote cause *as remote*.

I conclude first that in this chain of causality, the first cause is *superior* in all respects: it is more perfect, it is less limited. Duns Scotus does not say that it is prior in duration. On the contrary, he maintains that essentially ordered causes are simultaneous. So God is prior in all respects. The order God — sun — lower creatures is fixed in the sense that the sun does not cause without God, and the reverse, that God does not create without the sun, and that the effect is directly caused by the sun.

Second, there is an *indirect* causation, for God is indirectly related to the effect. God causes the sun, the sun the lower effects. God cannot produce an effect without the created cause, so in this sense God depends on the created cause; in Himself, however, God is superior.[61]

Criticizing Averroes Duns Scotus says[62] that only imperfect things can be produced by an equivocal cause, and that, just because of their imperfection. Here by "imperfect things" he means not men, animals and so on but the products of putrefaction; and by an equivocal cause he means God, into whose definition the notion of putrefaction does not enter. It is called "equivocal" because it is is not caused itself. In his theory of causation Duns Scotus emphasizes order in reality; only imperfect things can be produced by something of another nature than the thing itself.[63]

Duns Scotus says elsewhere[64] that the first cause *contains virtually (continere virtualiter)* both the second cause and the effects, and Ockham at least had the impression that according to Duns Scotus, these effects can be deduced from a higher cause.[65] In Duns Scotus' works "virtual containment" is the primary notion used to express the relation between first and second causes.[66] He uses the notion of *intention* only for instrumental causation (e.g. of a living organism, using its hand to feed itself).[67]

A problem many Medieval philosophers found difficult was how God could produce *changeable* things different in species and number, without Himself being multiplied or changed. A fundamental conception in Duns Scotus' works is that a thing *in itself* is ontologically prior to any *manifestation* of the thing, or to the thing in its outward relations. According to these

---

61 Ockham gives Scotus' view from Scotus' *Ordinatio* I (see above, § IV. 3. 1).
62 Duns Scotus, *Ordinatio* I, dist. ii, pars 2, qu. 4, ed. *Vaticana* II, esp. p. 322 [n. 327].
63 *Cf.* below, § IV.4.3.
64 *E.g.* Duns Scotus, *Lectura*, prologus, pars 2, qq. 1 - 3, p. 26 [n. 66].
65 *Cf.* L. Honnefelder, *Ens in quantum ens. Der Begriff des Seienden als solchen als Gegenstand der Metaphysik nach der Lehre des Johannes Duns Scotus* (Series: Beiträge zur Geschichte der Philosophie und Theologie des Mittelalters, Neue Folge, Band 16), Münster in Westfahlen 1979, 5 - 7.
66 *Cf.* above, note 11.
67 *Opus Oxoniense*, liber IV, dist. VI, qu. 5, n. 6 - 8.

principles God in Himself is *immutable*, whereas He can produce mutable things. God's mind changes insofar as he forms acts of intellection.[68]

IV. 3. 3. *Conclusion*

In Duns Scotus' works, contingency and God's omnipotence do not play a part in the same degree as they played in Ockham's works, as we shall see below.[69] The central notion is that of a hierarchical order among causes, though in some cases there is no influence from the higher cause to a lower, for instance in the generation of a child, where there is no influence from the father on the mother,[70] and in the production of an act of knowledge.[71] Duns Scotus emphasizes the order in reality which is determined by God. For instance, an accidental property (be it corporeal or incorporeal) is less perfect than a substance; in a chain of essential causation a first cause is equivocal (because it is not caused itself) and therefore more perfect than the second causes. Accidents and second causes cannot act without the action of a substance and first cause.[72] Unlike Thomas Aquinas for instance, Duns Scotus defends the view that a first cause acts simultaneously with a second. The first cause has the primacy of influence. He probably means that the first cause can act without the help of a second cause, but he is not very clear on this point. He does allow this type of causality when *imperfect* effects are caused, for instance the effects of putrefaction can be produced without the help of a second cause.[73]

IV. 4. *William of Ockham*

This part of my article runs parallel to that on Duns Scotus in order to facilitate a comparison. As has been said in the introduction, Ockham's interpretation of the first proposition of the *Liber de causis* primarily separates the concepts *priority in duration* and *causation*. The background is the problem of the relation between first and second causes.

IV. 4. 1. *The texts*

There are three passages in which Ockham explicitly discusses the problem: (1) *Reportatio* II, qq. iii - vi: (qu. iii: "Whether God is the first and immediate cause of everything"; qu. iv: "Whether God is a natural or a free agent"; qu. v: "Whether God is the cause of everything according to the intention of the

---

[68] *Ordinatio*, liber I, dist. viii, pars 2, qu. unica (*Opera omnia*, ed. *Vaticana* IV, 1965, 321 [n. 293]).

[69] See below, § IV. 4. 2.

[70] *Ordinatio* I, dist. iii, pars 3, qu. 2, p. 496.

[71] *Ordinatio* II, dist. xxxvii, qu. 2, n. 7.

[72] *Opus Oxoniense* IV, dist. xii, qu. 3, nn. 13 - 15 (ed. *Wadding* VIII, 744 ff.); *Reportatio Parisiensis* IV, dist. xii, qu. 3, nn. 9 - 11 (ed. *Wadding* XI, p. 686).

[73] See also below, § IV. 4. 3.

philosophers"; qu. vi: "Whether it is a contradiction: a creature has the power to create");[74] (2) *Ordinatio* I, distinction ii, qu. x: "Whether there is just one God";[75] and (3) *Quaestiones in Physicam,* qq. 132 - 134 (qu. 132: "Whether in essentially ordered causes the second cause depends on the first"; qu. 133: "Whether in essentially ordered causes the superior cause is more perfect"; and qu. 134: "Whether essentially ordered causes are necessarily simultaneously required to produce an effect with regard to which the causes are essentially ordered"[76]). Of these texts the *Reportatio* was written, according to the modern editors[77] in 1318 or somewhat earlier, the *Ordinatio* in about 1317 - 1319,[78] the *Quaestiones in libros Physicorum Aristotelis* was written 1323 - 1324.[79]

IV. 4. 2. *Ockham on God's priority in causation*

In answer to the opponent's interpretation of the first proposition of the *Liber de causis*[80] Ockham first says, that, though God, as first cause, has primacy of perfection and of limitlessness. He need not be prior in duration to a second cause, because the causality *may* be *simultaneous.* Simultaneity, he says,[81] is accepted by Aristotle. Traditionally it was said[82] that a first cause operates in time *before* a second cause.

This conclusion follows from Ockham's definition of causality. In our text, the definition is very meagre: "if a cause does not exist, an effect does not exist."[83] Though this definition seems to apply to the efficient cause, Ockham

---

74 Liber II, qq. iii - vi, *Opera Theologica* V, 1981, 50 - 98.
75 William of Ockham, *Scriptum in librum primum Sententiarum, Ordinatio,* dist. ii-iii edidit S. Brown adlaborante G. Gál *(Opera theologica* II), St. Bonaventure, N.Y., dist. II, qu. x, 1970, 337 - 356.
76 *Opera Philosophica* VI, 1984, 753 - 762.
77 See the introduction to the edition, p. 26*.
78 See William of Ockham, *Ordinatio, prologus et distinctio prima, Opera Theologica* I, 34* - 36*.
79 See the modern edition, *Opera Philosophica* VI, 41*. Some scholars have raised problems concerning the *Quaestiones in Physicam.* According to G. Leibold, 'Zum Authentizität der *Quaestiones in libros Physicorum* Wilhelms von Ockham', *Philosophisches Jahrbuch* (1973), 368 - 378 it is a collection of older texts of Ockham, not arranged by him. He adduces some passages to show that the texts can be found elsewhere in Ockham's works, and that no doctrinal development is involved. Vl. Richter agrees with Leibold (Vl. Richter, 'In Search of the Historical Ockham: Historical Literary Remarks on the Authenticity of Ockham's Writings', *Franciscan Studies,* vol. 46, Annual XXIV, 1986 (William of Ockham (1285 - 1347), Commemorative Issue, Part III, 1988), 93 - 106, 96) writing as if Leibold had denied the authenticity of the questions in any strong sense, in § VI, 2 of the modern edition of Ockham's text, Brown argues that the *Quaestiones* is, contrary to Leibold's opinion, authentic. A. Goddu *(The Physics of William Ockham,* Leiden - Köln 1984, 5) thinks it is indeed a compilation, and authentic. I add that it may be a compilation, and that nobody, Leibold included, denies this, but there are (albeit small) changes and developments in the *Quaestiones* (1984, 5), so parts of the text may be of an early date, *i.e.* those that can be found in the *Ordinatio,* see below, § IV. 3. 5
80 See above, § III.
81 Ockham, *Ordinatio,* liber I, dist. ix, qu. iii, *Opera theologica* II, 1970, 299, 3 - 4; Ockham does not explicitly refer to a specific passage in Aristotle's works.
82 *Cf.* above § IV. 2. 2.
83 *Cf.* M. McCord Adams, *William Ockham,* 1987, 798.

often calls the cause *causa productiva* ("a producing cause"), which is a more general formula.[84] Thomas Aquinas notes that Proclus uses the verb *"producere"* to express the causality alone of the efficient cause,[85] so no specific kind of causality is meant. In his omnipotence God can produce any creature immediately and totally, Ockham says. He criticizes Aristotle because, in his opinion, Aristotle only accepts mediate causation.[86]

In his commentary Ockham also concludes that a cause may be *later* than its effect, as when the activity of the sun is suspended by God's omnipotence and when the sun exercizes its conserving function later. Here the sun is the cause of an effect which already exists, because the effect has already been created by God. In his *Reportatio*[87] Ockham adds that the case of a cause being later than its effect cannot be maintained assertively, probably because he is speaking of things that are not according to the established laws of nature and that are completely in God's power. Here Ockham abandons a strictly hierarchical chain of causation as it is found in Duns Scotus.[88]

Ockham is interested to safeguard God's *immediate causation*. Beyond this, God gives creatures a causation of their own: He co-operates with them in a joint causality. He does not exercise his full power, however. Ockham gives the example of a father and a son carrying a burden of ten[89] stones. The father could carry the stones alone; he carries most of the burden, and carries it directly and immediately. However, the father does not exert his full strength, for he lets his son play his own part. If the son fails, the son is to be blamed, whereas the father is not.[90] In the same way God co-operates with created causes, hence God and creatures are *de facto partial* causes of an effect.[91]

In the Prologue of his *Commentary on the Sentences*, Ockham criticizes Henry of Ghent for advocating that there are two total causes of the same effect. Ockham opines that, when God is the indirect or remote cause and a lower cause is a proximate cause of the same effect, both are partial causes. In the modern edition[92] it is noted that numerically the same son can be the son of one or another father, Duns Scotus implies, it seems, that either can be the total cause. This remark may have misled Ockham.

Like Duns Scotus, Ockham says that, although God can produce something without the help of a second cause, in the present circumstances He

---

[84] *Cf.* G. Leff, *William of Ockham,* 1975, 388 - 390.

[85] Thomas Aquinas, *Super Librum de causis expositio,* ed. 1954, 8, 29 - 9, 1.

[86] See *Reportatio* II, qu. v, *Opera Theologica* V, 1981, 87, 2 - 12.

[87] William of Ockham, *Reportatio* II, qq. iii - iv, *Opera Theologica* V, 1981, 64, 7.

[88] See above, § IV. 3. 2.

[89] For "ten" *(decem)* in "ten" stones: this addition is based on the *apparatus criticus, ad locum,* version in manuscripts G and L (Olmutii, *Bibliotheca Capitularis,* C. O. 327 of the modern edition).

[90] *Reportatio* II, qu. iii - iv, *Opera Theologica* V, 1981, 72, 3 - 20.

[91] *Ibid.,* II, 3, 63, 19 - 25.

[92] P. 64, note 2.

co-operates, which is also a partial cause, with a second cause, also being a partial cause.[93]

IV. 4. 3. *Ockham's criticism of Duns Scotus*

In two passages Ockham criticizes Duns Scotus' theory about the relation between first and second causes. The first passage is in book I, dist. ii, qu. x.[94]

A. The first main point of criticism is Duns Scotus' argument that the second cause was dependent on the first in its causation. Ockham rejects this view. He says that there are three possible interpretations of "dependence".

1. The first is that a first cause is *necessary to* the causality of a secondary cause; however, this is not always the case. In many cases a first cause also needs a second cause (*e.g.* the sun can not act without other created causes in producing an effect). Though Ockham criticizes Duns Scotus on this score, Scotus in fact said the same.[95]

2. The second interpretation is that a second cause is dependent *for its existence* on a first cause. According to Ockham (2. 1) this is only applicable to accidental causes (*e.g.* the relation of father to son) and (2. 2) along these lines, the cause of a cause would be the cause in itself of an effect. The miracle of the eucharist, however, shows that sometimes the substance, notably the substance wine, which is the cause of accidents such as its quality red, is not the cause of the effects that are caused in the sacrament, because the substance has changed into the substance of the blood of Christ.

3. The third interpretation is that a second cause *receives influence, or active power* from a first cause. This cannot be, Ockham says, because (3. 1) often a second cause does not receive a form from the first. The example Ockham gives is the sun and lower second causes, such as a father, who does not receive the form of the sun. It should be noted, however, that Duns Scotus acknowledges this case.[96] (3. 2) Another example is an object of learning and the intellect which are two partial causes of an act of intellection. The object, Ockham apparently means, is the second cause, the intellect a first cause; both causes act according to their own power, however. Here, Ockham criticizes Thomas Aquinas, as Bannach was correct in thinking.[97] Duns Scotus also acknowledges this case.[98]

B. The second main point of criticism is Duns Scotus' claim that a first cause is more perfect than a second cause. Ockham replies: either (1) the first cause is primary in respect of perfection, and then the phrase is tautologous; or (2) a first cause is less limited than a secondary cause. And this is false. A less

---

[93] *Reportatio* II, qu. iii - iv, *Opera Theologica* V, 1981, 63, 19 - 25.
[94] See above, § IV. 4. 1. He repeats the criticism in his *Quaestiones in libros Physicorum*, qq. 132 - 134 (*Opera Philosophica* VI).
[95] See above, § IV. 3. 3.
[96] See above, § IV. 3. 3.
[97] Kl. Bannach, *Die Lehre der doppelten Macht* ..., 1975, 293.
[98] See above, § IV.3.3.

limited cause (*e.g.* the sun) is not more perfect than a limited cause (*e.g.* a man or an ass), for a living being endowed with senses is always more perfect than an unanimated being without senses. Duns Scotus did not pay attention to this counterexample, it seems. Perhaps he thought only in terms of a hierarchy of causes, where the higher cause is more universal and more perfect.

C. The third main point of criticism is Duns Scotus' claim that a first cause never acts without a second cause, so that causation is simultaneous. Ockham denies this, for, he says, there is the counterexample of spontaneous generation where a universal cause acts without a particular cause. Ockham accuses Duns Scotus of a contradiction,[99] because, according to Ockham, Duns Scotus did acknowledge the counterexample. Duns Scotus, however, only accepts it for the case of the production of imperfect beings.[100] Ockham acknowledges God's direct causality without the help of second causes with respect to all existent creatures, whereas Duns Scotus accepted it only for imperfect beings, namely the products of putrefaction.[101].

In an objection it is said, that a second cause would be superfluous. Ockham denies this. He refers to his *Reportatio*, liber II, questions iii - iv, in which he emphasizes the part played by the second partial causes in the present order of creation. It is only according to his absolute power that God is a total cause. Here, Ockham takes miracles into account.

Elsewhere, Ockham criticizes[102] Duns Scotus' view[103] that everything would be *virtually contained* in the first subject of a hierarchy. This first subject, God, is the first cause, and every second cause and every effect would be in some way contained in it. This view seems to imply that everything is demonstrable by way of the first subject. Ockham clearly thinks that this way of thinking leads us away from any empirical knowledge: everything would be logically deducible from the highest principle.

In the *Reportatio* II[104] the problem is raised of how God can produce many things given that He must remain the same, and given that from one thing only one thing results, whereas a plurality of effects implies a plurality of powers, which is impossible in the case of God.[105] Ockham solves this problem by saying that according to faith God can produce many things immediately, and, moreover, that the opponent's view is against reason. The will is a single power with a plurality of effects, since it is a power both to will and not to will.

---

[99] Ockham apparently refers to Duns Scotus', *Ordinatio, liber primus, distinctio prima et secunda, Opera omnia* II, Civitas Vaticana, liber I, dist. i, qq. i - iv, n. 327 - 37, 1950, 322 - 328.

[100] *Ibid.,* 327; McCord Adams (*William Ockham* ,1987, 783) does not discuss the passage and therefore fails to give a more detailed description of Duns Scotus' view.

[101] *Cf.* above, § IV. 3. 2.

[102] See esp. *Opera Theologica* I, 229.

[103] See § IV. 3. 2.

[104] P. 56, 12 - 13.

[105] *Cf.* above, § IV. 3. 2. See *Reportatio* II, qq. iii - iv, *Opera Theologica* V, 1981, 56, 13 - 19.

Similarly, a natural cause like the sun can produce many things while in itself remaining the same, and, finally, one cause can have specifically different effects.[106] For a cause remains the same in producing many things that are specifically or numerically different. Ockham's conclusion is the same as that of Duns Scotus, though his principles of explanation are different: he does not distinguish a thing in itself and its manifestations as different ontological levels.

To my mind, Ockham does not accept the traditional distinction between essentially and accidentally ordered causes, for his notion of *causality* is that of efficient causality, in which forms or intentions do not play a part.

V. CONCLUSIONS

At this point it is possible to draw some conclusions.

1. In Ockham's text discussed above (*Reportatio* II, qq. iii - iv), Ockham's definition of "cause" (*i.e.* "when a cause does not exist, an effect does not exist") is of what he prefers to label a "producing cause" which strongly resembles Aristotle's "efficient cause".

2. Ockham does not, it seems, accept a distinction between essentially and accidentally ordered causes.

3. Unlike Thomas Aquinas, for instance, Ockham does not assign primacy in duration to the first cause. The first cause may be simultaneous with the second cause (in this respect Ockham agrees with Duns Scotus)

4. Ockham allows for a cause to be after its effect, though this is not a case of normal causality, but happens only rarely as a result of God's absolute freedom (*de potentia absoluta*).

5. One of Ockham's principles is that a cause may have specifically or numerically different effects while the cause in itself is not changed. Ockham argues for this conclusion from different principles than Duns Scotus.

6. Ockham defends God's immediate causality with respect to his own effects and the effects of second causes. In other words, Ockham strongly rejects Duns Scotus' theory of indirect causality by a first cause, when it operates together with a second cause.

7. Ockham rejects what he — wrongly — sees as Duns Scotus' idea of one effect having two total causes.

8. Ockham denies Duns Scotus' notion of virtual containment in causes that are essentially ordered.

9. He denies any absolute superiority of higher realities (e.g. the sun as opposed to a man). The second cause is not ontologically higher than its effect

---

[106] That one cause can have two specifically different effects, and that one effect can be produced by two specifically different causes is a fundamental and often recurring doctrine about causality in Ockham's works.

in all respects, as philosophers before him, especially the thirteenth century, had held.

SOURCES

Aegidius Romanus, *Opus super authorem de causis Alpharabium*, ed. Venetiis 1550.

Al-Fârâbî, *De intellectu et intellecto*, ed. in É. Gilson, 'Les sources gréco-arabes de l'augustinisme avicennisant', *Archives d'histoire doctrinale et littéraire du moyen âge*, 4 (1930), 115 - 126.

Al-Ghazâlî, *Metaphysica*, in: *Algazel's Metaphysics*, a Medieval Translation by J.T. Muckle, New York, 1933.

Albertus Magnus, *De intellectu et intelligibili*, ed. P. Jammy, *Opera omnia* V, Lyons 1651, 239 - 262.

Albertus Magnus, *De causis et processu universitatis*, ed. A. Borgnet, *Opera omnia* X, Paris 1890, 361 - 619.

Albertus Magnus, *De praedicabilibus*, ed. A. Borgnet, *Opera omnia* X, Paris 1890, 1 - 148.

Albertus Magnus, *De sex principiis*, ed. A. Borgnet, *Opera omnia* X, Paris 1890, 305 - 372.

Albertus Magnus, *Ethica*, ed. A. Borgnet, *Opera omnia* VII, Paris 1890.

Albertus Magnus, *Liber de natura et origine animae*, ed. B. Geyer, *Opera omnia* XII, Münster in Westfahlen 1955.

Albertus Magnus, *Metaphysica*, ed. B. Geyer, *Opera omnia* XVI, pars I, Münster in Westfahlen 1960; XVI, pars II, Münster in Westfahlen 1964.

Albertus Magnus, *De anima*, ed. Cl. Stroick, *Opera omnia* XVII, pars I, Münster in Westfahlen 1968.

Albertus Magnus, *Super Ethica, Commentum et Quaestiones, libros quinque priores* edidit. W. Kümel, *Opera omnia* XIV, pars I, Münster in Westfahlen 1968 - 1972.

Albertus Magnus, *De caelo et mundo*, ed. P. Hoßfeld, *Opera omnia* V, pars I, Münster in Westfahlen 1971.

Albertus Magnus, *Super Dionysium De divinis nominibus*, ed. P. Simon, *Opera omnia* XXXVII, pars I, Münster in Westfahlen 1972.

Albertus Magnus, *De fato*, ed. P. Simon, *Opera omnia* XVII, pars I, Münster in Westfahlen 1975.

Albertus Magnus, *De XV problematibus*, ed. B. Geyer, *Opera omnia* XVII, pars I, Münster in Westfahlen 1975.

Albertus Magnus, *Summa theologiae sive de mirabili scientia Dei*, ed. D. Siedler P.A. collaborantibus W. Kübel et H.G. Vogels, *Opera omnia* XXXIV, pars I, Münster in Westfahlen 1978.

Alexandre d'Aphrodise, *Épître des principes du tout selon l'opinion d'Aristote le Philosophe*, trad. A. Badawi, in: A. Badawi, *La Transmission de la philosophie grecque au monde arabe*. Cours professé à la Sorbonne en 1967 (Études de Philosophie Médiévale 65), Paris 1987, 135 - 153.

Aristote, *Ethique à Nicomaque*, nouvelle traduction avec introduction, notes et index par J. Tricot, Paris 1959.

Aristote, La *Metaphysica, nouvelle édition* entièrement refondue, avec commentaire par J. Tricot, 2 tômes, Paris 1953.

Aristote, *Les Topiques*, trad. J. Tricot, in Aristote, *Organon* V, Paris 1965.

Aristoteles, *Ethica Nicomachea*, translatio Robertus Lincolniensis, in: Albertus Magnus, *Super Ethica Commentum et Quaestiones, tres libros priores Opera omnia* XIV, pars I, ed. W. Kümel, Münster in Westfahlen 1968.

Aristoteles, *Metaphysica* (Lib. I - IV, 4), translatio Iacobi sive vetustissima cum scholiis. Translatio Composita sive vetus, ed. G. Vuillemin-Diem, (*Aristoteles Latinus* XXV 1/1a), Leiden 1970

Aristoteles, *Metaphysica* (Lib. I - IX; XII - XIV), translatio anonyma sive 'Media', ed. G. Vuillemin-Diem (*Aristoteles Latinus* XXV 2), Leiden 1976.

Augustin, *Cité de Dieu*, Texte de la 4e édition par B. Dombart et A. Kalb, introduction générale et notes par G. Bardy, traduction française par G. Combes (Bibliothèque Augustinienne 34), Paris 1959.

Augustinus, *De Genesi ad litteram*, ed. J. Zycha (CSEL 28), Vienna-Leipzig 1894.

Augustinus, *De diversis quaestionibus LXXXIII*, ed. A. Mutzenbacher, Turnhout 1952.

Augustinus, *De Trinitate libri XV*, cura ac studio W.J. Mountain auxiliante Fr. Glorie, 2 vols., Turnhout 1968.

Averroes, *Aristotelis Stagiritae Metaphysicorum libri XIV cum Averrois Cordubensis in eosdem Commentariis* (...), Venetiis 1552.

Averroes, *Metaphysica*, ed. G. Darms (Thomistische Studien 11), Freiburg, 1966.

Avicenna, *Logica*, ed. Venetiis 1508.

Avicenna, *Liber de philosophia prima sive scientia divina* I - IV, édition critique de la traduction latine médiévale par S. van Riet *(Avicenna Latinus)*, Louvain-Leiden, 1977; V - X, édition critique de la traduction latine médiévale par S. van Riet *(Avicenna Latinus)*, Louvain-Leiden, 1977;

Avicenna, *Metaphysica*, ed. S. van Riet *(Avicenna Latinus)*, Louvain-Leiden, 1980.

Berthold von Moosburg, *Expositio super Elementationem theologicam Procli: Prologus, propositiones* 1-13 (Corpus Philosophorum Teutonicorum Medii Aevi VI, 1), ed. M.R. Pagnoni-Sturlese and L. Sturlese, Hamburg 1984. Propositiones 14 - 34, (Corpus Philosophorum Teutonicorum Medii Aevi VI, 2), ed. L. Sturlese, M.R. Pagnoni-Sturlese and B. Mojsisch, Hamburg 1986.

Chartularium Universitatis Parisiensis, I, ab anno MCC usque ad annum MCCLXXXV, édité par H. Denifle et A. Chatelain, Paris 1889.

Damascius, *In Phaedonem* , ed. L.G. Westerink, Amsterdam 1977.

Damascius, *Vitae Isidori reliquiae*, ed. C. Zintzen, Hildesheim 1967.

Damascius, *De primis principiis*, ed. L.G. Westerink, Paris 1989.

Dietrich von Freiberg, *De cognitione entium separatorum et maxime animarum separatarum*, ed. H. Steffan, Dietrich von Freibergs Traktat *De cognitione entium separatorum*, Studie und Text (Diss.), Bochum 1977, 107 - 317

Dionysius Areopagiticus, *De divinis nominibus*, Patrologia Graeca 3, ed. J.P. Migne, Paris 1857.

Eustratius, *In Primum Aristotelis Moralium ad Nicomachum*, ed. H.P.F. Mercken (Corpus Latinum Commentariorum in Aristotelem Graecorum VI/1), Leiden 1973.

Eustratius, in: *Eustratii et Michaelis et anonyma in Ethica Nicomachea commentaria* edidit G. Heylbut, Berlin 1892.

Gilles de Rome, *see* Aegidius Romanus.

Guillaume d'Ockham, *see* William of Ockham.

Hermeias, *In Platonis Phaedrum Scholia*, ed. P. Couvreur, Paris 1901.

Hierocles, *In Aureum Pythagoreum Carmen Commentarius*, ed. F.W. Koehler, Stutgartt1974.

Iamblichus, *De communi mathematica scientia liber*, ed. N. Festa, Leipzig 1891.

Iamblichus, *De vita Pythagorica* , ed. L. Deubner, Leipzig 1937.

Iamblichus, *De mysteriis* , ed. E. des Places, Paris 1966.

Iamblichus, *In Platonis Dialogos Commentariorum Fragmenta*, ed. J.M. Dillon, Leiden 1973.

Iamblichus, *Protrepticus*, Paris 1989.

Iulianus, *Oratio VII, Contra Heraclium* , ed. J. Bidez 1932.

Johannes Duns Scotus, *Opera Omnia*, ed. L. Wadding (12 vols.), Lyons 1639 (reprinted Hildesheim 1968).

Johannes Duns Scotus, *Opera Omnia*. Editio nova iuxta editionem Waddingi XII tomos continentem a patribus Franciscanis de observantia accurate recognita (26 vols. in 13), Paris (Vivès) 1891 - 1895.

Johannes Duns Scotus, *Opera Omnia*, ed. C. Balic et alii, Civitas Vaticana I - ... (1950 - ...).

Johannes Duns Scotus, *Ordinatio, liber primus, distinctio prima et secunda, Opera omnia* II, Civitas Vaticana 1950.

Johannes Duns Scotus, *Ordinatio, liber primus, distinctio tertia, Opera omnia* III, Civitas Vaticana, 1954.

Johannes Duns Scotus, *Ordinatio, liber primus, a distinctione quarta ad decimam, Opera omnia* IV, Civitas Vaticana 1956.

Johannes Duns Scotus, *Lectura in primum librum Sententiarum, a distinctione octava ad quadragesimam quintam, Opera Omnia* XVII, Civitas Vaticana 1966.

Johannes Duns Scotus, *Ordinatio, liber secundus, a distinctione prima ad tertiam, Opera omnia* VII, Civitas Vaticana 1973.

Johannes Duns Scotus, *Abhandlung über das erste Prinzip,* herausgegeben und übersetzt von Wolfgang Kluxen, Darmstadt 1974.

Johannes Duns Scotus, *Lectura in librum secundum Sententiarum, a distinctione prima ad sextam, Opera Omnia* XVIII, Civitas Vaticana 1982.

Johannes Scotus Eriugena, *Periphyseon (De divisione naturae),* ed. I.P. Sheldon-Williams, Dublin 1968 - ...

John Wycliff, *Tractatus de universalibus,* ed. I.J. Mueller, Oxford 1985.

Liber de causis. Édition établi à l'aide de 90 manuscrits avec introduction et notes par Adriaan Pattin, *Tijdschrift voor Filosofie, 28.* Louvain 1966 (édition séparée).

Liber de causis: The *Book of causes,* Translated from the Latin with an Introduction by D.J. Brand, Milwaukee, Wisconsin 3233, [2]1984 (revised).

Macrobe, *Commentarii in Somnium Scipionis,* ed. J. Willis, Leipzig 1963.

Maïmonide, *Dux neutrorum sive Perplexorum,* anonymous translation, ed. by Augustinus Justinianus, Paris 1520.

Marinus, *Vita Procli,* ed. J.F. Boisonnade, Leipzig 1814.

Marsilius ab Inghen, *Quaestiones super quattuor libros Sententiarum,* Strasbourg 1501 (reprint Frankfurt am Main 1966).

Master Eckhart, *Die deutschen und lateinischen Werke,* hrsg. im Auftrage der Deutschen Forschungsgemeinschaft. Die deutschen Werke *(DW)* hrsg. von J. Quint; Die lateinischen Werke *(LW)* hrsg. von E. Benz, K. Christ, B. Geyer, J. Koch, E. Seeberg, K. Weiß, Stuttgart 1936 ff.

Nicolaus Cusanus, *De docta ignorantia* I, ed. by. E. Hoffmann and R. Klibansky, Leipzig 1932.

Olympiodorus, *In Phaedonem,* ed. L.G. Westerink, Amsterdam 1976.

Philippus Cancellarius Parisiensis, *Summa de bono,* ed. N. Wicki, Bern 1985.

Photius, *Bibliotheca,* ed. R. Henry, Paris 1962.

Platon, *Timée,* trad. J. Moreau, *in: Platon. Oeuvres complètes,* II, Paris [1]1950.

Platonis Timaeus a Calcidio translatus commentarioque instructus, edidit J.H. Waszink (in societatem operis coniuncto P.J. Jensen) (Plato Latinus IV), Londini et Leidae, 1962.

Proclus, *In Parmenidem commentarius,* ed. V. Cousin, Paris [2]1864.

Proclus, *In Platonis Rempublicam commentarii,* G. Kroll, Leipzig 1899 - 1901.

Proclus, *In Platonis Timaeum commentarii,* ed. E. Diehl, Leipzig 1903 - 1906.

Proclus, *In Platonis Cratylum commentarii,* ed. G. Pasquali, Leipzig 1908.

Proclus, *Procli Elementatio theologica translata a Guillelmo de Moerbeke,* ed. C. Vansteenkiste, *Tijdschrift voor Filosofie* 13, 1951, 263 - 302; 491 - 531.

Proclus, *In Parmenidem,* ed. R. Klibansky - C. Labowsky *(Plato Latinus* III), London 1954.

Proclus, *De providentia et fato,* ed. H. Boese, Berlin 1960.

Proclus, *The Elements of Theology, A revised Text with Translation, Introduction and Commentary* by E.R. Dodds, Oxford, [2]1963.

Proclus, *Eléments de théologie,* commentaire et traduction par J. Trouillard Paris 1965.

Proclus, *Théologie platonicienne.* Texte établi et traduit par H. D. Saffrey et L.J. Westerink. Livres I - V, Paris 1968 - 1987.

Proclus, *Commentaire sur le Parménide de Platon, trad. G. de Moerbeke,* ed. C Steel, Leuven 1985.

Proclus, *Elementatio theologica, translata a Guillelmo de Morbecca,* hrsg. von H. Boese, Leuven 1987 (Ancient and Medieval Philosophy, De Wulf-Mansion Centre, series 1, V).

Robert Grosseteste, *In Analytica Posteriora,* ed. P. Rossi, Florence, 1981.

Siger of Brabant, *Les Quaestiones super librum de causis de Siger de Brabant,* ed. A. Marlasca, Louvain - Paris (Philosophes Médiévaux xii), 1974.

Suidae Lexicon ed. A. Adler, Pars IV, Leipzig, 1935.

Syrianus, *In Aristotelis Metaphysicam,* ed. W. Kroll (Corpus Latinum commentariorum in Aristotelem Graecorum VI, 1), Berlin 1902

Thomas Aquinas, *Opera omnia* iussu Leonis XIII edita cura et studio Fratrum Praedicatorum, Romae 1882 ff.

Thomas Aquinas *Liber de causis: Sancti Thomae de Aquino super Librum de causis expositio,* ed. H.D. Saffrey, Fribourg (Sw.) - Louvain 1954.

Ulrich of Strasbourg, *De summo bono* II, tract. 1 - 4, hrsg. von A. de Libera (Corpus Philosophorum Teutonicorum Medii Aevi I, 2 (1)) Hamburg 1987; IV, tract. 1 - 2, 7, hrsg. von S. Pieperhoff (Corpus philosophorum Teutonicorum Medii Aevi I, 2 (4)) Hamburg 1987.

William of Ockham, *Scriptum in librum primum Sententiarum, Ordinatio,* Prologus et distinctio prima, edidit G. Gál adlaborante S. Brown (*Opera Theologica* I), St. Bonaventure, N.Y. 1967.

William of Ockham, *Scriptum in librum primum Sententiarum, Ordinatio,* distinctiones ii - iii edidit S. Brown adlaborante G. Gál (*Opera Theologica* II), St. Bonaventure, N.Y. 1970.

William of Ockham, *Scriptum in librum primum Sententiarum, Ordinatio,* distinctiones xix - xlviii, ediderunt G.I. Etzkorn et F.E. Kelley (*Opera Theologica* IV), St. Bonaventure, N.Y. 1979.

William of Ockham, *Quaestiones in librum secundum Sententiarum,* Reportatio, ediderunt G. Gál et R. Wood (*Opera Theologica* V), St. Bonaventure, N.Y. 1981.

William of Ockham, *Brevis Summa libri Physicorum, Summula Philosophiae naturalis en Quaestiones in libros Physicorum Aristotelis,* ed. S. Brown, (*Opera Philosophica* VI), St. Bonaventure, N.Y. 1984.

LITERATURE

Aertsen, J.A., 'Die Lehre der Transzendentalien und die Metaphysik', *Freiburger Zeitschrift für Philosophie und Theologie* 35 (1988), 293 - 316.

Aertsen, J.A., 'Die Transzendentalienlehre bei Thomas von Aquin in ihren historischen Hintergründen und philosophischen Motiven', in: *Thomas von Aquin*, ed. A. Zimmermann, (Miscellanea Mediaevalia 19), Berlin-New York 1988, 82 - 102.

Albert, K., *Meister Eckharts These vom Sein. Untersuchungen zur Metaphysik des* Opus tripartitum, Saarbrücken-Kastellaun 1976.

Altmann A., Stern, S.M., *Isaac Israeli. A Neoplatonic Philosopher of the Early Tenth Century,* (Scripta Judaica 1), Oxford 1958.

Armstrong, A.H., 'Plotinus', in: A.H. Armstrong, *The Cambridge History of Later Greek and Early Medieval Philosphy,* Cambridge 1967, 193-268.

Aujoulat, N., *Le néo-platonisme Alexandrin, Hiéroclès d'Alexandrie,* Leiden 1986.

Badawi, A., *Aristû cinda 'l-cArab,* Le Caire,1947.

Badawi, A., *La Transmission de la philosophie grecque au monde arabe.* Cours professé à la Sorbonne en 1967 (Études de Philosophie Médiévale 56) Paris 1987.

Ballériaux, O., 'Syrianus et la télestique', *Kernos* 2 (1989), 13 - 25.

Bannach, Kl., *Die Lehre von der doppelten Macht Gottes bei Wilhelm von Ockham. Problemgeschichtliche Voraussetzungen und Bedeutung.* Wiesbaden 1975.

Bardenhewer, O., *Die pseudo-aristotelische Schrift: über das reine Gute bekannt unter dem Namen Liber de causis,* Freiburg 1882 (Nachdruck Frankfurt, o. J.).

Barnes, J., 'Immaterial causes', *Oxford Studies in Ancient Philosophy* 1 (1983), 169 - 192.

Beierwaltes, W., 'Der Kommentar zum *Liber de causis* als neuplatonisches Element in der Philosophie des Thomas von Aquin', *Philosophische Rundschau* 11 (1964), 192 - 215.

Beierwaltes, W., *Proklos. Grundzüge seiner Metaphysik,* Frankfurt am Main 1965, ²1979

Beierwaltes, W., *Platonismus und Idealismus,* Frankfurt am Main 1972.

Beierwaltes, W., *'Deus est esse - Esse est Deus.* Die onto-theologische Grundfrage als aristotelisch-neuplatonische Denkstruktur', in: *Platonismus und Idealismus,* Frankfurt am Main 1972, 5 - 82.

Beierwaltes, W., *Identität und Differenz,* Frankfurt am Main 1980.

Beierwaltes, W., *Plotin. Über Ewigkeit und Zeit,* Frankfurt am Main ³1981.

Beierwaltes, W., *Denken des Einen. Studien zur neuplatonischen Philosophie und ihrer Wirkungsgeschichte,* Frankfurt am Main 1985.

Beierwaltes, W., 'Einheit und Identität als Weg des Denkens', in: *L'uno e i Molti,* a cura di V. Melchiorre, Milano 1990, 3 - 47.

Bielmeier, A., *Die neuplatonische Phaidrosinterpretation,* Paderborn 1930.

Boese, H., *Wilhelm von Moerbeke als Übersetzer der* Stoicheosis theologike *des Proclus,* Abhandlungen der Heidelberger Akademie der Wissenschaften, phil.-hist. Klasse, Jg. 1985, 5. Abhandlung, Heidelberg 1985.

Breton, S., 'Le théorème de l'Un dans les *Eléments de théologie* de Proclos', *Revue des sciences philosophiques et théologiques* 58 (1974), 561 - 583.

Brisson, L., 'Proclus et l'Orphisme' in: *Proclus, lecteur et interprète des Anciens* , Paris 1987.

Brunn, E. zum et al., *Maître Eckhart à Paris. Une critique médiévale de l'ontothéologie,* Paris 1984.

Burkert, W., *Lore and Science in Ancient Pythagoreanism,* Cambridge (Mass.) 1972.

C. Guérard, C., 'La théorie des Hénades et la mystique de Proclus', *Dionysius,* 6 (1982).

Cameron, A., *Literature and Society in the Early Byzantine World,* London 1985.

Charrue, J.M., *Plotin, lecteur de Platon,* Paris 1978.

Courtine, J.-F. 'Différence ontologique et analogie de l'être: le tournant suarézien', *Bulletin de la Société française de Philosophie,* 83e année, n°2 (Séance du 28 janvier 1989), Avril-Juin 1989.

Descartes, René, *Discours de la méthode,* texte et commentaire par É. Gilson, Paris 1925.

Dillon, J.M., *The Middle Platonists. A Study of Platonism 80 B.C. to A.D. 220,* London 1977.

Dillon, J.M., 'Porphyry and Jamblichus in Proclus' Commentary on the *Parmenides*' in:*Gonimos. Neoplatonic and Byzantine Studies presented to L.Westerink,* ed. by J. Duffy and J. Peradotto, New York, 1988.

Dodds, E.R., *Proclus. The Elements of Theology.* A Revised Text with Translation, Introduction and Commentary, Oxford 21963.

Dondaine, A., et Bataillon, L.J., 'Le manuscrit *Vindobonensis lat.* 2330 et Siger de Brabant', *Archivum Fratrum Praedicatorum* 36 (1966), 153 - 261.

Dondaine, H.F., *Le Corpus dionysien de l'université de Paris au XIIIe siècle,* Rome 1953.

Ebeling, H., *Meister Eckharts Mystik. Studien zu den Geisteskämpfen um die Wende des 13. Jahrhunderts,* Stuttgart 1941.

Faraggiana di Sarzana, G., 'Le commentaire à Hésiode et la Paideia encyclopédique de Proclus, in: *Proclus, lecteur, et interprète des Anciens,* Paris 1987.

Festugière, A.J., *Commentaire sur le Timée de Proclus.* Trad. et notes, 5 tômes, Paris 1966-1968.

Festugière, A.J., 'Contemplation philosophique et art théurgique chez Proclus' in: *Studi di Storia religiosa della tarda Antiquità,* Messina 1968, reprinted in: *Études de philosophie grecque,* Paris 1973, 585-596.

Festugière, A.J.,'l'Ordre de lecture des dialogues de Platon aux Ve/VIe siècles', *Museum Helveticum* 26 (1969), 281-296, *Études de Philosophie grecque ,* 535-550.

Flasch, K., 'Eine (das), Einheit II', in: *Historisches Wörterbuch der Philosophie,* Teil II, Darmstadt 1972, 367 - 377.

Flasch, K., *Die Metaphysik des Einen bei Nikolaus von Cues. Problemgeschichtliche Stellung und systematische Bedeutung,* Leiden 1973.

Flasch, K., 'Die Intention Meister Eckharts', in: *Sprache und Begriff, Festschrift für Bruno Liebrucks,* hrsg. von H. Röttges, B. Scheer, J. Simon, Meisenheim 1974, 292 - 318.

Foscari, A., e Tafuri, M., *L'armonia e i conflitti. La chiesa di San Francesco della Vigna nella Venezia del '500,* Torino 1983.

Gauthier R.A., et Jolif, J.Y., in: Aristote, *L'Ethique à Nicomaque,* Commentaire, Louvain-Paris 1970.

Gersh, S., *From Iamblichus to Eriugena,* Leiden 1978.

Gilson, É., *Being and Some Philosophers,* Toronto 21952.

Gilson, É., *Jean Duns Scot. Introduction à ses positions fondamentales,* Paris 1952.

Gilson, É., see: René Descartes, *Discours ...*

Giocarinis, K., 'Eustratius of Nicaea's Defense of the Doctrine of Ideas', *Franciscan Studies,* 12 (1964), 159 - 204.

Goddu, A., *The Physics of William Ockham,* Leiden-Köln 1984.

Goulet-Cazé, M.-O., 'L'arrière-plan scolaire de la *Vie de Plotin* 'in:*Porphyre, La Vie de Plotin I,* ed. L. Brisson, Paris 1982.

Guthrie, W.K.C., *A History of Greek Philosophy* V: 'The Later Plato and the Academy', Cambridge etc. 1978.

Haas, A.M., *Meister Eckhart als normative Gestalt geistigen Lebens,* Einsiedeln 1971.

Haas, A.M., *Sermo Mysticus,* Freiburg (Switserl.) 1984.

Hadot, I., *Le problème du néoplatonisme alexandrin, Hiéroclès et Simplicius,* Paris 1978.

Hamesse, J., *Les* Auctoritates Aristotelis, *un florilège médiéval,* étude historique et édition critique, Louvain-Paris 1974.

Hankey, W., 'Aquinas' First Principle: Being or Unity?', *Dionysius* 4 (1980), 138 - 172.

Hedwig, K., 'Negatio Negationis. Problemgeschichtliche Aspekte einer Denkstruktur', *Archiv für Begriffsgeschichte* 24 (1980), 7 - 33.

Henle, R.J., *Saint Thomas and Platonism,* A Study of the *Plato* and *Platonici* texts in the writings of Saint Thomas, The Hague 1956 (reprint 1970).

Hoenen, M.J.F.M., Marsilius van Inghen († 1396) over het goddelijke weten. Zijn plaats in de ontwikkeling van de opvattingen over het goddelijke weten ca. 1255-1396, Deel I: Studie, Deel II: Tekstuitgave van: Marsilius van Inghen, *Quaestiones super Quattuor Libros Sententiarum,* Lib. I, quaestt. 38 en 40, Nijmegen 1989 (Diss.).

Honnefelder, L., *Ens in quantum ens. Der Begriff des Seienden als solchen als Gegenstand der Metaphysik nach der Lehre des Johannes Duns Scotus,* (Beiträge zur Geschichte der Philosophie und Theologie des Mittelalters, Neue Folge, Band 16), Münster in Westfahlen 1979.

Horst, P.C. van der, *Les vers d'or pythagoriciens,* Leiden 1932.

Imbach, R., *"Deus est intelligere". Das Verhältnis von Sein und Denken in seiner Bedeutung für das Gottesverständnis bei Thomas von Aquin und in den Pariser Quaestionen Meister Eckharts,* Freiburg (Switserl.) 1976.

Imbach, R., 'Le (néo-)platonisme médiéval, Proclus latin et l'école dominicaine allemande', *Revue de théologie et de philosophie* 110 (1978), 427 - 448.

Kaiser, R., 'Die Benutzung proklischer Schriften durch Albert den Großen', *Archiv für Geschichte der Philosophie,* 45/1 (1963), 1 - 22.

Kaluza, Z., 'Le Chancelier Gerson et Jérôme de Prague', *Archives d'Histoire Doctrinale du Moyen Age,* 51 (1984), 81 - 126.

Kaluza, Z., 'Le *De universale reali* de Jean de Maisonneuve et les *epicuri litterales',* *Freibürger Zeitschrift für Philosophie und Theologie,* 33 (1986), 486 - 489.

Kaluza, Z., Les Querelles doctrinales à Paris. Nominalistes et réalistes aux confins du XIVe et du XVe siècles, (Quodlibet 2), Bergame, 1988.

Kern, O.*Orphicorum fragmenta,* Berlin 1922.

Koch, J., 'Meister Eckhart. Versuch eines Gesamtbildes', in: *Kleine Schriften,* Roma 1973.

Koch, J., *Platonismus im Mittelalter,* Krefeld 1948.

Kremer, K. *Die neuplatonische Seinsphilosophie und ihre Wirkung auf Thomas van Aquin,* Leiden 1971.

Kremer, K., '*Bonum est diffusivum sui.* Ein Beitrag zum Verhältnis von Neuplatonismus und Christentum', in: *Aufstieg und Niedergang der römischen Welt,* Teil II: Principat. Band 36, 2, Berlin-New York 1987, 994 - 1032.

Kremer, K., *Die neuplatonische Seinsphilosophie und ihre Wirkung auf Thomas von Aquin,* Leiden 1966, [2]1971.

Kroll, W., *De oraculis Chaldaicis* , Bratislava 1894.

Le Blond, J.M., *Logique et méthode chez Aristote,* Paris 1939, [3]1973.

Le Fèvre de Boderie, G. *L'harmonie du monde,* Paris 1578.

Leff, G., *William of Ockham. The metamorphosis of scholastic discourse,* Manchester 1975.

Leibniz, G.W., Lettre à N. Remond (datée du 11 février 1715), in: C. Gerhardt, *Die philosophischen Schriften von G.W. Leibniz,* III, Berlin 1887.

Leibold, G., 'Zur Authentizität der *Quaestiones in libros Physicorum* Wilhelms Ockham', *Philosophisches Jahrbuch* 80 (1973), 368 - 378.

Lewy, H., *Chaldaean Oracles and Theurgy.* New edition by M. Tardieu, Paris 1978.

Lévêque, P., *Aurea Catena Homeri,* Paris 1959.

Libera, A. de, 'Le problème de l'être chez Maître Eckhart: Logique et métaphysique de l'analogie', *Cahiers de la Revue de Théologie et de Philosophie* 4, 1980.

Libera, A. de, 'Théorie des universaux et réalisme logique chez Albert le Grand', *Revue des Sciences Philosophiques et Théologiques* 65 (1981), 55 - 74.

Libera, A. de, *Introduction à la mystique rhénane d'Albert le Grand à Maître Eckhart,* Paris 1984.

Libera, A. de, 'Ulrich de Strasbourg lecteur d'Albert le Grand', *Freiburger Zeitschrift für Philosophie und Theologie* 32/1-2 (1985), 122 - 124.

Libera, A. de, 'Les sources gréco-arabes de la théorie médiévale de l'analogie de l'être', *Les études philosophiques* 3-4 (1989), 319 - 345.

Libera, A. de, 'Philosophie et théologie chez Albert le Grand et dans l'École dominicaine allemande', in: *Die Kölner Universität im Mittelalter,* ed. A. Zimmermann (Miscellanea Mediaevalia 20), Berlin-New York 1989, 49 - 67.

Libera, A. de, *La philosophie médiévale,* (Que sais-je? 1044), Paris 1989.

Libera, A. de, 'Albert le Grand et Thomas d'Aquin interprètes du *Liber de causis',* *Revue des Sciences Philosophiques et Théologiques* 74 (1990), 347 - 378.

Libera, A. de, *Albert le Grand et la philosophie,* Paris 1990.

Libera, A. de, 'Ex uno non fit nisi unum. La Lettre sur le Principe de l'univers et les condamnations parisiennes de 1277', à paraître dans: Historia Philosophiae Medii Aevi, ed. B. Mojsisch et O. Pluta (Bochumer Studien zur Philosophie), Amsterdam.

Linley, N., Ibn At-Tayyib, Proclus' Commentary on the Pythagorean Golden Verses, Buffalo 1984.

Lloyd, A.C., 'Porphyry and Jamblichus', in: A.H. Armstrong The Cambridge History of Later Greek and Early Medieval Philosophy, Cambridge 1967, 283-301.

Lloyd, A.C., 'Procession and division in Proclus', in: H.J. Blumenthal and A.C. Lloyd, eds.,Soul and the structure of Being in late Neoplatonism, Liverpool 1982.

Lohr, C.H., 'Medieval Latin Aristotle Commentaries', Traditio, Studies in Ancient and Mediaeval History, Thought and Religion 23 (1967) - 30 (1974).

Lossky, Vl., 'La notion des analogies chez Denys le Pseudo-Aréopagite', Archives d' histoire doctrinale et littéraire du Moyen Age 5 (1931), 279 - 309.

Lossky, Vl., Théologie négative et Connaissance de Dieu chez Maître Eckhart, Paris 1960.

Marg, W., Timaeus Locrus, De natura mundi et animae, Leiden 1972.

Markus, R.A., 'Marius Victorinus and Augustine' in: The Cambridge History of Later Greek and Early Medieval Philosophy, Cambridge 1970, 327 - 419.

Maspéro, J., 'Horapollon et la fin du paganisme égyptien', Bulletin.de l'Institut français d'Archéologie Orientale 11 (1914), 163 - 195.

Matthews, J. F., 'Olympiodorus of Thebes and the History of the West (A.D. 407-425)', Journal of Roman Studies 60 (1970), 79 - 97.

Maurer, A.A., Master Eckhart - Parisian Questions and Prologues, Toronto 1974.

McCord Adams, M., William Ockham, 2 vols (Publications in Medieval Studies, The Medieval Institute),.Notre Dame (Indiana) 1987

Meijer, P.A., 'Stoicism in Plotinus' Enneads VI, 9, 1', Quaderni Urbinati di Cultura Classica, 58 (1988), 61 - 76.

Meijer, P.A., 'Some Problems in Proclus'Theologia Platonica II, ch. 7', Rheinisches Museum für Philologie, 132 (1989), 182 - 203.

Mojsisch, B., Meister Eckhart. Analogie, Univozität und Einheit, Hamburg 1983.

Morrow, G.R., and Dillon, J.M., Proclus' commentary on Plato's Parmenides, Princeton 1987.

O'Meara, D.J., Pythagoras revived. Mathematics and Philosophy in Late Antiquity, Oxford 1989.

Pelzer, A., 'Guillelmus de Leus (de Levibus), Frère Prêcheur de Toulouse', in: Aus der Geisteswelt des Mittelalters. Studien und Texte Martin Grabmann zur Vollendung des 60. Lebensjahres von Freunden und Schülern gewidmet (Beiträge zur Geschichte der Philosophie und Theologie des Mittelalters, Supplementband III), Münster in Westfahlen 1935, 1065 - 1079.

Pépin, J., 'Plotin et le miroir de Dionysos (Enn. IV 3 [27], 12, 1 - 22)', Revue Internationale de Philosophie, 24 (1970), 304 - 320.

Pouillon, H., 'Le premier traité des propriétés transcendantales. La Summa de bono du Chancellier Philippe', Revue néoscolastique de philosophie 42 (1939), 40 - 77.

Praechter, K., 'Hermeias', in: Pauly-Wissowa. Bd. 15 (1912), 732 - 735.

Praechter, K., 'Das Schriftenverzeichnis des Neuplatonikers Syrianos bei Suidas',Byzantinisches Zeitschrift, 26 (1926), reprinted in Kleine Schriften, Hildesheim-New York 1973.

Purnell jr., F., 'The Theme of Philosophic Concord and the Sources of Ficino's Platonism', in: Marsilio Ficino e il Ritorno di Platone, Manoscritti, Stampe e Documenti, Firenze 1984 (Acts of the colloquium Marsilio Ficino e il Ritorno di Platone) a cura di G.C. Garfagnini, Firenze 1986, 397 - 415.

Richter, Vl., 'In Search of the Historical Ockham: Historical Literary Remarks on the Authenticity of Ockham's Writings', Franciscan Studies vol. 46, Annual XXIV, 1986 (William of Ockham (1285 - 1347), Commemorative Issue, part III, 1988), 93 - 106.

Rijk, L.M. de, 'Abailard's Semantic Views in the Light of Later Developments' in English Logic and Semantics from the end of the Twelfth Century to the Time of Ockham and Burley, ed. H.A.G. Braakhuis, C.H. Kneepkens, L.M. de Rijk, Nijmegen (Artistarium, Supplementa I) 1981, 1 - 58.

Rijk, L.M. de, 'Semantics and Metaphysics in Gilbert of Poitiers. A Chapter of Twelfth Century Platonism'(1),*Vivarium* 26 (1988), 73 - 112 and (2) *ibid.* 27 (1989), 1 - 35.

Rijk, L.M. de, *La philosophie au moyen âge*, Leiden 1985.

Rijk, L.M. de, *Plato's Sophist. A Philosophical Commentary*, Amsterdam 1986.

Rist, J.M., *Plotinus . The Road to Reality*, Cambridge 1967.

Romano, F., 'L'ermeneutica dell' ineffabile' in *Questioni Neoplatoniche* a cure di Francesco Romano e Antonio Tiné, Catania 1988.

Romano, F., *Proclo. Lezioni sul "Cratilo" di Platone. Introduzione, Traduzione e Commento"*, Catania 1989.

Rosán, L.J., *The Philosophy of Proclus. The Final Phase of Ancient Thought*, New York 1949.

Ruh, K., *Meister Eckhart. Theologe, Prediger, Mystiker*, München 1985, [2]1989.

Saffrey, H.D., 'Introduction' in: *Sancti Thomae de Aquino Super Librum de causis expositio* (Textus Philosophi Friburgenses 4/5), Fribourg-Louvain 1954.

Saffrey, H.D., 'Der gegenwärtige Stand der Forschung zum *Liber de causis*, als einer Quelle der Metaphysik des Mittelalters', in: *Platonismus in der Philosophie des Mittelalters*, hrsg. von W. Beierwaltes (Wege der Forschung 197), Darmstadt 1969, 462 - 483.

Saffrey, H.D., 'La *Théologie platonicienne* de Proclus, fruit de l'exégèse du *Parménide*,'*Revue de Théologie et de Philosophie*, 116 (1984), 1 - 12.

Saffrey, H.D., 'Proclus, diadoque de Platon', dans *Proclus, lecteur et interprète des Anciens* , Paris 1987.

Schmitt, Ch.B., '"Prisca Theologia" e "Philosophia Perennis": due temi del Rinascimento italiano e la loro fortuna' in: *Il pensiero italiano del Rinascimento e il nostro tempo* , Firenze 1970, 211 - 236.

Schönberger, R., *Die Transformation des klassischen Seinsverständnisses. Studien zur Vorgeschichte des neuzeitlichen Seinsbegriffes im Mittelalter*, Berlin 1986.

Schütz, L., *Thomaslexikon*. Sammlung, Übersetzung und Erklärung der in sämtlichen Werken des h. Thomas von Aquin vorkommenden Kunstausdrücke und wissenschaftlichen Aussprüche, Paderborn 1895.

Schwyzer, H.R., 'Corrigenda ad Plotini Textum' , *Museum Helveticum* 44 (1987).

Sicherl, M., 'Ein neuplatonischer Hymnus unter den Gedichten Gregors von Nazianz', in: *Gonimos, Neoplatonic and Byzantine Studies, presented to L. G. Westerink at 75*, Buffalo, New York 1988, 61 - 83.

Sleeman, J.H., et Pollet, G., *Lexicon Plotinianum* , Leiden-Leuven 1980.

Spruyt, J., *Peter of Spain on Composition and Negation. Text, Translation Commentary*. Nijmegen 1989.

Sturlese, L., 'Proclo ed Ermete in Germania da Alberto Magno a Bertoldo di Moosburg. Per una prospettiva di ricerca sulla cultura filosofica tedesca nel secolo delle sue origini (1250-1350)', in: *Von Meister Dietrich zu Meister Eckhart*, hrsg. von K. Flasch, (Corpus Philosophorum Teutonicorum Medii Aevi Beihefte, 2), Hambourg 1984, 22 - 33.

Sturlese, L., '*Homo divinus*. Der Prokloskommentar Bertholds von Moosburg und die Probleme der nacheckhartschen Zeit', in: *Abendländische Mystik im Mittelalter*. Symposion Kloster Engelberg 1984, hrsg. von K. Ruh (Germanistische Symposien, Berichtsband 7), Stuttgart 1986, 145 - 161.

Sturlese, L., 'Il dibattito sul Proclo latino nel medioevo fra l'università di Parigi e lo Studium di Colonia', in: *Proclus et son influence*. Actes du Colloque de Neuchâtel, juin 1985, eds. G. Boss and G. Seel, Zürich 1987, 268 - 269.

Sturlese, L., 'Tauler im Kontext. Die philosophischen Vorausetzungen des Seelengrundes in der Lehre des deutschen Neuplatonikers Berthold von Moosburg', *Beiträge zur Geschichte der deutschen Sprache und Literatur*, Band 109, Heft 3, Tübingen 1987, 390 - 426.

Taylor, R.C., 'Causation', in: *The Encyclopedia of Philosophy* ed. by P. Edwards, vol. II, New York-London 1967.

Taylor, R.C., 'St. Thomas and the *Liber de causis* on the hylomorphic composition of separate substances', *Mediaeval Studies* 41 (1979), 506 - 513.

Taylor, R.C., 'The *Liber de causis*: A Preliminary List of Extant Manuscripts', *Bulletin de Philosophie Médiévale* 25 (1983), 63 - 84.Taylor, R.C., 'The Kalâm fî mahd al-khair

(*Liber de causis*) in the islamic philosophical milieu', in: *Pseudo-Aristotle in the Middle Ages. The Theology and other Texts* (Warburg Institute Surveys and Texts XI), London 1986, 37 - 52.

Thesleff, H., *The Pythagorean Texts of the Hellenistic Period,* Åbo 1965.

Trouillard, J., 'Un et être', *Les études philosophiques* 15 (1960), 185 - 196.

Trouillard, J., *L'un et l'âme selon Proclos,* Paris 1972.

Trouillard, J., *La mystagogie de Proclos,* Paris 1982.

Trouillard, 'Un (Philosophies de l')', in: *Encyclopaedia universalis,* Paris 21988, 427 - 429.

Vansteenkiste, C., 'Il *Liber de Causis* negli scritti di San Tommaso', *Angelicum* 35 (1958), 325 - 374.

Vogel, C.J. de, 'Some reflections on the *Liber de causis*', *Vivarium* 4 (1966), 67 - 82.

Wackernagel, W., *Imagine denundari. Éthique de l'image et métaphysique de l'abstraction chez Maître Eckhart,* Paris 1991.

Walker, D.P.,*The Ancient Theology* , London 1972.

Westerink, L.G., 'Hierokles II', in: *Reallexikon für Antike und Christentum,* Lieferung 113, col. 109 - 117, 1989.

Westerink, L.G., *Anonymus Prolegomena to Platonic Philosophy,* Amsterdam 1962.

Westerink, L.G., *Porphyry, The Cave of the Nymphs in the Odyssey,* (Seminar Classics 609 of SUNY at Buffalo), Buffalo 1969.

Westerink, L.G., *Proclus commentateur des Vers d'Or* in:*Proclus et son influence,* ed. G. Boss et G. Seel, Neuchâtel 1987, 61 - 78.

Wilson, N.G., 'A Chapter in the History of Scholia', *Classical Quarterly.* 17 (1967) 244-256.

Wilson, N.G., 'The Relation of Text and Commentary in Greek Books', *Il Libro e il Testo* , Urbino 1984, 103-110.

Wind, E., *Art et Anarchie* , Paris 1988.

Wyller, E.A., 'Henologie', in: *Historisches Wörterbuch der Philosophie* III, Darmstadt 1974, col. 1059 - 1060.

Zorzi, F., *L'harmonie du monde,* par G. Le Fevre de la Boderie, Paris 1578.

INDEX

PHILOSOPHIA ANTIQUA

A SERIES OF STUDIES ON ANCIENT PHILOSOPHY
EDITED BY J.J. MANSFELD, D.T. RUNIA
W.J. VERDENIUS AND J.C.M. VAN WINDEN

32. WELLIVER, M. *Character, Plot and Thought in Plato's Timaeus and Critias.* 1977. ISBN 90 04 04870 7

33. BOEFT, J. DEN. *Calcidius on Demons.* (Commentarius Ch. 127-136). 1977. ISBN 90 04 05283 6

34. EPIKTET. *Vom Kynismus.* Herausgegeben und übersetzt mit einem Kommentar von M. Billerbeck. 1978. ISBN 90 04 05770 6

35. BALTES, M. *Die Weltentstehung des platonischen Timaios nach den antiken Interpreten.* Teil 2. Proklos. 1979. ISBN 90 04 05799 4

36. BILLERBECK, M. *Der kyniker Demetrius.* Ein Beitrag zur Geschichte der frühkaiserzeitlichen Popularphilosophie. 1979. ISBN 90 04 06032 4

37. O'BRIEN, D. *Theories of Weight in the Ancient World.* Four Essays on Democritus, Plato and Aristotle. A Study in the Development of Ideas 1. Democritus: Weight and Size. An Exercise in the Reconstruction of Early Greek Philosophy. 1981. ISBN 90 04 06134 7

38. O'BRIEN, D. *Pour interpréter Empédocle.* 1981. ISBN 90 04 06249 1

39. TARÁN, L. *Speusippus of Athens.* A Critical Study with a Collection of the Related Texts and Commentary. 1982. ISBN 90 04 06505 9

40. RIST, J.M. *Human Value.* A Study in Ancient Philosophical Ethics. 1982. ISBN 90 04 06757 4

41. O'BRIEN, D. *Theories of Weight in the Ancient World.* Four Essays on Democritus, Plato and Aristotle. A Study in the Development of Ideas 2. Plato: Weight and Sensation. The Two Theories of the 'Timaeus'. 1984. ISBN 90 04 06934 8

43. NILL, M. *Morality and Self-Interest in Protagoras, Antiphon, and Democritus.* 1985. ISBN 90 04 07319 1

44. RUNIA, D.T. *Philo of Alexandria and the* Timaeus *of Plato.* 1986. ISBN 90 04 07477 5

45. AUJOULAT, N. *Le Néo-Platonisme Alexandrin: Hiéroclès d'Alexandrie.* Filiations intellectuelles et spirituelles d'un néo-platonicien du Ve siècle. 1986. ISBN 90 04 07510 0

46. KAL, V. *On Intuition and Discursive Reasoning in Aristotle.* 1988. ISBN 90 04 08308 1

47. LONDEY, D. and JOHANSON, C. *The Logic of Apuleius.* Including a Complete Latin Text and English Translation of the *Peri Hermeneias* of Apuleius of Madaura. 1987. ISBN 90 04 08421 5

48. EVANGELIOU, CH. *Aristotle's Categories and Porphyry.* 1988. ISBN 90 04 08538 6

49. BUSSANICH, J. *The One and Its Relation to Intellect in Plotinus.* A Commentary on Selected Texts. 1988. ISBN 90 04 08996 9

50. SIMPLICIUS. *Commentaire sur les Catégories.* Traduction commentée sous la direction de I. Hadot. I: Introduction, première partie (p. 1-9, 3 Kalbfleisch). Traduction de Ph. Hoffmann (avec la collaboration d'I. et P. Hadot). Commentaire et notes à la traduction par I. Hadot avec des appendices de P. Hadot et J.-P. Mahé. 1990. ISBN 90 04 09015 0

51. SIMPLICIUS. *Commentaire sur les Catégories.* Traduction commentée sous la direction de I. Hadot. III: Préambule aux Catégories. Commentaire au premier chapitre des Catégories (p. 21-40, 13 Kalbfleisch). Traduction de Ph. Hoffmann (avec la collaboration d'I. Hadot, P. Hadot et C. Luna). Commentaire et notes à la traduction par C. Luna. 1990. ISBN 90 04 09016 9

52. MAGEE, J. *Boethius on Signification and Mind.* 1989. ISBN 90 04 09096 7

53. BOS, E.P. and MEIJER, P.A. (eds.) *On Proclus and His Influence in Medieval Philosophy.* ISBN 90 04 09429 6

54. FORTENBAUGH, W.W. (ed.) *Theophrastus of Eresos.* Sources for His Life, Writings, Thought and Influence. ISBN 90 04 09440 7

55. SHANKMAN, A. *Aristotle's* De insomniis. A Commentary. ISBN 90 04 09476 8

DATE DUE

HIGHSMITH 45-220